Language and Learning:
The Home and School Years

SECOND EDITION

Terry Piper
MEMORIAL UNIVERSITY OF NEWFOUNDLAND

Merrill, an imprint of Prentice Hall

Upper Saddle River, New Jersey   Columbus, Ohio

Library of Congress Cataloging-in-Publication Data

Piper, Terry.
    Language and learning : the home and school years / Terry Piper.
—2nd ed.
       p.   cm.
    Rev. ed. of: Language for all our children. © 1993.
    Includes bibliographical references and index.
    ISBN 0-13-863903-5
    1. Children—Language.   2. Language arts.   3. Language acquisition.
    4. Linguistics.   5. home and school.   I. Piper, Terry.
    Language for all our children.   II. Title.
    LB1139.L3P53   1998
    372.6—dc21   97-29947
                                            CIP

Editor: Bradley J. Potthoff
Production Editor: Julie Peters
Production Manager: Patricia A. Tonneman
Design Coordinator: Julia Zonneveld Van Hook
Text Designer: Angela Foote
Cover Designer: Russ Maselli
Illustrations: Carlisle Communications, Inc.
Director of Marketing: Kevin Flanagan
Marketing Manager: Suzanne Stanton
Advertising/Marketing Coordinator: Julie Shough

This book was set in Revival 565 by Carlisle Communications, Inc., and was printed and bound by Quebecor Printing/Book Press. The cover was printed by Phoenix Color Corp.

 © 1998 by Prentice-Hall, Inc.
Simon & Schuster/A Viacom Company
Upper Saddle River, New Jersey 07458

Earlier edition, entitled *Language for All Our Children*, © 1993 by Macmillan College Publishing Company.

Printed in the United States of America

10 9 8 7 6 5 4 3 2 1

ISBN: 0-13-863903-5

Prentice-Hall International (UK) Limited, *London*
Prentice-Hall of Australia Pty. Limited, *Sydney*
Prentice-Hall of Canada, Inc., *Toronto*
Prentice-Hall Hispanoamericana, S. A., *Mexico*
Prentice-Hall of India Private Limited, *New Delhi*
Prentice-Hall of Japan, Inc., *Tokyo*
Simon & Schuster Asia Pte. Ltd., *Singapore*
Editora Prentice-Hall do Brasil, Ltda., *Rio de Janeiro*

To the memory of my dear friend

Gail Davis Harkavy

whose intellect inspired me, whose sense of humor delighted me,

whose love sustained me, and whose daughter provided

delightful data on language learning.

Preface

This book is about children's language acquisition from the time they are born throughout the years of schooling. It is also about and for teachers. This is not a methods text; it is a foundational book about how children learn language, how we teach it, and how these two processes are sometimes at odds. It tracks language acquisition from birth through the school years, using the experiences of a number of different children to exemplify stages and sequences of development.

No author ever escapes bias, and I will declare both of mine here on the first page. The first is my belief, based on research and experience, that there are more similarities than differences between first and second language acquisition. There are undeniable parallels, and these should not be overlooked in the classroom. You won't find a chapter at the back of this book telling you what to do about ESL children in your classrooms. In this book you will find some separation but largely you will find the description and discussion integrated. You will meet several children whose stories inform and exemplify the language processes. Lucy, Janet, Quy, Michael—these are all children I knew and worked with. Jani, I did not know, although I know enough of her story to regret that I did not.

My second bias is related to the first. Although I am a lifetime advocate for public education, I am also convinced that we have failed when we need not have. The approach of generations of educators, particularly on the North American continent, has been to change the child. When children fail at school, the reason often given is that they aren't "ready" or that they came from "disadvantaged" homes. When we fail in our efforts to teach children to read and write, we blame the child or home. Then we set up programs to try to change the child to fit the mold of the school. This has always struck me as strange. Why do five-year old children have to bear the responsibility for their failure when it is completely out of their control? The people who *do* have control of the materials, the teaching, and the curriculum do not bother to try to fix the school to meet the needs of the child; they are too busy trying to "fix" the child to fit the school. And mostly they fail.

This failure is most obvious in literacy. Even at the end of the twentieth century, when we should know better, I hear educators blaming everyone but themselves for what appears to be a falling literacy rate. Parents, television, social breakdown, poverty, computers. Everything but education. Of course, all these factors greatly influence children's ability to learn, particularly if we persist in using our traditional methods, and we would be foolish to ignore them; but unless educators assume full responsibility for educating children just as they are, then we won't make much progress. This is my belief and it permeates the book, particularly the last few chapters.

The language and learning of every child is the rightful concern of teachers, and the more teachers know about first and second language acquisition, the better able they will be to plan for effective education for every child they meet. I have sought to achieve a balance between theory and practice, between first and second language acquisition, between showing and telling. It is the book I wrote for myself as an educator of teachers, and I hope that other teachers and future teachers will find it useful.

ACKNOWLEDGMENTS

My first and biggest debt of gratitude is to Susan Hicks, my secretary and friend, who protected me from intrusions and who formatted the thousand pages of the manuscript. I know that there were times that she was "poisoned with" the job, as they say in Newfoundland, but she kept smiling. I cannot begin to thank her properly either for her work or for her sunny disposition. I am also grateful to Bernadette Power, my very able executive assistant, who shouldered more of the work load than she should have during the time I worked on this book, and to Elizabeth Maddox whose willingness to help out in so many ways made my life and writing so much easier. My research assistants at Memorial, Colleen Hickey and Susan George, spent more hours in the libraries, the one with books and the virtual ones, than I ever could have. For that I am indebted. I must also thank the faculty members who kindly overlooked my occasional lapses in attention to their concerns. Although it was several years ago and they have both moved on in their careers, Kim Rebane and Chris Grant made a substantial contribution to the research that gave me the descriptions of Lucy, Quy, and Michael. By being the best teacher I've ever encountered, Mary Kennedy of Calgary, Alberta, gave me inspiration and hope for the future of education. She also helped to shape my views about the education of children.

I would also like to extend my thanks to the reviewers of the second edition manuscript: Marion Crowhurst, University of British Columbia; Trevor J. Gambell, University of Saskatchewan; Maria J. Meyerson, University of Nevada, Las Vegas; Beverly Otto, Northeastern Illinois University; and D. Ray Reutzel, Brigham Young University.

And finally, I would like to acknowledge the support of Jaap Tuinman, my mentor and "boss," who has always talked sensibly with me about the business of education.

Contents

Chapter One / Why Is Language Special?   1

    LANGUAGE IS UNIQUELY HUMAN   2

    LANGUAGE IS LINKED TO COGNITION   3

    LANGUAGE IS NATURAL   5

    LANGUAGE IS CULTURALLY BOUND   6

    LANGUAGE HAS MANY VARIETIES   8

    LANGUAGE HAS STRUCTURE   10

    LANGUAGE AND THE CHILD: AN EXAMPLE   12

        Lucy   13

    IF LANGUAGE IS SO NATURAL, WHAT IS THERE TO TEACH?   18

        The Remainder of the Book   19

    QUESTIONS FOR DISCUSSION   19

Chapter Two / Linguists and Language   21

    LINGUISTS   22

        Descriptive and Theoretical Linguists   22

        Historical Linguists   23

        Psycholinguists   25

        Neurolinguists   27

Sociolinguists   28

Applied Linguists   29

LANGUAGE STRUCTURE   30

Phonology: The Sound System   30

Morphology: The Structure of Words   39

Syntax: The Structure of Sentences   40

Morphemes, Sentences, and Other Languages   49

Pragmatics   51

QUESTIONS FOR DISCUSSION   53

Chapter Three / Learning One Language   **55**

INTRODUCING JANET   56

INFANCY   57

The Precursors to Language   57

Janet as an Infant   58

THE PRESCHOOL YEARS   61

Overview of Development   61

Janet from 1;0 to 1;6   63

Janet from 1;6 to 2;0   66

Janet from 2;0 to 3;0   68

Janet from 3;0 to 4;0   75

Janet from 4;0 to 6;0   80

THE SCHOOL YEARS   82

CONCLUSION   89

QUESTIONS FOR DISCUSSION   90

Chapter Four / Learning Two or More Languages   **91**

HOME BILINGUALISM   93

SCHOOL BILINGUALISM   96

Immersion   97

FLES   99

Two-Way Immersion   99

Bilingual Programs   100

Submersion   101

ISSUES IN SECOND LANGUAGE ACQUISITION THEORY 103

    Learner Variables 104

    Krashen's Monitor Model 112

    How the Variables Fit Together 116

    Language Reacquisition 116

QUESTIONS FOR DISCUSSION 117

Chapter Five / Stories of Second Language Learners **119**

QUY'S LANGUAGE LEARNING 120

    Quy from Birth to 22 Months 120

    Quy from 1;10 to 3;0 121

    Quy from 3;0 to 4;0 123

    Quy from 4;0 to 4;9 123

    Quy in Kindergarten 124

LUCY'S LANGUAGE LEARNING 128

COMPARING LUCY WITH QUY 131

JANI FROM LABRADOR 134

THE CONDITIONS FOR SUCCESSFUL
    SECOND LANGUAGE ACQUISITION 136

QUESTIONS FOR DISCUSSION 139

Chapter Six / Theoretical Perspectives on Language Acquisition **141**

BEHAVIORIST THEORIES 143

    What Behaviorists Believe 143

    The Case Against Behaviorism 145

LINGUISTIC NATIVISM 149

    What Nativists Believe 149

    The Case Against Linguistic Nativism 153

COGNITIVE THEORIES 155

    Piaget's Cognitive Theory 155

    Luria and Bruner 157

    Information Processing 157

    The Case Against Cognitive Theories 158

SOCIAL INTERACTION THEORY 159

    What Social Interactionists Believe 159

The Case Against Social Interaction Theories   162
WHAT THEORY HAS TO SAY ABOUT LANGUAGE
   LEARNING AND ENVIRONMENT   163
CONCLUSION   164
QUESTIONS FOR DISCUSSION   164

Chapter Seven / Michael's Miracle   **167**

LANGUAGE DISORDERS IN MONOLINGUAL
   AND BILINGUAL CHILDREN   167
   Disorder or Difference?   168
   Four Types of Communicative Disorder   169
LANGUAGE PROBLEMS OF BILINGUAL CHILDREN   175
MICHAEL'S LANGUAGE DEVELOPMENT   179
   Comprehension   181
   Accuracy   182
   Fluency   183
   Communicative Competence   185
PRINCIPLES AND GUIDELINES FOR ASSESSING
   BILINGUAL CHILDREN   186
CONCLUSION   189
QUESTIONS FOR DISCUSSION   189

Chapter Eight / Language and the Society of Home and School   **191**

PRAGMATICS IN THE SCHOOL YEARS   192
   Building Conversational Skills   192
   Learning to Construct Narrative   195
LANGUAGE FUNCTIONS   196
THE FUNCTIONS OF LANGUAGE IN CHILDREN'S LIVES   197
   Four Perspectives on Language Function   197
   Five Functions of Language   199
   Language Functions Across Cultures   203
CONCLUSION   204
EXERCISES AND QUESTIONS FOR DISCUSSION   204

Chapter Nine / Language and Cognitive Growth   **207**

THE ROLE OF LANGUAGE IN MEMORY DEVELOPMENT   208

  Basic Capacities   208

  Memory Strategies   210

  Metamemory   211

  Language, Memory, and the Child's Perspective   212

THE ROLE OF LANGUAGE IN CONCEPTUAL DEVELOPMENT   214

  Psychologists' and Linguists' Views Compared   214

  Language and Conceptualization from the Child's Perspective   216

THE ROLE OF LANGUAGE IN THE DEVELOPMENT

  OF ACADEMIC SKILLS   217

  Early Learning of Mathematics   217

  Early Learning Associated with Reading   218

  Early Learning Associated with Writing   225

  Language and Academic Skills from the Child's Perspective:

    Six Characteristics of Children's Preschool Learning   226

CONCLUSION   231

EXERCISES AND QUESTIONS FOR DISCUSSION   232

Chapter Ten / Schooling and Language Growth   **233**

THE ATTITUDES OF SOME EDUCATORS   234

  Change the Child   235

  Change the Language   236

WHAT'S WRONG WITH LANGUAGE IN SCHOOL   238

  "No Talking" and Other Unfriendly Signs   238

  Teachers Value Talk   241

  Dishonest and Manipulative Talk   242

  Teacher Talk Is Teacher Talking   244

  School Talk Is Homogeneous   247

  School Talk Intimidates   248

  School Language Is Disembodied   250

LANGUAGE IN SCHOOL: THE POSITIVE SIDE   251

Whole Language Defined   251

  Whole Language in Practice   251

The Debate: Whole Language or Phonics?   257

Whole Language in (Mis)practice   259

Public Perceptions and Whole Language   261

SIX CHARACTERISTICS OF LEARNING: A COMPARISON   262

QUESTIONS FOR DISCUSSION   266

Chapter Eleven / Language, Technology and Schooling in the 21st Century   269

THE FUTURE IS NOW: SCENES FROM THE PRESENT   270

HOW DOES TECHNOLOGY AFFECT CLASSROOM INTERACTION?   273

What Is the Impact of Technology on Literacy?   274

The Computer as a Tool in Remediation   276

How Is the Teacher's Role Changing?   279

What Does the Future of Education Look Like?   280

QUESTIONS FOR DISCUSSION   282

Chapter Twelve / Language and Learning: Reconciling the Home and School Years   285

TEN PRINCIPLES FOR RECONCILING DIVERSE VIEWS   285

Principle #1: Second Language Acquisition
  in Children Bears a Strong Resemblance
  to First Language Acquisition   287

Principle #2: Know Why You Do What You Do   289

Principle #3: Remember that Language
  Learning Is a Whole-to-Part Enterprise   290

Principle #4: But Don't Forget the Parts   292

Principle #5: A Second Language Is an
  Asset Some Children Bring to School   292

Principle #6: Make Sure that the Method of Evaluation
  Corresponds to What Happens in the Classroom   293

Principle #7: Involve Parents and the Community   296

Principle #8: Don't Be Dogmatic   298

Principle #9: Be Professional   299
Principle #10: Remember That You Are
    Teaching Children, Not Language   300
CONCLUSION   300

Bibliography   **311**

Subject Index   **345**

Author Index   **351**

CHAPTER ONE

Why Is Language Special?

The following sentence appeared in the first paragraph of the first edition of this book:

> In most elementary teachers' daybooks, time for language arts is blocked
> in alongside arithmetic, science, and social studies, and it is what goes on
> in that period of time which is the concern of most college or university
> methods courses in language.

While a great many primary and elementary teachers still divide the children's day in this manner, many have also experimented with and adopted the integrated approach to organizing their curricula. I'll take this up in more detail in Chapter 10, but the integrated curriculum deserves mention right here on page one because, as you will see, it represents a significant step toward creating a school environment that parallels children's real-life experience of language. In attempting to break down the traditional subject area boundaries, teachers have recognized that children's real-life learning is not segmented into artificial units or categories of study but is a seamless journey of enquiry. They have also begun to realize that the true uniqueness and potential of language in children's lives does not lie in the additional 10 minutes it may have warranted in the traditional school day.

One of the things that makes language special is that while it *can* be a rather fascinating subject of study, it is also a prerequisite for the study of all other subjects. To put it very simply, "The talk that students engage in during school lessons goes far to shape what they learn" (Barnes, 1995, p. 2). Language is the foundation to thinking about and learning math, or science, or social studies, and in this respect it is unique. Language plays a central role in children's learning because it is a partner to those central mental processes of perception, comprehension, attention, memory, and that somewhat amorphous activity we call thinking. I am not exaggerating to claim, in fact, that children's success in school depends to a very large degree on their facility with the four modes of language—listening, speaking, reading, and writing.

The converse is not true, of course. Although language is needed to study other subjects, children do not require prior facility with math, science, or any other subject area before they can learn language. There are prerequisites, of course, cognitive as well as social, and we will examine these more closely in Chapters 4 and 6, but it is obviously and significantly true that children need not be conversant with theories of mathematics or even know how to count before they learn the language of counting. Rather, they learn basic counting concepts *as they learn* the language for counting. This is true of much of children's learning—the concepts and the language required to talk about them are learned simultaneously.

When children begin school, they have already begun the lifelong task of acquiring language. This is true of the other subjects in the curriculum in only a very rudimentary sense. More significantly, they have acquired their language without being taught. Children learn a great deal about the world without being formally taught by others, but they are able to do so in large part because they ask questions, they hear people talking, and, eventually, they read about their world and others' experience of it. In short, they rely on language for their learning. This cognitive basis of language makes it unique, whether it is a discrete subject in the school curriculum or, more appropriately in my view, integrated into a seamless web of learning. There are other unique characteristics of language, of course. I have identified five other attributes that are especially important to our understanding of the importance and uniqueness of language. I begin with the fact that language belongs exclusively to humans because in justifying that claim, I must provide at least a rudimentary definition of language. Since language is the subject of this book, it seems appropriate to begin by being very clear what we are talking about.

LANGUAGE IS UNIQUELY HUMAN

Language belongs exclusively to human beings. I know that in writing such a blunt statement I run the risk of offending animal lovers, some of whom are convinced that their pet dog (cat, pig, hedgehog) speaks more sense than some of their relatives. If this is true, then it is more a comment on the content of their kinfolk's discourse than it is on the pet's linguistic abilities. Certainly, some animals have systems of communication, but these differ from human language in fundamental ways.

Human language has many attributes, but for the purpose of comparison with animal communication, three are definitive. First, language has **semanticity.** It conveys meaning through its capacity to represent ideas, objects, and events with symbols. Second, human language is **productive.** Speakers can understand and produce utterances they have never heard before, and they can also create new utterances by recombining elements they already know. In other words, in acquiring a language, speakers acquire the ability to generate new and unique utterances, with no limit on the number of original utterances they can create. Third, human language, as opposed to other communication systems, has the capacity of **displacement,** meaning that it can be used to create messages that are not tied to the immediate environment. Many animals have the ability to communicate in some limited ways. For the purpose of comparison we will look briefly at how bees and jackdaws communicate and how this differs from human language.

The **waggle dance** has been studied by scientists of many different disciplines in attempts to understand the functions it serves and to compare it with the functions of language in humans. Bees use the waggle dance to tell other bees the direction and approximate distance to the nectar they have discovered. The information is contained in the movements of the bee's dance. A westward movement tells the other bees to move west, a round dance consisting of alternating circles to the left and right indicates that the source of nectar is near, and tail-wagging tells them that it is farther away. Dancing bees don't lie about the direction or distance to the flowers, and presumably, the "listeners" don't misunderstand. Neither do dancing bees, nor the bees in their audience, comment on the quality of the nectar or hazardous flying conditions. They do not introduce any other topic of conversation or wander off topic. They communicate a particular kind of information that all bees understand. Their message is **iconic,** meaning that it looks like what it is conveying, and it is always located within the context of nectar-gathering. While it does have limited semanticity, it fails on criteria of productivity and displacement.

Jackdaws, relatives of crows, have three kinds of calls. One is the mating or courting call (self-explanatory, I think). Another is a call they use when they fly away, and the third is a warning call used before attacking any creature carrying a dangling black object. Like the dance of the bees, the communicative call of the jackdaw has meaning to its users (and thus some semanticity), but it is very strictly bound to the context of the present, failing on the criteria of displacement and productivity.

Many animals besides bees and jackdaws have communication systems. Whales, dolphins, sticklebacks, gibbons and meadowlarks (not to mention the family dog) have also been found to possess intricate ways of communicating. But none meets the three basic criteria that define human language. Not even chimpanzees, far closer to humans on the evolutionary scale, have more than an extremely rudimentary capacity for symbolic representation.

As interesting as it is to speculate on animal language and to compare human and animal communication systems, for teachers, other attributes of language are perhaps more relevant, particularly the fact that language is linked to cognition.

LANGUAGE IS LINKED TO COGNITION

It is almost impossible to study human cognition without considering language, although psychologists have been a little slower than linguists to recognize this link. Language and cognition are not the same, of course. Some cognitive development is possible without language, but from the time children begin to acquire language, it affects all aspects of their mental development. Vygotsky (1962) would claim, for example, that speech and thought have different roots and develop independently of one another up to a particular point. At this point, thought becomes verbal and language becomes rational (p. 44). When children develop rational language, they use it not only to express their needs but also

> to manipulate their perceptions of the world by mentally manipulating language . . . . In the process, the perceptions themselves are sorted into categories that are available in the language. Thus, the language to some extent structures the child's developing life-view.
>
> *(Smith, Goodman, & Meredith, 1976, p. 15).*

This is not to say that children cannot or do not think without language but that language becomes the principal means of thought.

Linguistic and cognitive growth occur in tandem and influence each other in complex ways that make them inextricable. Learning, in short, comes to depend on language as we use it to organize our thinking and actions. We use language to shape our experiences, to store our experiences, and to reshape them when we recall them from memory. We talk our way through difficult tasks (and some that are not so difficult), we talk aloud to clarify our thinking, and, indeed, to find out what we think. Through language we share and increase our experience and learning. As teachers, we rely on children's language to tell us what order they see in the world and what sense they are making of their experience of living in it.

When I talk about how language is linked to cognition, I refer not only to oral language but to reading. Dickinson, Wolf, and Stotsky (1989) observe that "Reading represents one of the most interesting and cognitively complex systems and, as such, has a great deal to teach us about cognition in general" (p. 231). Children's reading and writing are, in a very real sense, extensions of their oral language. They bring their life experiences, shaped first by oral language, to the task of learning to read and write, and so that learning is also cognitively driven. Another sense in which written language is linked with cognition is in children's learning of it. In learning to read and to write, they are active participants. Indeed, we have known for some time that children in Grades 1 and 2 are capable of assuming responsibility for their own learning to read and write (see Hansen, 1983, for example). We have also come to view reading and writing, like oral language, as essentially processes of the interactive construction of meaning (Tierney & Pearson, 1984, p. 68). Once they have learned to read and write, children can use written language in much the same way as they use oral language— to shape, store, and recall experience. Reading is one of our most important ways of increasing our experience. For those of us who love to read, "Some of our best memories never happened," (with apologies to Frank Zappa).

In Chapters 8, 9, and 10, I will talk more about the role language plays in learning, first outside the school as children unencumbered by the formal requirements of schooling learn to use language in a variety of social contexts; and then as they encounter literacy and other less contextualized language demands of schooling.

LANGUAGE IS NATURAL

I recall a doctoral oral many years ago in which much of the candidate's time was spent defending this simple assertion. One of the examiners, a science educator, took this statement to mean that science was somehow unnatural. That was not, of course, the point, but it made for an interesting debate. To say that language is natural is not to suggest that other subjects in the curriculum are not. What is meant is that children's learning of language is part of their nature in ways that no other human learning is. First, of course, is the fact that language is learned by all children with normal or near-normal mental and physical abilities, and it is learned very early in their lives when those abilities are far from fully developed.

Second is the fact that no active intervention is required. In fact, most of us who have watched our own children grow are very grateful that we were not charged with the task of teaching them their native language. Even the finest teachers among us would likely fail, such is the enormity of the task and the magnitude of their accomplishment at so young an age. Many theorists have speculated, in fact, that children possess innate mechanisms that give them a head start on the task of language learning, that to talk of their learning language makes no more sense than to talk of a tulip bulb learning to become a tulip. Children are born with the biological potential to acquire human language and will overcome great handicaps to do so.

Evidence gathered in Nicaragua provides very strong support for the claim that language is instinctive. Rutgers University linguist Judy Shepard-Kegl discovered a group of deaf children in that country in 1985 who were in the process of developing a sign language of their own. A decade later, the language is so well developed that a dictionary of the signs is about to be published. According to newspaper reports in *The Globe and Mail* (Canada) and the *Daily Telegraph* (Britain), the researcher did not publish her findings in the early years for fear that someone would go to Nicaragua and try to teach the children American Sign Language, help they apparently did not need. The naturalness of language is a subject that we will explore in greater depth in Chapter 6.

An especially interesting question does arise, however, with regard to written language. Specifically, educators and theorists have debated for several decades whether written language is as natural as oral language. Smith (1984), Goodman (1984), and others have argued that it is, contending, for instance, that preschool children "know how to learn to read and write because written language presents them with problems similar to those they solve with spoken language" (Smith, 1984, p. 143). There is an obvious counterargument, though: Whatever similarities may exist between written and spoken language, the simple fact remains that most children do not learn to read and write without instruction. Still, it would be a mistake to focus on what may turn out to be a minor difference when research is beginning to point to the correspondence between the way oral and written language are acquired.

Even before they come to school, children already know a great deal about reading and writing and, especially, about the nature of literacy itself. They have a good idea about why people read books and the stories to be found in them, about why people write, and most have some general idea about the correspondence between squiggles on paper and meaning. Before they come to school, they have spent time drawing and labeling pictures (even though the adult reader might not know what the label says), marking on pavements, walls, newspapers, and magazines. Hand a child a crayon or chalk on the first day of school and chances are good that she will know what to do with it. Children come to school wanting to write. Donald Graves (1983) claims that these early marks, undecipherable to teachers and parents, proclaim "I am" (p. 1).

It would appear, then, that acquiring language—oral and written—is part of children's nature. The stories of Helen Keller and of a girl named Genie who managed to acquire her first language at the age of 13.5 after nearly 12 years spent in isolation, speak to the intensity of the human drive to acquire language. Language is so very much a part of human nature that the most interesting thing about language acquisition may be the *failure* to acquire it. Later, in Chapter 7, we will meet a child who overcame a major environmental deficit to acquire language, a testament to the overwhelming human motivation to communicate.

This emphasis on the naturalness of language should not be read as an invitation to ignore language in the school curriculum. Rather, it should be read as a challenge to design language programs in school that build upon children's real experience of learning and using language and to integrate oral and written language across all subjects in the curriculum.

LANGUAGE IS CULTURALLY BOUND

The fact that Inuktitut has more words for *snow* than English and that Arabic has more words for *camel* are often cited as evidence for language being culturally bound. In other words, language is shaped to meet the needs of the speakers who use it. In the British Isles, where English originated, as in most places where it is now spoken, there is relatively little need to talk in great detail about snow—other than its presence or absence, amounts, and how soon it is likely to be removed. Similarly, we are more likely to cross the Mojave Desert in a Jeep or a Side-Kick than on a camel, and we have little need to talk about them except in biology classes or with the travel agent in planning exotic trips to the Middle East or Africa. When the conversation does turn to camels, we muddle along with the words we have, talking about one-hump and two-hump camels or, if we are only recently graduated from our biology classes, Arabian (or dromedary) and Bactrian camels.

Anyone who has ever studied a second language has discovered that learning a language necessarily involves learning something about the people who speak that language and the society in which they live. While it is possible to learn the verb forms and syntax of a language independent of its culture, that kind of learning constitutes only a very small portion of language learning. Some would argue, in fact, that it is really learning *about* the language rather than the language itself. That is a valid distinction. As a linguist, I studied and passed examinations in a number of languages before getting my doctorate. I know quite a lot about French, Spanish, Japanese, and

Mandarin, and yet I can claim proficiency only in English. Understanding the literature of a language and learning to communicate in it require some understanding of the people who speak the language and whose lives are reflected in its writings.

We don't have to seek examples in other languages, however. The evidence that language is culturally bound exists right within the boundaries of our own language. Although a language may have a great many words for talking about a particular subject, only speakers who are interested in or familiar with the subject will have the experiences that give them the detailed vocabulary to talk about it. Five years ago, there were few people on the planet who knew (or cared) what a *URL* was. Outside the computer industry, most people still believe that *java* refers to coffee. Likewise, it had to be pointed out to me recently that the Toledo Mudhens are the farm team of the Detroit Tigers who, I was also told, play baseball. While the two men engaged in the conversation I heard about the Mudhens used no words I had not heard and used before, I did not have the background culture to give me access to the meaning. That is the nature of language; it exists to meet the communicative needs of the speakers who use it, and it would be very odd indeed if it were unable to meet those needs.

There is another very important perspective from which to view language and culture. Children learn very young that ". . . the language we speak identifies us as members of a particular group. Members of different clubs, of different communities, do not speak in the same way. Our own particular language is an emblem of all our cultural ties" (Smith, 1988, p. 6). Children acquire their first language within their society of language users—that ever-widening circle that begins with the immediate family. They learn language in order to become a part of that society, and their learning entails a variety of social functions of language. For instance, they learn greetings, leave-takings, apologies, and excuses, and the only way they can do so is within the context of use. They hear people around them greeting and leaving each other and making apologies and excuses for their behavior, they observe the conditions under which these activities take place and the bodily gestures that accompany the language. Children acquire not only the language of their community but the customs and values as well, and these customs and values vary somewhat among groups who speak the same language.

There is mounting evidence that culture plays an equally important role in the acquisition of literacy. Stressing that "literacy learning is influenced by one's language and cultural background," Strickland (1994) recommends the use of literature that reflects a wide variety of cultures, and especially their own (pp. 332–333). Her view is supported by research evidence. The work of Schieffelin and Cochran-Smith (1984), for instance, suggests that children's interest in print emerges from a particular cultural orientation in which literacy is assumed. Children are socialized to be literate. Reporting on their study of nursery school children's early experiences with print, they observed that

> . . . in cultures where adult-child dialogue is characteristic of language learning, children's caregivers initially accept almost any response as the child's part in a conversation. . . . These actions provide some insight into the way the nursery school children were acquiring

literacy. Adults initially played all the parts in literacy events, completely producing and comprehending print for the children and behaving as if the children themselves intended for print to be used in particular ways and as if the children themselves were using the print. Little by little . . . the nursery school children took over the various roles in literacy events and need less and less help from adult intermediaries. (p. 8)

The culture in which a child grows has a profound influence on language development, particularly written language. Children learn to read and write when they are socialized in a literate environment. Not all children are so fortunate. While most children develop normal oral language in almost any kind of environment, the absence of a literate culture in the preschool environment may have a negative impact on a child's success in learning to read and write in school. This is a topic of considerable importance that will receive fuller treatment in Chapter 10.

LANGUAGE HAS MANY VARIETIES

No one knows exactly how many different languages are spoken by how many people in the world today. A number of factors make it very hard to judge. First, the number of languages is decreasing. A hundred years ago, there were several hundred North American Indian languages that no longer exist. Other continents have experienced similar losses. Second, the population of the planet is growing, and third, migration is increasing. Finally, the technological revolution has put television and the Internet into homes all over the globe and given people the opportunity, and often the necessity, to learn new languages. Given all these factors, it is not surprising that more people than ever speak English. In fact, more people speak English than any other language in the world today—not as a first language, but as either a first or additional language. It is not surprising that the number of non-white, non-English speaking children in North American classrooms continues to grow.

It is highly unlikely that a teacher will know all of the languages spoken by all the children he or she will encounter during a career. Twenty years ago when I taught ESL, the first question most people asked me was how many languages I spoke. They were always disappointed when I replied, "One." It is not necessary for ESL teachers or any other teachers to speak the native language of the children in their classes. What is important is to understand that languages can have very different structures from English, that the cultures they reflect and represent will also differ in significant ways, and that the child comes to school equipped with both.

As interesting as it is, language variation is not restricted to those differences which exist between distinct languages. A significant amount of variation exists among speakers of a given language, much of it due to the fact that language changes and the distance between communities that existed hundreds of years ago led to the development of distinct dialects. Even in the information age, these differences remain, and even to the untrained ear, there is a distinctive sound to Scots English, Australian English, and the English spoken in Alabama.

The reality of geographical dialects was illustrated for me just after I moved to Newfoundland, an island province of Canada in the North Atlantic ocean. English is the only language of the island and has been since John Cabot landed here 500 years ago. It is not, however, a variety of English that came easily to me despite my nomadic ways that have taken me from my beginnings in Missouri, to New Hampshire, Alberta, British Columbia, and Nova Scotia before landing on this easternmost of Canada's provinces. During my first months, I was stopped one day as I walked through the corridors to the University's founder's day ceremony. A colleague stopped me and asked, "Who's after dying?" The befuddled look on my face must have led him to believe that I was "stunned" (a Newfoundland word meaning "slow-witted"), and so he elaborated, "The flag's at half-mast." Then I understood that he was asking me who had died. I responded that no one had died, or at least not recently, but that it was founder's day. He then understood that the flag was at half-mast in honor of the dead of World War I in whose memory the university had been founded. There are many distinctive words and syntactic constructions that set Newfoundland English apart from its cousins on the mainland. Some of these words and constructions are much closer to its British cousins.

My experience in Newfoundland reminds us that language variation is sometimes marked by geographical bounds. That is not always the case. Within a geographical region, groups of people are sometimes identified by the language they speak. We may pretend that North America is a society without the social classes that characterize Great Britain, and certainly there is a less predictable relationship between social groups and language in North America than in the British Isles. Nevertheless, there are marked differences among the dialects spoken, for example, by Francophone children on the Port au Port peninsula in Newfoundland, by Puerto Rican children in southern Florida, by Mexican children in New Mexico, by Sarcee children in Alberta, and by African-American children throughout North America. These differences are caused not by where the children live but by the social and ethnic groups to which they belong. It is essential that teachers learn not to accept society's ill-informed judgments about linguistic diversity and, particularly, not to generalize them to judgments about the ability or the potential of the children whose language differs from their own. As Dorothy Strickland (1994) put it, "Competence isn't tied to a particular language, dialect, or culture" (p. 333). Language, ethnicity, and culture are topics that take up a great deal of space in the professional literature of teaching today. Rightly so. Throughout the remainder of this book, I will revisit these issues from a variety of perspectives.

Most dialect differences are neutralized in the written language. In other words, if there is a standard dialect of English, it is probably best represented by the written forms. But across languages, there is a great deal of variability in writing systems. The two basic categories are systems that show a clear relationship between sounds and graphic symbols (phonological systems) and systems that do not (nonphonological systems). Most of the languages of the world are represented by phonological systems. These include both syllabic and alphabetic systems. The smallest unit in syllabic writing systems is the syllable. Japanese *kana* and Cherokee have syllabic writing systems.

The smallest unit in alphabetic systems is the letter, but languages vary in the degree of predictability between the letter and the sound. Spanish, for instance, has a very regular correspondence between sound and symbol. But any bilingual Spanish speaker will tell us that English does not. How could we possibly explain the spelling of *tough* if it did? Modern nonphonological writing systems are mostly logographic. In these, the graphemes represent words. Chinese and Japanese *kanji* script are some of the better known of these languages.

Children who have been born and attended school in non-English-speaking countries have probably learned a different language and a different writing system. Even another alphabetic system may be based on a different script. Cyrillic (used for Russian), Arabic, and Greek are good examples. If education is to be universally accessible and equally effective for *all* children, then teachers must understand the cultural and linguistic diversity of their students and plan and act accordingly.

We know, for example, that the dialect and language differences that influence children's speech also influence their comprehension of what they hear and read. This is not an insignificant point for teachers, who must keep in mind that such differences reflect, in part, differences in experience and world view that lead, in turn, to interpretations that may differ from those of the teacher or other children in the class from the dominant culture. Later in the book, in Chapters 4, 5, and 10, we will return to the subject of the child who speaks a language other than English.

LANGUAGE HAS STRUCTURE

Obviously, we cannot base a claim for the uniqueness of language on the fact that it has structure. Almost everything in our lives is structured in some way. Language structure is special, however, because it is so very complex, and despite the complexity, children manage to learn it at a very young age. Language structure has always been of special interest, not only to linguists but to average language users. Many of the latter seem to be preoccupied with finding out what among competing forms is the *correct* form, not understanding that what they are really talking about is a standard—mostly written—versus a dialectical variation. Here in Newfoundland, *saw* as the past tense of *see* is rarely heard in the spoken language, except among highly educated speakers. Visitors to the island may conclude that their hosts are using an incorrect form, but if they listen more closely they will discover that this rich dialect has its own structure that differs in other important ways from the standard written form. In speech, they favor, for example, a past tense that has its roots in Irish English and is rarely heard on the North American continent. The earlier example, "Who's after dying?" illustrates this form as do sentences such as "It's after snowing ten inches last night" or "He's after buying lottery tickets for twenty years." There is nothing *incorrect* about any of these sentences, but my Newfoundland-born colleagues at the University tell me that any English teacher worthy of the name devoted her career to eradicating such forms from the language. Unsuccessfully, as it turned out, and happily, I think, for the language is richer for having such variation. This anecdote should tell us something about teaching. Provide a good model of standard English and opportunities to learn it, but respect the linguistic heritage that children bring to the classroom.

While we may remember school grammar lessons as tedious and boring, most of us will admit to a certain curiosity about the structural peculiarities of the language we speak. But language structure is also important from another perspective. It helps us to appreciate the enormity of children's accomplishments in acquiring language. Language is systematic in a myriad of ways. It consists of sounds that are strung together to make words that are strung together to make sentences that are, in turn, strung together to form discourse—not that this is what we do in normal language production. The point is that no human language allows this stringing together to be done in random fashion. There are laws governing the ways in which elements at every level can be combined. In English, for example, we cannot combine the sounds *m* and *b* in that order unless there is a syllable boundary between them. Swahili, however, permits this combination, leading more than one Swahili speaker to conclude that the correct syllable division for *hamburger* is *ha/mburger.* Nor in English can we combine words in random order. Try it and note the looks of confusion on the faces of your listeners.

Somehow children in the first 5 years of life must figure out enough about these structures to make sense of what they hear. The fact that language seems so complex to the adult, whether linguist or person-on-the-street, and yet seems so easily learned is something that makes language truly unique. By the time children come to school, they have mastered much of the structure of their first language (and sometimes another), and it is the task of the school to extend this understanding to new uses. As teachers, we are likely to underestimate the importance of our task. Because children's language accomplishments have thus far been so very impressive, we tend to assume that they can understand the highly abstract language of the school when, in fact, they do not. How many young children correctly interpret the opening lines of *The Star Spangled Banner?* How many children have any idea what *pledge* or *allegiance* mean or what they are promising when they utter them in the pledge to the American flag? Canadian children are equally bewildered by their own national anthem even though the language is more contemporary. More importantly, how many teachers think about and take the time to explain what they are doing to children in language they can understand? Stories about children's interpretations of the language they hear can be very revealing of the mismatch that frequently occurs between what is said and what children understand.

In the first edition after reading my story of Maria, a child who came home from Sunday School with a picture she had drawn of a teddy bear with very strange looking eyes, a number of people confessed that they were in junior high school before they realized that there was no hymn in the hymnal called *Jesus the Cross-Eyed Bear.* Another story from that edition, illustrative of the assumptions children sometimes make about adult language, bears (oops!) repeating in its entirety.

Three brothers, 6, 8, and 9 years old, were sitting on the floor playing cards. Several times during the play, I heard them say "I'm going to drop one card" or "I'm going to drop two." In every way, the rules of the game they were playing seemed to mirror those of poker. Finally, I asked what they were playing.

Paul: Drop poker.
Me: Is that the same as "draw poker"?
Paul: I don't know that game.
Me: Why is it called "drop poker"?
Paul: (Shrugging) 'Cause you drop the cards you don't want, I guess.

In the example of the cross-eyed bear, the child's interpretation is structurally correct and is far more consistent with her own experience than is the intended meaning. In the second example, Paul's interpretation is also structurally sound. He has assumed that the "p" that begins the word *poker* also ends the previous word. This kind of boundary confusion is perfectly normal in continuous speech because we do not, as we sometimes think we do, pause or leave any space between words. This interpretation was accepted by the children since to *drop* cards made more sense than to *draw* cards, especially if they knew only the most obvious meaning of *draw*.

While it is not important for elementary school teachers to know the structure of English in the detail that a linguist does, they should understand the relationship between form and meaning, to what degree and how children have come to master that relationship before starting school, and how to build on their understanding so that it will serve not only their linguistic needs but their other learning needs as well.

One of the ways in which the school extends children's understanding of language structure is in teaching them to read and write. But written language shares only some of the structural properties of oral language, and one of the jobs of schooling is to teach, or to help children to discover, those new structures. Many children come to school knowing a great deal about the structure of text—most know, for instance, how stories are organized—but they still have much to learn about creating that structure in their own writing. We will return to a discussion of language structure in Chapter 2.

LANGUAGE AND THE CHILD: AN EXAMPLE

The title of this chapter raised the question *Why is language special?* In the first few pages, I attempted to answer that question by describing some of the ways in which language is set apart from other subjects in the school curriculum. But the question might be better answered from a more personal perspective. Sensible decisions about curriculum and teaching are impossible to make on the basis of theories and descriptions about language. We have to consider the significance of language in the life of the child. After all, as we saw earlier, language is natural and the child needs neither the school nor the teacher to learn it and to function in it. In this section, we will consider further why language is special in the life of the child.

Lucy

A few years ago when I was conducting research in a Kindergarten in a small community in coastal British Columbia, I met a young Portuguese-speaking child who taught me a great deal about the role language plays in children's learning. About half the children in the Kindergarten arrived in September knowing little or no English. Lucy was one of these children, and she caught my attention right away. Every day, she was brought to school and then taken home again either by her mother or by her friend Jenny's mother. In the brief greetings and leave-takings, both girls and their mothers spoke only in Portuguese. I learned from the ESL consultant, who visited the homes of the ESL children, that Lucy's family had been in Canada for only a few months and spoke no English at all. I expected, therefore, that Lucy and Jenny would speak Portuguese at school, at least when talking to each other.

I was wrong. During the first month of school, I never once heard them speaking Portuguese. Actually, I heard Jenny say very little at all, not surprisingly since she knew no English. But Lucy was a different story! Not knowing English didn't even slow her down. She chattered away, using the few words she acquired each day in a variety of ways. To an adult English speaker's ears, Lucy made many mistakes. She didn't bother with past tense endings or with the third person singular marking on verbs. She had no time for plural suffixes either. She was too busy learning the words that matter to bother with the frills of grammatical nicety. And she made those words do double and triple duty. Initially, she used *teacher* to refer to any adult and then she used it to refer only to her teacher, assuming, perhaps, that it was a unique name. Eventually she sorted out the appropriate referents, but in the meantime she managed to communicate very effectively. Her few verbs, *be* and a couple of action verbs (*go* and *get* were predictable favorites of this active child) were used in whatever way she needed them.

All the time she was busily acquiring English, Lucy made do with the language she had at her disposal, but her language grew impressively, with notable changes taking place almost daily. Early in October, Lucy's mother gave birth to a baby boy. On Halloween, I had the following conversation with Lucy about her new brother:

Lucy: He cry. All the time cry.
Me: Who cries?
Lucy: My baby.
Me: Oh, right. Your new brother.
Lucy: Yeah. All the time he cry.
Me: What do you do?
Lucy: I pat him. Hims back. (She pats her own back.)
Me: Does that help?
Lucy: (She nods.) He can't talk.
Me: No, not yet. But he lets you know when he wants something, doesn't he?
Lucy: (Doesn't seem to understand.)
Me: Can you tell when he's hungry?
Lucy: Yeah. He cry.

Me: Right. That's his way of talking right now, isn't it?
Lucy: Yeah. I not cry.
Me: No, you know how to talk, don't you? Lucy, how many languages do you speak?
Lucy: (Looks puzzled.)
Me: How many different languages do you know?
Lucy: One!
Me: Which one?
Lucy: Mine!

My last two questions to Lucy were silly ones to ask a 5-year-old child simply because answering them required her to think about language as an object apart from herself. Gradually children acquire what we call *metalinguistic awareness* (the ability to think about language as language), but she had not done so at this point. Much of what goes on in classrooms demands metalinguistic thinking that is even more sophisticated than in this example. Most 5-year-olds just beginning Kindergarten are limited in their capacity to think in this way. Lucy's answer makes it clear that using language is much higher on her agenda than talking about it. And so it should be. Even if she had spoken seven languages in addition to English and Portuguese (and perhaps she did!), her answer would have been the same. To her, language was part of her thinking, something so much a part of her that it could not be objectified and counted.

Lucy's answer also provided a clue as to why she never spoke Portuguese in school. One of the things children learn very quickly is to shift registers in different situations. In other words, they learn very early that the language of the playground may have to be modified for the classroom and yet again for the home. Children make these adjustments in register quite easily, and that seems to be precisely what Lucy was doing as she shifted from Portuguese to English and back to Portuguese again. The languages were no more different to Lucy than the different registers of English used by a native English-speaking child moving from "Gimme the ball" to "Would you please pass the potatoes?"

From this brief dialogue, we see once again how natural is the business of acquiring language. We also see how central a role a child plays in the process. She is by no means a blank sheet on which some adult imprints language. In the uttering of only 17 different words, Lucy has demonstrated that she knows a great deal about English and its use.

Lucy's Utterances Were Unique

Although it is true that Lucy must have previously heard the 17 distinct words she used here, it is unlikely that she had ever heard them combined in exactly the same way. In fact, given the absence of grammatical markings in her language, it is extremely unlikely that she had heard exactly the same sentences uttered before. Lucy combined the words to create the meaning she wanted to make at that particular time, meaning that was relevant to the conversation she was having with me.

If we compare Lucy's sentences to those an adult native speaker would use, we see that Lucy's are different. Forms such as *hims* are considered to be developmental forms (rather than errors) and are noteworthy for several reasons. First of all, the presence of developmental forms makes it clear that for Lucy, what she says is more important than how she says it. In this dialogue, as in all her language use, Lucy does not concern herself with grammatically perfect utterances. As far as she is concerned, although most likely she is unaware of it, she is constructing her utterances in response to the situation, that is, to communicate with me about her baby brother. This centrality of meaning and communication in children's language acquisition is a topic to which we will return throughout this book.

Second, Lucy was not taught such forms as *hims*, and it is unlikely that she ever heard them. She created them based on her observation of other forms in the language. In this case, she had correctly worked out that English nouns and many pronouns require an *-s* ending for the possessive form. She had not yet worked out the details of the pronominal system that would prevent *hims*. Lucy was constructing her own language rules based on the observations she had made. In other words, she was not parroting back fully formed utterances she had heard before. She was creating them anew to meet the communication need before her. To do so, she had to have created her own set of rules for using English, a task requiring her to hypothesize about the structure and meaning of the language around her, test her hypotheses, and either discard or modify those found faulty. While there is little doubt that hypothesizing is one way in which children come to recreate the full set of linguistic rules that govern language, there is also little doubt that an hypothesis-testing model is inadequate to explain all the learning they do. In Chapter 6, we will look at hypothesis-testing and some alternative language learning strategies.

In the brief dialogue with Lucy, I did not correct her "hims" nor her "he not cry." This is not unusual behaviour for an adult talking with a child. Research tells us that parents and teachers rarely correct children's language unless there is an error in content. Research also tells us that correcting either grammar or pronunciation is a futile act. Numerous anecdotes attest to children's resistance to such correction, one of the most famous of which is provided by Berko and Brown (1960), came to be known as the *fis* phenomenon:

> One of us, for instance, spoke to a child who called his inflated plastic fish a fis. In imitation of the child's pronunciation, the observer said: "This is your fis?" "No," said the child, "my fis." He continued to reject the adult's imitation until he was told "That is your fish." "Yes," he said, "my fis." (p. 531 quoted in Reich, 1986, p. 58)

If Lucy had referred to her baby brother as her *sister*, then I might have corrected her, but for the same reasons that she did not understand the questions I asked her *about* language, she would not have responded to the correction of the grammatical *forms* of her language.

One other point should be made about developmental forms. It is tempting to think about the mismatches between children's and adults' language forms as deficits or flaws in children's language. To do so, however, implies a particular view of language learning, one that is at odds with much of the evidence we now have about child language acquisition. According to this view, the task of children in language acquisition is to mimic adult production, coming progressively closer to adult forms. This view considers the child's system as a lesser variant of the adult's, and in doing so, ignores the systematic integrity of the child's *own* system, obscures the facts about that system, and minimizes the child's accomplishment. The enormity of this accomplishment and the conditions under which it occurs are topics for discussion in Chapters 3 through 7.

Lucy Understood the Language Spoken to Her

In the brief dialogue, I used a total of 68 words, 45 *different* words, and a variety of sentence types. In addition to the statements, I asked Lucy nine questions of three different structural types, five of which required more than *yes* or *no* responses. Of the four that did require *yes* or *no*, two were tag questions, meaning that there was a question tagged onto the end of a statement, and I merely required confirmation. The remaining two also required yes/no answers but they also asked for information. Even when Lucy failed to understand the question, it is clear that it was not the structure of the question that was problematic but the meaning. She understood far more words than she produced or was able to produce. This is an important observation about language learning: Children are almost always able to understand more than they are able to produce, but the reverse is never true.

When we consider all that is involved in comprehension, we begin to appreciate what the child has accomplished. Lucy had to recognize the incoming sounds as speech, segment the unbroken stream into potentially meaningful units, work out the structure that would give those units meaning, and interpret that within her understanding of my intent in the context of our conversation. The comprehension she exhibited during the brief exchange was in itself an impressive psycholinguistic feat.

Lucy's Language Was Situationally Appropriate and Showed Cultural Awareness

I said above that Lucy responded appropriately to my questions. Not only did she give the linguistically expected response, but a socially accepted one appropriate to the conversation as well. Consider an example. Lucy nodded in response to my question "Does that help?" and introduced a new but related topic into the discourse with "He can't talk." This may seem trivial, but given that she had been in contact with English speakers for only a few weeks and considering the range of inappropriate responses she might have given, it is a noteworthy demonstration of her linguistic competence. This aspect of linguistic competence dealing with the appropriateness of utterances is often overlooked in the literature on language acquisition, but much rides on children's acquiring it.

Lucy's Pronunciation Was Clear and Accurate

Because I did not transcribe the session phonetically, the reader cannot judge the quality of her pronunciation. Each session I had with Lucy was tape recorded, however, and the recording of this dialogue revealed very little of what we commonly call a foreign accent. In eight short weeks, Lucy had effectively mastered the sound system of English, a system that is appreciably different from that of her native Portuguese. In doing so, she accomplished something that most adult learners never do. This accomplishment is partly cognitive, partly linguistic (because there is an underlying system or grammar to the sound system as well as to the sentence), but it is also a physiological feat. Of course, Lucy did not begin as an infant would. She had already mastered the sounds of Portuguese. But English has different sounds, requiring different kinds of articulatory control, and these she mastered in a very short time.

Lucy's Second Language Acquisition Strongly Resembled First Language Acquisition

This is not to say that Lucy's speech was in any way infantile, and certainly the rate of acquisition was much faster than it would be in an infant. This speed can be attributed not only to her age and more advanced cognitive ability but to the simple fact that she had already learned one language. She merely had to engage the mechanism again. There is abundant evidence that first and second language strongly resemble one another, so much in fact, that much of the next several chapters is devoted to drawing parallels.

The case for the similarity between first and second language will be made later in this book, and it will be made on theoretical as well as practical grounds. Here, however, it is useful to consider the most obvious reasons for the similarity between Lucy's second language acquisition and her first. Perhaps the most conspicuous reason is the language learning environment. Many linguists who study second language acquisition believe that there is a difference in kind between second language learning in an informal environment and in a structured environment such as an ESL class. Although Lucy did acquire her language in school, the environment of the kindergarten did not constitute the kind of formal, structured language class that we think of when we think of formal environments. It may well be the case that especially for young learners, the less contrived the language learning environment, the easier the task of learning. The fact that Lucy learned so rapidly and that she apparently experienced little crossover or interference from her native Portuguese suggest that the informal, talk-centred atmosphere of the kindergarten class comprised as friendly an environment for acquiring a second language as the home did for acquiring her first language.

Lucy's teacher organized a kindergarten classroom that was demonstrably friendly to second language learners. She did not believe in structured language lessons but took her cue from observations of children acquiring their first language and provided a rich environment for language to grow. Drawing on her knowledge of cognitive development in young children, she provided concrete materials and experiences for them to think and talk about, but she also allowed them to share their own experiences. The language in the sample dialogue was not, thus, a result of repetition drills or of vocabulary lessons with flash cards. It was made possible because Lucy spent many hours in a classroom where there was much to do and to talk about, where the teacher nourished the natural functions of language in each child's life.

In Chapters 8 and 9, we look at the uses to which children put language and how they acquire them. Then, in Chapters 10, 11, and 12, we return to the issue of language in the school and examine how some teachers have created healthy environments for language growth. We will also visit a Grade 2 class where children from eight different countries talk and learn together.

IF LANGUAGE IS SO NATURAL, WHAT IS THERE TO TEACH?

The dominant theme of this chapter so far has been the uniqueness of language, the major argument being that it forms a natural part of human existence in a way that no other subject in the school curriculum does. If that is the case, one might wonder, then why bother to teach it? Or, more precisely, what exactly is there to teach? One answer to the first question is that we should not teach it. Certainly if what is meant by *teaching* language is to sit children in rows and drill language structures and spelling lists into their heads, it *would* be better not to teach language. If, on the other hand, by teaching language we mean creating an environment that is sensitive to the demands children place on language and to their use of language as a medium for their other language, then it is of utmost importance in the primary/elementary curriculum.

One of the most significant demands, of course, is cognitive. Oral and written language enable almost all other learning that children do through their school years and, indeed, in life. We will see in the remainder of this book that this is so. Even, or *especially*, in the computer age, schools are text places. Whether they are reading books from the class library or material that has been downloaded from the Internet, children must have a high degree of literacy to succeed in school. That literacy depends to a large degree, as we shall also see, on the child's having established a solid foundation of oral language. In an article on speech problems and the danger of ignoring them in the mistaken belief that a child with early language problems may be "the strong silent type," Gary Fowlie made this stark observation.

> I do know that Johnny's going to need all of his strength to survive in a school system where the best indicator of his academic success at 18 is how good his language skills are when he walks in the door at age 5.

This observation offers the best answer to the question raised in the heading above. Language deserves special attention precisely because it *is* natural and because it is essential to school success. Giving language a prominent place in the school day permits teachers to exploit the naturalness of language to the child's benefit. In other words, since language learning comes more easily to children than any other kind of learning and since language is the foundation for success in other learning, it makes good sense to ensure that the foundation is solid and strong.

The Remainder of the Book

In the preceding pages, I have given the very briefest introduction to the issues that are raised and discussed throughout the text. My bias is clear. I hope my goals are also obvious. They are simply to help teachers and potential teachers to understand more about how the children we meet in our classrooms acquire language before they come to us and to understand how to build on that early experience to create a school environment in which every child has an equal opportunity to succeed.

The first seven chapters look at language acquisition, both first and second as well as extraordinary and from a practical, or "case," as well as a theoretical perspective. Chapters 8–11 consist of a close examination of what happens and what *should* happen to children's language in school. The final chapter of the book takes us on a visit to a school in Atlantic Canada, a school that embodies many of the ideals set forth earlier. From that visit, we are able to extract a set of concluding principles or guidelines for making learning a positive experience for all our children.

QUESTIONS FOR DISCUSSION

1. The author claims that animal communication differs from human language in three fundamental ways. Can you think of other similarities or differences?

2. The author refers to Lucy's *hims* as a "developmental form." Why does she distinguish between developmental forms and errors? Would it ever be appropriate to call a child's form that differed from an adult form an *error?*

3. Some mathematicians claim that mathematics is a *pure language.* In what ways does it qualify as a language, according to the author's definition of language, and how does it differ from human language?

4. What other instances of the *fis* phenomenon have you witnessed, and what did they reveal about language acquisition?

5. The author writes, "Children are almost always able to understand more than they are able to produce, but the reverse is never true." Why can the reverse never be true? Why is this an important observation (for teachers, especially) about language acquisition?

CHAPTER TWO

Linguists and Language

There is something about language, possibly the fact that it serves so many purposes in our lives, that makes people interested in it. Humans are nothing if not self-absorbed, and what could be more fascinating as an object of study than this intimate yet observable facet of our humanity? Language is as compelling a subject for scholars as it is for everyone else, and they study it for many different purposes. Poets study it or, more accurately, push the boundaries of its use in exploring the human experience. Psychologists study it to gain insights into human understandings and behaviors. In between are novelists and biographers, journalists and playwrights, anthropologists, sociologists, psychiatrists, educators, and, among many others, linguists of various ilk.

For every aspect of language we might identify, there is someone interested in studying it. The number of perspectives on language study grows steadily as it becomes more and more specialized. Ten years ago, for example, there were few, if any, people studying *hacker* language. In fact, there were few if any who could define it, so recently has it been added to our lexicon. Today, however, there is an entire dictionary devoted to this language used by people who work with computers, and it is an everchanging one. Other scholars are studying the effects of word processing, email, and other Internet communication on the written English and on children's ability to write. Rhetoricians and sociologists are also studying the effects of instant communication on language use, and doubtless a generation from now, we will have to revisit first language acquisition to learn what effect being on-line has had on first (and subsequent) language learners in much the same way that researchers 30 and 40 years ago studied the effects of television on oral and written language development.

In describing some of the more current directions language study has taken, I am by no means implying that all enquiries of a more traditional nature have been answered. Despite all the scholarly attention language has received over the past few centuries, we still know relatively little about language processes or about individual languages, and no one runs any risk of running out of questions or data to study—even if they eschew the computer revolution.

In this chapter, I will describe some of the perspectives from which various people attempt to define and find answers to these questions, especially those areas whose insights about language influence us in our teaching. I will begin with a description of practitioners of the parent discipline, theoretical linguists, a group of scholars whose numbers have greatly diminished in recent years but who are in no immediate danger of extinction.

LINGUISTS

Descriptive and Theoretical Linguists

Foundational to the work of all linguists is a rational, accurate description of language structure. This work of descriptive and theoretical linguists provided invaluable insights into the structure of language and in doing so have advanced our understanding of children's language acquisition as well as our understanding of how they comprehend, speak, read and write. By giving us a clearer picture of the structure—or *possible structures*—of language, these linguists bring us some appreciation of the enormity of the task. Because there are competing descriptions within any one language, the structures also provide alternative bases from which to try to understand language learning.

Traditional descriptive linguists have contributed more directly to language teaching practice. Traditional phonics instruction, for instance, is based not only on the observation that there is some degree of correlation between sound and symbol but on basic concepts from phonemics as well. Though English presents certain problems for phonics instruction because the sounds of English do not correspond exactly to its spelling, this is hardly the fault of the linguists who have clarified our understanding of what correspondence does exist. Whatever we might think about the appropriateness of phonics, we cannot deny that our understanding of sound-symbol correspondence is largely attributable to the work of this group of linguists. (We will return to a fuller description of phones and phonemes later in this chapter.)

Theoretical linguists are also concerned with philosophical issues such as the essence of language, the relationship between language and formal logic, and the existence and nature of universal properties of language. While their field of enquiry might seem further removed from the day to day realities of teaching practice, we must not undervalue their contribution to our work. Noam Chomsky (1975), for example, taught us that language and language behavior were rule-governed and that we could learn a great deal about children's understanding of the rules by observing the language they produced. A descriptive and theoretical linguist, historian, and philosopher, Chomsky was arguably the first of the true psycholinguists. He challenged us to view child learners as actively instructing themselves in language. He argued further that they were so successful because they were innately endowed with brain mechanisms directed specifically to language learning. In the years since he articulated this position, there have been many persuasive arguments against innatism, but the observation that children are active participants in their own learning has become part of the canon of teaching.

All linguists work to some degree with language description and with theories about language. Many have specialized interests, however, that have especial relevance to teaching and learning. Those who practice the discipline of historical linguistics are among them.

Historical Linguists

Linguists who trace changes in language structure over time and help us to understand the origins of modern-day peculiarities of our language are historical linguists. There is no rational explanation for the regular past tense of *go*, for instance, unless we look several centuries back into our language's history. We find thus that there was once a verb *wend* which meant about the same thing as *go* and which is still used in certain expressions. The conjugation of *go* and *wend* somehow collapsed into a single one, retaining *go* and *gone* from *to go* and *went* from *to wend*. By looking at English from a historical perspective, linguists help us to understand why certain words that rhymed in Shakespeare no longer rhyme today. Throughout Shakespeare, *where* and *were* are treated as exact rhymes. In fact, it is Shakespeare's rhymes that give linguists some of their strongest evidence for how English words were pronounced during the early modern period of the language. Consider, for example, the following examples, the final two lines from five of Shakespeare's sonnets:

1. *O, him she stores, to show what wealth she had*
   In days long since, before these last so bad. (LXVII)
2. *For we, which now behold these present days,*
   Have eyes to wonder, but lack tongues to praise. (CV)
3. *If some suspect of ill mask'd not thy show,*
   Then thou alone kingdoms of hearts shouldst owe. (LXX)
4. *For I am sham'd by that which I bring forth,*
   And so should you, to love things nothing worth. (LXXII)
5. *Therefore, like her, I sometimes hold my tongue,*
   Because I would not dull you with my song. (CII)

While it is possible that Shakespeare was having an off day when he wrote the last two sonnets, it is more likely that his rhymes were as exact in those two sonnets as in the first three examples.

The kinds of questions that historical linguists try to answer in their research may seem to be of little direct relevance for modern language teachers. Issues such as which sounds might have existed in a language before it was written down, for example, or why the *th-* sound is relatively rare in the languages of the world seem far removed from the life of a 7-year-old child. But we also have historical linguists to thank for much of what we now understand about English spelling (although, unfortunately, we can't blame them for it!). What seems at times a chaotic and random system makes a great deal more sense when we understand that current English spelling is a product of its history.

A very brief look at that history reveals a language with a long and checkered history but one whose writing system was only standardized about 250 years ago. It is not possible to pinpoint a time when English was born, but most scholars choose a date around 450 A.D. when the British Isles were invaded (as they were often in subsequent centuries), this time by three Northern European tribes, the Angles, Jutes, and Saxons. Not a highly civilized crowd, these invaders managed to meld their various languages or dialects into the language we now call Old English. What has survived from Old English into modern times are the words that were needed in their daily pursuits, principally farming, once they stopped warring among themselves. Words such as earth, tree, dirt, and sheep all come from Old English as do most of the 100 or so most frequently used words in contemporary English. About 150 years after this invasion, St. Augustine landed in Britain, bringing with him Christianity and Church Latin. The establishment of monasteries had a profound influence on language and culture in the British Isles, and some influence on the English language which learned monks began to write down. England rose as a center of learning and culture throughout Europe and the publishing capital of the world, but the books were mostly written in Latin.

By the end of the millennium, Britain had survived the Viking invasion, which brought the Danish language to Britain, and had begun another renaissance led by Alfred the Great. This wise king encouraged the printing of books in the vernacular—Old English.

The Middle English period began with yet another invasion, the Norman Conquest of 1066. The major linguistic effect of this invasion was the introduction of French. Although French was used mainly at court, a great number of words that we use today—approximately 40% of our vocabulary—were brought to the English language by William the Conqueror. Words for cuisine, for example, such as *beef* and *pork* (cf. French *boeuf* and *porc*) came to be used instead of the perfectly utilitarian *cow* and *pig* that Anglo-Saxons would have used. There remains today, incidentally, a certain snobbery attached to the use of French words *de cuisine* leading us to shun the perfectly descriptive *snail* in favour of *escargot* or *cake* in favour of *gateau* (in Britain), and don't even bother thinking about the English equivalent of *hors d'oeuvres* (although with the mangled pronunciation most of us inflict on the last term, the French might be excused for thinking it *is* English).

The Norman Conquest furthered Britain's claim as a cultural center, and by the 14th century the demand for books was growing. When Caxton brought the printing press to England in 1476, the subject of how to spell English words became important. It had been a fairly flexible affair before that and after the introduction of the printing press remained so. The fact that the early printers emigrated to Britain from what is now the Netherlands and spoke Dutch did little to add precision to an already lax system. To complicate matters further, at the time that the printing press was introduced to Britain, the pronunciation of a great many English words was in flux as a result of what has come to be known as the *Great Vowel Shift*. Understanding how modern spelling came to represent the spoken language depends to some degree on knowing what happened in the development of English vowels. Moreover, if Bear et al. (1996) are correct in asserting that children's learning of the spelling system parallels the historical development of spelling, then it is useful to look at the Great Vowel Shift a little more closely.

Sometime during the period of early Modern English, a change occurred in the pronunciation of the vowels that we typically characterize as *long*. As a result of the Great Vowel Shift, words that had been pronounced with an /e/ sound as in modern *lake* came to be pronounced with an /i/ as in modern *leek*. *Sheep*, in middle English, would have sounded more like modern *shape* and today's *boot* would have sounded to the modern speaker like *boat*. This shift did not affect the pronunciation of short vowels such as the ones in *it, bet,* or *fat*. We can begin to understand certain vowel alternations better when we consider the simple fact of the Great Vowel Shift. Consider, for example, *sheep* and *shepherd*. We typically think of vowels as occurring in long/short pairs. The long vowel in modern day *sheep* is represented as [i]. Its corresponding short vowel is the vowel in *sit*, which linguists represent as [I]. In Middle English, however, the vowel in *sheep* would have been [e] (as in *shape*), the short version of which *is* the same vowel as is still found in *shepherd*. The language is replete with examples of alternations that would have been quite regular in Middle English but are no longer so today. The alternation between the vowels in *bite* and *bit* provides another good example. In Middle English, the sound that today is the diphthong [ai] would have been [i] as in modern *beet*. The Great Vowel Shift changed the long high vowels [i] and [u] into the diphthongs [ai] (as in *bite*) and [au] (as in *cow*). The corresponding short vowels were unaffected so that the alternation between long and short vowels in these words is not the natural one it once was. Shakespeare's seeming indifference to spelling can thus be explained. He was writing at a time when the pronunciation of the language was going through a major change, it was printed by foreign printers who doubtless imposed some of their own pronunciations, and most of the population of Britain was still illiterate.

It was not until the modern English period and the publication of Samuel Johnson's *Dictionary of the English Language* in 1755 that English spelling was standardized. And since then, although the pronunciation of the language has gone through some major changes, the spelling has remained more or less constant. There are some exceptions, such as the American spellings of *favour, honour, colour,* etc., but these had nothing to do with regularizing sound-symbol correspondence.

Even though the facts of language change interest some young children, most teachers would not use the information in this way but to inform their own understanding. Knowing that English is much more regular and predictable than it first seems makes us less likely to treat it as a puzzle without a solution.

Psycholinguists

Although the label of their discipline is somewhat daunting, psycholinguists probably speak more directly to the language concerns of educators than any other type of linguist. Unlike theoretical/descriptive and historical linguists whose data come mainly from printed language that occurred sometime in the past, psycholinguists work for the most part with oral language in the present. They are more interested in the people and processes that create the data. Psycholinguists study the three processes that comprise human language behavior—language acquisition, comprehension, and production.

Psycholinguistics have increased our understanding of how these processes work, and in doing so have had a significant impact on language teaching practice. In fact, among the ranks of psycholinguists today can be found a great many educators, and I would count as practicing psycholinguists most effective elementary teachers, although I doubt that many would be aware of it or share my view. Let's examine this notion more thoroughly. In claiming that a good elementary teacher is a psycholinguist, I make no assumptions about the scholarly publications she might read or write. She may never attend a conference of linguists; she may never have even seen the *Journal of Psycholinguistic Research*. But in the course of a day, as she talks, instructs, or tells and reads stories to the children in her class, she is mindful of making herself understood by listeners who do not have the same level of competence that she does. She is, thus, concerned with oral language comprehension, with the developmental level of the children, and about how to modify her own speech appropriately for each situation. In teaching children to read, in evaluating their miscues and deciding what, if anything, to do about them, she has to think about how fluent readers get meaning from text. When she wonders why Sarah still substitutes a /w/ for some of the /l/ and /r/ sounds in her speech, she is posing a question that a great many psycholinguists have posed about the nature of and the relationship between language *perception* and *production*. When she observes that some of her Asian learners seems to have the same difficulty with these sounds as Sarah, she is really asking whether the Chinese sound system is interfering with English or whether the child is merely experiencing the same kind of developmental behavior as Sarah.

As teachers, we owe much to psycholinguistics for our understanding of the reading process. Recognizing that reading involves an interaction between reader and text was a major change from earlier beliefs about the nature of reading and methods of teaching it. In the past, the identification of sounds and words dominated the teaching of reading, a practice that had a limited psycholinguistic basis itself because it assumed that the reader made mental connections between the printed symbol and the language sound. It was a far cry, however, from the kind of active cognitive processing assumed by more recent educators and psycholinguists who have given the child more mental work to do in the business of learning to read.

Every teacher of young children is aware of and worries to some degree about the relationship between children's language development and their general cognitive growth, a question that goes to the heart of current psycholinguistics. It is common practice, for example, to make a preliminary assessment of children's cognitive development by assessing their language ability. We know this is true when we witness the difficulty in assessing the educational level or readiness of a non-English-speaking child. In fact, all these questions with which the elementary teacher routinely deals are asked by psycholinguists as well. It is to be expected, then, that psycholinguistics is the branch of linguistics that does most to inform our teaching practice and why I claim that good teachers are also linguists.

Since psychology is a science of the mind, it would be reasonable to expect that psycholinguistics would include the study of the relationship between language and brain functions. There was time when this was so, when some psycholinguists did venture into brain study, but the major work in this area today is now done by neurolinguists.

Neurolinguists

I said earlier in the book that humans are self-absorbed, and our interest in our own language is, in part, a product of our egocentricity. Nowhere is this more evident than in our fascination with the human brain. Physicians, of course, have a legitimate and critical interest in the brain. In treating traumatic and other kinds of neurological mal-functioning, they need to learn as much as possible about how the human brain functions. Often, their interest is linguistic as when a patient has suffered language loss from a stroke. In this case, they also need to know about language processes. In fact, we owe much of our understanding of neurolinguistic processing to the work of physicians and other health care professionals working with patients who have suffered brain trauma. On the other hand, the work of neurolinguists has begun in recent years to inform the medical profession. Neurolinguists further their understanding, and ours as educators, through their study of brain structure and how it influences language learning and processing and how damage to the brain affects language learning, production, and comprehension.

It is problematic, of course, that most of neurolinguistic data about linguistic functioning necessarily comes from people who have suffered some degree of damage to the brain. It is rarely possible, thus, to do more than to speculate on normal brain functioning as it affects language acquisition, production, and comprehension. But if neurolinguists contribute nothing more, they raise important questions and alert us to the potential of brain research for language education.

There are two major types of neurological research that have some potential for informing language education. One relates to brain maturation and addresses the question of how the parameters of brain maturation contribute to our understanding of language acquisition in monolingual and bilingual persons (Whitaker, Bub, & Leventer, 1981, p. 59). The other has to do with neurological bimodality and addresses two different questions. The first is, broadly, how the two hemispheres of the brain contribute to the learning of either a first or a subsequent language. The second is how teaching methods might best be constructed to correspond with what is known about hemispheric functioning. Danesi (1988a), for example, has made the claim that the failure of many second language teaching methods is due to the fact that they appeal to, or are directed to, only one side of the brain. He stresses the importance of developing bimodal approaches or methods, but recognizes at the same time that in order to do so, we must be very clear about what kinds of techniques would be appropriate for which hemisphere. Other researchers point out that because the brain is such a highly complex structure, questions about such gross distinctions as hemisphericity are immaterial. Some

Canadian researchers have postulated, moreover, that the distinction between the front and back of the brain has as much or more potential for understanding linguistic and behavioral differences as left/right hemisphericity.

While I am sceptical that our understanding of brain functioning is sufficiently detailed or accurate to dictate sound teaching practice, I am convinced that as our understanding of the brain improves, we will eventually find the basis for a closer correspondence between the human "hardware" and the educational "software." At this point, we can only trust in some very basic tenets, and these serve more as guidelines about what *not* to do than what *to do*.

1. Second and subsequent languages are acquired in much the same way as the first with allowance for known differences in cognitive strategies in use at different ages of learners.
2. The same regions of the brain are involved in all language acquisition.
3. The aging of the brain during childhood does not negatively affect the ability to learn the vocabulary, syntax, or pronunciation of a second language, and no period of the life span is more critical than another to the acquisition of a second or subsequent language.
4. Any "greater plasticity" of the immature brain relates to the ability to compensate for structural loss of brain tissue and has no impact on the functioning of the intact brain. (Adapted from Kinsbourne, 1981, p. 56)

While brain research is progressing rapidly, the relationship between brain science and cognition and learning remains imprecise. Nevertheless, neurolinguistics is interesting for the questions it raises and for the potential that exists for contributing to our understanding of how the brain learns.

Sociolinguists

Sociolinguists study language in relation to social factors such as age, sex, ethnic origin, social class, and educational level. These are all factors that educators must take into account in all their educational activities. Sociolinguists might study some of the same general issues as psycholinguists and neurolinguists, but they would do so from a different perspective. All three, for example, might be interested in bilingualism. A psycholinguist might ask how bilinguals process their two languages, what cognitive strategies are involved, or whether they are the same for the two languages. A neurolinguist would wonder about the physical effects of bilingualism—whether there is a measurable difference in the brains or in the cerebral functioning of bilinguals. A sociolinguist would likely be more concerned with how the community of language users influence the individual's language learning or use; or about the linguistic indicators of socioeconomic class.

Another area of overlap between sociolinguists and psycholinguists is **discourse analysis.** While the psycholinguist may be interested in "discovering the intellectual processes we use in understanding [spoken or written] narratives" (Hatch, 1983, pp. 150–151), the sociolinguist is more likely to be interested in studying the conversational differences between men and women or between doctor and patient. There is, in fact, an entire domain of research known as unequal power discourse that studies speech events during trials, doctor-patient encounters, and in classrooms.

An important area of research undertaken by sociolinguists (and by applied linguists) is the interaction that takes place between mother, or other caretaker, and child. From sociolinguistic studies we have learned, for example, that many aspects of mother-child interaction and maternal expectations are culturally determined (Harris, 1985). Freedman (1979) observed, for instance, differences in the ways Native American and European descent mothers attracted the attention of their infants. These, together with studies showing differences in the way Native American children interact with adults, constitute a major contribution to educational practice.

Broadly speaking, sociolinguists study how members of a community interact linguistically. Of particular interest to us is the community of the classroom and how the social environment of the classroom contributes (or not) to literacy in children. In the final analysis, however, it is educators and not linguists who determine just what that environment will be. Sociolinguists have the task of describing the interaction that occurs in classrooms. Educators have the task of evaluating those descriptions and implementing changes they think appropriate.

Sociolinguists are also interested in the language varieties that may exist within a community. These varieties may be different languages as they are in bilingual communities throughout Canada, or they may be dialects of a single language. Dialectic variation will be found in nearly all communities, certainly in all urban communities. Language variety is another area of overlap between sociolinguists and teachers. Educators tend to talk about "linguistically different" children, implying (perhaps) that there are few of these children. This implication is not borne out by the statistics available in the United States and Canada where there are many communities with a majority of linguistically different children. In Toronto, Vancouver, Los Angeles and other large North American cities, more than half the children in city schools may speak a language other than English. If we consider children who speak a nonstandard dialect as well, we have a very large population of linguistically different children. In coping with the linguistic and educational needs of these children in school, educators necessarily rely on insights from sociolinguists.

The appropriate application of the research findings of sociolinguists (as well as other linguists) is the job of educators. We are helped, however, by another group of linguists, the applied linguists.

Applied Linguists

Applied linguists take information from other subdisciplines of linguistics and use it in various ways. There are several varieties of applied linguist. One applies the principles and theories of linguistics to second and foreign language learning and teaching. Another studies the role of language in practical problems such as lexicography, translation and speech pathology. Still others, sometimes called educational linguists, are concerned with aspects of language research that have broad application in education. Literacy, for example, is a primary concern of educational linguists. They have to borrow greatly from psycholinguistics, neurolinguistics, developmental psychology, and educational theory in their attempts to explain how children learn to read and write.

The aim of educational applied linguistics is not to tell teachers how to teach language. How to teach, and to a large degree *what* to teach, remain the prerogative of teachers and teachers of teachers who study children, classroom interactions, approaches, methods, and techniques of instruction in the classroom environment. Rather, the aim of educational linguistics is to provide the language teacher with the latest theories and the findings of quality research that serve to inform educational practice. Applied linguists, especially educational linguists, must be conversant with their parent discipline and sometimes several. Because there are so many areas to be taken into account, the educational linguist may choose not to conduct original research, although it is certainly possible to do so, but may interpret the scholarship of other areas for use in education. That is no easy job for it requires sufficient expertise in the different branches of linguistics to be able to evaluate and interpret the various studies intelligently; and sufficient expertise in education to be able to suggest reasonable, appropriate applications. For our purposes, the issue is what kind of insights we can hope to gain from applied linguistics and how we translate them into practice.

LANGUAGE STRUCTURE

There are many reasons for studying language structure, but the most compelling for teachers is to understand what children accomplish in acquiring language. Here we will examine five aspects of language structure and talk briefly about their importance to teaching. They are phonology, the study of the sound system; morphology, the structure of words; syntax, the structure of sentences; semantics, the structure of meaning; and pragmatics, the study of language as it is used in actual communication.

I am extremely reluctant to separate language in this way because to do so is quite alien to children's experience of learning it. They do not learn the sound system before attempting to put words together or master a large vocabulary before attempting sentences. The structure of English (or any language) is so complex, however, that separating it into these various levels makes it easier to deconstruct. One caveat is necessary. This is not a text on linguistics and so this is the barest of introductions to a topic about which thousands of volumes have been written, but I am hopeful that this brief introduction to language structure will provide a useful overview and generate sufficient interest for further reading. We begin with the sound system.

Phonology: The Sound System

If we think about the sound system from the perspective of children acquiring language, the question is, quite simply, what has to be learned? Broadly, children must come to understand and produce the sounds necessary for communicating meaning in their language. At the onset of speech, it is unlikely that their attention is commanded by any unit smaller than the word or the syllable; there is evidence that phonetic segmentation is difficult for pre-reading children. Eventually, of course, children learn to distinguish among all the individual speech sounds—the consonants and vowels of their language—a task which they prepare for throughout the babbling period but one which is more complicated than it seems. Every speaker a child encounters utters each sound a little differently from every other and a little differently in some words than in others. Children must figure out which sounds are distinctive and which are not—in other words, which differences in sound signal a changed meaning. They also have to learn that a great deal of the variation between the speech sounds they hear can be safely ignored. An example of the latter is the different pronunciations of -*ing* at the ends of words. Speakers of several dialects of English regularly pronounce -*ing* as -*in* while other speakers produce the standard form. Yet both mean the same thing and children learn to ignore this non-distinctive difference.

In the first edition I wrote that "children must also learn to combine sounds in syllables and words." Taken literally, that is, of course, erroneous, as I must have known at the time. The evidence beginning to emerge then and well established now is quite the opposite: It is the larger units, either the syllable or the rime (discussed below) that children learn first. Eventually they learn finer segmentation but mostly as a result of learning to read. In the acquisition of oral language, a child does not "combine sounds in syllables and words." They do not learn to pronounce [p] and [l] and eventually combine them to produce [pl-] which is eventually combined with vowels to produce words such as *play* and *plum*. Their early difficulty with pronouncing the cluster [pl-] is not a problem with *combining* sounds because to the child, the unit is a single one. It is simply hard to produce just as the *th-* sound is hard to produce. Talking about children's learning to combine sounds is an adult linguist's perspective on what is done because in terms of describing the sound system, that is what is easiest to do.

Another aspect of the sound system that children must master is the stress and intonation patterns of their language, a skill that they began preparing for in the crib. If a child is Chinese, the task is very different than it is for an English-speaking child, but for both, learning the meaning conveyed by these more subtle cues is an essential part of language learning. In the next few pages, I offer the briefest introduction to the English sound system, concentrating on those units that are central to understanding childen's acquisition of both the spoken and written language.

Minimal Pairs and Phonemes

English has many pairs of words which differ from each other by only one sound. These are called minimal pairs, and they tell us which sounds are distinctive. For example, we know from the following list of words that the consonants /p,b,g/ are distinctive because substituting one for the other changes the word meaning. For the same reason, we know that the two vowels, /I,a/ are distinctive sounds.

pill	pall
bill	ball
gill	gall

On the other hand, each consonant and vowel sound has several possible and permissible pronunciations. We articulate the /g/ in *gill*, for example, just a little differently from the same sound in *gall*. In the first, the tongue touches the roof of the mouth near the hard palate while in the second, the tongue touches the roof of the mouth farther back, near the soft palate or velum. Substituting the /g/ sound in *gill* for the one in *gall* will result in a distorted pronunciation which will sound strange to the native speaker but will not change the meaning.

For every distinctive sound in the language, there are many permissible articulations, but all articulations of each are distinct from all articulations of any other. These distinctive sounds of a language are called **phonemes,** linguists indicate them with slashes (//), and every language has a different set. Phonemes can be classified into two broad categories, consonants and vowels. There is also a third and smaller category of sounds which resemble both consonants and vowels, called semivowels. Linguists would point out that people do not actually speak in phonemes. Rather, each phoneme serves as a categorical name for the group of sounds speakers use and recognize as the same. They describe actual speech in terms of *phones*, and each phoneme is made up of many different phones all of which would be identified by native speakers as the same sound despite the many variations among them. For convenience here and because the literature on reading uses the term, I will use *phoneme* to refer to individual sounds.

Individual phonemes are described according to how the airstream is modified to produce them. During speech, as air moves from the lungs through the mouth or nose, it is modified in a number of ways to produce different sounds. In the articulation of consonants, the airstream is either partially or totally blocked in the mouth. In the production of vowels, the air from the lungs is not blocked at all, but the shape of the mouth gives each vowel its characteristic sound. Semivowels, as their name suggests, resemble vowels and are produced with only very slight interference.

In producing **consonants,** the airstream coming from the lungs is obstructed to some degree, and this obstruction may occur anywhere in the oral cavity. One other alteration to the airstream is made by the vocal folds in the larynx. If the folds vibrate, as they do with the articulation of /z/ and /m/, for example, the sound is voiced. If they do not, as in /s/ and /f/, the sound is voiceless. The consonants of English can be distinguished from one another, then, on the basis of three modifications to the airstream—the place in the oral cavity where the air is impeded, the manner in which it is impeded, and voicing.

Vowels are very different from consonants. To begin with, because the airstream is not impeded, they are highly resonant and all voiced. They are easier to hear, and it is easier to distinguish between them. A common example demonstrates that this is true. This morning when I telephoned an airline to make a reservation, I had to spell my name with names (P as in Peter, I, P as in Peter, E, R as in Reindeer). I had to tell them the additional information about the consonants because the telephone does not transmit sound well enough to distinguish, for instance, between /p/ and /t/. There is no problem hearing the correct vowel because they are so resonant and dissimilar. (It probably wasn't necessary to add Reindeer because /r/ is more resonant than the other consonants in my name. I did so because of the wide variations in the pronunciation of /r/.)

The particular quality of each vowel is achieved by changing the shape of the resonator, that is, the oral cavity. Vowel quality depends on which part of the tongue is raised—front, central, or back—and on how far the tongue is raised—high, mid, or low. High front vowels are those in which the front part of the tongue is raised almost to the roof in the mouth, as in the vowel sounds in *cheap* and *chip*. To distinguish these two vowels, another feature is required. This feature refers to the amount of muscular tension in the vocal tract, principally the lower jaw. Vowels which are produced with a relatively greater degree of movement and with greater tension are called **tense vowels** and those produced with less movement and less tension are called **lax vowels.** This is a particularly salient distinction for elementary teachers because it corresponds roughly to the categories "long vowel" and "short vowel" used in phonics. The short (or lax) vowels are produced with comparatively little movement or tension and include the vowels in *bit, blood, put, bat, bought,* and *father.* Long vowels are those produced with greater movement and muscular tension and include the vowels in *beep, brood, bake,* and *boat.* Also in the category of long vowels are the *diphthongs* in *boy, bite,* and *bout.* Diphthongs are treated like single vowels, but they are really two vowel sounds produced with one gliding into the other. Because they are produced with a gliding motion of the tongue, diphthongs are tense. My description of vowels is based on the standard of mid-East-Coast United States and much of eastern Canada. Throughout the English-speaking world, and even in these areas, there will be variations from these descriptions. The vowel \e\, for instance, is diphthongized in much of North America to \e^1\.

Semivowels are produced with only very slight interference of the airstream in the oral tract. These sounds are, in fact, more like vowels in their articulation, but in English they function like consonants. They include the initial sounds in *wax* and *yaks*.

Syllables

The consonants, vowels and semivowels are not the only units of the sound system. Another important one is the **syllable,** a unit which people intuitively recognize. There are even writing systems based on syllables. English syllables are, however, rather difficult to define formally or even to identify consistently. Does *chocolate,* for example, have two syllables or three? The answer depends on at least two variables—the dialect the individual speaks and how carefully he or she pronounces the word.

English has a number of different kinds of syllables. A syllable can be composed of a single vowel and no consonants (*Oh!*—remember, we are talking about sound, not writing), or a vowel with one or more consonants on either side (*car, scar,* and *scars* are all single syllable words). English permits up to three consonants before the vowel (e.g., *strip*) and up to four following the vowel (*texts*—pronounced "teksts").

Although syllable structure is somewhat awkward to describe, evidence is growing that children cope well with syllables at an early age. Children's early ability to rhyme points to the way in which they cope with syllable structure: a syllable consists of an onset followed by a rime. An **onset** is the initial consonant or cluster in a syllable, and a **rime** is the vowel and any consonants that follow. Thus the word (and syllable) *plant* consists of the onset *pl-* and the rime *-ant*. Similarly, *rub* consists of the onset *r* and the rime *ub*. Onsets and rimes seem to have greater psychological validity to children than do phonemes. Preschool children, for example, are generally good at rhyming. They can produce *rub, grub, club, sub, flub,* and *hub,* and perhaps some made-up syllables in a rhyming game. Goswami (1993) and other researchers (cf. Kirtley, Bryant, MacLean, & Bradley, 1989; Bowey & Francis, 1991; Treiman, 1985) have provided a great deal of evidence that when children come to school they already have phonological knowledge about onsets and rimes. They are not so good, however, at phonemic analysis—telling how many different sounds in *grub* or *club* or even *rub* or choosing the odd member of a set of sounds when the unit of sound is smaller than an onset or a rime. Children who have learned to read are better at this level of phonemic analysis, suggesting that it may be a product of learning to read rather than a prerequisite. This is important and a subject to which I will return in Chapter 3.

Phonological Processes

The task of learning the individual sounds and the syllable structure of a language is a complex one, and it is made more so by the fact that the actual pronunciation of speech sounds varies under different conditions. For example, we may pronounce a vowel one way when it is stressed and another when it is not. Whether the vowel is stressed depends, in part, on the prefixes or suffixes which are present. The process by which a vowel sound becomes neutralized to schwa when it loses its stress is called **vowel reduction.** This process occurs with certain words when they change their part of speech (their grammatical role in a sentence). Consider these pairs of words:

receive (v.)	reception (n.)
conceive (v.)	conception (n.)
cleave (v.)	cleft (adj.)
bereave (v.)	bereft (adj.)
sustain (v.)	sustenance (n.)

Notice that in each pair, the same syllable is stressed but when an additional morpheme is added in order to change the part of speech, the quality of the vowel changes. This process is called **vowel alteration** and is very common in English. We see it in the conjugation of certain irregular, or strong, verbs:

leave, left, left	break, broke, broken
lose, lost, lost	sink, sank, sunk
ring, rang, rung	sing, sang, sung
write, wrote, written	bite, bit, bitten

Consonant sounds are also reduced in various ways in continuous speech. In the sentence,

Alma and Fred will have the dog groomed next week

unless the speaker is articulating very precisely, the final /t/ in *next*, normally pronounced *nekst* in citation form, will be left out. A similar process occurs in the pronunciation of *dog groomed*. Here, because the final consonant of *dog* is the same as the first consonant of *groomed*, speakers will often reduce the two sounds to a single /g/. This is one of several types of assimilation, or the changing of one speech sound to become more like another sound in its immediate environment. If the speaker is from parts of Britain or New England, he or she may also introduce an /r/ sound between *Alma* and *and* (producing something akin to "almarand"). This is a kind of **dissimilation,** the opposite of assimilation, and apparently occurs to break up two similar or identical sounds. Although both assimilation and dissimilation are natural processes, the first to reduce and somewhat simplify the stream of speech, it is curious that the processes occur in different contexts in different dialects.

The Sound System and Literacy

There is a great deal of speculation about the relationship between children's phonological awareness and their later ability to read and write. Certainly, in the broadest sense, it is true that in learning to read and write children must be able to manipulate speech sounds in print. It requires, however, a giant leap in reasoning to reach any conclusions about the nature of the phonological awareness they need in advance. Some researchers and educators define phonological awareness as a child's "ability to reflect upon and manipulate components of spoken words" (Snowling et al., 1994, p. 161). This definition is of a metalinguistic ability (the child's ability to think *about* language) rather than a linguistic ability (the child's ability to use language) and still begs the question of what kind of knowledge is required. What seems to be the case is that while there is a relationship between early phonological awareness and learning to read, that awareness does not necessarily mean the ability to identify and manipulate individual phonemes. Rather, there is growing evidence that early sensitivity to rhyme is the determining factor in learning to read. Wimmer et al. (1994) found, for example, that children's ability to identify rhymes, as measured before the onset of reading instruction, was a predictor of their ability to read at the end of Grade 3. Their ability to isolate onsets, on the other hand, was significantly correlated, albeit barely, with their ability to read at the end of Grade 1 but had lost all predictive power by the end of Grade 3. This is consistent with the findings of other researchers that the ability to segment by phoneme is a consequence of rather than a prerequisite to reading, though it is necessary to learning to spell (Bradley & Bryant, 1983; Goswami & Bryant, 1990; Snowling et al., 1994). Goswami and Bryant (1990) have demonstrated that preschoolers' performance on rhyme and alliteration tasks predicts their later ability to read. They have argued rather convincingly that at the earliest stage of learning to read, children need to be able to discriminate onsets and rimes. Other researchers insist that the ability to isolate and manipulate individual sounds, i.e., phonemes, is what is required of children (e.g., Yopp, 1988). On the whole, emerging research supports onsets and rimes as the salient unit of phonology for literacy.

Studies of children learning to read English after first learning to read a nonalphabetic language are useful in determining the effect of prior learning on alphabetic decoding. Comparing British children with children from Hong Kong, Huang and Hanley (1994) found that British children had more difficulty in deleting the first phoneme from an initial consonant cluster (i.e., *s-* from *sp-*) than did children from Hong Kong. In contrast, the British children found it easier to isolate the *s-* from *sit* and to perform similar tasks than the Chinese children. It would seem that English-speaking children viewed the initial consonant cluster, common in English phonology, as an integral unit while the Chinese children remained true to their phonology, that does not have consonant clusters. More importantly, however, was the finding that phonological awareness contributed only to the reading of an alphabetic language. This is important because most of the studies use correlation methodology, and this methodology has an inherent weakness in interpretation. Specifically, even though the relationship between rhyming and alliterative ability on the one hand and reading ability on the other has been demonstrated through correlation, it is always possible that another undetected variable is influencing both phonological awareness and reading ability. If that were the case, as Huang and Hanley (1990) point out, this undetected variable should cause an equally strong relationship between phonological awareness and the reading of a non-alphabetic language. Since this is not the case, they argue, there is good reason to believe that "phonological awareness is a primary cause of differences in reading ability amongst children who read an alphabetic script" (p. 92).

Most children acquire the sound system quite easily despite its complexity. When reading and writing become part of children's language awareness, the sound system gets more confusing because the sound-symbol correspondence is not always predictable. One of the seeming irregularities is related to that strange phenomenon known as the silent letter. The silent letter is primarily a reading rather than a writing concept. In other words, the issue of the silent letter first arises when we are decoding printed text into sound units, and it might be tempting to try to rid the language of such culprits. It is fairly easy to demonstrate, however, that many letters which are silent in one form of a word make plenty of noise in another. Consider the following pairs:

sign	signature
autumn	autumnal
column	columnar
bomb	bombard

The pronunciation of the words in the second column would suggest that were we to change the English writing system to make it strictly *funetik*, we might well complicate it instead, since the relationship between such pairs of words would be far less obvious. Other kinds of silent letters exist, of course, for less obvious reasons. Many phonics rules are intended to make sense of the silent letters in very common words. *When two vowels go walking, the first one does the talking* tells the beginning reader that the first vowel of a digraph "says its name" while the second is silent, thus telling a child who encounters words such as *beak, leaf, braid,* or *boat* how the vowel is pronounced. The concept is virtually useless when it comes to trying to figure out the spelling of these words as children's invented spellings will tell us.

Stress and Intonation

Another important aspect of the English sound system is the prosody, or the stress and intonation patterns of the language. *Stress* refers to the force with which a syllable is articulated. When stress serves to distinguish the otherwise identical inVALid from INvalid, for example, it is said to be distinctive. It is also predictable to a certain degree in that there are very general rules which tell us which syllable of a word to stress. For example, for two-syllable words which end in two consonants (words such as *deduct, resent, result, adapt,* and *report*), stress usually falls on the second syllable. In contrast, two-syllable words which end in a single consonant (such as *exit, cancel,* and *festive*) are stressed on the first syllable. The rule is, however, more complicated than that. Consider, for example, *erase, refrain, align,* and *remove*. Stress on these words is on the second syllable despite their single final consonant (once the reader has figured out that the *g* in *align* is silent). This is because the vowel is tense (or long).

Unfortunately, this rule for assigning stress to two-syllable words is complicated further by the existence of many noun-verb pairs in English which are identical but for their stress. Unlike the example of inVALid/INvalid given above, these pairs are related in meaning. They include words such as:

NOUN	VERB
PERfume	perFUME
TORment	torMENT
CONvict	conVICT
REcord	reCORD
SUBject	subJECT

The rules for assigning stress to words in English are complex and they have many exceptions. It is unlikely, however, that children learning the language have to be concerned with learning the rules. The pronunciation of the word includes its stress placement, and it is likely that this is part of what we call "lexical" learning. In other words, the matter of learning individual words is *not* a matter of learning a rule which will apply widely (as is learning to pluralize, for example), but of simply learning the phonetic configuration which identifies that word as unique from all others. Stress is part of that configuration and presents no particular problem to children. Not, that is, until the child begins to read. When faced with the task of matching up the words on the printed page with the words stored in their memories, children are introduced to the systematicity of stress. Similarly, in trying to sound out an unfamiliar word, children begin to come to terms with stress assignment rules.

Intonation refers to the pattern of stress and rising and falling pitch which occurs in connected speech. Intonation can also be used for special purposes such as emphasis. Consider, for example, the different meanings which result from the shift of stress in the following sentence:

WHAT are you doing here? (It looks pretty strange to me!)

What ARE you doing here? (You should be somewhere else!)

What are YOU doing here? (I was expecting Arnold.)

What are you DOING here? (Whatever it is, you shouldn't be doing it!)

What are you doing HERE? (Instead of Baghdad!)

This use of stress is called contrastive stress, and it is used to give emphasis to a particular part of the sentence. Another intonation feature which conveys meaning is pitch. Rising pitch is normally used at the end of a question and is also used to signal uncertainty or doubt in statements or single-word utterances.

The Sounds of Other Languages

The sound systems of the world's languages vary greatly. Some have a large number of distinct sounds while others have very few. Some Polynesian languages, for example, have as few as 11 or 12 segments, including both consonants and vowels. There is a language, Xu, in the Khoisan family, on the other hand, with 141 different segments, 24 of which are vowels.

Another way in which sound systems vary is in the particular consonants and vowels which occur. Most languages have between five and seven vowels, a fact which may surprise English speakers since English and many of its relatives have from 10 to 15. Some languages distinguish nasal vowels (resonance in both the oral and the nasal cavity) from oral vowels. But in general, it is the consonants that give learners more difficulty.

Speakers of other languages sometimes complain that English has especially troublesome consonants. Certainly English has some relatively rare consonants, including the th- sounds. Speakers of German, French and a host of other languages experience difficulty with these sounds which are also difficult for very young children just gaining control of their articulators. On the other hand, most English speakers would find the clicks found in Zulu difficult, although they are quite capable of making very similar sounds when starting horses or clucking disapproval.

It isn't only the individual sounds that distinguish the sound systems of languages. In more than half the languages of the world, it is possible to change the meaning of a word simply by changing the pitch at which it is articulated. These languages are called tone languages, and there are a number of possible tones and combinations of tones ranging from two to six. In Mandarin, which has four tones, the word mai can mean either to buy or to sell, depending on the tone. Mai, meaning to buy, is articulated with falling-rising tone while mai, meaning to sell, is articulated with falling tone. In general, speakers of tone languages have less difficulty in learning non-tone languages than speakers of non-tone languages have in learning tone languages.

Syllable structures also vary from language to language, and these pose certain problems for second language learners. In Mandarin, for example, syllables normally consist of a consonant followed by a vowel. The only consonants permitted at the end of a syllable are nasals. When Mandarin speakers learn English, they frequently drop or fail to produce the consonants at the ends of words such as *cat, dog,* and *rob* but produce words such as *can, sing,* and *rum* correctly. These errors occur as a result of their applying the syllable structure rules of their language to English.

The job of learning the sound system is a formidable one for both non-native and native learners. Learners must acquire motor control of the articulators as well as all the cognitive aspects of phonology. Neither children nor second language learners learn the sound system in isolation. They learn it as part of the process of learning words and larger communication units. One of the central of these is the morpheme.

Morphology: The Structure of Words

If we were to ask people who have not studied language structure what the smallest meaning-carrying unit is, most would probably say that it is the word. The word is, after all, the smallest unit that can normally stand alone in speech or in writing. It is not the word, however, but the **morpheme** that is the smallest unit of meaning. Some morphemes happen to be words—*cat, banana,* and *trigger* are all words consisting of a single morpheme, that is, they stand alone but cannot be reduced further without loss of meaning. Other morphemes may be equally meaningful but cannot stand alone as words. *Bio-, semi-,* and *-logy* are examples of non-word morphemes and are called **bound morphemes** because to function in the language they must bind themselves to another morpheme. All the examples in this paragraph are of **lexical morphemes** and are the earliest kinds of morphemes children learn. Bound morphemes include morphemes such as *bio-* (meaning *life*), *phot-* (meaning *light*), and *anti-* (meaning *against*) and have lexical meaning but must be attached to another morpheme to be used.

There are other ways of classifying morhemes. When children learn that a *dusty road* is a road layered with dust, they have learned a **derivational morpheme.** The addition of the morpheme {-y} to words such as *dust, rust, might, trust,* and *dirt* to form *dusty, rusty, mighty, trusty,* and *dirty* is highly productive in the sense that it is widely used in English to change nouns to adjectives. There is not a great deal of meaning carried by this morpheme; it serves principally to change the part of speech. Although most derivational processes are highly productive, they can be problematic for first or second language learners. The same /-y/ sound, for example, that can change a noun to an adjective turns the adjective *full* into the adverb *fully.* The {-er} that turns the verbs *teach, write, play,* and *sing* into *teacher, writer, player,* and *singer* takes a different form in *actor* and still another in *lawyer.* It also sounds just like the morpheme that turns *cold* and *bold* to *colder* and *bolder.* This latter morpheme, however, is an **inflectional morpheme.**

Inflectional morphemes, like derivational morphemes, serve more as grammatical indicators than as meaning bearers. Inflectional morphemes include the plural suffix, the past tense suffix, the possessive suffix, the third-person plural suffix, -ing and the present perfect form, as well as the comparative and superlative forms, {-er} and {-est}. Learning the grammatical inflections is an important aspect of morphological learning. When they learn a new noun, children do not have to be told what the plural form is. Assuming that the word takes a regular plural ending, they can figure out the correct form because they already know how nouns are pluralized in English. Nor do they have to wonder about the past tense of a new verb; knowledge of the inflectional system tells them exactly how it is formed. There are irregular plural forms, such as *women* and *children,* and irregular past tense forms such as *bought* and *rode.* But learning the regular inflections gives children a head start on the business of word learning.

Another important aspect of what children learn about English morphology is how words combine to form **compounds.** At first blush, the process seems simple enough. *Milk* and *man* combine to form *milkman,* the man who brings the milk (ignoring for the moment that the person may be a woman). Except to the native speaker, however, this relationship may not be at all obvious. A *snowman* is *not* a man who brings snow but a man who is made of snow. We would not be too pleased, either, if the *garbage man* were to deliver garbage nor if he were made of garbage. A *doorman,* on the other hand, does not deliver nor remove doors; neither is he made of them. Words in English combine in myriad ways to form new words, but the meanings of combined forms are not nearly as predictable as we might assume.

English, in fact, abounds with words that don't always mean what they should! An **idiom** is an expression whose meaning cannot be worked out from its individual parts, and the learning of idiomatic expressions is a major challenge for both children and for non-native learners. *Hit the road* is a good example. Knowing every possible meaning of each component of the phrase is of little value in making sense of the expression. Similarly, what sense is the child who has just learned about roots in the garden, for example, likely to make of the expression *root for the home team?* Non-native speakers find learning the idioms of English one of the greatest challenges in the task of language learning. Learning the appropriate use of idioms requires knowledge not only of word meanings but of how sentences are structured as well.

Syntax: The Structure of Sentences

Most native speakers consider the basic unit of expression to be the sentence despite the fact that they frequently do not speak in complete sentences. They believe they do, and they recognize the sentence as the means by which they make themselves understood. The study of how morphemes combine to form sentences is called **syntax.** Notice that I wrote *morphemes* and not *words.* This may seem somewhat confusing since I also said above that morphemes combine to form words and am now talking about how they combine to form sentences. While it is the case that the word is an important constituent of the sentence, it is also true that in order to understand how grammatical sentences are formed, it is necessary to examine the behavior of smaller units. Consider the following example:

The nurse gave the patient an injection
The doctor gave the patient an injection.

The cod disappear from the waters of Newfoundland.
The cod disappeared from the waters of Newfoundland.

It would be misleading to describe the difference between the first pair of sentences in the same way as the second. What differentiates the first pair of sentences is a single word, the subject or agent of the verb. What differentiates the second pair of sentences is a unit smaller than a word, a morpheme that changes the tense of the verb from present to past tense. In both pairs, there is a meaning difference, but the quality of the difference is greater in the first sentence than in the second.

What children must learn in order to understand and produce sentences they have never heard before is a great deal of knowledge about how sentences are formed. If that language is English, they must acquire two kinds of knowledge. They must know the linear order of morphemes in sentences and they must know something about the hierarchical structure of sentences.

Linear order is an obvious aspect of sentence organization in English. Rearranging the words in an English sentence can have amusing, confusing, or even disastrous results. There is, after all, a significant difference in meaning between *Baby eats goldfish* and *Goldfish eats baby*. Less obvious but equally important is **hierarchical structure,** which refers to the ways in which the morphemes in a sentence are organized into coherent groupings or units that are themselves organized into larger groupings or units. These units are referred to as **constituents** of a sentence. In the sentence, *Spike caught the mouse under the deck*, we can see that there are a number of groups of words that have meaning. We can also see that not all sequences of words make up sentence constituents. For example, most native speakers would agree that *caught the mouse under the deck* has some meaning of its own and, more significantly, contributes to the meaning of the sentence in a coherent way. Specifically, it tells us what Spike (my Siamese cat) did; it is the predicate of the sentence.

We can further divide the predicate into constituents. Native speakers would likely agree that the next two major constituents are *caught the mouse* and *under the deck*, even though they might not be able to explain why this is the case. They could even break these two constituents down further if asked.

What is it about these groupings that marks them as constituents? First of all, they *do* have some meaning of and on their own and could serve as answers to questions. To the question *Who caught a mouse under the deck?* one might well answer *Spike*. Or to the question *Where did Spike catch the mouse?* one would likely respond not with the entire sentence but *Under the deck*. In contrast, it is difficult to imagine the question to which *mouse under* might be the answer, although those words appear in that order in the sentence.

A second way in which we know that these are true constituents is that parenthetical expressions can be used between them. We might say, for instance, *Spike, amazingly enough, caught a mouse under the deck* or *Spike caught a mouse, which she seemed to think was a major threat, under the deck.* Conversely, the sequence *Spike caught the, I was surprised to see, mouse under the deck* would be highly unlikely in English. In general, we cannot insert parenthetical comments *within* grammatical constituents.

A third attribute of constituents is that often they can be replaced with a single word. For example, in answer to the question *Who caught the mouse under the deck?* we could answer with the full sentence, although we would be unlikely to, or we could answer *Spike.* We could also say *Spike did.* In this case, *did* stands in for the entire predicate. Constituents, then, are more than just words or words in sequence. They are meaningful units which are hierarchically arranged in the sense that a single constituent may be part of a larger constituent which may in turn be part of a still larger constituent.

Returning to the full sentence, we can see that *deck* is a constituent of the larger unit *under the deck* which is a constituent of *mouse under the deck*, etc. We could demonstrate this and the other hierarchical relationships in the sentence with brackets.

[[Spike][caught the mouse under the deck]]
[[Spike][[caught][the mouse under the deck]]]
[[Spike][[caught][[the mouse][under the deck]]]]
[[Spike][[caught][[[the][mouse]][[under][the deck]]]]]
[[Spike][[caught][[[the][mouse]][[under][[the][deck]]]]]]

This is one way of representing constituent structure, but it does not convey the hierarchical relationship in an easily discernible way. Most linguists today use the tree diagram to show the linear as well as the hierarchical structure of sentence elements. In the tree diagram, each constituent of the sentence forms a branch. The simplified tree diagram (Figure 2.1) conveys exactly the same information as the brackets.

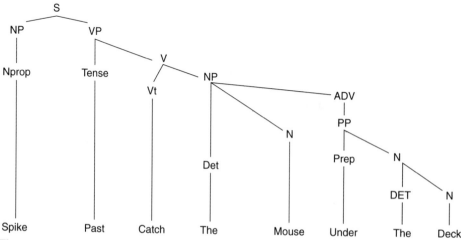

Figure 2.1. Tree Diagram of *Spike caught the mouse under the deck.*

Ambiguity. Tree diagrams are especially useful for demonstrating the different constituent structures of ambiguous sentences, that is, sentences which share a common expression but have two or more distinct meanings. The sentence *Mad dogs and Englishmen go out in the noonday sun,* for example, has two interpretations. In one, both dogs and Englishmen are mad, and in the second only dogs are mad (although both go out in the noonday sun). The tree diagram for each meaning is shown in Figure 2.2.

Sentences that are syntactically ambiguous look the same but have two (or more) different meanings.

Even the sentence used earlier, *Spike caught the mouse under the deck,* could be construed as ambiguous, but it is a grammatical ambiguity that does not greatly change the meaning. The brackets and tree diagrams assume one meaning, that is, that *under the deck* modifies *mouse.* A paraphrase of this meaning might be *Spike caught the mouse that was under the deck.* A second meaning would be represented on the tree diagram shown in Figure 2.3. Here, *under the deck* modifies both the noun and verb phrases. A paraphrase of this meaning might be *It was under the deck that Spike caught the mouse.*

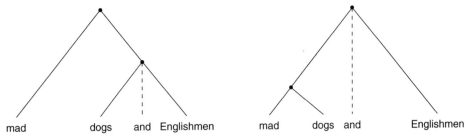

Figure 2.2.   Two meanings of *Mad dogs and Englishmen go out in the noonday sun.*

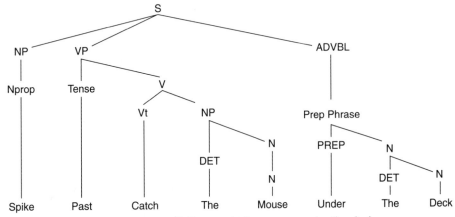

Figure 2.3.   Alternate meaning for *Spike caught the mouse under the deck.*

In these examples, sentences that appear to be the same actually have different underlying structures and meanings. Just the opposite relationship exists in sentences that are syntactic paraphrases of one another.

Sentences that are syntactic paraphrases of one another share certain properties: They comprised the same main lexical items; they have essentially the same meaning; and other sentences of the same structure can be paraphrased in exactly the same way. Consider, for example, the following sentences:

The soothsayer made the prediction.

The prediction was made by the soothsayer.

What the soothsayer made was a prediction.

It was a prediction that the soothsayer made.

Each of these sentences has a different form, but they all have the same principal words—*soothsayer, made,* and *prediction.* They all express the meaning that a soothsayer made a prediction, and they are all related to each other in such a way that every other sentence with the same structure can be transformed in the same ways.

Cats chase mice.

Mice are chased by cats.

What cats chase are mice.

It is mice that cats chase.

All these sentences have the same basic, or **underlying,** structure which may be represented as shown in Figure 2.4.

It is not sufficient that the syntax of English demonstrate the common underlying structure for these kinds of sentences. It must also demonstrate how that common

Figure 2.4. Deep structure for four syntactic paraphrases.

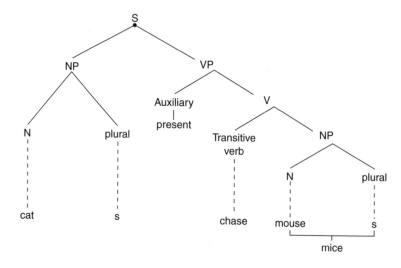

structure can be transformed in so many ways without changing the core meaning. Ambiguity and paraphrase, then, impose two very different demands on a syntactic description. Ambiguity requires that the syntax account for the fact that two superficially identical sentences may have very different constituent structures. Paraphrase, on the other hand, requires the syntax to account for the fact that a number of superficially different sentences may have a common constituent structure. But the demands do not stop there. Certain sentences are related to each other in systematic ways but involve changes in meaning. Questions and negatives are good examples of these kinds of sentences. The systematic relationship between affirmative declarative sentences and various kinds of questions is easy to see.

1. Uncle Harry wrote the book in prison.
2. Did Uncle Harry write the book in prison?
3. Who wrote the book in prison?
4. What did Uncle Harry write in prison?
5. Where did Uncle Harry write the book?

Certain regularities can be seen among all four questions. The question word is always at the front of the sentence whether the question requires a yes/no answer, as in 2., or specific information, as in 3., 4., and 5. Notice that in 2., the past tense of *do* has been inserted at the beginning of the sentence because English word order does not permit *Write the book in prison . . .?* although Middle English did allow such a form. In Modern English, a verb cannot begin a question unless it is a form of *be, have,* or *do.* Likewise, in 4. and 5., *did* has been added just after the question word. This addition is not required in 3. because the question word replaces the subject noun phrase (Uncle Harry) and the verb *wrote* is already near the beginning of the sentence and does not have to be moved. The same regular pattern occurs throughout the language.

The relationship between affirmative sentences and negatives is systematic in a similar way. The following sets of sentences demonstrate the regularity.

6. The jury acquitted Uncle Harry on appeal.
7. The jury didn't acquit Uncle Harry on appeal.
8. Uncle Harry's books sold well.
9. Uncle Harry's books didn't sell well.
10. Aunt Maud is angry with Uncle Harry.
11. Aunt Maud isn't angry with Uncle Harry.
12. Uncle Harry has many original ideas.
13. Uncle Harry hasn't many original ideas.
14. Uncle Harry doesn't have many original ideas.

Once again, a form of *do* is required to support the negative in sentences without *be* and may be used in sentences with *have* (some dialects require it). We can see, then, that both questions and negatives are related to affirmative statements in a regular and predictable way. These kinds of systematicity must also be reflected in a complete description of English sentences. This might be accomplished in a number of ways, but the most efficient is through a two-level system of grammar such as the one proposed by Noam Chomsky (1965) and refined by linguists and teachers over the past 25 years.

Transformational-Generative Grammar (TG)

One of Chomsky's major goals in conceiving his bi-level grammar was to account for sentences that appeared to have the same structure but in fact had different underlying meanings. He used the sentences *John is eager to please* and *John is easy to please* to demonstrate that sentences which appear to be structurally identical may in fact, have radically different constituent structures. His aim was to provide a way of analyzing sentence structure that accounted for these divergent underlying structures. One level of structure was intended as a way of representing the meaning. This was the underlying structure of the sentence which he called the generative component, or base component.

The base component consists of a set of phrase structure rules which are intended as general statements about how the most basic or core sentence patterns of a particular language are constructed. They consist of statements such as *A sentence consists of a noun phrase and a verb phrase* and *A noun phrase consists of an optional article and a noun which may be singular or plural*. Linguists use a notational system that simplifies the writing of phrase structure rules, and would represent these two as:

$$S \rightarrow NP + VP$$
$$NP \rightarrow (Det) + N + (Plural)$$

Using this notational convention, ( ) indicates optionality, that is, elements that may occur in some constituents but not others. The phrase structure rules serve as *directions* for constructing the trees we saw earlier, more properly called *phrase markers*. The structure that results from applying the phrase structure rules is called a *deep structure*.

An example will be useful in understanding how the second level of the grammar operates. Let's consider two of the syntactic paraphrases from an earlier example.

Uncle Harry wrote the book in prison.

The book was written by Uncle Harry in prison.

Because they are syntactic paraphrases, they have the same deep structure, the one shown in Figure 2.5.

The surface structure of the first sentence will look essentially the same as its deep structure but in order to show the surface structure of the second sentence, a number of changes must occur. Briefly, they are to

1. Reverse the order of the subject and object noun phrases

2. Add *by*

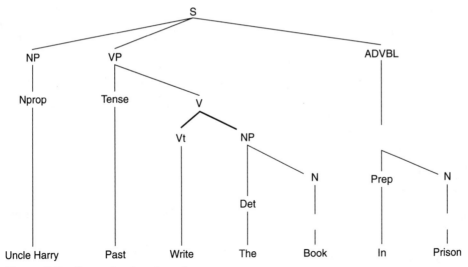

Figure 2.5. Deep structure tree diagram.

3. Add a form of the verb *to be*

4. Add the past participial ending to the main verb.

The transformational component of the grammar makes these alterations to the deep structure, resulting in the following tree diagram (Figure 2.6). Remember that this is *not* a tree diagram showing deep structure but a diagram showing the structure of the sentence *after* it has been transformed into a passive sentence. Transformational rules add, delete, and move sentence elements, but although they may result in slight meaning changes, they do not change the core meaning of the sentence. The structure which results from applying all relevant transformational rules is called the *surface structure*.

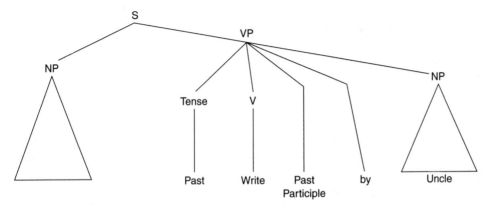

Figure 2.6. Surface structure tree diagram.

Recursion

A complete syntactic description of a language should account for all possible sentences in the language. This is no minor undertaking since it is theoretically possible to string any number of elements together to form compound, complex, and compound-complex sentences. Stringing noun phrases together forms compound subjects or objects.

Raymond chased the weasel.

Raymond and Alice chased the weasel.

Raymond, Alice, and Harriet chased the weasel.

Raymond and Alice chased the weasel and caught the toad.

Raymond and Harriet chased the weasel, caught the toad, and spent Tuesday at the pound.

We can also conjoin complete sentences.

Raymond ate his tuna and Alice ate the squid.

Raymond ate his tuna and Alice ate the squid, but Harriet stayed on her diet.

In theory, using conjunctions such as *and*, *or*, and *but*, it would be possible to conjoin subjects, predicates, and complete sentences indefinitely. In this way, the number of possible sentences in English would be infinite. But conjunction is only one way of creating new sentences. Another way is to embed one sentence within another, and English has several ways of doing this. Consider the following sentences.

The man sleeps on the park bench.

The man is my uncle.

Assuming that *the man* in each sentence refers to the same person, we can combine these two sentences by embedding one within the other.

The man who sleeps on the park bench is my uncle.

We could embed still another sentence.

The man who sleeps on the park bench which the city painted last year is my uncle.

And another.

The man who sleeps on the park bench which the city painted last year is my uncle whom my mother disowned in 1962.

There are other ways of embedding sentences within sentences. English has an entire class of verbs, in fact, which take sentences as their objects. Verbs such as *know, be-*

lieve, imagine, deny, and *claim* take sentences, frequently beginning with *that* as objects. For example, in the sentences *The Senator denies that he lied to the Senate* and *Sheila claimed that the Senator lied to everyone*, the object of the verb is a complete sentence. *He lied to the Senate* is the object of *denies* in the first sentence and *the Senator lied to everyone* is the object of *claimed* in the second. The fact that English sentences can be embedded within other sentences is another reason why the number of possible sentences is infinite. This being the case, we can easily see that an adequate syntactic description of English must include a mechanism for describing recursion. Otherwise, we would have to generate an infinite number of rules to account for an infinite number of sentences.

A complete syntax of English is beyond the scope of this book. The purpose here has been to introduce the notions of linearity, hierarchical structure, sentence constituents, ambiguity, syntactic paraphrase, and recursion as well as to give a broad indication of the types of rules linguists use to represent the role each plays in English sentences.

Morphemes, Sentences, and Other Languages

One of the principal ways in which languages differ is in their rules for combining morphemes into words. In English, we are able to combine a number of morphemes in a single word, and these morphemes may impart either grammatical or lexical meaning. The word *dialogues,* for example, consists of three morphemes—{dia-} meaning *two,* {logue} meaning *to speak,* and {-s} indicating that the noun is plural. Some languages are far more ambitious in the number of morphemes which can be combined in a single word. In one Invit language, for example, the word *angyagh-llangyugtuq* consists of five separate morphemes and means *he (-tuq-) wants (-yug-) to acquire (-ng-) a big (-ghlla-) boat (angya-)* (Crystal 1987, p. 90). Eskimo is what is called an *agglutinating language,* meaning that words are made up of long sequences of morphemes with each expressing a particular grammatical function or meaning.

Mandarin, to illustrate another extreme, is an *isolating language,* meaning that there are no endings on words, and word order is used to show the relationships among words in a sentence. The sentence *We sold the horses to the teacher* would be rendered in Mandarin *wo men ba ma mai gei lao shi le.*

wo	1st person pronoun
men	plural
ba	object indicator
ma	*horse*
mai	*sell*
gei	benefactive case marker
lao	*venerated*
shi	*master*
le	past tense marker

Between the two extremes are the *inflecting* or *synthetic* languages such as Greek, Latin, and Arabic. In these languages, grammatical relationships are expressed by changing the structure of words. As the name suggests, this is most often accomplished by using inflectional endings. The Latin word *amo* conveys, literally, *I love*, but also that the verb is in the present tense, is active and indicative.

English is somewhat difficult to classify. Because it has been influenced by a number of other languages over the centuries, it shares some of the characteristics of agglutinating, inflecting and isolating languages. It is agglutinating in the sense that it can build words out of several morphemes (such as *nonreturnable, humanitarianism*, and *neurolinguistically*). It is inflecting in the sense that some grammatical relationships are expressed with word endings (plural, past tense, present progressive, etc.), and it resembles isolating languages because the basis of its grammar is word order.

Whichever language a child learns to speak, the learning will entail the ability to understand and to produce novel sentences. Language would be very boring to use and difficult to learn if we had to rely on a memorized store of sentences for communication. The ability to generate a new utterance at will and to understand whatever utterances one hears lies at the heart of language acquisition and use. No amount of learning about sentence structure will be sufficient, however, to the task of making and understanding meaning.

Semantics: The Structure of Meaning

Semantics refers broadly to the study of meaning. Of course, it is impossible to study *any* aspect of language without considering meaning, but in linguistics, semantics is concerned with word meanings, with meaning that results from combining words in various ways, and with how language represents real-world meaning. The study of semantics is particularly fascinating, then, because in talking about semantics we are talking about how people represent reality. And reality is defined by individual and cultural experience—meaning categories of a language are specific to that language and the culture it represents. It sometimes comes as a shock to a monolingual to discover that speakers of other languages may not share the same reality. As an example, speakers of English have relatively few words for the fluid chemists identify as H_2O. If it happens to be falling from the sky we call it *rain*, but otherwise we make do with *water* whether it is in a bathtub, an ocean, or a glass with ice. The Japanese language, in contrast, differentiates between hot water (*oyu*) and cold water (*mizu*), and it is impossible to talk of water without specifying which is intended. Clearly this distinction has, or had at some time, particular significance for Japanese speakers.

Colors offer especially rich distinctions among languages, in large part because they offer direct evidence of differences in perception. English has the distinction between red and pink, pink being the color red to which sufficient white has been added to change the English speaker's perception of the color. Blue, however, is blue whether it be navy, sky, powder, or baby. In Russian, the exact opposite holds true. Blue and light blue are expressed by two distinct words, as different as *red* and *pink*, but for the Russian speaker, adding white to red results only in light red.

While to a large degree word meanings are culturally agreed upon, there are subtle differences in the meanings words hold for individual speakers of a language. These differences are largely a function of experience. An English-German bilingual once explained to me that the English word *lap* had little meaning for her beyond the dictionary definition (the front of a sitting person, from waist to knees). The German equivalent, *schoss*, on the other hand included memories of being held and cuddled by her German grandmother. She also explained that her reading of the Biblical "bosom of God" had only literal meaning for her, but the German translation, which replaced *bosom* with *schoss*, conveyed a very special message.

These cultural and individual variables have contributed to the frustration that linguists experience in trying to formalize semantics in the same way as they have formalized phonology, morphology, and syntax. But there are other reasons why semantics resists precise formalization. Chief among these is that meaning resides in so many places—in words, sentences and in larger discourse units and in all of them at once. Nevertheless, some linguists have attempted to describe the structure of meaning independently. Working under the assumption that semantics and syntax are distinct language components that can be described independently of one another, they have developed models that are called *interpretive*. Other linguists believe that the distinction between syntax and semantics is artificial, and that a description of the two language components must be integrated. Their work has led to *generative* theories and to *case grammar*. Both these theories hold that syntax is determined by semantics and that it is impossible to consider syntactic structures independent of meaning. While their arguments are compelling, they are beyond the scope of this text.

A certain amount of meaning in a language is semantic in the sense that it resides in the language—in words and sentences—somewhat independent of particular speakers and hearers in particular contexts. Another aspect of meaning is communicative meaning, and it resides in social situations and in the relationship between particular speakers and hearers. The study of this communicative meaning is commonly called *pragmatics*.

Pragmatics

Pragmatics refers to the use of language for real communication in real time and encompasses almost any linguistic aspect of human society. Although they are less well formalized, there are rules or conventions that govern language use in a variety of situations. These range from the conventions for interpreting syntactic paraphrase to gender issues to the use of language for manipulating thought. Unlike other levels of language description, pragmatics cannot be discussed independent of human language users.

Bolinger lists a total of four such conventions that account for the meaning differences conveyed by minor variations in word order, but there are many others. Certainly it is possible to get by in English without any conscious awareness of these conventions, but in order to become effective speakers and writers, we do learn and follow these subtle rules even though they are rarely taught.

In the section on syntax, we saw that when sentences are related to one another in systematic ways, they are called syntactic paraphrases. But in actual language use, they are seldom true paraphrases at all. Bolinger (1980) points out that English has conventions for arranging sentence elements to signal meaning. These are not grammar rules but usage conventions, and they include, for instance, the following rule.

> When a modifier goes before a noun, it characterizes the noun, says something about the way the noun "really is." When it follows, the "really is" quality is neutralized. *The corner house* is the house that belongs on the corner; *the house on the corner* could be one in the process of being moved, perhaps parked there overnight. *The people ready were picked up* refers to a temporary state of readiness; *The ready people were picked up* sounds strange because it implies that "being ready" is something you have with you as part of your nature, not just a temporary condition. Sometimes the same adjective can be used both ways: the only handy tool and the only tool handy. (p. 29)

These pragmatic conventions of language use must be acquired by children, a task that is a lifelong process, as many college and university English professors will attest. Yet another aspect of learning the pragmatics of language is learning how to manipulate the language for specific purposes. English abounds in opportunities for doing so. It has been pointed out repeatedly that there are many more pejorative words in the language for talking about females than for talking about males. But sexism is embodied even in the "neutral" words. To borrow another example from Bolinger,

> If a woman driver makes a bad maneuver, a man may be heard to say *What does that woman think she's doing!* with *woman* lengthened and pronounced with a rise-fall-rise intonation—which makes it an expression of disregard. A similar use of *man* would be taken as an emphatic way of expressing the emotion of the whole sentence, not as a reflection of the man's sex. (p. 93)

Even if children were not exposed to sexist language in the home (an unlikely prospect given the fact that a significant degree of sexist bias is inherent in the language), they would encounter it as soon as they started school. The stories and books they read emphasize sex roles and the language uses masculine pronouns and other male terms with far greater frequency than female terms. As Bolinger observes,

> . . . when adults write for one another, they refer to young people as *children*, almost as often as they call them *boys* and *girls*. When writing books and stories for children, however, adults use the gender words *boy* and *girl* twice as often as the neutral words *child* and *children* . . . . (p. 93)

Bolinger goes on to cite studies showing that in schoolbooks, the ratio of use of he/him to she/her was almost four to one (Graham, 1975) and that the same disproportion occurs in the 200 million achievement tests commonly given in U.S. schools (Tittle, 1973). While the feminist revolution may have had some impact on the language of books, it takes only a cursory look at the books on the shelves of any elementary school to see that the bias has by no means been eliminated.

A more subtle form of manipulation comes in the language of commercial advertising. Bolinger's (1980) delightful example, "We reduced the size because we didn't want to increase the price" (p. 58) is an example of the kind of doublespeak to which we are exposed daily. Because they are to some degree innocent believers in the voices of authority, children are more prone to commercial manipulation than are adults, though, obviously the target of Bolinger's example was the adult population. I am not sure which is more alarming, the fact that advertisers *believed* that such a slogan would work or the likelihood that with some of the population, it probably did.

Because most language manipulation has a negative impact on society, it might seem best not to learn it or to learn about it. It is hard to justify, for example, the language of sexism and racism. On the other hand, not all manipulation is negative, and more importantly, if language users do not learn to recognize the ways in which language can be used to influence thought, beliefs and behavior, they have little protection against being manipulated themselves.

Finally, children learn very early the fallacy of the playground taunt "Sticks and stones may break my bones but words will never hurt me." Part of their lifetime language learning is not only to realize but to take responsibility for the fact that words do indeed wound—to learn, in other words, the paradox that oral language is at once ephemeral and permanent. Words find their targets and inflict their wounds, and while the wounds may heal, the act which inflicted them cannot be undone. Counselors and educators alike now recognize that while verbal abuse may not be life-threatening in the same way as extreme physical abuse, it can do extreme damage to children, damage that may take a lifetime to heal if it heals at all.

QUESTIONS FOR DISCUSSION

1. The author claims that descriptive linguists advance our understanding of how children learn and use language by providing "a clearer picture of the structure—or *possible structures*—of language . . ." What does she mean by *possible structures*?

2. In Portia's famous "Quality of mercy" speech from *The Merchant of Venice*, Shakespeare wrote the following.

   The quality of mercy is not strain'd;
   It droppeth as the gentle rain from heaven
   Upon the place beneath: it is twice bless'd . . .

   What is the function of the apostrophe in *strain'd* and *bless'd*? Why is it no longer used today?

   Why would a historical linguist insist on keeping the anachronistic forms when changing the words to *strained* and *blessed* would not alter the intended sound or meaning of the language?

3. The author explains how *went* came to be the past tense of *go*. Have you ever wondered about the strange conjugation of other common verbs such as *to be*? Try to find out what historical explanation there is for the diverse forms *be, am, was,* and *were*.

4. The author expresses her view that good teachers of young children are necessarily practicing psycholinguists. Can you find further evidence in support of this position?

5. The author uses an example of an English-speaking child (Sarah) and an Asian child, both of kindergarten age and both having difficulty with /l/ and /r/. Consider a third child, an Asian child of 11 or 12, having the same difficulty, and speculate about the degree to which the source of the problem in each is similar. See if your answer changes after reading Chapters 3 and 4.

6. What is *neurological bimodality* and why is it an important notion for teachers?

7. The author says that a Chinese-speaking child learner and an English-speaking child learner face different tasks in learning the intonation of their languages. Why is this true? Does it mean that the task is easier for an English-speaking child? Why?

CHAPTER THREE

Learning One Language

Those of us in the English-speaking world may find it hard to believe that children to whom this chapter title refers are in the minority. Indeed, most of the children in the world acquire more than one language before the end of schooling. Often that second language is English, accounting for the fact that more people in the world speak English than any other language. That is not to say that more people speak English as a first language, for this is not the case. But if we were to take a census of the world's population and have them list every language they speak and counted the result without regard for whether the language is native, English would win. Given that the world's largest national population speaks Chinese, this is an impressive statistic. The children many of us teach are, then, members of a minority if they speak only one language and a member of the majority of world speakers who speak English.

This chapter is about children who grow up monolingual. My example is of an English-speaking girl named Janet. We meet Janet as an infant and trace her language growth right through the school years. Language learning does not end with graduation, whether from high school, university, or graduate school. It is a lifelong undertaking. But for our purposes here, what is important is language learning in the school years and the earlier learning that has such a profound impact on those years. While I maintain that Janet's experience is a typical one, some readers of the first edition pointed out that Janet's intact family with university-educated parents is hardly typical of children beginning school at the end of the 20th and beginning of the 21st centuries. Unfortunately, they may be right in pointing out that the educational level and the high degree of literacy in Janet's home put her in a minority of North American children. Nevertheless, I maintain that Janet's history is instructive. In the first place, data from Janet's experience are contextualized within experiences of other children and other studies. Second, there is a great deal of evidence that children's early oral language development runs a similar course whatever the educational level of the parents. Success in school is another matter, but that is a fact that I will confront directly. Third, we have to ask the question, which child's experience is typical? Each child has a unique learning experience. However typical the child's environment might be, there will be some differences between one child's language development and that of any other. The best a researcher can do is to present the most complete data that exists and within the analysis speculate about how much or how little can be generalized to other children. As you will see, in Janet's case, I believe that her experience of language learning is substantially similar to that of other children. In any case, it is instructive.

The organization of this chapter is for the most part chronological. Each section covers a particular period of time, usually 6 months to 1 year, and is introduced by a general overview of the course of language development during that time. This broad sketch is followed by a description of Janet and her language learning during the same period. This, in turn, is followed by a more detailed description and discussion of the course of language acquisition in most children of the same age.

INTRODUCING JANET

Janet was born in Dover, New Hampshire, in January of 1972. Most of the observations that follow are based on notes and transcripts of my own interaction with her and on her mother's diaries, kept in detail until Janet was 7 years old and sporadically until she was 14. Janet's only sibling, her brother Matthew, was 21 months old when she was born. Their father was a research physicist and their mother a lecturer in the English department at a nearby university. Janet arrived 3 weeks before her expected date of arrival, on her mother's 26th birthday. She weighed exactly 6 pounds, and her mother's diary entries during her first 6 months tell of a fairly untroubled infant. Janet cried when hungry, and seemed to be hungry every 4 hours around the clock, but otherwise slept well. She was alert and a real charmer with big blue eyes and a winning smile. She was a responsive child, particularly to her mother and to the antics of her older brother. The family spoke only English and that was the only language Janet was exposed to until the age of 18 months when she had an occasional Spanish-speaking babysitter.

Between Janet's second and third birthdays, her family moved to another state. There, living in a city of approximately 750,000, Janet attended a Montessori school from the time she was 3 until she began public kindergarten in the September before her fifth birthday. Following first the father's and then the mother's career, the family moved again when Janet was 9 and again when she was 13. Her schooling was thus interrupted several times. Although she experienced a brief troubled period during her early teens, Janet graduated from an International Baccalaureate program with very high marks. She completed a university degree in biology and is currently a graduate student in biochemistry at a western Canadian university. Although she was a science major, Janet took sufficient courses in English to qualify for a minor, and her professors often lamented that she was not an English major, such was her facility with and obvious interest in the language. That fascination with language began in infancy.

INFANCY

When I was first a student of language acquisition, the study of children's linguistic development began with the first words. Except for a brief description of babbling, there was little attention given to what, if anything, of importance might occur before the utterance of the first word. Even today, when parents talk about their children, the question "Is she talking yet?" refers to the first word. Appropriately so, I might add. If, however, the question were rephrased in broader terms that encompassed the child's early understandings and responses, then the answer would be very different. It would also be more consistent with our current understanding of the seamlessness of the language learning experience, an experience that begins at birth or possibly before. In recent years we have come to realize that the first year or so of a baby's life are not idle ones by any means. Much of the infant's behavior during this period signifies cognitive processes that make the acquisition of language possible. It is a period during which we observe behavior that is precursory to true language development.

The Precursors to Language

Children before the age of approximately one year are not yet able to produce language as we traditionally think of it—as words or utterances with intentional meaning. They do, however, demonstrate a great deal of sensitivity to and awareness of language. We see in that first year behavior that appears to form the foundation for later language growth. This is not true linguistic behavior but *precursory* behavior. Somewhat paradoxically, it differs in kind from true language, and yet it is essential for the growth of true language.

There are two important differences between precursory linguistic behavior and true language. Although children during their first year perceive and produce sounds, learn about events, objects, and relationships and interact with others in their environments, they do not use the conventions of language in doing so. In the first year of life, infant behavior is largely related to observable events. Crying when wet, hungry, or tired is common behavior in infants, and there is often a direct and observable relationship between the cry and the condition. This begins to change in the second year when a *conventional mapping relation*—or language—begins to occur. The events and situations are still observable, but there is a new and more sophisticated verbal interaction or response with them.

The second crucial difference between the first and second year of life has to do with intent. Before the age of approximately one year, the infant "reflects feelings and states more that it intends a representation of affect and changes in affect." In the second year, in contrast, the child begins to communicate intentionally (Bloom & Lahey, 1978, p. 71). We refer, therefore, to Janet's language learning in the first year as precursory, not to underestimate its importance, for it was vital, but to emphasize the difference between this and later learning.

Janet as an Infant

When she was only a few weeks old, Janet seemed to respond to her mother's voice. Her mother's diary notes that Janet would usually stop crying when her mother made soothing noises. By 2 months, Janet would stop gurgling or crying and appear to be listening when her brother was in the room and talking.

Janet demonstrated the abilities that all normal babies have in her responses to her mother's voice. At only a few days old, most infants respond to human voices, and by the time they are 2–4 months old, they respond to different tones of voice. Research has shown, too, that babies as young as 1 month are able not only to discriminate between speech and non-speech sounds but to discriminate between speech sounds as similar as /p/ and /b/ (Eimas et al., 1971). This early perceptual sensitivity to the sounds of language makes it possible for them to learn the relevant phonological distinctions they will need to understand and to form intentional utterances as they get older.

But it is not at all clear just how this early perceptual ability is related to their later learning, since children appear to lose their ability to make certain discriminations. Research has shown, for example, that while infants of 1–4 months are able to distinguish between voiced and voiceless pairs of consonants, two-year-old children find it one of the most difficult distinctions to make in discrimination experiments (Shvachkin, 1973; Garnica, 1973; Graham & House, 1971).

At about the same time as they are manifesting these perceptual abilities, infants begin to vocalize. This was the case with Janet. During the first 2 months, most of the sounds she produced were cries, but she did sometimes gurgle and seem to coo or shriek with delight when something pleased her. From 6 weeks to 3 months, her cooing and shrieking behavior increased. Her mother also noted that Janet's cries became differentiated during this period, i. e., her cry when she was wet or hungry differed from the late afternoon fussy cry which her mother attributed to fatigue or frustration.

We know from numerous studies that the vocalizations of infants younger than 6 months or so are likely to be cooing sounds. In fact, spectrographic analysis has shown them to be quite unlike human speech sounds (Titone & Danesi, 1985, pp. 64–65). Nevertheless, cooing plays an important role in later development of speech by serving as a rehearsal of the tongue movements which are necessary for the production of speech.

Even Janet's crying behavior provides important insight into her language development. If her mother was right about her using different cries for different purposes, then we have evidence of precursory language use—purposefully using language for different functions. In adults, the practice is easy to observe. Even in young children just slightly older than Janet was at this time, we see evidence that they use a single word to serve a variety of purposes. They may stress it differently, lengthen the vowel, or vary volume or accompanying gestures to make a single word (from the adult's perspective) serve a variety of different purposes. The difference, of course, is in intent. The older child clearly intends to signal different meanings, but there is no evidence to suggest such intent on the part of the infant.

One of the more interesting questions about Janet's language acquisition at this age is the role played by those around her. Specifically, what effect did Janet's mother and her older brother have on her early phonological development? This is never an easy question to answer. Her mother's diary and my own research notes from Janet's first year mention a number of occasions on which Janet was heard to imitate her brother. He would make a request, for example, and Janet would *sing* the intonation pattern of his utterance. Later, when she began to produce words, she would often mimic a single word from one of Matthew's utterances. In one instance, he said, "Want to watch Big Bird," and Janet promptly piped up, "Buh" (bird).

Babbling

At around 5 months, Janet began to babble. At first, her babbling sounded to the adults around her like random noises, some of them English-like, but others quite foreign. She seemed particularly fond of glottal sounds during the first month or so, and she combined them most imaginatively. By the time she was 6 months old, she was producing a great many labial sounds, particularly /b/ and /m/ in utterances such as *babababa* or *mumumum*. Gradually, both the rhythms and the speech sounds she produced became more English-like. The intonation patterns took on the quality of English discourse. The similarity between the sounds infants make in babbling and the sounds of the language around them appears to be universal babbling behavior. It is evidence that the *input* language is having an effect, that infants are attending to the sounds of language. During these early months, children may be highly inventive in their production and combination of speech sounds, and they seem to be busily learning the intonation of their language as well as training their articulators for producing the individual segments.

What, then, did Janet's babbling contribute to her learning of the system of her language? Ingram (1976) would say that she had completed the first of six stages of development that run parallel to cognitive stages of development, as described by Piaget (1962). Ingram views phonological development not as beginning with the first word and ending at around age 6, as many linguists have traditionally done, but as beginning at birth, and ending at around age 16—extending, in other words, most of the way through the school years.

The first stage is what we have seen thus far in Janet—producing the various sounds of her language (and many others besides) and imitating the intonation contour of the language around her. She was also making a great many unobservable perceptual distinctions. Gradually, as her babbling increased in frequency and in length, her phonology also improved. There is also evidence that her babbling became differentiated at around eight months. Janet's mother notes in her diary that Janet sometimes seemed to be singing and just playing with sounds. This behavior occurred when she was lying in her crib, either at nap time or upon awaking in the morning. At other times, especially when she was sitting on the floor playing with her toys, Janet's stress and intonation would sound more "purposeful, almost as if she were giving orders sometimes" (Diaries).

Apparently it is not uncommon for infants to babble differentially. Menn (1976, 1989) has pointed out such behavior is common in the later stages of babbling when children typically demonstrate two different types. In the first, *sound play*, children appear to be vocalizing for its own sake, presumably for the sheer pleasure of making and listening to the sounds. There seems to be little connection between the sounds they produce in sound play and intentional communication. In *conversational babble*, on the other hand, children really sound like they are talking even though the listener would be hard pressed to identify any of the words. As they engage in conversational babble, children use eye contact, gestures, and the intonation contours of normal speech—all the elements of conversation except meaningful words. "Conversational babble can clearly convey requests for aid, rejection of food or toys, desire to direct attention to ongoing events" (Menn, 1976, cited in Menn 1989, p. 73). It is possible, of course, that to the child, the words *are* differentiated but that the immature articulators are as yet unable to distinguish them for adult listeners. Even in this early stage of development, then, we find not only the precursors to language structure but also the foreshadowing of meaningful language used for different purposes.

In discussing precursory language behavior, we have focused on the infant's awareness of the sound system. Obviously in babies who do not yet produce words, or who produce only a few single-word utterances, it is difficult to speculate about their awareness of syntax. Many researchers believe, however, that infants do exhibit precursory syntactic awareness. Bloom (1973) reports observing a 16-month-old child early in the two-word stage of speech. This child used an interpretable word, /wid / in combination with other common words in the child's vocabulary. The unusual word always occurred in second position, and it only occurred with certain of the child's words such as *Mama, Dada, more*, and *no*, but not with other frequently used words. The child's utterances also indicated her awareness of the stress patterns in English. Bloom interpreted the child's behavior as evidence "that she had learned something about word order—with /wid /, which was consistently in second position, and with the few words that appeared with /wid /, which were always in first position" (Bloom, 1973, cited in Bloom & Lahey, 1978, p. 91).

The child Bloom observed, however, was 16 months old and arguably past the precursory period and into the stage of true language development. Evidence for syntactic awareness in children of around 1 year or younger is sketchy, but several researchers have made the claim that infants use intonational changes to signal the differences in meaning that will later be signaled by word order. Engel (1973) claimed, for example, "that her son used humming with 'sentence intonation' before he used words, using rising pitch for requests" (cited in Sachs, 1989, p. 45). Nakazina (1962) reported that infants of 8 months imitated adult pitch contours, an observation that is consistent with those made by Janet's mother (above). Nevertheless, it is difficult to claim with any degree of certainty that such behavior is evidence of early syntactic awareness. It does, however, indicate a strong sensitivity to *language*, and whether it is sensitivity to phonology or syntax seems hardly to matter.

Before her first birthday Janet had begun to show signs of moving from precursory language to true language acquisition. As mentioned earlier, the two main differences between precursory and later language acquisition have to do with the use of conventions and intent. Researchers have identified a number of behaviors that they believe indicate communicative intent. They include the increased use of eye contact during gesturing or vocalizing, the emergence of consistent sound patterns in vocalizations, appearing to wait for a response after vocalizing or gesturing and persisting in attempts to communicate (Bates, 1979; Bruner, 1973; Harding & Golinkoff, 1979; Scoville, 1983, all cited in Sachs, 1989, p. 47).

Janet exhibited some of these characteristics. A month before her first birthday, she was sitting on her mother's lap while her mother read to her. They had just finished reading *The Cat in the Hat* and her mother started to put the book down. "No," insisted Janet, trying to retrieve the book. When she failed, she looked directly into her mother's eyes and said again, "No!" This simple exchange is evidence that Janet was becoming a true language user—she knew what she wanted and she communicated it effectively.

Transition: First Words

By the time Janet was 8 months old, she was producing long strings of babbling, with intonation patterns that sounded very much like English conversation. When she began to produce her first words, a few days before her first birthday, she produced them not as part of her stream of babble but independently. That is, she continued to babble, particularly at night or nap time when she was alone in her crib, but she also began to produce the occasional word in isolation.

After the "No!" which Janet produced in the example above, and which she used a great deal for the next two years, the first word that Janet's mother believed to be intentional was *weo*. Janet was sitting on the floor watching her older brother play with his cars and trucks. When he rolled a large yellow dump truck toward her, Janet giggled and shouted *Weo! Weo*, (wheel), which was also her brother's word for wheels, cars, or anything that had wheels. She also encountered the word in the title of a favorite book, Dr. Seuss's *Bears on Wheels*. A single word, but it marked the beginning of a period of rapid and very impressive language learning.

THE PRESCHOOL YEARS

Sometime after their first birthday, most children begin to combine their growing inventory of single words into two-word utterances. This is the point at which most people think language learning has truly begun. While we have seen that it is in fact already underway, it is certainly true that the rate of learning seems to increase. By the time they begin school, most children are producing well-formed, simple and complex sentences expressing a variety of meanings and fulfilling a number of communicative functions. They have gone from pre-linguistic infants to fully participating members of their language community in five short years.

Overview of Development

As children grow from infants to school-age, their worlds expand to include people other than family and frequent visitors, and places other than their own homes. Their linguistic and communicative needs grow as well. This is the period during which children acquire near-adult phonology and the complex rules they need to express the meanings they want to express in the increasingly varied situations in which they find themselves. They go from babies who point and produce a single, sometimes unintelligible *word* to children able to produce sentences such as "Shelly gots no bear like mine to play with" (Janet 5;2). While not quite perfectly formed, the sentence clearly and correctly expresses a number of propositions. More importantly, it is not grounded in the here and now. Neither her friend Shelly nor the bear was present; Janet was simply reporting to her mother about her visit to her friend's house.

The preschool years encompass a wide spectrum of language development. Because children vary so greatly in the ages at which they achieve certain linguistic milestones, researchers commonly describe stages of language development independent of age. A common way of doing so is by mean length of utterance (MLU), or the average number of morphemes a child produces in an utterance. This is the approach taken by Brown in his impressive two-volume work (1973) and by a number of researchers before and since. It has the advantage of making comparison easier among children. One of the children in Brown's study, for example, reached an MLU of 2.8 at 22 months while another reached it at 35 months (p. 55). It was thus easier and more useful to discuss language development in terms of MLU rather than age. During the preschool years, then, Brown identified five stages of language development, from an MLU of 1.75 to an MLU of 4.0.

Other researchers, however, break down the preschool years differently. Ingram (1976) identifies three distinct subperiods of development during the preschool years. The first corresponds with the latter part of the period that Piaget calls the Sensorimotor period. Linguistically, the child enters the period of one-word utterances and acquires a vocabulary of approximately 50 words. The second subperiod, lasting from approximately 1;6 to 4;6, he calls the period of Preconceptual Thought. This marks children's earliest symbolic behavior and results in their pretend play—an alphabet block becomes a table, a house, or even a car, for example. For children at this stage, language is grounded in the here and now of the immediate environment. It is also a period of rapid growth "during which the child progresses from putting two words together to the point around 3;6 to 4;0 when most simple sentences are well formed by adult standards" (Ingram, 1976, p. 13). At the same time, children experience a period of impressive phonological growth for it is during this time of expanding vocabulary that children face the first real need for a phonological system.

The third subperiod begins at around age 4 and continues to age 6 or 7. This is the period during which children begin to come to grips with reality and "to abandon the dominant use of symbolic play. Rather than modify reality through play, the child begins to use play to express reality" (Ingram, 1976, p. 13). Children begin to enter into social games at this time although they may still not understand that there are arbitrary conventions which govern these games. Any parent who has tried to explain the rules of turn-taking in tag to a 5-year-old who doesn't want to be "It" will understand very well the limitations of the child's ability to comprehend abstract rules.

In language, more complex sentence structures begin to appear. Verb complements (*Gurgles thinks that's silly!*) appear along with a few relative clause structures (*Shelly want the doll that's mine!*), but the chief way of combining propositions is conjunction. Thus conjoined sentences such as *Shelly want the bear and she took it home and I want it back* account for most of the longer sentences children produce during this period. In the pages that follow, I have assumed Ingram's divisions and terminology, but for the sake of clarity, I have presented the time periods in shorter segments.

Janet from 1;0 to 1;6

Within a few weeks of uttering her first word, *weo*, Janet added to her vocabulary *baba* (bottle), *mumum* (mummy), *gaga* (Gurgles, the name of her stuffed bear) and *du* (juice). Interestingly, with the exception of *weo* and *du*, these words were of the reduplicated form common in the babbling of children between six months and one year of age.

First words have long interested researchers, who have recorded and categorized them in a number of languages. Although there is variation between cultures and, indeed, between children in the same culture, it seems to be universally true that children's first words identify or label particularly salient objects or people in their immediate environments. Broadly, these include family members or frequent visitors, food, actions, body parts, clothes, animals, toys, vehicles such as cars or trucks, and locations. Assigning children's early words to such categories requires, of course, that the researcher, or in the case of Janet, her mother the diarist, make judgments about the meanings and functions which these words serve. These judgments are susceptible to bias in the sense that the adults' preconceptions about what the child intends may influence their reporting. For this reason, it is important to have as much contextual information as possible about the conditions under which these early words are produced.

The number of words in Janet's vocabulary increased dramatically after her first birthday. By the time Janet was 16 months old, her mother had recorded a total of 24 different words. Table 3.1 shows the words, a phonetic transcription, a *gloss* or meaning, and in some instances a brief note about the situation in which the word was uttered.

There are a number of ways of classifying Janet's first two dozen words. Most appear to be nouns for naming things in her immediate environment. Her use of verbs (*stop* and *go*) adjectives (*more* and *dirty*) and the negative indicates that her communicative ability was well in advance of the naming stage. From her mother's diary and my own incomplete observational notes made at the time, it would seem that Janet's early words were used largely in the presence of the named object, that is, she used *gaga* when pointing to her bear and not in its absence. Even *go* was used in what seemed to be an observational sense, that is, when she saw her father with his coat on preparing to leave, she said *go*. There was no indication that she was asking to go with him. *Stop*, the other action word, however, she used in an attempt to direct her brother's behavior, ordering Matthew to stop tugging on her blanket on one occasion. Similarly, *more* was used to demand more of almost anything she wanted, initially cookies or juice.

These first 24 words also reveal a great deal about Janet's developing phonology. We see a number of instances of reduplication (discussed below). We also see instances of homophony, or two different words that sound the same, such as *du* for

Table 3.1   Janet's First Words

Weo	/wio/	'wheel'	car, truck, bus or anything with wheels
Baba	/baba/	'bottle'	bottle, milk, glass
Gaga	/gaga/	'gurgles'	Janet's stuffed bear
Mumum	/mamamam/	'Mummy'	Janet's mother
Du	/du/	'juice'	juice of any kind, coffee, any liquid other than milk
No	/no/	'no'	negatives of all kinds
Dada	'dædæ'	'Daddy'	Janet's father or other adult males
Buh	/bə/	'bird'	Big Bird
Da	/dæ/	'cat'/'dog'	From *The Cat in the Hat,* also used for neighbor's dog and for other Dr. Seuss books
Mo	/mo/	'more'	used also to indicate she didn't want an action to cease
Doe	/do/	'go'	
bop/ba	/bap/ba/	'stop'	used only when playing with Matthew
Dee	/di/	'street'	*Sesame Street*
Bubba	/bəbə/	'bubbles'/'water'	bubbles for her bath, water, ginger ale, soap
Wimu	/wimu/	'window'/'door'	
Du	/du/	'shoe'	
By	/bai/	'pie'/'cake'/ 'pudding'	
Da	/dæ/	'Janet'	
Guh	/gə/	'cup'	
dye	/dai̯/	'diaper'	
didi	/didi/	'dirty'	
Kuku	/kuku/	'cookie'	
Du	/du/	'Matthew'	Janet's brother

shoe and *juice.* This homophony results from the child's simplification of the adult system. In this case, Janet substituted [d], which she was able to produce, for both [S] and [J] that she was still unable to produce. Such substitutions typified Janet's speech at this stage, and are, in fact, very typical of children at this and the next stage of development.

Ingram points out, however, that development during this period differs in significant ways from later development. During the early part of this period, for example, the child uses words with shifting reference. A "bow-wow may refer to a dog one day, a horse another, or even a clock the next . . ." (Ingram 1976, p. 12). We see this to be true of Janet in her use of *pie, cat, bubble* and *window,* each expressing a number of meanings.

In comparison with the next stage of development, the child's sound system at this time is relatively primitive, consisting of a limited inventory of individual sounds and of syllable types. Although there is a great deal of variability among English-speaking children, their early consonants tend to be alveolar and labial stops, particularly [b]. Ferguson and Garnica (1975) have pointed out that [w] is also one of the earliest sounds acquired. Children at this stage of development may have as few as two vowels or as many as six, but [i] (the vowel sound in *feet*) and [a] (the sound in *tot*) are among the most frequent.

In Janet's speech of this period, we find rather extensive vowel development with five vowels and a diphthong. Her consonants included both labial stops as well as [w] and [m]. In addition to the alveolar stop [d], she also produced the voiced velar stop [g] and the alveolar nasal [n], but only in the word *no*. In *window*, she substituted [m], suggesting that [n] was not yet fully established.

Although she did produce some CVC syllables, in her versions of *street* and *mummy*, and a vowel as the second syllable of *wheel*, she overwhelmingly preferred CV syllables at this stage. Ingram reports that this is the preferred syllable configuration for the first 50 words or so, but VC may be found as well. His child Jennika used a great many VC syllables while Janet and the children studied by Menn and by Velten rarely did so. We see in Janet's speech another process which is characteristic of children in this stage. When she produced words of more than one syllable, she did so by duplicating the first syllable. *Reduplication* is a common phonological process in children under 2 years of age although not all children use the process and others use it to varying degrees.

Two other aspects of phonological development are noteworthy at this stage. Sometimes children appear to regress in their phonological development so that their early approximations of new words are closer to the adult forms than later attempts (Ferguson & Farwell, 1975). Leopold observed that his daughter Hildegard's attempts to pronounce the word *pretty* were better formed at ten months than at 1;3 and even 1;10 (cited in Ingram, 1976, p. 21). Piper (1984a, b, c) reports a similar phenomenon in 5-year-old children acquiring English as a second language. At first blush, this may seem to be a strange occurrence. But perhaps not.

The explanation appears to be that at first children are imitating and do not yet have a productive phonological system of their own. Later, as they attempt to come to terms with the *systematicity* of sound, they use a number of regular processes to simplify the adult system and thus their pronunciation appears to deteriorate. We see in Janet's speech at this point only one exemplar of this process, her pronunciation of *stop*. She first produced [bap] and then a few days later deleted the final consonant to produce [ba]. Admittedly, this is slim evidence for regression, and Ingram notes that it is not well documented in the research literature, but it is one that raises important questions about how the child creates an early phonological system.

A second noteworthy aspect of children's phonology at this stage concerns their selection of words. Ferguson and Farwell provide evidence suggesting that children select words that fall within their current phonological capabilities and avoid those that do not. One of the children they studied acquired words beginning with [b] but no words beginning with [p]. Leopold's Hildegard exhibited apparent *avoidance* of the same sound, and although Smith (1973) does not mention it, his account of his son's phonology from age 2 shows only three words beginning with [p] at the earliest stage but a great many more beginning with [b]. It would appear that many children consider sound patterns in choosing the words they acquire, or at least words that they produce since there is no evidence that they fail to understand words beginning with particular sounds.

In describing and discussing the first subperiod in the preschool years, we have focused on the phonological system. This is true because at this stage it is the most *visible* of the child's language systems. This is not to say that the child knows nothing about word or sentence structure but only that it is not yet apparent to the observer. In the next 6 months, however, as Janet began to combine words, we are able to make interesting observations about her syntactic as well as her phonological development.

Janet from 1;6 to 2;0

The onset of this age period is marked by a rapid increase in vocabulary and by the child's combining of words into early sentences. According to her mother's diary, Janet added a new word or two each week and at 1;6 uttered her first two-word sentence, "No nap." Table 3.2 shows excerpts from her mother's diary when Janet was 1;10. Here we find both an expanded vocabulary and evidence of two-word sentences. From this sample we can see that Janet had added *go, there, doggie, cold, nap,* and *kitty* to her vocabulary. The diary recorded that she had also produced the words listed in Table 3.3. These new words brought her observed productive vocabulary at age 1;10 to 38 words.

Table 3.2 Janet's First Sentences

1. Weo go.	[wio do]	Wheel go.	(She is rolling a toy car.)
2. Buh dere.	[bədɛ]	Bird there.	
3. Tu no.	[tuno]	Matthew, no.	A directive to Matthew to stop some action.
4. Dada go.	[dædæ do]	Daddy go.	
5. Dada weo.	[dædæ wio]	Daddy wheel.	Her father's car.
6. Goggie go.	[gagi do]	Doggie go.	
7. Su dode.	[tu kod]	Shoe cold.	Her mother has put a shoe on her that has been on the mud porch.
8. No nap.	[no næ]	No nap.	
9. Tu weo.	[tu wio]	Matthew's wheel.	Matthew's car.
10. Kiki dere.	[kiki dɛ]	Kitty there	

Table 3.3 Janet's New Vocabulary at 1;10

Hi	[hai]
Byebye	[baibai]
Up	[də]
Down	[dæ]
Sock	[dak]/[da]
Oscar	[aka]
Crayon	[ge]
Book	[bu]

Syntax and Semantic Relations

Once children begin to combine words, we can attempt to describe and to understand the rules governing their syntax. Researchers have shown a great deal of interest in the meanings conveyed by children in their two-word utterances. An obvious question that has arisen is the degree of universality in these early expressions. In other words, when they first begin to combine words, do children produce the same types of sentences? Apparently, there are similarities in the early meanings conveyed, but there is a great deal of variation among individual children. Some of the more common meanings include:

An Agent performing an Action	*Katie eat.*
An Action affecting an Object	*Kick ball.*
An Object being given a location	*Baby there.*
A Person or Object being described	*Katie cold.*

(Crystal 1987, p. 243)

The danger in describing children's utterances in this way is that we cannot always be sure what meaning is intended. In the utterances above, for example, the child *could be* doing essentially the same thing in the first and last sentences, namely describing some attribute of Katie. It may be only an adult's imposition of structure on the child's language to assume that a verb is used in one case and an adjective in the other.

Using the categories from Crystal's example, we see that Janet was conveying similar meanings:

An Agent performing an Action	*Daddy go.*
An Action affecting an Object	*Wheel go.*
An Object being given a location	*Kitty there.*
A Person or Object being described	*Shoe cold.*

We also see additional meanings in the sentences in Table 3.2. Possession is expressed in sentences five and nine and negative intent in sentences three and eight. Janet appeared to be telling Matthew, in the third sentence, not to take her stuffed mouse, and in sentence eight, she was telling her mother that she didn't want to take a nap. Not only was Janet able to create a number of meanings, we see even at this two-word stage clear evidence of early syntactic variety. In 10 utterances consisting of only 12 different words, Janet was effectively using six different sentence structures.

Although the first two-word utterances tend to consist of verb and object (or action and object), very shortly after two-word utterances appear, many children start using two-word noun phrases. The first expansion of the noun phrase usually occurs with the addition of an adjective (*bad doggie*) or a quantifier (*more juice*). After these come, more or less in order, the ordinals (*other spoon*), cardinals (*two bears*), the demonstratives (*this cookie*) possessives (*my hat*), and finally the articles *a, an* and *the*. All these may occur as early as age two. By 2;6, children may produce noun phrases with two modifiers before the noun (*this old hat*), and by 3;0 their noun phrases may have three or even four prenominal modifiers.

Phonology

With the addition of new words, we also find changes in Janet's phonology. She had added to her inventory of sounds two consonants. One was [t] which she now used instead of [d] in *Matthew* and the other was [h] in *hi*. She also used a new vowel, [ɛ] in *there*. Although she still showed an overwhelming preference for CV syllables, she did produce the occasional CVC syllable, in *sock* and *cold*. In *sock*, however, the CVC syllable alternated with the CV syllable, suggesting that she hadn't fully *settled* on the CVC form. Indeed, we find a few weeks later that she had chosen [da] as her pronunciation. We also see that she still uses reduplication as a strategy for producing two syllable words such as *kiki* (kitty) and *dada* (Daddy).

Janet from 2;0 to 3;0

Sometime around their second birthdays, many children begin to produce three- and four-word sentences. Obviously, once they begin to produce these longer utterances, more complicated syntax is needed to describe them. Children now begin to add questions and commands to the statements that characterized the two-word stage. Although children at this stage may be *telegraphic* in their tendency to omit grammatical morphemes such as the verb *to be* and the conjunctions, this tendency has largely disappeared by the time they are 3 years old.

Syntax

Two months before her second birthday, Janet produced her first three-word sentence, and by the time she was 2;0, they appeared regularly enough in her speech that her MLU was approximately 2.2. Considering that she still produced a number of single word utterances, this MLU showed rapid development. When Janet was 2;6, her mother's diary included the list of sentences in Table 3.4.

Table 3.4 is not a complete list of Janet's three-word sentences at this age; it consists of those sentences for which phonetic or near-phonetic transcriptions were available. These were representative, however, of all the semantic relations recorded between 2;0 and 2;6. The meanings expressed in these items included:

Agent Action Object (1,2,4,5,12)
Possessor Possession Locative (3) *
Possessor Possession Attribute (6,7)
Action Entity Attribute (8)
Action Entity Locative (11)
Action Object Attribute (9) *
Negative Agent Action (10) *

Table 3.4   Janet's Sentences at 2;6

1. Janet eat cookie.	[dæ i kuku]	2;3
2. Matthew eat cookie.	[tu i kuku]	2;3
3. Matthew cookie there.	[tu kuku dɛ]	2;4
4. Mummy see kitty.	[məmi si kiki]	2;4
5. Daddy go wheel.	[dædæ go wio]	2;5
6. Matthew face dirty.	[tu ses dədi]	2;5
7. Daddy big wheel.	[dædæ bɪk wio]	2;6
8. See big wheel.	[si bɪk wio]	2;6
9. Want Matthew gum.	[wã tu kəm]	2;6
10. Mummy no go.	[məmi no go]	2;6
11. See doggie there.	[si dagi dɛ]	2;6
12. Daddy chase Matthew.	[dædæ ses tu]	2;6

Most of these relationships are typical of those found in children beginning to form three-word sentences. Except for those marked with *, all were identified by Brown (1973) as prevalent in the speech of children at this stage. Once children reach the three-word stage, it is possible to view their sentences as having hierarchical structure. The sentence *Daddy chase Matthew*, for example, would traditionally be viewed as having two major constituents with *chase* and *Matthew* forming the VP constituent. That is the adult's way of parsing the sentence, but what is the evidence that it is the child's? In other words, how do we know that the action (*chase*) is more closely bonded to the object (*Matthew*) than it is to the agent (*Daddy*)? Martin Braine (1971b) has suggested one kind of evidence, the *build up* or expansions the child sometimes makes.

Eat cookie. . . . Janet eat cookie.

Unfortunately, this is an isolated instance in Janet's language and we do not know whether it is a common hierarchical structure. Another type of evidence could be sought in her two-word sentences. If it were the case that action and object were more closely bonded in her three-word utterances, it would likely also be the case that these were the predominant relationships in her two-word utterances. Returning to her two-word utterances, we find both agent-action and action-object bonding. This is consistent with research evidence showing that some children form stronger action-object bonds and others stronger agent-action bonds.

There was another important dimension of syntactic development apparent in Janet's speech at this age, and that was her use of pronouns. Although there are no pronouns in the language data reproduced in Table 3.4, Janet did begin to use pronouns during this year. Most children use *it*, *this* and *that* before the personal pronouns, and Janet was no exception, using these pronouns before she was 2 years old. The personal pronouns, specifically *he*, *she*, *him* (sometimes *hims*), *I*, and *me* all appeared with some regularity in her speech by the time she was 2;8. Young children's learning of the first person pronouns is an especially impressive feat. As Perera (1984) points out, children hear themselves addressed as *you* yet must learn to address themselves as *I* or *me*. Parents don't always provide much help, using names rather than pronouns in sentences such as *Mummy will put Lindsey to bed* (p. 104).

Grammatical Morphemes

Before the age of about 2;6, Janet's speech was usually devoid of grammatical *frills*. At about this time, however, she began to produce two grammatical inflections: The progressive form, *-ing*, and the possessive inflection on nouns appeared on certain words. These first appeared, as shown in Table 3.5, in two-word sentences—but note that the number of *morphemes* in each utterance remains three.

The period during which children acquire the inflectional morphemes has been of considerable interest to researchers. Perhaps the most thorough piece of scholarship in this area was conducted by Roger Brown in the 1970s. Brown (1973) recorded and analyzed the order in which three children, Adam, Eve, and Sarah, acquired 14 grammatical morphemes. A number of other researchers have followed his procedures in both longitudinal and cross-sectional studies. This period, when children are between 1;9 and 2;10 and the MLU is approximately 2;5, finds them typically adding a few prepositions, principally *in* and *on*, an article or two, and perhaps the plural and possessive forms. Other grammatical morphemes follow as the child marks finer syntactic distinctions. These remaining morphemes are acquired during a time when the child is between approximately 2;0 and 4;0 and the MLU is between 2;0 and 2;5 (Brown 1973, p. 271).

The procedure that Cazden (1968) initiated and Brown (1973) modified for determining the order of acquisition of grammatical morphemes is a rigorous one that has not been applied here. It is useful to note, however, that the earliest grammatical morphemes to appear in Janet's language were the progressive inflection on the verb and the possessive inflection on the noun. This is consistent with Brown's finding that

Table 3.5 Early Grammatical Morphemes

1. Matthew playing.	[tu pen]	2;6
2. Matthew's wheel.	[tus wio]	2;6
3. Janet's shoe.	[dæns su]	2;6
4. Janet's baby.	[dæns bebi]	2;7
5. Mummy's juice.	[məmis du]	2;7
6. Shoes there.	[sus dɛ]	2;8
7. Shoe in bed.	[su ɪn bɛt]	2;8
8. Gurgles in bed.	[gagas ɪn bɛt]	2;8
9. See in window.	[si ɪn wɪno]	2;9
10. Got two book.	[ga tu bʊ]	2;9
11. Doggie got Gurgles.	[dagi ga gagas]	2;10
12. Matthew's shoe there.	[tuz su dɛ]	2;10
13. Matthew chasing doggie.	[tu sesɪn dagi]	2;10
14. Sit on bed!	[sitɔn bɛt]	2;11
15. Gurgles jumping!	[gagas dəmpln]	2;11

two of his three subjects acquired the present progressive before any of the other inflectional morphemes. The possessive came higher in the acquisition order for Janet than for Brown's subjects, but she was well within the age range during which they acquired the possessive. Following shortly were the plural (although *shoes* was the only form to appear for some time) and the prepositions *in* and *on*. It is interesting to note that in learning *in*, Janet seems to have acquired not one but two prepositions. In sentences 8 and 9 in Table 3.5, we find her using two very different senses of *in*.

Phonology

Although certain infantile pronunciations remained, Janet rapidly added to her inventory of sounds. She maintained her earlier pronunciation of *Matthew, cookie* and *kitty* but improved upon her *Mummy* and *doggie*. Notice that the second syllable of *Mummy* is no longer reduplicated and the initial consonant of *doggie* is now a [d]. While she was still unable to produce consonant clusters, such as the *pl-* in playing, we can see in Table 3.5 that she had added the individual sounds [k,s,o] and stabilized her use of [n], using it instead of [m] in *window*, for example. Another kind of instability appeared, however, as she began her acquisition of the possessive. As she added to her inventory of individual sounds, Janet inevitably began to produce a greater variety of syllable shapes. In the language samples in Tables 3.4 and 3.5, CV syllables still dominate, but we also find CVC, VC and even a CVCC syllable.

Researchers have investigated the order in which children add to their basic inventory of the previous stage, both in naturalistic case studies and in experimental studies. Despite variation among children, certain patterns of development seem to hold true. Vowels, for example, are acquired first and are usually fully in place by the time a child is three. Janet had acquired the full inventory of vowels by 2;3 although she did not always follow adult pronunciations. For example, she maintained her pronunciation of *kitty* as [kiki] even though the vowel [I] was in her inventory. She also continued to pronounce *cookie* as [kuku] although she had both [U] and [I] in other words.

Because vowels occur singly in syllables, an acquisition order is relatively easy to establish. For consonants, such an order is more difficult to describe because they may occur in sequences in syllables and in a great many configurations. Moreover, children do not acquire individual sounds but sequences of sounds. As might be expected, children generally acquire single consonants before clusters. Templin studied 480 children ranging in age from 3 years to 8 years and found that by the age of 4, children have acquired most single consonants with the following exceptions: [t] between vowel sounds (as in *eating*), the *ch-* sound, the *j-* sound between vowels (as in *budgie*), the *th-* sounds, [v] and [z] at the beginning and end of words, the middle consonant in *leisure*, and word-final [l] and [s] (Templin, 1957 cited in Ingram, 1976, pp. 26–27).

By 2;6 Janet had acquired [p,b,t,d,s,k,g,m,n,w] but not in all positions. She still showed a tendency to delete or to devoice word-final consonants, producing [ga] for *got* and [bIk] for *big*. She was still missing a number of single consonants, notably [n,č,ǰ,r,l] but she used words with these sounds nevertheless. She did so by substituting sounds she could manage and by simplifying sequences of sounds. Her pronunciation of *playing* as [pen] illustrates: She substituted [n] for [ŋ] and reduced the initial cluster to a single [p]. This behavior highlights one of the most interesting aspects of phonological development at this stage, namely the appearance and gradual loss of certain regular processes.

At this age, children are not able to produce perfectly formed imitations of adult speech. Rather, they simplify adult sound sequences to ones which they can manage with their immature cognitive and articulatory abilities. There seem to be certain universal tendencies which govern the ways in which children accomplish this simplification. By studying the relationship between the forms produced by the child and the corresponding forms of the adult speaker, researchers have been able to describe the regular and fairly consistent processes children use in reducing the full range of adult sounds to a smaller and more manageable set. These phonological processes resemble those described in Chapter 2, but these are developmental and get left behind or suppressed as children become more proficient at producing adult forms.

Developmental processes are of three basic types. Children use one type to simplify the structure of syllables. Because English syllables may consist of consonant sequences that are very difficult to pronounce and because young children find CV syllables much easier to pronounce; there is a universal tendency to reduce syllables to the CV type (Stampe, 1979; Grunwell, 1982). For children learning English, this tendency may be realized in a variety of ways. A two-year-old who produces [du] for *juice* or [ti] for *cheese* is simplifying a CVC syllable to a CV syllable by deleting the final consonant. This is a very early process in children's speech and may not appear at all in some children. Grunwell reports that it has usually disappeared by the age of 3;0 or 3;3. Janet was still reducing some syllables to CV at 2;9 ([ga] for *got*), but the process had disappeared by 3;0.

Not all syllables are reduced to CV, of course, and even when the CVC syllable is mastered, there remain cumbersome consonant clusters to be dealt with. Often, children deal with these clusters by deleting one of the sounds in the cluster. For example, if children produce *top* for *stop*, they are simplifying a CCVC syllable to a CVC syllable by deleting the first sound in the cluster. Such deletions are rarely random. In two consonant clusters beginning with -*s*, for example, it is usually the /s/ which is deleted; words such as *pot* for *spot* and *kate* for *skate* are common in children under the age of three. In two consonant clusters beginning with a stop and followed by a liquid, it is usually the liquid that is deleted, producing forms such as *bick* for *brick* and *go* for *glow*. We see this type of reduction in Janet's pronunciation of *playing* and her earlier *crayon* as [ge].

In the early months of language acquisition, children produce mainly one syllable words but attempt many words of more than one syllable. Sometimes these early attempts involve deleting the unstressed syllable. Most of us have heard children pronounce *banana* as *nana*, but *ap* for *apple* is also possible in the very young child (Grunwell, 1982, p. 170). This process is called *weak syllable deletion*. Although this is an early process, we see a remnant of it in Janet's pronunciation of *Cinderella* as [sIndrɛlə] at 4;0 (Figure 3.2).

Simplifying the syllable shape is not the only way in which children simplify the adult phonological system. Through *assimilation*, or making one sound more like another, children effectively reduce the total inventory of sounds they have to produce.

Although there are several types of assimilation possible in child speech, two are very common. In the first type, one consonant in a word affects the pronunciation of another. The following examples come from Janet's speech:

Janet's Form	Adult's Form
[gagi]	'doggie'
[kiki]	'kitty'
[ses]	'chase'
[dæns]	'Janet's'

In each of these words, the initial consonants become the same as or more similar to the following consonant in the word. Young children have, incidentally, a preference for voicing consonants that precede vowels (Ingram 1976, p. 36), and this is also a kind of assimilation: Just about the only way of making a voiceless consonant more like a vowel without completely changing its character is to voice it. Janet, for example, pronounced [s] as [d] in *sock* and [k] as [g] in *clock*.

A second very common type of assimilation involves the devoicing of stop consonants at the ends of words. This process is assimilatory because by losing its voicing, the consonant becomes more like, or anticipates, the silence that follows it.

Common examples of this process include:

Janet's Form	Adult's Form	Age
[gək]	'bug'	1;11
[bɛt]	'bed'	2;8
[bIk]	'big'	2;6
[pɛk]	'Peg'	2;2
[bæt]	'bad'	2;0

The third major type of phonological process by which children simplify the adult sound system is substitution. In assimilation processes, children substitute one sound for another, but the sound that they substitute is influenced by another in the immediate environment. With substitution processes, however, they replace one sound with another apparently without reference to surrounding sounds. This is another way in which the total inventory of sounds is temporarily reduced, allowing children to produce simpler sounds or those that they can better approximate for more difficult ones.

Substitution, like assimilation and syllable structure processes, is rarely random. Children behave in similar ways in replacing one sound for another. Ingram (1976) reports, for example, that the process of stopping, or replacing fricatives and affricates with stops, is common in both normal children and in those with phonological disabilities. This process accounts for Janet's pronunciation of *juice* as [du], *jumping* as [d mpIn], and *sock* as [dak]. Notice that the stop is articulated in the same place as the fricative or affricate which it replaces.

Another type of substitution, also very common in the speech of young children, is called **fronting** and is apparently the result of a universal preference for consonants articulated near the front of the mouth. The most common realization of this process is the substitution of an alveolar consonant for a velar one, resulting in pronunciations such as the following:

Child's Form	Adult's Form	Source
/bæt/	'back'	Menn (1989)
/tæt/	'cat'	Menn (1989)
/tek/	'cake'	Hills (1914)

This was a process that Janet appeared to use only rarely and only when she was very young. Her pronunciation of *go* as [do] at 1;10 was the only reported incident of fronting. That it was not a process she generally favored is shown in Table 3.2. At the same time she was saying [do] for *go* she was also correctly producing [k] and [g] in *cold, kitty,* and *doggie.* Other researchers have noted that although consonant fronting is a well-attested process in the speech of young children, it is also one which does not occur in all children. Smith (1973) conducted a careful, detailed study of his son's phonological development and found virtually no instances of fronting. In children who do exhibit the process, it usually disappears by the age of 2;6; Grunwell (1982) reports that velar consonants (the ones affected by fronting) are mastered by all normal children by the age of 3;3.

Most of the examples used so far in describing the more common simplification processes children use in mastering the sound system have involved a single process. In real speech, however, children frequently apply a number of phonological processes at once. Ingram (1976) has reported as many as seven processes operating in a single word, and certainly two, three, or four are common. In a child's pronunciation of *scratch* as *tæt*, for example, we can see three processes operating. The initial consonant cluster is reduced to a single consonant, the /k/ sound in that cluster is fronted to a /t/, and the final affricate is replaced by a stop, /t/ (Grunwell 1982, p. 182). In Janet's pronunciation of her own name as [dæ] at 2;3 (Table 3.4), we see the substitution of an alveolar stop, [d], for [ǰ] as well as weak syllable deletion.

Identifying the processes which link children's pronunciations with the corresponding adult pronunciations depends to a large degree on how well we *hear* children's speech. Of course, just as we hear a foreign language through the filter of our own language, we also hear children's speech through the filter of our adult perception. Even trained transcribers must exercise caution in transcribing children's speech. Using machine analysis, Macken and Barton (1980) demonstrated, for example, that some children who appeared to be using voiced stops at the beginnings of words where they should have used voiceless stops were actually attempting to produce the correct form. What this suggests is that children may be farther along their path to phonological mastery than they seem to be, given what we hear as their pronunciations. This is a caution that we would do well to keep in mind as we view children's language data.

We cannot help but view it from our adult bias, and in doing so, we run the real risk of underestimating their accomplishment.

Janet from 3;0 to 4;0

This was a year of impressive progress for Janet in all areas of language acquisition. She continued her learning of the inflectional and grammatical morphemes, she continued to combine words into sentences which grew in length to seven and eight words. She gained control of the phonology of her language, leaving only a few minor distinctions unmarked. Two transcripts, one taken the day before her third birthday and the other a week or so after her fourth, provide a good indication of the magnitude of her progress.

Janet was making giant strides forward in pragmatics, syntax, morphemic structure, and phonology. These are apparent in comparing the conversations reported in Figures 3.1 and 3.2.

Pragmatics

During this stage, Janet became far more sophisticated and resourceful in her uses of language. In Figure 3.1, we see her clarifying her question when her mother doesn't understand. She was not yet able to say, "No, that's not what I meant," but she very deftly let her know that she wasn't asking about the next number in the sequence but about the color of the paper liner. In the year between the first and the second conversation, we find that Janet has become increasingly adept at using language for a variety of purposes. The child who used language largely to report and comment on the present has evolved into one who attempts to manipulate her mother and then play with the situation and the language in her opening line of *Cinderjanet*. While Janet at age 3 still relied heavily on repetition of her mother's phrases, by age 4 she was initiating utterances without direct reliance on her mother's words or structures.

Syntax and Semantic Relations

Janet's syntactic development was no less remarkable. By the time they are 3, most children take or have taken a giant grammatical leap forward as they begin to produce sentences with more than one clause. These clauses are still largely conjunctive, i.e., linked by *and*, and may run on and on. Janet was nearly a textbook case when it came to conjunction. Her mother's diary records the following sentence at 3;6:

> *Matt want my baby and I said he can't have her and he take Gurgles and I take his book about bears and he hit me.*

Children of this age are also capable of producing sentences with subordinate clauses, principally with *because ('coz)*, sometimes correctly:

> *My baby cry 'coz she want me* (Janet, 3;4)

Janet is standing on a chair helping her mother bake cupcakes for Matthew to take to
his kindergarten class.
Mother: You want to help?
Janet: Me help?
       [mi hɛlp]
M: Yes. You can put these in here. (The paper liners in the tins.)
J: Like this?
       [laik dɪs]
M: Right. Can you count them?
J: Count. One, two, three . . . what this?
       [kãut wən tu twi wa dɪs]
M: Four?
J: No. This one yellow. This one yellow, too. This one
       [no dɪs wən yɛwo dɪs wən yɛwo tu dɪs wən]
M: Oh, the color. That one's pink. You know pink.
J: Yeah. Pink. This one pink. Me taste?
       [yɛ pɪŋk dɪs wən pɪŋk mi tes]
M: You want to taste? Just a minute while I get you a spoon . . . There. What do you
     think? Is it good?
J: (Nodding) Good. Mat?
       [gʊd mæ]
M: Matt? Oh yes, these are for Matt to take to school.
J: Me too!
       [mi tu]
M: You want to go to school?
J: (Laughing) No. I want this one. (Points to cupcake.)
       [no ai wan dɪs wən]
M: Oh, you want a cupcake. Well, when they're baked, you can have one. Okay?
J: Okay. This one.
       [okei dɪs wən]

Figure 3.1   Janet at 3;0

and sometimes not:

> *Spike bite me 'coz it hurt.* (Kate, 2;9)

Before they can use constructions such as these correctly, a great deal of grammatical
knowledge is required. Similarly, as they begin to produce longer and longer utterances, greater syntactic sophistication will be required to prevent the kind of muddle
of tenses experienced by this child of 3;9 reported by Crystal (1987, p. 243):

> *If Father Christmas come down the chimney, and he will have presents when
> he came down, can I stay up to see him?*

Matthew and Janet have been begging to stay up to watch a children's special on television. Matthew has conceded the battle and headed toward bed, but Janet continues to argue with her mother while getting dressed for bed.

Mother: Which gown do you want?

Janet: Don't want *any* gown!
   [dõt wãn Ini gawn]

M: Well, that's up to you, but you might get cold.

J: I don't care. (She sits down on her bed and sulks.)
   [ai dõt kɛr]

M: I see. Do you care which story I read?

J: Nope. I don't care. I want to watch Charlie Brown.
   [nop ai dõt kɛr ai wãt tu watʃ tʃarli brawn]

M: I'm sorry, it's on too late. But you'll be able to see Charlie Brown another time. Don't forget, he's in the comics every Sunday.

J: I want to see him *now!*
   [ai wãt tu si hIm naw]

M: We're through talking about Charlie Brown, Janet. Now do you want me to read to you or not?

J: I'll read.
   [ail rid]

M: You'll read to me? What will you read?

J: How about Cinderella?
   [haw bawt sIndrɛlə]

M: That's a pretty hard one. Do you think you can read all of it?

J: (Defiantly *reading*) There was a mean wicked mother and she had a poor little girl named Cinderjanet.
   [ðɛr wɔz ə min wIkld məðɚ ænd ʃi hæd ə poːr lIto gɚo nemd sIndɚ-dʒænIt]

Figure 3.2   Janet at 4;0

At age 3, Janet's utterances were from two to seven morphemes in length, and she had begun to produce negatives, declaratives, and questions. It is usual for children to begin to produce different types of sentences at about the same time as the grammatical morphemes begin to appear. We saw that Janet had begun to produce certain grammatical morphemes at 2;6, and the transcript from 3;0 shows her beginning to use questions and some negatives. We still see, however, evidence of telegraphic speech, typical of infancy or the earliest preschool period. When she said *Matt?* with rising intonation, she was letting the single word carry a very large semantic burden, one that her mother recognized in her subsequent expansion of Janet's question.

By her fourth birthday, Janet's utterances ranged from 2 to 16 morphemes in length and most of her sentences were well-formed. Certainly those reproduced in Figure 3.2 were nearly perfect. At the same age and for several months previous, she had been producing a variety of syntactic forms including questions, negatives, negative questions, imperatives, and negative imperatives. There is no record of Janet's producing passive constructions during this time, although the dialogues recorded

Mother: What happened here?
Janet: It broke.
M: All by itself?
J: What?
M: Was the glass broken all by itself?
J: No. I broke it.

Janet: Your car broken?
Daddy: Yes, it was hit in the parking lot at work.
J: Who hit it, Daddy?

Figure 3.3   Understanding of Passives

when she was 3;5 and 3;6, respectively, in Figure 3.3 show her quite capable of understanding at least some passive constructions

This is not to say that Janet's syntactic development was complete. She still relied heavily on conjunction for linking related propositions rather than relative or reduced relative clauses. That is, she typically produced sentences such as *Matt took Gurgles and Gurgles had a sore ear and I told him not to!* (3;11) and *I saw Daddy's car and it was broken 'coz the wheel was on the ground and now he's going to fix it* (4;0).

The semantic relations expressed in Janet's sentences at age three were no longer restricted to the seven simple ones of 6 months earlier. She was producing well-formed SVO sentences (*I want this one*) although she did not yet produce the copula (*to be*). A moment's reflection explains why this might be the case. With *I want this one*, Janet was making her wishes known. Arguably, she could have done so without the first person pronoun, but the verb, object (*one*) and even *this* were essential to her specifying, and getting, exactly what she wanted. The copula, *is*, in the sentence *This one yellow* is clearly expendable. It is entirely redundant for expressing the meaning she wished to express. This is to say that children cannot learn *all* the grammatical conventions of language at once, and so the order in which they *do* acquire them is to a large degree determined by the meaning they wish to make.

It is possible to make certain observations about Janet's learning of the grammatical morphemes. We saw earlier evidence that she had acquired or was well on her way to acquiring the progressive, the possessive, and the prepositions *on* and *in*. Before the age of 3, she had added the plural form and certain irregular past forms such as *broke, saw, ate,* and *took*. Sometime around age 3 she had added the demonstrative article, *this* (see Figure 3.1) but still produced sentences without the copula (*What this?*). In the next year, however, Janet added the contractible auxiliary (*I'll read*), the contractible negative (*Don't want any*), other prepositions including *about, with, under, over,* and *beside*, as well as the copula in both the present and past tenses. She even made a stab at a complex sequence of tenses reminiscent of the example used earlier from Crystal.

> *When Daddy would come home if Matthew is not home from school is it—*
> (at this point, she gave up and started again)

When Daddy would come home and Matthew wouldn't come home, can I go with him to feed the horses? (4;2)

If we were to examine this excerpt for its errors or deviations from the correct adult form, we would do Janet a grave disservice. Even though neither sentence is perfect when compared with the adult model, both represent tremendous syntactic growth. In this short excerpt, we find Janet using auxiliary verbs, complementary structures (*go with him to feed the horses*), and making an attempt to express conditional relationships. She has come a long way from the child who only 18 months earlier was producing mainly two-word sentences.

Vocabulary

Children at this age are also busily acquiring a great many new words, and in the process sometimes get a bit muddled.

Exasperated Mother: Will you *please* behave?
Christopher (age 3): I *am* being hayve!

It is estimated that children of 3 have a vocabulary of between 800 and 1,200 words; by the time they are four, that total will have risen to between 1,500 and 1,900 words (Crystal 1987, p. 232). Assuming the lower end of each estimate, this means that children learn approximately two new words every day during this year. Parents of 3- and 4-year-olds will not be surprised by these estimates. If language use contributes to language learning, as it undoubtedly does, then most children have plenty of opportunity to learn. German researchers have reported that children of 3;6 produce nearly 38,000 words during a 12-hour day (Crystal, 1987, p. 244).

Phonology

Janet's phonological development at age 4 was mostly complete. Only a few individual sounds gave her any difficulty. She sometimes substituted [d] for the interdental sound in *this* or *there* but at other times produced it correctly, indicating that she had not yet fully gained control of the interdental. She also substituted [w] for [l] at times, but her mother's diary notes that she usually did this when she was playing with her dolls and was, perhaps, engaging in baby talk. We see in Figure 3.2 her pronunciation of *little* as [lIto] and *girl* as [gəro]. This substitution of a vowel, usually [u] or [o], for a consonant, usually [l] or [r], is called vocalization. It is common among younger children but it is not known how frequently it occurs in children of 4. This is true in part because the process results in a sound that is not greatly deviant, and most adults do not notice it (Grunwell, 1982, p. 171). The fact that Janet's vocalization appeared to be restricted to certain words, e. g., *girl*, *little*, and *wheel* and did not influence *I'll* or *call*, suggests that it was attached to certain lexical items which she had learned early and was likely in the process of being lost. By the time she reached her fifth birthday all traces of this process had been lost.

By the age of 4, Janet could produce most sequences of consonants and, thus, most syllable shapes. She would still occasionally omit or substitute a consonant in a three-consonant cluster such as *spring* which she produced sometimes as [spwin] and other times as [spin] at 3;11. She also pronounced *scream* as [skwim] until just before her fourth birthday.

Janet from 4;0 to 6;0

During these last 2 years in the preschool period, children develop remarkably in every way—physically, cognitively, and linguistically. The tentativeness of the word *toddler* no longer applies to these young children whose language is marked by major growth. The smaller building blocks of language are largely in place, and development during this period occurs largely in syntax and vocabulary.

Syntax

By the age of 4 and for the next year or two, children gradually solve some of the more complex grammatical puzzles of their language. At this stage, certain kinds of overgeneralizations appear as they work out the details of their rules-in-process.

Heidi gots too many.

Kate didn't went.

Mummy wented to gets Daddy.

That children of this age are capable of actively working on the rules is evidenced by Janet at 4;4 trying to tell her mother that Spook, the family cat, had not eaten her food (see Figure 3.4.)

The overgeneralizations in *gived* and *gaved* provide evidence that she was working on the regular past tense form. Her two self-corrections suggest that she was intentionally doing so and that her past tense and third person singular rules were still in progress, i. e., that she hasn't yet worked out the exclusiveness of the past tense and third person singular inflections. Crystal (1987) notes that this kind of "sorting out" of grammatical forms "is a particular feature of 4-year-old speech" (p. 243), and Janet's mother's diary abounds with examples of such grammatical struggles. Sometimes during the sorting out process, children revert to word order typical of an earlier age. Janet, for example, was heard at 4;4 to ask *Where goes Daddy's car?* But at the same time, she was producing syntactically sophisticated sentences such as the last one in Figure 3.4 in which she used an imperative and a well-formed relative clause.

Relative clause formation begins during the preschool years, chiefly as a way of specifying information about the sentential object. The sentence Janet uses to tell her mother what kind of food to feed the cat is a good example. In three separate studies, Menyuk (1971), Limber (1973), and Bloom et al. (1980) found that preschool aged children never use relative clauses to provide additional information about the subject noun (as in *The dog that bit me is in the garden*). This construction develops during the school years. But the researchers also found that the total number of relative clauses actually produced by the children they studied was very small. This was also true of Janet, and the reason may be that children tend to avoid the relative construction because it *is* difficult.

Janet: Spook doesn't like this food.
Mother: How do you know?
J: Well, you gived—gaved it to her last night and she doesn't ate—
   no, she didn't ate it.
M: Oh, well I guess you're right. What should we do?
J: Give her some different food that she likes!

Figure 3.4   Evidence of Rules in Progress

Consider the sentence *The cat that ate the tuna is mine*. To create this sentence, the child has to figure out how to create two sentences and embed one somewhere in the other without losing track of the first one. Assuming that the child has worked out the appropriate placement for the embedded sentence (relative clause), a decision dictated by the meaning, several other decisions need to be made. What is the appropriate relative pronoun? *That, which, who*, and possibly *whom* and *what* are all possible candidates to the child learner. Knowing which one to use requires a lot of sophisticated grammatical knowledge. Similarly, the choice of verb form has to be made. In this example, the choice is easy but adult speakers are often tangled up in tense puzzles with relative clauses, particularly those involving a choice between *who* and *whom*.

Another syntactic structure that begins to develop during this time is the passive, a construction relatively rare in oral speech. It is used mainly to emphasize the object of the sentence by making it the surface subject. In the speech of young children, the passive appears so infrequently that researchers find it impossible to study unless they deliberately try to elicit it in experimental situations (Tager-Flusberg, 1989, p. 153). Such experiments were not performed with Janet, and there was only one recorded instance of her producing a passive construction. At 4;9, she ran into the house to tell her mother that *Spook almost got hit by a car!* In this sentence, the agent was specified, but in general, young children produce more truncated passives, or sentences without agents, than full passives, or sentences with passives (Horgan, 1978).

We saw that Janet's preferred syntactic device for expressing longer utterances had been conjunction for some time. This preference continued between ages four and five when she continued to use *and* to link a variety of propositions. Table 3.6 shows examples of the conjoined sentences she used during this period.

As this table shows, the conjunction *and* can be used to express a number of different relationships between the two clauses. Researchers have identified at least four relationships marked by *and* in the speech of young children. They have also found that there is a largely invariant order in which they are acquired (Bloom et al., 1980 cited in Tager-Flusberg, 1989, p. 156). The earliest relationship expressed is simply additive. Sentences 1 and 2 in Table 3.6 illustrate this kind of relationship. The second *and* that children use expresses a relation of time between the two elements in sentences such as *Daddy gave me a dime and then I went to the store*. The third sentence in Table 3.6 is an example of this relationship. The fourth sentence may be an example of the same relationship or it may be an example of the next one to develop,

Table 3.6 Examples of Conjunctive *And*

1. I sawed Big Bird and he was talking to Cookie.	4;1
2. Mummy made cookies and I helped.	3;11
3. Matt come home from scool and then he wented.	4;4
4. Daddy fixed his car and now it will go.	4;6
5. Spook didn't sleep with me and I'm mad at her.	4;7
6. Grammy was here and now she's not.	4;5

causality. The fifth sentence more clearly expresses a cause-effect relationship and the sixth could be simply temporal or it could be an example of a contrasting or adversative relationship, the final one to appear. Tager-Flusberg gives the example of "'Cause I was tired and now I'm not tired" (1989, p. 156), but Janet's intent was less clear.

Vocabulary

If Janet was typical of children her age, and there is no reason to suppose otherwise, her vocabulary during this year grew from approximately 1,500 words to over 2,000 (Crystal, 1987, p. 232). Her words also became more complex as she learned most of the remaining grammatical inflections and some of the derivational ones as well.

Phonology

By this time, children have acquired a reasonably effective sound system, although they will continue to refine it for a number of years. From 4;0 to 6;0, they discontinue the simplification processes described earlier and their pronunciation becomes more adult-like. As they learn to cope with longer words that result in part from their increasing sophistication with inflectional and derivational morphemes, they will demonstrate that their language is still under construction. There are numerous examples of children's difficulty with longer words that show them relying on the same simplification processes. At 4;7, Janet announced to her friends that her mother worked at the "unibersity" and that her father was a "searching fizzlist." Certain words continue to be problematic for most children until they begin school or even after. Ingram (1976) reports creative pronunciations of *thermometer* and *vegetables* for children up to 5;11 (p. 45). Janet's pronunciation of *vegetables* as [vej boz] at 4;0 and [vej blz] at 5;1 are both typical. There is no evidence that she had any difficulty with *thermometer*, either because she did not talk about thermometers much or, as the daughter of a "searching fizzlist," she had no trouble with the word *thermometer*.

THE SCHOOL YEARS

By the time children reach school, they are adept language users. They understand the functions and uses of language and have mastered most of its syntactic structures. They have acquired most of its individual sounds as well as most of its intonational features, and so their learning of the sound system during the next several years will be of the finer distinctions marked by intonation and stress. They will begin to understand irony, for example, and other kinds of subtle meaning changes signaled by intonational changes. The most remarkable linguistic achievement during the school years, however, will be the sound symbol correspondence necessary for reading. Partly through reading and partly through the broader experiences they will have in school, they will add daily to their already substantial vocabulary.

Pragmatics

As they grow older, children's social circles widen, placing greater demands on their language. Even in these days of daycare, nursery schools, and preschools, there is still something very special about going to school. For a variety of reasons, the onset of formal schooling represents a new milestone in the acquisition of pragmatics. Not only does it present children with new social and learning situations with which to cope but it provides a great many new people and opportunities from which to learn.

When Janet, who did not go to preschool, went to kindergarten, she hurried home every day for the first few weeks with a "Did you know?" question. She excitedly reported all the routines of the Kindergarten, not realizing that what was new to her was known to the others in her family. She added the vocabulary of the school, words such as *recess*, *tardy*, *show-and-tell*, etc. And she gradually learned the rules of usage associated with the social structure of the school. Janet observed after her first encounter with the school principal, "She's sort of the boss and we have to be *very* quiet when she comes in."

Learning the roles of the principal, vice-principal, one's teacher, other teachers, janitors, secretaries, older children, and all the people who populate the school also means learning the register of speech appropriate to each as well as the subjects one might talk with them about. Children who do not already know learn very quickly that there may be severe penalties for breaking the sociolinguistic rules. Because she is a native speaker of English, Janet did not make the mistake of a little non-English-speaking girl in her class by answering the teacher's "Would you please be quiet now?" with the seemingly reasonable "No, thank you, I don't want to." Over the next several years, and to some degree for the rest of their lives, children will continue to learn the social rules governing language use.

To become competent language users, children must also learn the rules for initiating and maintaining conversation. They eventually must learn, for instance, that they will likely get off on the wrong foot if they try "That wart on your nose sure is ugly" or "Have you thought about wearing a more flattering wig?" as an opening gambit. They have to learn that turning and walking away without comment from a conversation that has begun to bore will have social ramifications. Conversational rules, if broken, can result in more severe communicative and social breakdowns as broken phonological, morphological or syntactic rules.

The school years are also the years during which children learn the subtle differences conveyed by syntactic paraphrases or *equivalents*. They learn that "The invasion was ordered by the president" imparts a slightly different message than does "The president ordered the invasion" and that there are reasons why governments might choose the truncated form, "The invasion was ordered," over either of the other versions. They learn that they can paraphrase "The cat is black" by saying "The black cat," but if they name the cat, the syntactic rule changes. Thus, "Spike is white" is all right, but "white Spike" sounds child-like. These are pragmatic rules that border on the syntactic, which brings us to the next major area of accomplishment.

Syntax

We have seen that by the time children begin school, they have mastered the basic syntactic structures of English. There is still a great deal to be learned, however, and over the next several years, they will learn to understand and produce more complex sentences including those that serve specific functions in the language, such as the passive and cleft sentence. Although it is possible to consider this learning from a number of perspectives, here we will concentrate on two broad areas of syntactic change—the global clause structure of sentences and development within their two major constituents, the noun phrase and verb phrase.

Clause structure refers to the patterns that children use in constructing their sentences—Subject-Verb-Object, Subject-Verb-Object-Complement, etc. Research has shown that although children are able to understand and to produce a wide range of clause patterns by age 6, they typically produce only a few. The predominant ones are transitive SVO sentences either with or without a sentence adverbial. They also produce a number of intransitive sentences, with and without adverbs, but other structures, such as sentences with two objects (*Matthew gave Spook the food* or *Grammy gave that book to me*) are less common.

Adverbs play an important role in young children's clause structure, and the use of adverbs has been widely studied. The kinds of adverbs children use appear to be established by age 6 and remain unchanged throughout the elementary school years. The proportion of adverbs denoting place, time, manner, and cause or condition is largely predictable from the order in which they were acquired—place and time first at about 2;6 followed closely by manner adverbials and those expressing cause or condition later. What does change from the age of 6 until the age of 14 or so, is the number and placement of adverbs children use. According to Strickland (1962 reported in Perera, 1984, pp. 94–95), children not only use more adverbials as they grow older, they are more likely to "include an adverbial within the verb phrase, e. g. *have been always trying*," behavior that is rare among 6-year-olds. (Perera, 1984, p. 94). While there were only sporadic entries in her mother's diary after Janet began school, an earlier entry shows her constructing a sentence of just this form. This and other samples of Janet's adverbial constructions appear in Figure 3.5.

Perera mentions one final interesting change in clause structure during the school years. The structure is the recapitulatory pronoun in which the noun phrase is repeated when the grammar doesn't require it (in sentences such as *These students with five classes they shouldn't work*). It appears less frequently in children's language as they grow older. Cotton (1978) found that children between 7;9 and 9;9 use this construc-

Grammy doesn't come always on Sunday.	5;2
Daddy won't go with me never!	4;4
Kick the ball over here!	4;6
Matthew and Daddy will come later?	5;8
Bears on Wheels isn't anywhere!	3;10
I did looked everywhere.	4;4

Figure 3.5   Adverbials in Janet's Speech

tion in speech (it is far less common in writing) but use it less with age (Perera, 1984, pp. 96–97). There are a few recorded instances of Janet's using this construction.

Spook she threw up on the floor.	5;4
Matthew and Daddy they left me here.	5;6
That mean boy outside he hit Spook.	5;10
Mummy and me we went to see Grammy.	6;0

The changing structure of the noun phrase is another indication of maturing syntax. Researchers generally believe that the use of complex subject noun phrases is a mark of linguistic maturity. Loban pointed to the fact that the most capable of the 12-year-old children in his study produced eight times as many expanded noun phrases in subject position as did the less capable (Loban, 1963 cited in Perera, 1984, p. 100). Complex noun phrases such as *The little dog with the bow on its collar* are more commonly found in writing than in speech, both in children and adults. This fact suggests that complexity in the noun phrase *may* result from some aspect of schooling, either literacy or overt teaching practice, such as sentence-combining exercises or editing of written work.

Another interesting aspect of noun phrase development is the acquisition of articles. As most non-native learners of English will attest, the rules governing the use of English articles are complicated, and native speakers do not work out all the rules until age eight or even later. Rules such as the one requiring *an* before a word beginning with a vowel and the plural agreement rule for *this* and *these*, for example, may not be perfectly learned even by age 12. Janet appeared to have worked out both rules before age 12, but at age 7;5, she produced the following sentences:

Matt said that he wanted a apple.
This ones are almost dead.

Another common error that children continue to make until age 8 or, more rarely, 10 or 12, is to use an article denoting definite reference, i. e., *the*, for something which is unspecified for the listener. Normally, for the article *the* to be used, the noun following it must have been previously introduced into the conversation or be clearly known to both speaker and listener. Hence, to say *The house was painted white* implies that both speaker and hearer know *which* house is under discussion. Children learn gradually during the school years that the use of *the* is restricted in this way. They also learn that the same restriction applies to *this*, *these*, and *those*, although colloquially, *this* is coming to be used as an indefinite determiner, as in "I was on the bus and I saw this man looking at me" (Janet 14;5). In this sentence, it is not at all clear that Janet had committed a reference error. It is more likely that she was using the language of her peer group which permits the use of *this* with a non-specified noun.

Verb phrase expansion in English refers mainly to the use of auxiliary verbs. Children master certain auxiliary verbs early. *Is, can, will,* and *could* are acquired early (by about 2;6) largely in negatives and questions. Major (1974, cited in Perera, 1984, p. 110) demonstrated that by the age of 5, most children have acquired *can, could, will, would,* and *should,* but many will not acquire *shall, may, might,* and *ought to* until age 8 or later. By 7;5, Janet appeared to have acquired all the modal auxiliaries, but at 6;9, she produced the following:

Mrs. Baker should might bring it to school.
Matt will might let me ride his bike.

Other kinds of difficulties with the modals persist well into the teenage years in some children. Conditionals and the hypothetical past presented particular problems for Janet.

If it would rain, the rain will get in under the tarp. (11;5)
Uncle Jack can't had left early or he'd be here by now. (11;0)

In fact, many native speakers fail to master the modals fully. Sports figures and other celebrities whose careers and fame depend upon something other than their facility with language might well produce a sentence such as this one: *If I would have known in advance, I wouldn't have come.*

Morphophonology

During the early school years, children add the few remaining sounds to their phonetic inventories. By age 7, or 8 at the latest, they can reproduce the full range of English sounds. If words such as *thermometer* and *vegetables* still give them difficulty, it is because they have not mastered all sequences of sounds in all environments. The most interesting aspects of phonological development during the early school years is closely connected with morphological growth. For example, children begin to learn the rules for the plural, past tense, and other inflectional and derivational morphemes that are phonologically governed.

Although this learning continues well into the teens, children between 4 and 7 make major gains. They master two of the three plural forms (the syllabic form which follows words ending in sibilants is learned a little later) and at least the same two forms of the possessive morpheme. Interestingly, children at this stage are better at producing the correct possessive form of *boss* than they are at producing the plural, although they sound exactly the same. Obviously, children are learning something more than phonetic patterns.

When children reach the age of 6 or 7, a stage of rapid morphophonemic growth begins. This period lasts for 5 to 7 years and it is during this stage that children acquire many of the derivational morphemes. We saw in Chapter 2 that regular sound changes occur with the addition of certain derivational morphemes. For example, when we add {-ity} to *divine* to produce *divinity*, the pronunciation of the vowel in the root word changes. Vowel alternation is one of the many morphophonemic processes that children learn during this stage, and it is one that Moskowitz (1973) studied in children between 5 and 12 years old. Specifically, her study asked whether children have knowledge of the rules governing vowel alternation and at what age they are acquired. Using a method that required her subjects to add the suffix *-ity* to nonsense forms, she found that 5-year-olds have no knowledge of the vowel alternation rule. She also found evidence that the 7- to 12-year-olds knew the rule, and that information about the rule is attained gradually.

Another kind of morphophonemic information acquired during this stage is how stress is used to differentiate compound nouns from noun phrases in pairs such as *BLACKboard* (compound noun) and *black BOARD* (noun phrase). In a study to test their ability to discriminate between such pairs, Atkinson-King (1973) showed children from kindergarten to Grade 6 paired pictures of blackboards and boards painted black, red socks and members of the Boston baseball team, etc. She found that the youngest children could detect a difference but could not correctly signal the difference in any consistent way (cited in Menn, 1989) even though they could accurately imitate each pair. Atkinson-King found that children develop their knowledge of this morphophonemic stress rule gradually from Grade 1 to Grade 6.

By age 7, then, children have not yet completed their acquisition of phonology; they gradually learn more complex morphophonemic rules until age 12 or so. At around this age, they move into the final stage of phonological development. Ingram (1976) identifies this as the Spelling Stage. It is at this time that children master (or come close to mastering) the spelling of English, a process that has begun much earlier. Ingram links this stage with Piaget's period of formal operations (roughly 12 to 16 years) and with the stage at which the child

> *becomes capable of making intuitional reflections on . . . language. . . . Decisions of grammaticality can be made. In phonology, the child can also begin to decide what is a possible sound change and what is not.*
>
> *This probably also has an effect on spelling, which develops markedly during this period.* (Ingram, 1976, p. 14)

Vocabulary

As they acquire the ability to understand and to use derivational morphemes, children's vocabularies show a dramatic improvement. Estimates of the vocabulary of an average school-aged child vary from approximately 2,500 different words (Crystal 1987, p. 232) to as many as 8,000 (Gleason 1989, p. 4). This variation is caused not only by a wide range of actual vocabulary size in children this age but by disagreement among researchers on what should be counted as a different word, or type. Does one, for example, count only root or base words or does one count all plurals, possessives, past tenses, etc. as separate words? Whatever the true figure, it is clear that children understand several times more words than they produce (Crystal 1987, p. 232). The size of both receptive and productive vocabulary will increase dramatically over the next several years in large part as a result of learning to read.

Literacy

Literacy is, of course, the dominant language learning task children face after the age of 5 or 6. In a real sense, learning to read and write is like learning another language since it involves learning another symbolic system. It is made easier, of course, by the fact that children have learned oral language. Otherwise, the task of learning to read and write would be a great deal more difficult than it is.

Janet learned to read at some point before she began Grade 1. From the time she was born, she was surrounded by books, magazines, and newspapers. Her parents read to her long before they had any hope that she understood the words. We saw Janet at age 4 pretending to read *Cinderella*. Sometime in the next 2 years, the pretend reading gave way to real reading. Janet's mother tells the story of Matthew having to learn a short poem for the Christmas play at school. He brought the poem, which he had printed onto lined paper, home with him to study it. She went into the family room to find Matthew reciting the poem and Janet following the written page. "No, Matt, it doesn't say that," Janet said when Matthew made an error. "It says 'the snows *lay* deep and white,' not *were* deep and white." Janet's mother checked the script and found that Janet was right. Janet was one month short of her fifth birthday; Matthew was not quite 7.

While it is tempting to claim that some children learn to read by mere exposure, there is a danger that in doing so we underestimate their accomplishment and fail to consider the factors that contribute to their success. Recent research indicates that oral activities, particularly rhyming, may contribute significantly to later success in reading. In particular, children who are able to produce rhyming segments and to identify non-rhymes at ages 4 and 5 are, in general, better readers 2 years later than children who lack such ability. Peter Bryant and colleagues at Oxford University have found that rhyming and alliterative abilities are distinct from general language ability and from sociolinguistic background. In other words, it seems to be the case that children's ability to recognize and produce rhymes and alliterative forms is independent of factors such as being read to in the home. This is not to say, however, that what happens in the home is of no consequence. It is highly likely, for instance, that rhyming and alliterative abilities can be encouraged and practiced in very young children. Many of the popular Dr. Seuss books (such as *The Cat in the Hat*) provide excellent exposure to rhyme and alliteration. The fact that they are nearly universally loved by children points to the fact that children find rhyming activities natural and fun.

Educationally, the fact that preschool children are good at rhyming is significant for two reasons. As Bryant, MacLean and Bradley (1990) point out, the fact that children have this ability indicates that they are able to analyze the constituent structure of words. Both rhyming and alliteration require the child to isolate the initial segment, the onset, from the vocalic nucleus, the rime, and thus shows that they are able to recognize sound units smaller than the word. The ability is also significant because research demonstrates that "there is a powerful connection between these abilities and the progress that children make later on when they learn to read and write" (p. 239).

Research linking rhyming and alliteration to reading is important because it suggests that early factors other than level of home literacy help to determine later success in reading. It is an exciting finding for educators because it points the way toward an intervention that might have a positive effect. More precisely, it causes us to rethink our position on phonics, whether pro or con, and to reconsider the kind of phonics instruction that might be effective. This is a subject to which I will return in Chapter 10.

All of this is not to say that home literacy is unimportant, for it remains a highly significant factor. It is only to say that other kinds of oral language appear to be important as well. It may be the case that Janet learned to read on her own simply by being exposed to print. Or it may be the case that the early exposure to children's books together with a rich oral culture in the home ignited the spark that already existed.

In order to learn to read, the majority of children need some teaching. This teaching is easier, of course, if the children know the purposes of reading and have been exposed to a great deal of print and simply learn on their own. Torrey (1973), Ferreiro and Teberosky (1982), and Bissex (1984) all report studies of children who apparently learned to read without instruction. Some had the advantage of *Sesame Street* and *The Electric Company*, as did Janet, but others did not. What they all did have in common was the view that learning to read presented a challenge that they wanted to meet and being questioners. As Pflaum (1986) reports, it seems to be a characteristic of early readers that they "ask very specific questions and . . . receive specific answers to those questions" (p. 65).

We come then to the importance of social interaction. While social interaction is clearly an important factor in children's learning to speak, it might be thought of as less important for learning literacy. Reading and writing, unlike speaking, are, after all, activities that can be carried out in isolation from others. But apparently, learning to read and write are facilitated by social interaction.

CONCLUSION

We have seen in this chapter a sketch of Janet's language development from the time she was born until she reached her teenaged years. While a full description of her language growth at each stage would warrant an entire book, even the brief examples provided in this chapter have served to mark significant milestones in her acquisition of pragmatics, syntax, morphology, and phonology of her native language.

We saw Janet grow from an infant whose precursory behavior was essential to the development of real language to a school-aged child already established as a lifetime member of her language community. Throughout the chapter, Janet's story has served as a springboard for more general discussion of the course of normal language acquisition. In the next chapter, we will see that this course is very similar for other kinds of language learning as well.

QUESTIONS FOR DISCUSSION

1. On p. 67, the author identifies four types of syntactic/semantic structures Janet has used. Are there alternative descriptions possible for any of the sentences?

2. What is a cleft sentence and why might it be used instead of another form?

3. Collect a short speech sample from a child in kindergarten. Analyze the adverbs used to see if they follow the pattern described by the author.

4. The author makes the following statement:
   "Interestingly, children at this stage are better at producing the correct possessive form of boss than they are at producing the plural, although they sound exactly the same."

   Why might this be true? Have you heard other instances of this apparent anomaly?

5. The author states that learning to read and write are facilitated by social interaction. What evidence from your own experience suggests that this is true?

6. The author writes that research on children's knowledge or alliteration and rhyme is promising "because it points the way toward an intervention that might have a positive effect." What kind of intervention would be appropriate?

7. The author refers to language as a "conventional mapping relation." Explain what this means and how it pertains to language.

8. What research methods might be employed to determine that very young infants are able to discriminate between similar speech sounds such as /p/ and /b/?

CHAPTER FOUR

Learning Two or More Languages

There is a tendency among North American educators to consider monolingualism as the normal outcome of schooling. This view is common in certain parts of society despite the fact that Canada, among other nations of the world, is an officially bilingual country that functions well in both English and French without insisting that all its citizens be bilingual. Educators and governments, especially in English-speaking countries, give the impression that multilingualism is unusual. The growing popularity of *English Only* legislation in the United States reflects this view very clearly. While there are very likely some legitimate safety and bureaucratic grounds for such laws, there is also a darker intolerance and ethnocentricity among some who support establishing these laws. There is also a great deal of misunderstanding about the nature of and importance of bilingualism. One of the aims of this chapter is to examine the facts about children who acquire more than one language, either simultaneously or successively. Throughout this chapter, I use the terms *acquisition* and *learning* interchangeably, although I am well aware that some theorists, particularly Stephen Krashen, mark a distinction between the two.

People learn their languages for a variety of reasons and under a variety of conditions, but the fact that they do so suggests that there cannot be anything especially difficult about learning an additional language. Yet, in North America, we seem to find foreign language teaching, and even English as a second language, particularly challenging. Anyone who claims to be bilingual is considered slightly exotic. And yet the fact is that most of the world's population learns and functions in two, three, or more languages (Crystal 1987, p. 360). There is, however, no clear agreement on what it means to be bilingual. Some authors use the term to refer to people with *any* proficiency, even if it is only a few words, in a second language. Others insist that native-like control of both languages is necessary. But, in fact, McLaughlin (1984) is correct when he says, "Bilingualism is best described in terms of degree" (p. 9). For our purposes, we will adopt Haugen's useful definition, also used by McLaughlin: "the ability to produce complete and meaningful utterances in the other language" (Haugen, 1956, cited in McLaughlin, 1984, p. 8). This definition does not assume balance. It is not uncommon even for young children to be more fluent in one language or to reserve one language for use in certain situations. It only assumes that children are able to communicate easily in either language at a level appropriate to their age.

There are many routes to bilingualism. Many children acquire two or more languages before they reach school. I have known a number of Canadian families in which a Francophone mother and an Anglophone father (or vice versa) bring up a bilingual child who speaks the appropriate language with each parent. Which language eventually dominates—and usually, one will—depends on what language is spoken in the surrounding community. Another young couple I know emigrated from China and speak only Chinese in the home. Yet their child, when she reaches school age, will be bilingual, having acquired English from her playmates, from television, and the sheer preponderance of English around her. Still another set of parents in a small community in Labrador speak both English and Inuktitut with their children. With only limited exposure to English-language television and no native English speakers in the small community, the parents believe that their children's eventual success in school and, indeed, in the predominantly English society, will be jeopardized if they begin school without some prior knowledge of English. They thus assume the responsibility for their children's second language learning. All these children are learning their two languages simultaneously.

The distinction between *simultaneous* and *successive* or *sequential* bilingualism is generally made in the literature on second language acquisition. It is probably accurate to say that educators tend to pay more attention to the latter. The reason is obvious: Educators believe they need not be particularly concerned about teaching a second language if the child has already acquired it before coming to school. In fact, this thinking is misguided. Teachers should be acquainted with both kinds of bilingualism for the same reason that they should have some understanding of first language acquisition. It is important to know as much as possible about children's cognitive development, and bilingualism has a significant impact on cognition. Also, by understanding the conditions in which children acquire their first and second languages simultaneously, they might gain insights to guide them in creating successful language learning environments in school.

In this chapter, we examine childhood bilingualism and the issues surrounding it. The first two sections correspond with the distinction noted above. Next we examine the issues that an adequate theory of second language acquisition must address. Because the focus of this book is *children's* language learning, we concentrate on the conditions affecting their second language learning, although in the description of the issues affecting theory, there will be some discussion of adult learning.

A critical factor in assessing these conditions is the age at which the child begins acquiring a second language, for most other conditions will be influenced by that one. The distinction already noted between acquiring languages simultaneously and sequentially (McLaughlin, 1984; Vihman & McLaughlin, 1982) is not always clear-cut.

It is not easy to assign an arbitrary age at which the acquisition of two languages ceases to be simultaneous and becomes sequential. Are children who begin to learn another language at age 2 or even age 3 adding a language to an established first language? Or are they acquiring two languages at the same time? We could adopt McLaughlin's arbitrary age 3 as the point after which children are assumed to be adding a second language. Certainly the child has a good head-start in the first language by that time.

We saw in the last chapter, however, that a significant amount of first language growth occurs between age 3 and the end of the preschool years. More importantly, there is a major difference between the conditions or environment for second language acquisition that occurs in the home and in the school. The former has been termed *natural language learning* and the latter *formal language learning*. While recognizing that these distinctions are sometimes useful, I have chosen instead to mark the distinction between **home bilingualism** and **school bilingualism**. The first refers to children who acquire two languages simultaneously from infancy or at other times before they begin formal schooling, even in daycare or preschool. The latter refers to those children who begin to learn a second language at any time during the school years.

HOME BILINGUALISM

Children who acquire two languages from birth are not really acquiring either as a second language; they are acquiring two first languages. Children of bilingual parents who speak both languages with the child from birth are effectively learning two first languages. What may be more common, though, is the child whose parents speak the same language but who learns another language from a grandparent, nanny, or babysitter, if not perhaps from birth, from a very young age.

Studies of preschool children acquiring two languages (Ronjat, 1913; Leopold, 1939, 1947, 1949a, 1949b; Totten, 1960) strongly indicate that they are able to do so in much the same way as they learn different registers of the same language. Ronjat's detailed study of his son, Louis, learning his mother's language, German, and his father's language, French, indicates that the child learned German and French vocabulary, phonology and syntax simultaneously and without confusion. According to Ronjat's observations, the child could produce the phonemes of both languages correctly by 3;5 (McLaughlin, 1984, p. 75). As we saw in the previous chapter, this is well within the normal range for a monolingual child, and Ronjat's son was bilingual.

Ronjat reported following his friend's, Maurice Grammont's, advice to keep the languages strictly separated: "each language must be embodied in a different person" (cited in McLaughlin, 1984, p. 75). With his daughter Hildegard, Werner Leopold followed the same advice, speaking to her only in German and her mother speaking to her only in English. Although her learning in both languages was impressive, Hildegard never achieved the balance achieved by Louis Ronjat. This was likely because the family lived in an English-speaking environment and visited Germany only twice in her first 5 years. So while German was the language in which she communicated with her father, it apparently had little utility outside the home. There was some mixing of

Hildegard's two languages, most obvious in her early vocabulary development where she seemed for a time to adopt

> the strategy of giving things one name only. However, once she realized that there were two languages in her environment, this competition ceased and she managed to use the appropriate words in both languages (although the increasing predominance of English complicated this task).
>
> *(McLaughlin, 1984, p. 80).*

In general, however, Leopold found no evidence that bilingualism in any way influenced the development of either language. Each developed as they would in a monolingual.

Another study from early in this century is useful for comparison with Ronjat's and Leopold's. Madorah Smith reported in 1935 on the learning of English and Chinese by eight children from the same family. The parents were American missionaries, and all their children were born in China. The parents spoke both Chinese and English to the children, who apparently confused the two languages until about age 3. Their preference was for their parents' native English, but they sometimes used Chinese even when playing alone together. Unlike the Ronjats and the Leopolds, the parents of the children in Smith's study mixed the languages, each parent speaking Chinese at times and English at others.

Tabouret-Keller (1962) reported a more recent study of early bilingualism in a family where the parents mixed the two languages. The little girl's mother was raised in a poor rural area and spoke both her native German and the French she had learned in school. The child's father was a mine worker who had learned both German and French as a child. According to Tabouret-Keller's account, both parents mixed the two languages in speaking with the child, using French about twice as often as German. Not surprisingly, the child had a larger French than German vocabulary by the time she was 2 years old by a margin of about three to one. She also mixed German and French words in about 60% of her sentences. While mixing would be expected under the circumstances described, the amount of language mixing done by this child exceeded what would be predicted given the proportion of French she heard. But then, of course, the parents were not the only influence on their child's language growth. The family lived in an area where German was spoken and this was the language of the child's playmates.

Numerous other studies report the mixing of the child's two languages (Ruke-Dravina, 1965, 1967; Zareba, 1953; Totten, 1960; Engel, 1965) or three languages in the case of a trilingual environment (Murrell, 1966). One of these studies was particularly interesting for the conclusions it reached about the nature of language structure. Engel's son, who was learning both English and Italian, produced a number of hybrid words, usually English words with Italian endings, and experienced some semantic confusion between the two languages. The sound systems, however, were entirely distinct, leading Engel to conclude that the phonological system is somehow separate from the semantic and morphological systems.

Oksaar (1970) supported this conclusion in his study of a bilingual child. The child spoke Estonian with his parents and Swedish with his playmates. The sound systems of the two languages are similar, and it is usually the case that children have more difficulty keeping similar systems distinct. Even though the child was in constant contact with a Swedish-speaking playmate, Oksaar found no evidence that Swedish influenced her son's Estonian pronunciation. There was, however, evidence of mixing in his morphology and syntax. Like Engel's child, this one tended to add endings from one language to words of the other. In contrast, Itoh and Hatch (1978), studying the language development of a Japanese-speaking child learning English from 2;6, found an early confusion especially in the sound system. Specifically, they found that the Japanese sound system influenced his English pronunciation (pp. 80–83).

It seems that learning the sound system may be a different sort of task from learning other language systems. Analyzing the language development of a 3-year-old Spanish-speaking child acquiring English, Hernandez "found that the influence of the new sound system was initially pre-eminent, suggesting that acquisition of the sound system is especially important for a child of this age learning a second language" (reported in McLaughlin, 1978, p. 104). Hernandez also reported the more general observation that Spanish-speaking children attempting to speak English often resorted to using Spanish words and grammar with English pronunciation.

If children tend to keep the sound systems of their two languages separate, what about the other systems? While some children appear not to confuse or mix their two languages, early mixing seems to be much more typical. Crystal identifies three stages of development in early childhood bilingualism:

1. Children build a vocabulary of words from both language which only rarely are translation equivalents of each other.
2. When they begin to combine words in two- and three-word sentences, words from both languages are used within the same sentence. But the amount of mixing declines rapidly.
3. As the vocabulary grows larger in each language, children begin to learn translation equivalents, e. g., chat and cat or friend and amigo. (Crystal, 1987, p. 363)

For Crystal, these stages constitute evidence that acquiring a single language and acquiring two languages are different processes. On the face of it, this appears to be so. But if we think about the processes from a broader perspective, they don't seem quite so disparate. Both bilingual and monolingual children initially acquire a single label for common objects or actions and only rarely have synonyms in their early vocabularies. When they begin to combine words into sentences, bilingual children use the words they have. Assuming that they attempt to express the same semantic relations as monolingual children, and there is no evidence to the contrary, then they must necessarily mix their two languages. Otherwise, given the nature of their vocabularies, they would be limited in what they could express. As their vocabularies expand, monolingual children *and* bilingual children add synonyms. So while a case can be made for different *behavior* in bilingual and monolingual children, the different behavior may not signal different acquisition processes.

In addition to the ones cited here, there have been a number of other studies of early bilingualism, most of them case studies and thus inconsistent in their objectives, observations, and purpose. Even with such inconsistency, however, it seems that certain conditions facilitate the acquisition of two languages. In general, it seems to be the case that Grammont's advice to his friend Ronjat was sound. Young children experience less confusion between their two languages if those two languages are kept distinct. They seem to have little trouble learning the separate languages of their two parents, or the language of their parents and the language of their peers or other caretaker. The distinction, however, need not be embodied in people. Ruke-Dravina (1967) observed situational specificity in which children playing with the same playmates used their parents' language, Swedish, when playing in the home and Latvian, the playmates' language, when playing outside. The studies also agree that balanced bilingualism is rare and that sooner or later one language dominates. It also seems to be true that once a particular language becomes predominant, it is difficult for the child to switch back to the other language. There may even be a period during which child refuses to use either language, a silent period until some degree of balance is attained (Engel, 1966; Leopold, 1949b).

What is abundantly clear is that children who grow up bilingual or multilingual are neither linguistically nor educationally at risk. There is no evidence whatsoever that acquiring more than one language is detrimental. On the contrary, "By the time these children arrive in school, the vast majority have reached the same stage of linguistic development as have their monolingual peers" (Crystal, 1987, p. 363). In addition, they have another language. Bilingualism is clearly an advantage.

SCHOOL BILINGUALISM

The most obvious differences between home and school bilingualism are the age of the child learner and the setting in which the languages are acquired. These are, indeed, compelling differences, but common sense tells us that there are more. As every parent knows, children appear to perform amazing feats of learning—linguistic and otherwise—during the first few years of life. But as every primary teacher knows, the learning feats of young schoolchildren are no less impressive. Moreover, for all the emphasis we place on the home environment for language acquisition, we all know that there is a great deal of variability in children's homes in the amount and variety of talk and reading, for example. And yet, children from all homes learn one, two or more languages with apparent ease. All this argues that influences other than age and setting account for differences between home and school bilingualism.

One of the major differences between home and school bilingualism appears to be the kind of language that occurs in school. A number of researchers and educators have observed that the language used in schools is significantly different from the language used outside classrooms. Margaret Donaldson (1978) characterizes the difference in terms of children's thinking. They are quite capable thinkers before they begin school, but their thinking tends to be "directed outwards on to the real, meaningful, shifting, distracting world." Success in school, however, requires them to learn "to turn language and thought in upon themselves," to direct their own thought processes in a thoughtful manner. Linguistically, this means that children must be able not only to talk but to choose what they will say, "not just to interpret but to weigh possible interpretations." In short, they "must become capable of manipulating symbols" (pp. 87–88). Children must learn these new thinking and language skills in contrast with the language of the school, the formal, abstract language that is largely decontextualized, logical and expository. The informal language of the home is, in contrast, context-bound, sequential, and intuitive.

Learning language in school is made easier when children have been previously exposed to the literary functions of language by being around people who read and by having books read to them. Still, a great many children find the language demands of the school very difficult to meet. When the language of the school is also a second language for the child, the problem is compounded. Children learning a second language benefit, just as monolingual children, from literate homes. Monolingual or bilingual, children who know about books and the language of books, have a better chance of success. Unless, of course, the language of the school can be better suited to match the experience of the children. As we shall see, in school second language programs, this seldom happens.

The majority of children in North America achieve whatever degree of bilingualism they possess in school. Whether they are adding the dominant language (usually English) to their home language or adding a minority or foreign language, children may encounter any one of a number of different formal language programs. These include immersion, two-way immersion, bilingual, FLES (foreign languages in the elementary school) and a hands-off approach, sometimes called submersion.

Immersion

One of the most promising of the second language programs in elementary schools is immersion. The most comprehensive research literature comes from the Canadian experiment in bilingualism, French immersion. Swain (1976) listed 114 such research reports, and dozens more have appeared each year for the past two decades. Throughout Quebec in the 1960s, the protection of the French language became a sensitive political issue. It became apparent to Anglophone parents that their children's future in Quebec would be brighter if they spoke both their native English and the language of the majority of the population of Quebec, French. Thus began what has since become a national movement in bilingual education, the government-supported French immersion programs. The identifying characteristic of immersion is the exclusive use of the second language in school. Teachers must be bilingual for the children will initially speak only in English. Teachers, however, will respond in French and gradually children start to use French themselves. For the first few years, all instruction in all subjects is in French. For children who begin immersion in kindergarten, English is usually introduced in Grade 3 (or in Grade 4 in some programs) and the amount of English gradually increased until the proportion is approximately 60% English and 40% French.

The children in the first immersion classes are in or have completed university as of this writing. As might be expected, they have been rather extensively studied. The results are on the whole positive. Not only do children acquire a better level of competence in French than those in more traditional language classes, they also tend to have more favorable attitudes toward French-Canadians. But the research does not indicate that immersion is a panacea. Although their language proficiency is impressive, children from immersion classes are a long way from native proficiency, partly because they have extensive academic or school competence but less social language proficiency in French. One very important finding on which nearly all studies agree, however, is that the children's proficiency in English is not at all adversely affected by their acquisition of French in immersion programs. Although they may lag slightly behind their peers in Grades 2 or 3, by Grades 5 or 6, they catch up. Since the original immersion programs began, there have been other experiments with variations—early partial, delayed, late and double immersion among them. **Early partial immersion** begins either in kindergarten or Grade 1 with the day divided between the child's first and second language. Initial evaluations of English-speaking children in French partial immersion have shown that their English language skills are no better than peers in total immersion and that their French skills are worse (although better than children in FLES programs) (Genesee, 1983; Swain & Lapkin, 1982; Barik & Swain, 1974, 1975). Even though early immersion has been largely successful, the program has suffered very heavy attrition rates across Canada. The attrition rate suggests that immersion is not the right program for every child. Moreover,

> Clinical studies indicate that there may be a subgroup of children for whom early programs are not suitable. These children could be termed developmentally immature in the sense that their cognitive and linguistic skills are not developed adequately to meet the demands of a bilingual academic environment.
>
> *(Wiss, 1989, p. 518)*

Rather than have their children face the possible stigma of withdrawing from immersion, and worrying that their children's education may suffer if they begin French immersion too young, some parents prefer to delay French until later. **Delayed immersion** is essentially the same as early total immersion except that it begins in Grades 3 or 4. **Late immersion** is yet another alternative for some children. It begins in Grade 6 or later and lasts for 1 or 2 years. Results of evaluation studies of late immersion indicate that the students suffer no harmful effects to their native language, do very well in French and develop positive attitudes toward French-speaking people. They do not, however, do as well in French as children of the same age who have had either early or delayed immersion (Barik et al., 1976; Connors et al., 1978; Swain, 1974).

Success in immersion led some educators to experiment with **double immersion**. Taking the view that if immersion in one language works, some schools are trying immersion in two languages. A study conducted in Montreal of English-speaking children immersed in both French and Hebrew showed promising results in both languages without detriment to English (Genesee and Lambert, 1983; Genesee et al., 1976, cited in Reich, 1986, p. 222).

FLES

Although immersion is a fairly common educational program in Canada, it is not widespread on the continent. More familiar, perhaps, is the taking of at least one foreign language in school. These courses, unlike immersion and bilingual programs, do not attempt to teach other curricular subjects *in* the foreign language. Rather, language is treated as a subject in its own right. Typically, both the amount and the kind of exposure to the new language is limited in comparison to immersion. The time devoted to the foreign language might be as little as 20 minutes three times per week or as much as 50 minutes per day. During that time, teaching is likely to focus more on the language itself than on content or meaning.

McLaughlin (1985) reported that early FLES programs were not dramatically successful. Although there was greater acceptance of foreign language classes beginning in the elementary school, children did not learn the languages quickly and easily when taught for one hour per day. One study did report that students who began learning a second language in elementary school generally performed better than children who began in high school (Vocolo, 1967), but most evaluations reported that children lost interest by Grades 5 or 6 and motivation became a major problem (Page, 1966). These studies are strongly at odds with the immersion studies, and the reason likely lies in the teaching method. Until relatively recently, and even now in some schools, most FLES teachers used a behaviorist approach. As they grew older, the children tired of pattern drills and structure manipulation. Since these constituted the children's only exposure to the language, their learning declined. Such methods were never used in immersion where the focus was on the subject matter being taught rather than the structure of the language.

More recent FLES programs have employed different methods with more positive results, but the language proficiency level achieved is still far less than that in immersion programs. Recent FLES programs have also been less ambitious in their goals, emphasizing oral skills and cultural awareness. Full communicative competence in the target language is not expected, and both parents and students are told so from the beginning. The most common languages taught in current FLES programs are Spanish, French, and German, although Japanese, Cantonese, and Mandarin are gaining in popularity.

Immersion and FLES programs are intended for children who speak the dominant language to learn a second language. Educationally, they are important, but they are not critical to the life of the child in the way that language programs for minority speakers are. There are hundreds of thousands of children in both the United States and Canada who speak a minority language at home and then face schooling in English. The next two types of programs attempt to meet their needs.

Two-Way Immersion

An increasing number of school districts in the United States are experimenting with programs designed to develop language proficiency in two languages while promoting academic achievement. Such programs are popular because they are seen as an effective way of educating both majority and minority children. Borrowing from the principles of immersion, these programs integrate majority and minority children in classes that provide content as well as language development in both languages. This approach permits minority children to maintain and develop their language and majority children to acquire a second language. It also permits minority children to learn English. These programs are seen as empowering minority children because they officially sanction their first language. Christian (1996), in her review of two-way immersion programs, points out that "the social interactional features of two-way immersion programs support better opportunities for language development. Both L1 and L2 acquisition are facilitated by interaction between the 'novice' (the learner of the language) and 'experts' (fluent speakers of the language)" (p. 67). In other words, children are able to learn from one another in an environment that gives equal value to both languages. They benefit from having native speaker models of their own age and interests.

These programs are relatively new and rare. Christian reports only 169 schools in 92 school districts in the United States. Most of the schools with these programs offer them in Spanish and English in the elementary school level, and so it is still early to measure their effect. Emerging studies, however, "point to their effectiveness in promoting academic achievement for minority and majority students, along with high levels of bilingual proficiency for both groups" (Christian, 1996, p. 72). There is also growing evidence that children in these programs develop friendships that are defined by neither race nor ethnicity. This is, in itself, an argument for these kinds of programs. As you will see below, two-way immersion programs resemble certain bilingual programs. The difference is in the goals, particularly as they relate to the inclusion of majority English speakers in the model.

Bilingual Programs

Language programs intended to maintain the child's native language within an English-speaking environment or to ease the transition between the language of the home and the language of the school are commonly called bilingual programs. The introduction of English in school and the widespread use of English in the community may cause children to lose much of their native language proficiency, unless there is a concerted effort to maintain it. **Maintenance bilingualism** is intended to protect the native language while introducing English as the language of the school. Such programs are not popular in the United States, although a few exist in areas with concentrated non-English populations. There are also a few programs for Native American children, designed to maintain their native language and culture. A number of researchers report studies of children taking part in small experimental programs for Choctaw (Doebler & Mardis 1980), Navajo (Rosier & Farella 1976), and Hopi (Haussler et al., 1987). Some of these are maintenance programs while others might more appropriately be considered transitional (see below). In general, the researchers conclude that children benefit from such programs. Nevertheless, because of the small number of children and the limited print material available for educational purposes, the programs are not widespread. This is particularly unfortunate in the case of Native American languages, some of which have only a few hundred speakers left, many of them elderly. In

Canada, on the other hand, with its official policy of bilingualism and multiculturalism, there are a number of bilingual maintenance programs operating in languages including German, Ukrainian, Hebrew, French, Spanish, Italian, Cree, and Inuktitut.

A second type of bilingual program is termed **transitional.** In this type of program, the child's home language is used in the early years of schooling and the dominant language introduced later. Transitional programs are widely used. In India, for example, where more than 200 languages are spoken, at least 80 are used in schools, mostly in the first 4 years, after which students are switched to one of the major languages (Khubchandani, 1978, cited in Reich, 1986, p. 224). Canada also has a number of transitional programs in place for Chinese, Ukrainian, German, Hebrew, Italian and some Native American languages. The United States government as well as some state governments sponsor programs for as many as 58 different languages (Tucker & Gray, 1980), including Native American languages.

Surprisingly, very few evaluations of transitional bilingual programs have been published. The ones that have been, including one done in Mexico and one in the Philippines, addressed program effectiveness from the perspective of proficiency in the second language only. Not surprisingly, they revealed that the longer the children spent being educated in English (the second language in both places), the better their English. Neither the children's native language proficiency nor their attitude toward schooling were considered, and many educators would consider these to be important factors in the overall development and the education of the child. Similarly, a study on the effects of bilingual programming on Choctaw children measured only the children's performance in English. Even so, researchers Doebler and Mardis found that the bilingual program resulted in superior performance on two of five measures (social studies and science) and no significant difference on other measures. It should be pointed out, however, that in studies of bilingual programs, "no significance" is not negative. *No significance* means that there is no statistically significant difference between the scores of children in bilingual programs and children in monolingual programs. But as Zappert and Cruz (1977) pointed out, this in itself is significant since the bilingual children have the advantage of another language.

Although there are relatively few global studies measuring the effects of bilingual programs, there is an emerging body of research on the acquisition of literacy in such programs. Although most researchers and educators seem to agree that, in theory, a child learns to read a familiar language more easily than an unfamiliar one, the decision whether to introduce reading in the child's native language or English is not so easily answered. Haussler et al. (1987) argue very persuasively that the decision must be made on a case-by-case basis after considering a number of factors. A major one is whether children are "active participants in a biliterate environment" (p. 84). In other words, children need the support of an environment in which people practice literacy in both languages. If this condition is not met, success is less likely.

Submersion

The success of immersion in Canada and in some U.S. communities has led some educators to the erroneous conclusion that the best language-teaching program is none at all. In other words, if immersion children can learn the new language in an environment where they are taught all the school subjects in that language, can't minority children do the same with English? In **submersion,** children are placed in classes where all their subjects are taught in the language of the school even though they may not know the language at all. According to Reich, (1986) this is the predominant teaching method for minority speakers in Sweden, New Zealand, China, Belgium, Australia, and many other countries (p. 223). It is also the method by which many older immigrants learned English in the United States and Canada.

But is it effective? It is a great credit to the learning powers of children that it does work for some. But on the whole, it is neither an effective nor a humane way to learn a language. The U.S. Supreme Court recognized the inadequacy of submersion in the landmark *Lau vs. Nichols* case, proclaiming that submersion does not provide equal educational opportunity for children who do not speak English.

Although it may not be immediately obvious, there are several important differences between submersion and immersion. There are, in fact, more differences than similarities. In Table 4.1, summarizing the differences, we see that the only real similarity between immersion and submersion is that children are not initially proficient in the language of instruction. A major difference is that children in immersion classes are all at the same level of proficiency in the unfamiliar language while children being submerged in English will likely have had varying amounts of exposure to the language. Immersion children come from the dominant culture where their language is protected and respected, and when they begin school, they are permitted to speak in their native language for the first few months. Their bilingual teacher understands their first language and encourages them in their second. In contrast, children submerged in English come from minority cultures, and there is little if any protection or respect for their languages. When they begin school, they must use English from the first day, and if they do not, their teachers will probably not understand them.

Table 4.1   Comparison of Immersion and Submersion

Category	Criterion	Immersion	Submersion
Children	Same level of L1	No	Yes
	L1 protected	No	Yes
	Allowed to use L1 initially	No	Yes
	Members of dominant culture	No	Usually
	All speak same L1	Rarely	Usually
Teachers	Understand L1 and L2	Yes	Rarely
	Specially educated in L2 methods	Yes	Occasionally
	Understand children's culture	Yes	Rarely
Program	Optional	Yes	No
	Specially funded	Usually	Rarely
	Available to every child	Rarely	Yes
	Taught entirely in L2	No	Yes

In the immersion classroom, the teacher knows both the children's native language and the language being taught. The submersion teacher will know English and possibly one other language, but the children in the class will rarely all come from the same language background. The immersion teacher has been educated in language acquisition and in methods for teaching children who do not know the language in which she is teaching. Some teachers in the submersion situation may have had Teaching English as a Second Language (TESL) training, but many must rely on their usual teaching practices. Finally, immersion is optional and prestigious. If children or their parents are unhappy with the program or the children's progress, there are good educational alternatives. Immersion is also specially funded by a government anxious to promote bilingualism and enjoys an elitist reputation in the community. No one can make such claims for submersion.

We have seen that children acquire a second language under a number of different circumstances and that they do so with varying degrees of success. A number of questions are thus raised both for theory and for practice. The practical issues will be addressed in Chapter 5 after we have looked at the particular circumstances in which two children acquired their second language very successfully. In the remainder of this chapter, we will see how situation, proficiency and a number of other factors are addressed in theories of second language acquisition.

ISSUES IN SECOND LANGUAGE ACQUISITION THEORY

Complicated as it is, the task of formulating an adequate theory of first language acquisition is simple in comparison with the task of formulating an adequate theory of second language acquisition. This is true because the number of factors which may vary in second language acquisition is far greater than those in first language acquisition. Spolsky (1985) framed the problem by breaking down into its component parts the central question about second language learning: Who learns how much of what language under what conditions?

Who can be anyone of any age, ability, and intelligence and with any attitude or personality. *Learns* refers to the process itself and raises questions about the different kinds of learning there are, about innateness, about transfer between languages, and about conscious and unconscious learning, etc. *How much of* refers to the amount of language learning which takes place and what aspect of the language is learned (e. g., syntax, phonology, semantics, culture). *What language* refers to the target language being learned, and *under what conditions* addresses the kind and amount of exposure to the second language which leads to learning (pp. 269–270).

Because first and second language acquisition have two essential elements in common, namely learners and language, it is not surprising that the theories devised to account for them would have at least basic similarities. In general, they do, and some theories of first language acquisition fit the data of second language acquisition with little or no modification. For example, a behavioristic model has only the additional requirement that the habit of the first language be eradicated in the learning of the second. Second language acquisition theories, thus, are partly derived from first language acquisition theories, but because of the variability in the factors identified by Spolsky, they are necessarily more complex. In fact, no one theory has yet been put forward that is comprehensive enough to account for all these factors and the interactions among them. Nevertheless, there has been no reluctance to theorize about second language learning. The details of the many theories that have been advanced in recent years are well beyond the scope of this chapter. Table 4.2, however, identifies nine such theories together with the researchers usually credited with proposing them, sources for recent discussion or evaluation, and some indication of their scope.

Under the heading *scope* in the table are the designations *learner, process, proficiency, language,* and *condition.* These correspond to different aspects of Spolsky's question. Learner variables (*who*) are those attributes of learners which influence their success in language acquisition. These include, among others, age of the learner, cognitive style, and socio-psychological attitudes toward speakers of the target language. *Process (learns)* refers to the internal systems devised by the learner or the strategies used in learning, understanding, and producing the new language. *Proficiency (how much of)* refers to those things that affect the amount of learning that takes place and the level of mastery a learner attains. *Language* takes a slightly broader view than Spolsky's and includes features of the target language as well as the nature of the input to the learner. Finally, *conditions* addresses the situational factors, e. g., classroom or naturalistic environments, that influence second language learning. In the discussion that follows, I examine the variables in turn, noting the strengths of particular theories for dealing with each one.

Learner Variables

It is fairly obvious that there is more variation among second language learners than among first language learners. Because second language learners are older than first language learners, they will have had a variety of linguistic, learning, and life experiences that infants learning their first language will not. While any number of learner factors may influence the course of language development, researchers have identified a number of general factors believed to contribute to individual learner differences. Among these are age, aptitude, cognitive variation, and personality traits.

There is a vast body of research literature that attempts to describe and explain differences that are attributable to the *age of the learner.* The results are mixed, as might be expected, but what has emerged with some clarity are the findings that

> a) in general, the ability to learn languages does not diminish with age; b) more specifically, young children's superiority as language learners is restricted to their learning of the sound system
>
> *(see McLaughlin, 1981, pp. 23–32)*

Some researchers believe that **aptitude,** or some kind of specialized language learning ability, plays a central role in language acquisition. The research findings are

Table 4.2   Nine Theories of Second Language Acquisition

Theory/scope	Origin	Evaluation/discussion
Acculturation		
Learner Proficiency Conditions	Schumann (1978a, 1978b, 1981a, 1981b, 1982)	McLaughlin (1987) Ellis (1985) Larsen-Freeman (1983) Larsen-Freeman & Long (1991)
Accommodation		
Learner Conditions Proficiency	Giles et al. (1977) Giles & Byrne (1982)	Ellis (1985)
Behaviorism		
Conditions Language	Skinner (1957)	McLaughlin (1978, 1984, 1987)
Cognitive		
Learner Process	McLaughlin et al. (1983); McLeod & McLaughlin (1986); Segalowitz (1986)	McLaughlin (1987)
Discourse		
Learner Conditions Process	Hatch (1978c, 1978d)	Ellis (1985) Larsen-Freeman (1983)
Interlanguage		
Process Language Proficiency	Selinker (1972)	McLaughlin (1987) Ellis (1985)
Monitor Model		
Leaner Process Conditions Language	Krashen (1977a, 1977b, 1978, 1981, 1982, 1985)	McLaughlin (1987) Spolsky (1985) Ellis (1985) Larsen-Freeman (1983); Gregg (1984)
Neurofunctional		
Process Language	Lamendella (1977, 1979)	Larsen-Freeman (1983); Ellis (1985)
Universal		
Process Grammar Language	Chomsky (1980) Greenberg (1966, 1974); Wode (1981)	McLaughlin (1987) Gass (1984) Ellis (1985)

dubious, however, in part because it is impossible to know with any certainty just what cognitive abilities aptitude comprises. If there is an aptitude factor in second language acquisition, it is likely that it is a rather specialized aptitude that governs only the ability to learn in formal settings, and probably not all of these. Otherwise, there would not be so many successfully bilingual people in the world—in Asia and Europe, for example—who have learned their languages either at home or in school. For most educators, however, the question of aptitude is in practice not very important. Children need to and have the right to learn the language of the school whether or not some test judges them capable or not. The educator's major concern is not with measuring aptitude, if indeed such a thing could be done, but with planning a language learning environment which enhances every child's learning opportunities.

Cognitive style refers to the ways in which individuals process information or approach particular tasks. Although much of the literature on cognitive styles seems to suggest that they are dichotomous, i. e., that people tend to possess one trait or its opposite, it is more likely the case that people "show a tendency towards one pole or the other, with their scores on cognitive style tests arranged along a continuum between the poles" (Larsen-Freeman & Long, 1991, p. 192). A number of dimensions are included under the heading cognitive style including:

1. *types* of learning inherent in cognitive tasks,
2. variation in *strategies* individuals employ, and
3. variation in personal *cognitive styles* of learning. (Brown, 1980, p. 80)

Types of Learning. According to Robert Gagné (1965), people employ eight different types of learning for different tasks ranging from signal learning, involving a classically conditioned response, to problem solving, requiring "the internal events usually referred to as 'thinking' " (pp. 58–59 quoted in Brown, 1980, p. 81). Brown claims that learners use all eight types of learning depending upon a number of factors including the aspect of language being learned and the learner's previous experience of language learning. Because language learning is highly complex, it is unlikely that the different levels of learning will proceed independently.

Variation in Strategy. An important part of language learning is problem solving. People vary greatly in how they reach solutions. In general, we distinguish between two broad types of strategies—learning strategies and communication strategies. The former refers to the ways in which learners attempt to work out meanings and structures in language and to store them for later recall. The latter refers to how learners manage to encode and express meaning in order to communicate in a language. Learning strategies include such things as memorization, overgeneralization, and inference, and learners make use of different strategies and different combinations of strategies for different purposes. Moreover, it is likely that older children and adults have better developed processing capabilities and thus more to build on as they approach the learning of a new language (see McLaughlin, 1981, p. 30).

To communicate in a second language, learners generally rely on essentially the same strategies as they do in learning it. Brown (1980) claims, in fact, that learning and communication represent the input and the output of the same process. Nevertheless, there are differences. It is very common for second language learners to avoid structures or words about which they are uncertain or which they find difficult. This strategy obviously has no parallel in learning. On the other hand, generalization, e. g., from a known form to an unknown form, is a productive learning strategy that also occurs in communication, although it is difficult to detect because its use results in a correct form. Overgeneralization, in contrast, is not a successful learning strategy, but is all too apparent in communication since it results in an incorrect form.

Variation in Personal Cognitive Styles. The third dimension of cognitive style refers to the particular way in which a learner approaches a learning situation. In learning language, people may vary in the amount of explanation they want or need or in their preference for oral or written presentation. Other dimensions of cognitive style include field dependence vs. independence, reflectivity vs. impulsivity, tolerance vs. intolerance of ambiguity, and the tendency to either skeletonize or embroider in the recall of cognitive material (Brown, 1980, pp. 90–97; Hatch, 1983).

Personality traits are those attitudes, feelings and emotions which may influence an individual's learning. They are sometimes called the *affective variables* and include the learner's attitude toward the language being learned and its native speakers, motivation for learning the language, and ego factors such as self-esteem, degree of inhibition, and capacity for empathy, among others.

Obviously, a complete theory of second language acquisition must account for learner differences attributable to personality and cognitive factors. For educators, however, the concern is a more practical one. They need to understand how such factors influence second language acquisition in order to have some idea how to plan instruction for the introverted as well as the extroverted child, the analytic as well as the synthetic thinker.

Situation

Situational variables are those things in the language learner's environment that influence the learning and the use of the new language. In short, they encompass everything the learner sees and hears in the new language, and they are highly significant.

> The quality of the environment is of paramount importance to success in learning a new language. If students are exposed to a list of words and their translations, together with a few simple readings in the new language, they will perhaps be able to attain some degree of reading skill in language, but listening and speaking skills will remain fallow.
>
> *(Dulay, Burt & Krashen, 1982, p. 13)*

ESL teachers have long lamented the fact that language forms that students apparently master in class sometimes give them all kinds of trouble outside. Several years ago, I had a similar experience with a Chinese graduate student who was taking an oral examination for his master's degree. Throughout the examining period, he answered the questions well but continually confused the personal pronouns, producing sentences such as "English is a difficult language because she is very different from Chinese" and "My mother could speak only one language and he was happy when I learned more languages." I had never heard him make these errors in the two previous years I had known him. The question of why a tense situation causes errors has potential impact on our understanding of the very processes of language learning and production, for clearly there is an interaction between situation of use and the learner's ability to recall correctly a previously learned form.

It would be impossible to identify all the environmental factors that potentially influence language learning, but researchers have identified four broad categories of factors that are believed to have a significant impact. These include

1. the naturalness of the environment,
2. the learner's role in communication,
3. the availability of concrete referents, and
4. target language models (Dulay, Burt, & Krashen, 1982, pp. 13–43).

Naturalness of the Environment. Evidence suggests that learners perform better when they "are exposed to natural language, where the focus is on communication" rather than in "a formal environment, where focus is on the conscious acquisition of linguistic rules or the manipulation of linguistic forms" (Dulay, Burt, & Krashen, 1982, p. 42). Certainly, this conclusion is consistent with many of the studies reviewed earlier in this chapter and with the experiences of the children reported in Chapter 5. It also seems to be the case, however, that some exposure to the formal properties of language may be helpful for adult learners.

The Learner's Role in Communication. The quality of language learning is also affected by the types of communication in which the learner is most frequently engaged. Communication exchanges may be classified as one-way, restricted two-way or full two-way. One-way exchanges occur when the learner listens to or reads the target language but does not respond. Restricted two-way exchanges occur when the learner listens and responds either non-verbally, e. g., by nodding, or in a language other than the target language. In full two-way exchanges, the learner responds in the target language.

There is some evidence that in the earliest stages of language learning, one-way and restricted two-way exchanges may actually facilitate language acquisition for some learners. A silent period lasting until the learner is ready to speak seems to be beneficial in some classroom situations. Gary (1975), studying 50 English-speaking children learning Spanish, found that the children who did not engage in any oral response during the first 14 weeks of the course performed better in listening comprehension than did children in classes where oral responses were required. What was more surprising, perhaps, was her finding that the children who had kept silent did as well in speaking as their peers who had been speaking for 14 weeks (Gary, 1975, cited in Dulay, Burt, & Krashen, 1982, pp. 24–26).

The Availability of Concrete Referents. An important aspect of the language learning environment seems to be the availability of visible referents. It is much easier to understand a language in which one has limited proficiency if there is adequate context. I once witnessed Stephen Krashen illustrate this point in a simple counting task. He first stood before us and counted to ten in a language I didn't understand. He could have been giving directions for making a moon landing for all I knew. He then repeated the exercise holding up one finger, then two, etc. as he said the corresponding number. The second time he did so, I was able to remember 6 of the 10 numbers. As a counterexample, most of us could sit and listen to Radio Moscow for hours, days, or even weeks without ever learning six words of Russian. Talking about what is present and observable helps the learner to understand and is thus crucial to acquiring language.

Target Language Models. The fourth type of situational variable has to do with the source, or models, of language the learner encounters. The different people learners come into contact with influence the language they learn. It seems to be the case that learners neither learn nor even attend to all the language they are exposed to. Research on speaker models indicates that learners apparently prefer some sources over others. Milon (1975) reported, for example, that when a 7-year-old Japanese-speaking child moved to Hawaii, he learned the Hawaiian Creole English of the children around him rather than the standard English of his teacher. Immersion studies in the United States and Canada have reported similar findings and also speculated that a child's language development is actually hampered when the only models are adults. Children who entered immersion in kindergarten were found to have some grammatical deficiencies in French even after 7 years in the program (Bruck, Lambert, & Tucker, 1975). Remember that there are no native-speaking peers in immersion classes. Children seem to prefer peers as language models over both teachers and parents. There is evidence, too, that they make more use of models who are members of their own social or ethnic group than those who are not (Benton, 1964). This is consistent with the immersion findings. Having no native-speaking peer group, the children served as models for one another and their language reflected the fact that they were non-native speakers. Language itself is, then, an important variable in the acquisition of a second language.

Language. Learners are not solely responsible for their language learning. We saw in our discussion of social interaction theory in Chapter 3 that the attempts caretakers make to focus the child's attention or to focus their own language on what is occupying the child's attention contribute to the child's language learning. In second language acquisition, a great deal of research has gone into understanding the characteristics of the language input which promotes learning (*foreigner talk*) and into the feedback the learner provides and its effect on subsequent input (*discourse studies*).

Studies on language input focus on describing **foreigner talk**, or the modifications which native speakers make when talking with someone they perceive to have less than native proficiency in their language. A number of common modifications have been identified. For example, native speakers typically choose topics concerned with

Table 4.3 Foreigner Talk Modifications

Example	Modification
Wuxing: I need, uh, the book. Terry Piper: The book? Which book?	*Repetition.* She repeats part of his utterance even though she has understood him.
W: From class. Yellow, I think. T: The yellow book from class. Let me see. The book about reading in a second language? W: No. Uh. Not about that.	*Repetition* and *expansion.* She expands his fragment into a well-formed sentence.
T: Not about reading in a second language. Was it today or last week? W: Last week.	*Self-repetition.* She repeats her own previous utterance.
T: Last week. (Removing a book from her shelf.) This one? W: No, about universals.	*Repetition* and *"here and now."* She repeats her own previous utterance and then offers visual aids.
T: Oh, language universals? Was it by Hatch? Who wrote it? W: I don't know.	*Repetition* and *confirmation check.* She paraphrases to confirm that he has understood her question.
T: Was it this one? W: No.	*"Here and now."*
T: Well, have a look. Books about universals are there. W: Yellow.	*Short response.* *Repetition.*
T: Yes. But I don't classify them by color. Do you understand "classify"? W: Yes. But maybe I, uh, blind to color.	*Comprehension check.* She asks overtly whether he understands.
T: You're colorblind? W: Yes, maybe. (Laughing)	*Expansion* and *confirmation check.*

the present, they check more often to see whether they are being understood, they repeat or paraphrase both their own utterances and the other speaker's, and they give shorter responses. Hatch (1983) has pointed out that ESL teachers commonly speak more slowly and use intonation patterns which help the learner to identify syntactic groupings and boundaries. The conversation between Wuxing, a Chinese graduate student, and his teacher in Table 4.3 shows the teacher making several adjustments to her speech to accommodate Wuxing's level of English proficiency, as she perceived it.

Understanding the adjustments native speakers make in talking with non-native speakers contributes significantly to our understanding of input. But it is only one side of the coin. Native speakers do not determine input nor the course of conversation all by themselves. Learners provide feedback and this feedback influences the subsequent input they receive. It makes sense, then, to study the interaction which occurs in conversations between native and non-native speakers. **Discourse studies** examine conversational turn taking, how topics of conversation are nominated and developed, and how meaning is negotiated. They also examine the differences between interactions that occur between adult speakers and those which occur between an adult and a child.

Hatch (1978b) has identified certain characteristics of adult-child interactions. As she describes them, a typical interaction begins when the child requests the adult's attention. "Mummy, look!" would be a common way of opening the communication channel. The adult normally responds by naming the object which has attracted the child's attention: "Oh yes, a bluebird." At this point, depending upon the age of the child and the particular situation, this conversation might be abandoned and another *nominating sequence* begun, or it might be developed. Development usually proceeds with the adult requesting some comment on the established topic. "It's a pretty one, isn't it?" or "Why do you think it's sitting in the apple tree?" would invite the child to elaborate.

These conversational routines seem to help children to learn language, although it must be recalled that children in some other cultures learn language apparently without much overt assistance from adults. If children and non-native speakers learn language with these modifications to input and accommodation in discourse and if they also learn language without them, there must be a variety of processing strategies which are sensitive to variations in input and feedback.

Process. Essentially, there are two kinds of processes with which second language acquisition theory is concerned. *Cognitive processes* consist of the types of learner strategies discussed earlier. *Linguistic processes*, according to one view "involve universal principles of grammar with which the learner is innately endowed. They provide the learner with a starting point. The task is then to scan the input to discover which rules of the target language are universal and which are specific" (Ellis, 1985, p. 17). This is, in essence, a *nativist*, or *universal-grammar*, perspective on the nature of linguistic processes.

Interlanguage theory (Selinker, 1972) takes the notion of process beyond the *starting point*, referring to the learner's system at any one point in time and also to the system as it changes over time. This system is believed to be separate from the native language system and to be the product of five cognitive processes:

1. Transfer of some features from the first language;

2. Transfer from the teaching process;

3. Learning strategies;

4. Communication strategies;

5. Overgeneralization of linguistic material from the target language.

The interlanguage hypothesis applies to adults and to children who acquire their second language after the first is clearly established. Although it speculates about different influences on the system, the hypothesis makes little attempt to explain the learning process. Rather, it provides a useful framework in which to describe certain second language phenomena. Not so with **Krashen's Monitor Model.**

Krashen's Monitor Model

Krashen's model rests on five hypotheses, all of which relate to second language processing. The first, and in Krashen's view the foundational hypothesis, is called the acquisition-learning hypothesis. It makes the claim that there is a distinction between acquiring language in an informal setting where attention is directed entirely to meaning, much as the first language is acquired, and learning language in a formal setting such as the classroom where attention is directed to form. Furthermore, this distinction is believed to be independent of the age of the learner or other learner variables. It is important to note that Krashen is not merely stating the obvious, i. e., the fact of environmental differences. He claims that the learner actually processes and stores language differently under the two conditions. Acquisition leads to subconscious internalization of language structures and rules while learning leads to conscious learning. Although this distinction holds a certain intuitive appeal, there is little evidence to support it. The further claim that language which is learned (as opposed to acquired) cannot eventually become subconscious knowledge is not only unsupported but "flies in the face of the evidence" (Spolsky, 1985, p. 271). An even more serious shortcoming of the hypothesis is that while it specifies two distinct sources of input, it fails to elucidate how the processes responsible for acquisition and learning differ from one another.

Perhaps the most important and the most controversial claim made by this hypothesis is the one that relates it to the Monitor hypothesis. Krashen claims that the role of acquired language is to initiate utterances and control fluency while learned language is available only as an editor or monitor to correct the language output before it is uttered. What this implies is that there is no place for learned language in comprehension, and this too flies in the face of experience. Attempts to confirm the existence and use of a monitor in experimental situations have failed, and the hypothesis is further weakened by the doubt cast on the acquisition-learning hypothesis which supports it. Quite simply, if the monitor does not exist, there is no purpose for the acquisition-learning distinction and, conversely, if that distinction is false, then there can be no monitor.

The other three hypotheses, the natural order hypothesis, the input hypothesis, and the affective filter hypothesis, falter in similar ways. The natural order hypothesis makes the claim that learners acquire the rules of language in a predictable order. The evidence for the claim comes mostly from studies on the order in which certain grammatical morphemes are learned by non-native speakers (e. g., Dulay & Burt, 1974; Porter, 1977). Once again, the evidence cited in support of the hypothesis is dubious. First, there are serious methodological problems with the morpheme acquisition order studies, not the least of which is that some measured accuracy of use rather than order. Second, other research has demonstrated that structures in the learner's first language influence the order and the accuracy with which they acquire the grammatical morphemes of English (McLaughlin, 1984, 1987).

The natural order hypothesis is dependent upon the fourth hypothesis, the input hypothesis. Assuming, "as Krashen does, that learners progress through 'natural' developmental sequences, we need some mechanism to account for how they go from one point to another" (McLaughlin, 1987, p. 36). Krashen claims that learners proceed from their current level of proficiency (i) to the next level (i + 1) by understanding language that is just beyond their current level of proficiency. This is called comprehensible input and has the following characteristics: a) it is focused on meaning; b) it is roughly tuned to the learner's level of competence rather than finely tuned, and c) it is based in the here and now.

Among other evidence which Krashen states for the input hypothesis are the existence of simplified speech, the existence of a silent period and the fact that older learners seem to make faster progress in language learning than do children. None of these is really arguable. It does seem to be the case, as we saw earlier, that a period during which speech is not required facilitates learning for some children, simplified codes play an important role when they are available, and older children and adults learn at a faster rate than younger children. But even if all of this is true, does it constitute evidence for any particular internal process? McLaughlin, Spolsky and Ellis think not, pointing out the absence of any explanation about *how* the mapping from meaning to structure occurs.

The final hypothesis comprising the Monitor Model is the affective filter hypothesis, and that it is widely questioned will come as no surprise to the reader. The affective filter is identified as "that part of the internal processing system that subconsciously screens incoming language based on what psychologists call 'affect': the learner's motives, needs, attitudes, and emotional states" (Dulay, Burt, & Krashen, 1982, p. 46). The affective filter supposedly reduces the amount of input available for natural learning by limiting what the learner pays attention to, what will be learned, and the speed at which it is learned. In other words, if a learner is extremely nervous or tense, as was the case with the Chinese graduate student described earlier, the filter purportedly keeps the learner from paying attention to certain kinds of language data. Or if the learner harbors resentment toward speakers of the target language, the filter may limit the amount of learning that actually takes place. The learner may cling to a heavy accent, for example. But these are hypothetical instances and as with the earlier hypotheses, the hard evidence for this hypothesis does not exist.

Unfortunately, the task of evaluating the affective filter hypothesis is further complicated by vagueness. Krashen and his colleagues have never explained just how the filter screens language intake. It would seem that unless the filter screens randomly, it would have to have available some grammar or grammatical template in order to separate those language items to ignore from those to attend to and admit. That being the case, several questions arise, including two obvious ones: What grammar is available to the beginning learner? and How does the affective filter get constructed?

Fortunately, there are other theoretical approaches to processing issues. Cognitive theory takes a broader perspective than universal grammar, the monitor model, or even interlanguage, deriving its principles not from linguistic theory but from contemporary research in cognitive psychology. As we have seen, cognitive theories of language acquisition do not accord language a special status. Rather, learning a second language is viewed as learning a complex cognitive skill "because various aspects of the task must be practiced and integrated into fluent performance. This requires the automatization of component sub-skills" (McLaughlin, 1987, p. 133). Automatization is one of two central concepts in cognitive theory; the other is restructuring.

In order to produce a meaningful utterance, a speaker must coordinate information of many kinds from a number of sources while making a simultaneous plan for the structure of the utterance and for its articulation. In order for all this to be accomplished in the very short time before the listener loses interest, the speaker must have automatized most of the component tasks. McLaughlin (1987, based on Levelt, 1978) conceives of speaking as a hierarchical task structure in which the first order goal is to express a particular intention. The second is to decide on a task, and the third to formulate a series of phrases. Finally, the speaker must attend to lower order goals which include retrieving from memory the necessary words, activating articulatory patterns, utilizing appropriate syntactic rules and meeting pragmatic conventions. When we consider, further, that *each* of these goals entails a number of sub-tasks, then we begin to understand the importance of automatization. Automatization occurs as a result of practice, of the repeated "mapping of the same input to the same pattern of activation over many trials" (p. 134).

Restructuring refers to the constant reorganization of the internal system to accommodate new material. In second language acquisition, the internal system would be the grammar and lexicon of the target language. A beginning learner of English might, on the basis of limited exposure to English, construct the rule that all past tenses are formed by adding [d]. For *gaze, rhyme, fail,* and many verbs in English, this rule works. But then the learner encounters the past tense of *ring* and *sing.* The internal system must be restructured to accommodate this new information and the new rule might be that there are two past tense forms, with verbs rhyming with *ring* requiring a vowel change but no ending and all other verbs requiring [d]. The learner then encounters *bring* and *rust* and has to restructure the system yet again. And so on, and so on. This particular cognitive theory is essentially human information processing. Although it is not the only cognitive approach to understanding language acquisition, it rests on the central assumption that language is acquired in the same manner as other complex cognitive skills. But treating language as just another cognitive skill is a position about which some researchers and theorists are highly skeptical.

Hatch (1983), for example, questions the closeness of the bond between cognitive development and language acquisition. She argues that the relationship cannot be causal, i. e., language acquisition cannot be dependent on cognitive development, and cites various kinds of evidence. The first is a study by Yamada (1981) demonstrating that a child with low cognitive development (she was unable to count, although she could recite numbers, unable to give her correct birth date or age consistently, and could not name the days of the week) demonstrated complex syntactic ability (cited in Hatch, 1983, pp. 220–221). Hatch also points out that there is no evidence that the operating principles Slobin (1973) identified for figuring out language (such as "Pay attention to the ends of words" and "Avoid exceptions") are truly cognitive strategies. They might well be unique to language. She cites as additional evidence cases of Turner's syndrome children (mentioned in Chapter 3) in which children with severe cognitive problems in visual-spatial tasks have superior language ability and cases of hydrocephalics who have linguistic abilities far in excess of their cognitive abilities. Yet, to be fair, cognitively based accounts of language acquisition and processing are very young and Hatch's criticism is not addressed specifically to information processing (although clearly information processing would have to be accountable to the same evidence). There has not yet been sufficient research done to evaluate the theory's worth as an account of second language acquisition.

Proficiency. We come finally to the question of proficiency, or Spolsky's *how much.* Not all second language learners become fully proficient in the new language, and second language acquisition theory will ultimately have to account for the variability in levels of attainment. It is obvious that all of the variables we have discussed so far affect proficiency, and thus it may not seem necessary to address it separately. But two theories pay particular attention to the reasons that learners seem to stop learning. Acculturation and accommodation theory account for different levels of success in terms of social and psychological distance.

The acculturation model (Schumann, 1978a, 1978b, 1978c) is based on the belief that language learning is a central part of adapting to a new culture. Schumann argues that learners' success in acquiring a second language is controlled by their success at acculturating to the target language group. Further, both acculturation and second language acquisition are determined by the social and psychological distances that exist between the learner and the target language culture. Social distance depends on differences between groups in size, ethnic origin, political status, and social status. Psychological distance depends on such individual factors as culture shock, motivation, and language shock. Acculturation theory holds that

> social and psychological distance influence second language acquisition by determining the amount of contact with the target language that the learner experiences, and also the degree to which the learner is open to that input which is available.
>
> *(Ellis, 1985, p. 252)*

Thus, when social and psychological distances are great, the learning situation is poor and the learner makes little progress. Schumann terms the failure to progress beyond beginning stages the pidginization hypothesis, referring to the simplified form of language that develops under certain conditions when two language groups come into contact. He maintains that when there is a social chasm between learners and the target language group, and thus a reduced motivation to learn the language, language learning may fossilize.

In his accommodation theory, Giles takes a similar view, that the causes for fossilization are rooted in socio-psychological factors. The major difference between accommodation theory and acculturation theory is that the former is concerned with perceived social distance and the latter with actual distance. Both view motivation as central to determining success in second language acquisition, but they see it as having different roots. Schumann apparently treats the distance phenomena as absolute while Giles believes the important factor is the perception of social distance. Specifically, Giles claims that what is important is how the learner's social group defines itself in relationship to the target language community (Ellis, 1985, p. 256). Giles claims that language proficiency is governed by a number of key variables:

1. How learners perceive their status in their own ethnic group;
2. Whether learners make favorable or unfavorable comparisons between their ethnic group and the target language group;
3. How learners perceive the status of the ethnic group within the larger community;
4. Whether learners view the ethnic group as culturally or linguistically distinct from the target language group or as linguistically related;
5. The degree to which learners identify and perceive themselves as having status with other social categories, such as occupational, religious, or gender. (Adapted from Ellis, 1987, p. 256)

Both acculturation and accommodation theory are useful in helping to identify some of the possible reasons for the apparent limitations on second language learning which some people experience. Both are concerned to some degree with learner factors and with situational factors. But neither addresses the learning process itself and does not, therefore, constitute a complete theory of second language acquisition. As Table 4.2 shows, no one theory is complete, although several of them taken together represent a fair account of how it all *might* work. It might even be reasonable to say of them individually, as Ellis (1985) does about neurofunctional theory, that "they are perhaps best treated as affording additional understanding about SLA [second language acquisition], rather than an explanation of it" (p. 275).

How the Variables Fit Together

It should be obvious by now that the major factors which influence second language acquisition are neither simple nor independent. We have seen that they overlap and that they interact in complex and largely unknown ways. The task of theory is ultimately to weave them together into some coherent explanation of how second language learning takes place. Theory is not yet at that point, but Ellis (1985) has provided a clear framework from which to think about the relationships among the different variables. He sees situational, input, and learner factors as influencing learning processes which, in turn, influence the language produced (p. 276).

In the next chapter, we meet two children who have become bilingual under two different sets of circumstances. In witnessing the success of Quy and Lucy, perhaps we can come to a clearer understanding of what factors exert the greatest influence on second language acquisition in children and just what it is theory must account for.

Language Reacquisition

Before concluding this chapter, I would like to look at a relatively rare (at least in the research literature) but very interesting phenomenon known as *native language reacquisition*. Families who have spent any appreciable length of time abroad with a small child will have learned a great deal about second language acquisition. Most parents will notice that in comparison with their own faltering attempts at learning the local language, their young children seem to soak it up like sponges. Occasionally, parents who are able to communicate in the second language themselves will find that their children appear to lose their native language. Two studies of the phenomenon (Berman, 1979; Slobin et al., 1993) offer some insights into the language learning of preschool children. Both children were under three when they were initially exposed to the second language.

The first language of the child reported in the Berman study was Hebrew, and during the period in which she was exposed to English, she appeared to lose her ability to understand Hebrew. When she returned to Israel after 1 year (at age 3;11), she had to regain both her comprehension and production abilities. The child reported in the Slobin study spoke English and was taken to Turkey where he maintained his comprehension of English. When he returned to an English environment at 3;0 after 6 months of speaking only Turkish, he had difficulty with production. The Berman child, upon returning to Israel, had to function in both Hebrew and English while the Slobin child had only to function in English. Without going into detail here, the most interesting finding was the accelerated development of the Slobin child's first language. Any loss was quickly regained at a rate much faster than monolingual children experience. His speed of acquisition was also greater than the bilingual Berman child's, but this is perhaps to be expected given that the Berman child was effectively acquiring two first languages.

> This suggests that whatever the internal processes that may have been involved, they did not flow immediately into procedures for programming utterances for production. We would suggest, then, that serious attention be paid to the possibility that comprehension and production might play quite different roles in the processes of acquisition. (1993, p. 195)

The studies also demonstrate, once more, the amazing capacity that children have to learn language in the early years of their lives. Moreover, they serve to remind us that bilingualism is an asset, not a liability. The more we understand about how young children become bilingual, the better able we are to construct school curricula and activities that will build upon and foster language growth, in one language or in two.

QUESTIONS FOR DISCUSSION

1. Educators often encounter arguments such as "My grandfather came to this country without a word of English and he learned it all right. There were no high-priced ESL programs for him." Assuming that your school has or is planning to put into place an ESL or a bilingual program, how do you refute this argument?

2. It is often observed that in Canada, most fluent bilinguals were born into French-speaking families rather than English-speaking families. Why do you suppose this is true? Is there a comparable comment that can be made about U.S. bilinguals?

3. The author writes "Learners are not solely responsible for their language learning." In explaining why this might be true, discuss the relevance of age of the learner as a factor.

CHAPTER FIVE

Stories of Second Language Learners

In this chapter, I tell the stories of three children learning their second language under different circumstances. It would be a neater story if I had met them all at the same time in the same class. That way, with their shared classroom experience, I could have drawn some firmer conclusions about the influence of variables external to school on their language learning. I could have made some reasonable assumptions about the roles played by family, age of first exposure to English, and other societal factors. But unfortunately, only two of the three were in the same class. The third lived 4,000 miles away and was born a decade later.

Two of the children, Quy and Lucy, I knew personally, for a brief time. The third child, Jani, I never met. For her story, I rely, against my preferences as a scholar, on secondhand sources, principally the recordings and accounts of her parents and on the interviews that my own research assistant carried out with her parents and teachers. I'm sorry I never met Jani. Knowing Quy and Lucy, for even a brief time, provided a personal connection that made their stories easier to tell. There are also differences in the data I had available to work with, a fact that is especially important as time passes. I had more data on Lucy, much more firsthand data, than on either Quy or Jani, and more on Quy than Jani. Nevertheless, I will make every effort to describe the language learning experiences of all three children in as much relevant detail as possible. For one year during the early 1980s, I spent 2 or 3 days a week doing research in a kindergarten class in a school on the northern coast of British Columbia. It was there that I met both Quy (pronounced *Kee*) and Lucy. After only a few weeks, I was so struck by the progress they were making in English that I decided to study the two children more closely. What intrigued me then was the fact that this Vietnamese boy and this Portuguese girl, with such widely different experiences of both life and language, were coping so well with the demands of an English-speaking kindergarten. Their being in the same class as Michael, whom we will meet in Chapter 7, and whose second language learning was anything but smooth, made them all the more compelling as subjects of study. I decided to gather as much information as possible on their backgrounds, hoping that by so doing, I could come to understand more about the process of second language acquisition in children.

The account of both Quy's and Lucy's language learning from the time they began kindergarten is based on tape recordings made in their kindergarten class weekly for the first 3 months of the school year and once every two weeks thereafter. In most sessions, the children wore lavalier microphones during their regular classroom activities and also spent 15 to 20 minutes in private conversation with their teacher or with the researcher. These recordings are supplemented by the teacher's notes and formal evaluation reports, the latter written four times during the year, and by the observation notes taken by the researcher.

Quy's early language acquisition is based on his mother's recollections, recorded in interviews taken over a 2-month period in November and December of their kindergarten year. Her recollections were assisted by the diary she had begun to keep, at the suggestion of one of her new friends from their church, when she arrived in Canada. I was also able to interview two women who worked in the preschool which Quy attended from age 4;0 to 4;9. The account of Lucy's early language learning is also based on interviews, conducted with the help of a Portuguese interpreter. These were conducted less frequently but over the 4-month period between mid-September and mid-December.

QUY'S LANGUAGE LEARNING

Quy from Birth to 22 Months

Quy was born in a refugee camp in Malaysia. During the seventies and eighties, there was a massive exodus of people from Vietnam, and Quy's parents were among the earliest to leave, under conditions so horrific that Quy's mother would not talk about them almost 10 years after the fact. Quy's father did not survive the journey, and it is something of a miracle that his mother, nearing her eighth month of pregnancy, did. Quy was born a few weeks after his mother reached the camp. Quy and his mother lived in the camp for just over a year before being accepted as refugees to Canada. During that year, his mother took English classes offered in the camp, but she was not a beginner, having learned some English in the job she had held in Vietnam during the war.

During their time in the camp, Quy's mother spoke only Vietnamese. That was the language used all around them, and essentially the only language that Quy heard. A month after Quy's first birthday, the young widow and her child boarded a plane for Vancouver, B. C. to begin their new life in Canada.

They arrived in the pouring rain, and the 10° C (about 50° F) temperature must have seemed very cold to the young mother and her child. But the Vancouver weather was almost balmy in comparison to the climate to which they were going. A church group in Prince Rupert, a small coastal community in northern B. C., had agreed to sponsor Quy and his mother. They met the new arrivals, and after one night in Vancouver, the two representatives from the church, Quy, and his mother boarded a plane for the one hour journey north.

Quy's mother reported that she was in shock for several months. She was frightened about what the future held for her and her son and she found the weather very inhospitable. But not the people. She said that she seldom felt lonely, and was grateful for the English she had learned because it helped her to communicate with "the very kind people who wanted to help Quy and me." Her English improved rapidly, but she still spoke only Vietnamese with Quy. They did not have television, but Quy heard English spoken when members of the church group visited their home and when his mother took him to church.

When Quy was 16 months old, about three months after they arrived in Canada, Quy's mother found a job. She was determined not to rely on the charity of her new friends but to support her son herself. At first, Quy was cared for by another Vietnamese woman, a mother of four who also lived in Prince Rupert. The woman's husband was a fisherman whose income was sporadic, and she welcomed the few dollars that Quy's mother paid her. After about six months, however, there was a severe downturn in the fishing economy of the area, and the woman had to find a job that paid more. Quy's mother then placed Quy in daycare, and his English language learning began in earnest.

Quy from 1;10 to 3;0

Although Quy had been exposed to some English before he went to daycare, according to his mother, he spoke only Vietnamese. Before he entered the daycare center, he had been very talkative, chattering away in Vietnamese. When playmates asked him questions in English, he would respond not by speaking but by nodding or shaking his head. She was unsure, though, just how much English Quy really understood. She was naturally worried about how he would adjust to an English environment. Unfortunately, his behavior during the first few weeks did little to ameliorate her feelings of anxiety. For the first few days, Quy didn't want to go to the daycare center. While he was there, he tended to play quietly by himself. After a few weeks, he stopped complaining and seemed to be happy about going. Sometimes, he even seemed reluctant to get out of the church van that delivered him to his home.

Quy celebrated his second birthday at the daycare center, and his mother was able to attend the lunchtime party in his honor. She reported that Quy seemed to be pleased with the party, and especially with the cake and ice cream, but he said nothing during the entire hour she was there, except a few words of greeting in Vietnamese when she arrived. When she asked the attendants at the center, they told her that Quy never talked. He didn't even speak Vietnamese with the other Vietnamese child, a 3-year-old girl.

Initially, Quy's mother wasn't worried about his silence, but then she started to notice that he was talking less and less at home. By the time he was 2;3, Quy spoke only when his mother insisted and then only in English even though she spoke only Vietnamese. He refused to speak Vietnamese, and would sometimes respond to his mother's Vietnamese by saying "I don't know," which she took to mean that he didn't understand. Even though she knew that he did understand her Vietnamese, she reluctantly switched to English which he would speak.

When Quy was about 2;4, his mother once again visited the daycare center. There she found Quy, not exactly talkative, but responding to his playmates in English. He greeted her in English when she arrived, and the attendants reported that he consistently greeted and responded to them in English although he was still reluctant to initiate conversation. At home, he was still mostly silent and still refused to speak Vietnamese.

It was natural enough for Quy's mother to worry that his refusal to speak Vietnamese would eventually lead to his losing it. Even though she knew that Quy would have to learn English to survive in Canada, she was anxious that he not lose this important link with their culture and history. She felt trapped. On the one hand, she desperately wanted to preserve his Vietnamese, but on the other, he refused to talk to her in Vietnamese and she was worried about the effect of continued silence on her relationship with him.

Gradually, she relented and began to speak English with him. She would occasionally try to slip in a few words of Vietnamese, but he seemed to be intent on not understanding that language. Then an event transpired that Quy's mother marked as highly significant in Quy's emergent bilingualism (and which speaks to the importance of motivation!).

Just before his third birthday, Quy was excited by the prospect of getting the tricycle he badly wanted. He was in town with his mother on a Saturday afternoon, and they walked past a hardware store that displayed a bright blue tricycle in the window. Quy pointed to it excitedly, saying, "There, that. Mama, I want that, please." Quy's mother did not respond, so he repeated his request, again in English.

His mother thought for a moment and then responded in Vietnamese that she was sorry but she could not understand him. He looked puzzled and repeated his request in English. She repeated that she did not understand. Quy merely pointed to the tricycle and said "Please." Quy's mother then told him in Vietnamese that she assumed he wanted a tricycle, but that since it was winter, he wouldn't be able to ride it anyway. It was Quy's turn to think. Finally, Quy laughed as though they were sharing a great joke and repeated his request for the tricycle. He went on to explain that he could ride it in the basement. All this transpired in Vietnamese. In perfect Vietnamese, his mother reported. He had not lost his first language, and it had not apparently deteriorated. From then on, Quy spoke whichever language was addressed to him.

Quy seldom confused his two languages, except in one sense. Sometimes, when talking to his mother about something that had happened in daycare, he would insert an English word into a Vietnamese sentence. She surmised that he had learned the names of certain objects and actions in daycare and simply did not know the Vietnamese equivalent. She would occasionally interrupt and tell him the Vietnamese word which he would repeat and usually remember. It was her opinion that his

Vietnamese pronunciation was fine, but she felt unable to judge the quality of his English pronunciation. We do not know, thus, whether Quy's Vietnamese influenced his English pronunciation.

Quy from 3;0 to 4;0

Quy stayed in full time daycare until he was 4;0. During the year between his third and fourth birthdays, he made a great deal of progress in both his languages. At home, he increasingly spoke Vietnamese with his mother. Sometimes, she reported, when he began to tell her something in English, she would forget and respond in English. At the daycare center, he mostly spoke English. Just before his third birthday, however, two other Vietnamese children joined the daycare group. One, a girl of about the same age as Quy, spoke no English and was very shy. Quy began to speak to her in Vietnamese to which she eventually responded, and the daycare attendants credited Quy with easing her adaptation to the daycare environment. The two children spoke Vietnamese at first, but gradually she began to use English words partly as a result of Quy's "teaching." She was observed to ask him in Vietnamese what the English label was for various objects. He would respond in English and at other times take the initiative in teaching her English words.

Quy from 4;0 to 4;9

When Quy was 4;0, he began attending preschool each morning. His mother had changed jobs and was working only part time outside the home. She was thus able to be at home with him in the afternoons where she worked doing tailoring and alterations. They also acquired a television set. According to Quy's mother, the television set had a significant influence on Quy's language growth. Initially, she put no limits on television, but after a few months she became concerned that he was engaging in fewer activities. After that, she limited his viewing to *Sesame Street* and *The Electric Company* in the daytime and one 30 minute program that he watched each evening with her. Nevertheless, she noticed a dramatic increase in his vocabulary, particularly in the use of idiomatic expressions of the type that she, as a non-native speaker, did not commonly use.

When Quy was about 4;7, during their bedtime routine, Quy's mother asked him, in Vietnamese, whether he needed to go to the bathroom before she read him a story. He replied, in English, "No way José!" She asked him, still in Vietnamese, "Who is José?" This time he replied in Vietnamese, "I don't know. Maybe he's a man on television."

From about this time on, his mother had difficulty in tracking his language development in either language so great was his speed. She had worried, earlier, that his Vietnamese would suffer if she were his only contact with the language, but the church group sponsored other Vietnamese immigrants and there was soon a small community with whom Quy could communicate. His mother judged that Quy's two languages were pretty well balanced when he entered kindergarten at 4;9. She knew, however, that once he started school, English would win out. Not that it worried her. "In Canada," she observed, "that is necessary."

By the time he was 5 years old, then, Quy had acquired basic interpersonal communication skills in two languages. Strictly speaking, perhaps, Quy's accomplishment was different from the **home bilingualism** described in Chapter 4. He had, after all, learned his English not so much at home as in the daycare center and the preschool. On the other hand, his mother was bilingual, and although she was reluctant to do so, responded to his English as well as his Vietnamese. What Quy did have in common with Ronjat's Louis, Leopold's Hildegard, and other children who have learned two languages from an early age, was the embodiment of the two languages in separate people or situations. From the time he was 1;4, Quy used his two languages in two distinct environments, home and daycare, and with the exceptions already noted, mostly kept them separate. More importantly, however, was the fact that Quy, like Louis Ronjat and Hildegard Leopold, acquired basic interpersonal skills in English. He was different from Lucy, Michael and many other children in the sense that by the time he faced the task of acquiring the cognitive academic language proficiency demanded in school, he already had the more basic language skills to build upon.

Quy in Kindergarten

To this point, Quy's story is the one told mostly by his mother as she recalled it after the fact. From the day he entered kindergarten, however, I was a frequent witness to his language learning. I met Quy on his first day in kindergarten. Anticipating a number of children who did not speak English, the kindergarten teacher, Colleen MacKenna, had asked me to assist her in determining the language proficiency levels of the 16 children in her class. In evaluating the language of a second language learner, teachers normally look at a variety of factors. They consider comprehension of the spoken language, the accuracy of forms in comparison to native speakers of the same age, and fluency. The easiest way to evaluate all three is to talk to the child.

It is relatively easy to get a general indication of how much English a child understands by asking questions, as long as the teacher asks questions to which the child is likely to know the answers. Otherwise, it is not a test of language comprehension. Asking the child's name or the names of common objects is fairly safe. Some children, however, demonstrate culturally determined behaviors that may be misinterpreted. Some Asian children as well as some Native American and Canadian children may respond to questions inaudibly if at all. This behavior is sometimes interpreted as meaning that the child hasn't understood when in fact the child is only behaving politely within the tradition of their culture. Quy had been in Canada long enough to have adopted Canadian behaviors in school, and so there was no difficulty in getting him to talk. We determined very quickly that his comprehension was excellent.

Accuracy of form is a little harder to evaluate in children of Quy's age. The difficulty is that unless they happen to be quite talkative, children may not produce the particular structures that the teacher wants to evaluate. They have to be manipulated into producing the structures of interest. Means exist for doing so, as in the *Bilingual Syntax Measure* (Burt, Dulay, & Hernandez, 1975). Unfortunately, this measure and others of the same type provide only a few opportunities for a limited number of

> Tran nots here.
> Lucy doesn't gots the glue.
> My Mom, she boughted it at the co-op.
> Mrs. 'Kenna didn't wanted it.

Figure 5.1 Quy's Overgeneralizations at 4;10

structures to emerge. So while they may be useful for charting development of a limited set of morphemes over a period of time, they tell us very little about how well the child knows the structures of English. The BSM probably tells us more about comprehension, since the child has to answer a series of questions designed to elicit certain structures. In talking with Quy, we learned that most of the inflectional morphemes seemed to be in place, although he did show a tendency to overgeneralize certain morphological patterns as shown in Figure 5.1. When we compare the similar forms that Janet produced at 4;4 (Figure 3.4), we can see that Quy behaved just as a native speaker of English might. In fact, his behavior was so natural that I hadn't noticed it until I read the transcripts.

Fluency refers to the ease with which a speaker produces oral language, and it seldom requires a formal test to determine a second language learner's fluency. Certainly, it was clear enough that Quy had little difficulty expressing himself in English. A recording made of Quy retelling a story to his teacher during the third week in September shows why.

Terry Piper: Have you read this book, Quy? Do you know the story?

Quy: Yes. I know.

T: Will you tell me?

Q: Yep. There was a woman and she was—she didn't have much money. So she lived in a shoe. Great big shoe. She had lots and lots of uh, boys and girls–

T: Children?

Q: Yep. Children. She had lots and lots of them and they all gots hungry. Real hungry. (He hesitates.)

T: Yes? And so what did she do?

Q: I don't know.

T: You don't remember? Why don't you tell me what you *think* happened?

Q: (After thinking for a moment) She wented to the Co-op and boughted some turkey!

Fluency also entails a good, but not necessarily perfect, command of the grammar, vocabulary, and pronunciation of a language. Without administering any special tests, Quy's teacher and I could tell that Quy had near-native proficiency in all these areas. His pronunciation was native-like, although he had a slight tendency to devoice word-final consonants. This was apparent mainly in the plural ending on words such as *dogs* and *beds*. Since even native speakers have a tendency to a slight devoicing of word-final consonants, Quy's doing so was not a cause for concern.

The only other thing that revealed that English was not his first language was his hesitancy in providing the appropriate labels in English for certain body parts and items of clothing. Sometimes children who have learned these common lexical items at home in their native language will have trouble remembering the English equivalent. This is understandable since these are common vocabulary items that the child may not have been exposed to outside the home, or at least with any great frequency. This is likely the case with Quy. He had first learned the Vietnamese words for body parts and common articles of clothing. More familiar with the Vietnamese words, he had to search a moment longer for the corresponding English words. But he did know them, as we discovered when we administered the Peabody Picture Vocabulary Test (Dunn & Dunn, 1981). The PPVT was administered to all children who entered kindergarten with the exception of those who quite obviously did not know enough English to complete it. Quy's score on the test was 4;6, within normal bounds for his actual age of 4;9.

There were two other Vietnamese children in the class, a girl named Thuy (pronounced *twee*) and a boy named Tran. Thuy's family had insisted that she have an English name for school, and she had decided on "Doreen," although by Christmas she had changed it four times, to Dolly, Linda, Shelly, and Suzie. Just after she had decided to call herself Dolly, I recorded the following conversation between her and Quy.

> **Quy:** Thuy, give me the white glue.
> **Thuy:** Not Thuy. Dolly.
> **Q:** Why 'Dolly'?
> **T:** (Speaking in Vietnamese) Because I like it.
> **Q:** (Speaking in Vietnamese) Well, I don't. (Switching to English) I'm going to call you Thuy!

It is interesting to note that Quy switched to English even when he was talking about the girl's Vietnamese name. During the many hours of tape recordings of Quy, he only rarely spoke in Vietnamese, although he often played with the other Vietnamese children. He seemed to be reluctant to repeat the role of language teacher that he had played earlier at the daycare center. He was, however, willing to help out in other ways. An old hand at school, having spent 6 months in preschool, Quy sometimes provided rapid Vietnamese explanations of school routines. On one occasion, for example, he explained to Tran that he should wipe the finger paint off his hands with the paper towels kept at the teacher's desk. Although Tran's English was good enough for him to have understood, Quy chose to speak in Vietnamese, as he only rarely did. I wondered as I read the translation whether he had helped Tran to save face by not exposing his ignorance in front of the other children.

When I asked his mother which language he spoke when he was playing with these same children outside school, she replied that they switched back and forth, depending on what they were playing. In playing a traditional Vietnamese game which they enjoyed, for example, they used Vietnamese. When playing with G. I. Joe, with a soccer ball, or any of the games they had learned at school, they used English, even though the other two children were far less fluent than Quy.

Quy seemed to be in all respects comfortably bilingual. His English language development throughout kindergarten ran a parallel course to that of his monolingual peers. At home, he continued to speak Vietnamese with his mother and usually with the Vietnamese friends who visited them. With his Vietnamese playmates, he switched back and forth between languages as noted earlier. Quy was so obviously untroubled by his two languages that I had to wonder the degree to which he was aware of having them.

Other than the few instances of language switching cited earlier, only one other incident suggested that Quy was aware of his two languages. Once early in the year, the children were counting aloud. Quy, wearing his microphone, was counting along with the other children. They all reached 10, counting in English, and stopped. Quy paused, laughed, and continued in Vietnamese very softly, as if to himself. When I had the tape translated, I learned that he had continued counting to 20 in Vietnamese.

I wasn't about to repeat the mistake I had made with Lucy by asking Quy to think *about* language. I had learned that if I wanted to know if Quy felt his two languages to be distinct, I would have to find an indirect way. I devised a number of schemes. Once when we were sitting together looking at a Big Book, I began to point to various things in the pictures, asking Quy if he knew another word for them. I hoped thereby to get him to tell me a Vietnamese word. But Quy wasn't playing.

Terry Piper: (Pointing to a bird) Do you know what that's called?
Quy: A bird.
T: Do you know another word for 'bird'?
Q: Robin?
T: No, I don't think that's a robin. Can you think of *any* other word?
Q: Mmm. Seagull?
T: Well, that *is* another bird. Do you have a word for 'bird' in Vietnamese?
Q: (Looking puzzled) Bird. That's a bird.

At that point, Quy turned the page, fed up with my silly game. On another occasion, I enlisted the aid of his mother. I asked her to show him pictures and ask him to name them in Vietnamese and then to ask him for the English equivalents. She tried, but had little more success than I did. In desperation, I tried a trick. I explained to Quy the directions for making a Halloween pumpkin from construction paper. Knowing that Tran was far less able in English than Quy, I asked Quy to explain the directions to him. Translation is a highly complex cognitive skill requiring that the child keep in mind the entire message while simultaneously constructing a completely equivalent utterance in the other language. In order to translate, Quy would have to be aware that the two languages were separate. But instead of translating, he turned to Tran and in greatly simplified and somewhat pidginized English explained exactly what he was to do. I gave up.

Once I abandoned my tricks and turned to the transcripts, I found that even though there was no direct evidence of his being aware of having two languages, Quy did have some language awareness. Just before Christmas when the children were making Christmas decorations, Quy and Thuy were working together at a table. Quy began to sing a song that the class had been rehearsing for the school's Christmas pageant. Thuy joined in, singing "Shingle bell, shingle bell, shingle all the way. . . ." Quy interrupted her, "No, Thuy. It's not 'shingle.' It's jingle. It starts with *j-* not *sh-*." It is interesting to note that Quy did not tell Thuy that *bell* should be plural. The reasons are pure speculation, of course, but it is possible that the phonemic distinction was more salient to him than was the singular/plural distinction. Some support for this reasoning comes from evidence that awareness of the phonetic properties of language is one of children's earliest types of awareness, appearing in some children by the age of 3 (Dickinson, Wolf, & Stotsky, 1993).

Quy also joined eagerly in rhyming games, again showing awareness of the sound of language as it exists apart from meaning. Otherwise, I had only the indirect evidence supplied by his mother of his behavior when he was younger from which to make any judgments about his awareness of his bilingualism. It seemed reasonable to conclude that Quy treated his two languages as two registers of the same language, to be used for distinct purposes. As we shall see, this seemed to be Lucy's view of her two languages, one of which she began to learn much later than Quy.

LUCY'S LANGUAGE LEARNING

There are a great many children who enter school with little or no English who are not immigrants. Lucy was such a child, having been born in Vancouver, B. C. When she was a few months old, the family moved to the north coastal community where her father owned a large boat and employed a number of fishermen. Lucy's family, her mother, father, a sister 17 months younger, and a baby brother born during her kindergarten year, spoke Portuguese. Neither of her parents knew more than a few words of English, and since they lived and worked within the small Portuguese community, they had little reason to learn it.

Lucy's first extended exposure to English came when she attended a playschool for a few months during the year before kindergarten. Her mother reported using the playschool more as a babysitting service and that Lucy attended only occasionally, no more than once a week. The playschool teachers spoke only English as did roughly half the children. The others spoke a number of different languages, including Portuguese, Vietnamese, Chinese, and Italian.

When I first met Lucy in kindergarten, it was obvious that she understood some of what was said to her, but she was essentially a beginner in English. She did not have a sufficient vocabulary in English to reach even the minimum age-equivalent score of 2;6 on the PPVT. The school's ESL consultant (with an interpreter) visited Lucy's family at home and reported that Lucy was a very talkative child who was not at all shy and had a tendency to be a bit bossy toward her younger sister. She also reported that Lucy's family appeared to be well educated. There were many shelves of books in their home, and they subscribed to several Portuguese-language newspapers and magazines. While the ESL consultant and interpreter were visiting, Lucy brought out one of her books and started to read aloud. The interpreter was astonished to find that Lucy either had an excellent memory for a book that had been read to her many times or she really could read.

Given this kind of evidence about her use of Portuguese, I should not have been surprised by Lucy's progress in English. But I was. When she began, she could give her name when asked and could point correctly to most body parts and pieces of clothing. At this point there was no accuracy or fluency to measure since she said very little in English.

Just five weeks later, all that had changed. The teacher gave her the PPVT, and this time her score indicated that she had the English vocabulary of a monolingual child of 3;6. At this point, it occurred to me that Lucy's previous exposure to English must have had a greater effect than I had initially thought. Either that or Lucy was a phenomenal language learner. By the end of October, I was convinced that both explanations must be true. This time, the last time Lucy was given the PPVT, her score was 4;0. She was also given the BSM, and some of her responses to those questions, reproduced in Figure 5.2, demonstrate that her comprehension and accuracy were both excellent.

Terry Piper: What are these?
Lucy: Birds. [bəds]
T: What is the mommy bird going to do with the worm?
L: Give it to the birds.
T: Why?
L: 'Cause them hungry and crying.
T: Why's he so fat?
L: He eat too much.
T: And why's he so skinny?
L: He eat nothing.
T: What are these things?
L: Houses [hausəs].
T: And these?
L: Noses. [nozəz]
T: Why do you think this man lives in this house?
L: 'Cause that house fat.
T: What's he doing to the floor?
L: Wipin' it 'cause it all wet.
T: What did he do with his shoes?
L: Man wet them. (meaning 'He got them wet.')
T: Why is the dog looking at the king?
L: 'Cause dog hungry.
T: What happened to the king's food?
L: Dog eat it.
T: What would have happened to the food if the dog hadn't eaten it?
L: Then dog die.
T: What happened to the apple?
L: Dog drop it.

Figure 5.2 Lucy's responses to selected questions from the BSM

Well. Three pigs. One pig say he make house with straw. Hims brother pig say 'No good. I make house with mud.' Hims brother pig say 'No good. I make house with brick. Very strong.' Then the wolf came. He say 'I huff and I puff and I blow house down.' And he blow down straw house. Little pig cry and run away. He say 'I huff and I puff and I blow house down.' Then he blow down mud house. Other little pig cry and run away. Then wolf say 'I huff and puff and I blow house down.' He blow and blow and hims face look funny. But house toooo strong. So pig laugh and wolf cry and run away.

Figure 5.3   Lucy's telling of *The Three Little Pigs*

With one possible exception, Lucy correctly understood all the questions asked. She responded incorrectly to the question "What would have happened to the food if the dog hadn't eaten it?" Her answer showed her to be focusing on the dog in the sentence and not the food. Indeed, the dog figured as the subject of all her responses in this section of the BSM. Besides, the question *is* very difficult calling for the understanding of two conditionals and for a focus on the semantic object (the food) rather than the agent, (the dog). Lucy's response would not be unusual in a native English speaker of the same age.

For the most part, Lucy's responses indicated a high level of both accuracy and fluency. Notice that her syntax was, for the most part, excellent. She had a good command of basic sentence structure and deviated significantly from adult forms only by omitting frills—modals and the copula, for example. Her developmental errors tended to be morphological—using *them* for *they* and using the uninflected form of the verb in *eat* and *drop*. At first glance, it might seem odd that Lucy had such good control of English syntax at a time when she was still making a great many such errors in morphology. But when we look at what morphology Lucy *does* have, then we begin to understand the principle which guides her learning. She has the plural form; one bird differs from two and one cookie from a dozen. It is a meaningful distinction for her to mark. She has *that* in "'Cause that house fat." *That* is a demonstrative; it is used to indicate which object the speaker is talking about. In contrast, the morphology she does not yet have tends to carry less meaning. The modal *would*, for example, does not convey much meaning in the presence of *then* (*Then dog die*) and the copula is almost totally redundant semantically.

It might be argued that the overarching principle governing Lucy's second language learning is to pay attention first to those elements that are the most useful for expressing meaning. This makes sense as a comprehension strategy. When one does not have sufficient control of a language to attend to every lexical and grammatical feature, then one must focus on those that are most significant for understanding the message. These would, then, be the earliest items to appear in speech, given that the intent of children's speech is to convey meaning.

The answers she gave to the questions in Figure 5.2 give some indication of Lucy's fluency at this point. Her retelling of a story she had heard a number of times before is an even better indicator. Figure 5.3 reproduces part of a transcript of Lucy telling *The Three Little Pigs* during the first week in November.

> Once upon a time there was a boy and a girl. Hansel and Gretel were their names. One day they went for a walk to the woods. Their mother told them not to go to the woods 'cause bad people live there, but they were very bad children and so they went anyway. Then they went way, way back in the woods where it was very dark and scary and they were scared and Gretel says 'I'm hungry,' and Hansel says, 'Me too.' And then they see the witch's house and she came out and she had a big sore on her nose. She said 'Please come into my house.' And they did and so she gave them lots of things to eat—bread and meat and cookies and apples. Then they got sleepy and she put them into her oven to cook them. Then a man heard them crying and he came and he killed the witch and they went home. The end.

Figure 5.4 Quy's telling of *Hansel and Gretel*

One of the more revealing statistics of Lucy's story is the fact that she used only 40 different words in telling her story of 122 total words. She told it without major hesitations and entirely without false starts, both indicative of a fluent speaker. She was not yet a native speaker, however, and it might be useful to compare her story with one told by Quy at approximately the same time. His narrative, reproduced in Figure 5.4, differed from Lucy's in significant ways.

Quy's story had many features that Lucy's did not. First, he used more than twice as many different words (89) in his 164 word story. Since he had had far more exposure to English, a larger vocabulary would be expected. Quy's sentences were longer than Lucy's, mostly because of his use of conjunctive *and* and *then*. He also used the conventional ways of beginning and ending fairy tales. Lucy, at this point, did not. We know that Lucy had been read to and that she was an emergent reader in Portuguese. The fact that she did not use the standard frame for her story in English likely reflects her relative lack of experience with English stories. What is more important, though, is the strong sense of story conveyed by both children. It is obvious that neither child had memorized the story being told, although there is some evidence of semantic memory operating in repeated expressions such as "no good," "cry and run away," and "I huff and I puff and I blow house down" in Lucy's narrative. It seems likely that both children remembered the stories in episodes, that they had personalized the events in what is called **episodic memory** (Glucksberg & Danks, 1975).

COMPARING LUCY WITH QUY

There is no doubt that Quy was a more fluent speaker than Lucy at this time, but Quy was a more experienced second language learner. That Lucy was becoming rapidly fluent was obvious to her teacher. In class, Lucy was a real chatterbox. From the beginning, she made very full use of all the English-language resources she had. She was never heard to use Portuguese, even with her two Portuguese friends in the same class.

Jenny, Hilda, and Lucy played together both in and out of school, and most of the time when they were playing in one of their homes, they spoke in Portuguese. At school, however, Lucy always spoke English, at least until mid-January.

Many teachers have observed that ESL children who share a native language will often use that language when they are together and use whatever English they possess when they are talking with teachers or playing with English-speaking playmates. Such children may be following the principle *une personne, une langue* recommended by Grammont (Chapter 4). But there are also children who behave as Lucy did, coming to school with little or no English but learning it very quickly and using it exclusively in the school setting. They are also following a principle. They decide which language to use not on the basis of the native language of their playmates but on the situation or setting. That is, *if* they have a choice. Choice implies awareness, and there is little direct evidence that Lucy was aware of having two languages. There is, in fact, at least one suggestion to the contrary.

I was visiting Lucy's classroom a few weeks before Christmas and was sitting at a table with Lucy. She had been identifying some pictures for me as part of an informal vocabulary test, but as usual, she was impatient with the task and eager to talk about something else. On that day, the topic was her baby brother who had been born a few weeks earlier. She told me how tiny he was, that he always seemed to be hungry and that he woke her up before she was ready to get up—"before wake-up time" as Lucy put it. She also said that he couldn't talk at all. When I asked if she knew why, she replied that she didn't. I asked then how she knew that he was hungry, to which she replied, "'Cause he cry." I explained that his cries were his way of talking and promised her that eventually he would be able to talk just as she did.

On an impulse, I asked her "Which language do you think he'll speak?" She didn't appear to understand the question, so I tried again. "How many languages do you speak, Lucy?" Her response this time was prompt and very definite. "One."

"Which one?" I asked, although I really should have known better.

"Mine!" Lucy replied and let me know with her tone that she was not likely to put up with much more of this silliness!

This exchange provided a clue about how Lucy viewed her two languages. She seemed to treat her second language as a second register of *her* language. In other words, for Lucy, English and Portuguese may have been a single language with two registers, one for home and one for school. Many native English-speaking children do, after all, learn quite a different variety of English for use at school. It just happened that in her case one of the registers was Portuguese and the other English.

Under this interpretation, it would not be unusual to find some mixing of the two languages, yet her teacher could not recall ever hearing her speak Portuguese. Nor did the transcripts reveal any use of Portuguese at all until late January of the kindergarten year. When Lucy did begin to use her first language at school, however, it was for quite a specific purpose. It was also clearly apparent that Lucy had begun to mark a distinction between the two languages. After Christmas, a new child began kindergarten, another Portuguese speaker named Maria. Maria knew a little English, but it was clear that she did not always understand what was going on around her—clear to Lucy, anyway, who took it upon herself to teach her. Frequently when the teacher gave a direction,

Terry Piper: What do you see in this picture?

Lucy: There's Goldilocks playing with her toys. There's a big bed for papa bear, a middle size bed for mommy bear, and a weeny, weeny, tiny bed for baby bear.

T: Right. And what is Goldilocks doing?

L: Get in baby's bed. Trying them. Sleep. Now they're trying their porridge. Papa say in his loud voice "Somebody's eatin' my porridge." Mom's on the other side going "Somebody was eatin' my porridge." Pretty soon there's a tiny voice crying "Somebody's eaten my porridge and it's all gone." So Papa say in big voice "Somebody sleep in my bed." Mommy say in middle size voice "Somebody sleep in my bed." Baby bear, his tiny voice, "Somebody's sleep in my bed and here she is." She open her eyes and shouted "Who?" Then she ran home. The end. Do you want me sing a song?

Figure 5.5 Lucy's telling of *The Three Bears*

Lucy would turn to Maria and provide her the instructions in Portuguese. As noted earlier, translation is a highly complex cognitive skill, and it is unlikely that Lucy could have undertaken it without being conscious of the fact that her two languages were distinct. So whether or not she was aware of the distinction between her two languages earlier, by the end of January she was clearly treating them as separate.

From this point on, it would not have been uncommon to find some mixing of the two languages. If there was any, neither her teacher nor I heard it. Nor was there any evidence that her English language learning was in any way inhibited by her work as an unofficial translator. Lucy continued to make impressive progress with English, evident in the story she told me in early March. She was looking at a picture-only version of *The Three Bears* and, with very little prompting, told the story transcribed in Figure 5.5. Here we can almost hear the language spilling forth from Lucy. So eager was she to tell her story that she took grammatical shortcuts that eliminated some of the structural niceties of the language without damaging the meaning. Sometimes she spoke in short, telegraphic sentences, neglected a past tense ending, or left out entire phrases (*Baby bear, his tiny voice*). But because she demonstrated in the telling of the story that she had full command over highly complex morphological and syntactic structures (*Mom's on the other side going "Somebody was eatin' my porridge"*), it is likely that her shortcuts were just that. To put it in Chomskyan terms, her performance did not accurately reflect her competence.

The likelihood that Lucy initially considered her two languages as a single code and the fact that she kept them separate according to situation of use constitute an argument that Lucy learned her two languages in much the same way as younger children such as Quy and other simultaneously bilingual children, i. e., as two first languages. The best counterargument is her age. At 4;9, she clearly had a well-established first language, and so her subsequent language learning had to be successive rather than simultaneous. Yet the speed with which she learned the language and the apparent absence of interference from Portuguese suggest that she approached the learning of English in much the same way as she did Portuguese.

Fortunately, for educators, it doesn't matter how we designate either child's language learning. What is important is that we understand what motivated their learning and the circumstances under which they achieved their bilingualism. The story that follows is clearly one of school bilingualism. Unfortunately, there are fewer details available about Jani than Lucy and Quy. There is, nevertheless, much to be learned from Jani whose language learning experience has only just begun.

JANI FROM LABRADOR

When Jani began kindergarten in her Labrador community, Carla Doyle, the English-speaking teacher, became concerned after only a few days about her language abilities. Carla knew that Jani had only limited English, but she had observed her in the Inuktitut portion of the bilingual class and noted that she had little to say in that language either. Carla took up the matter with Mag, her Inuit co-teacher who taught the Inuktitut part of the class. The Inuit teacher was surprised by the assessment. Jani, she assured her, had very good language skills in Inuktitut. "How do you know?" Carla asked, having herself observed Jani to say very little.

"She does what I tell her," Mag responded.

Indeed, Carla thought, that seemed to be true. Yet she was surprised by how little evidence Mag seemed to require to ascertain that the child was proficient in her native language. So she persisted, "Does she ever say anything? I mean, how do you know that she has acquired Inuktitut?"

Mag looked puzzled but answered. "Well, this morning, when I told her to get the Big Book and put it on the stand so the other children could see it, she did. She also sat down when I told her to."

The misunderstanding between Carla and Mag is a cultural one. In Carla's culture, a child's language is usually assessed in terms of production. Parents busy themselves trying to figure out the meaning of the child's early utterances and tend to take their comprehension for granted. Inuit parents, on the other hand, judge their children's language acquisition by their ability to understand what they hear and to do what is asked of them.

Jani's success in school will depend, in part, on the ability of her teachers to match their teaching to her and her classmates' experience and background. For the first few years, she will have the benefit of a bilingual classroom, taught in this community where fully bilingual teachers are rare, by two teachers, one from the English-language and one from the Inuit culture. Later, in Grades 4 or 5, the language of instruction will be entirely English. Finding, or rather *creating* the match between home and school experience requires that Carla and the other English-language teachers whom Jani will encounter later come to understand more about Jani's world.

Like all the Inuit of Labrador (as well as those of Arctic Quebec), Jani speaks Inuktitut. Some linguists and anthropologists predict that this is "one of the few languages of native North Americans with a possibility of long term survival" (Foster, 1982; Priest, 1985 quoted in Crago, 1990). The Labrador community where Jani lives is harsh of climate and geography. The village where she lives is in a tundra-like land that is snow-covered from October until June. The people in the village of 200 live a very traditional existence, although it is obvious that their culture has been influenced by their Canadian and U.S. neighbors to the south.

Jani lives with her adoptive parents in an extended family of aunts, uncles, cousins and grandparents, 14 in all. As Crago (1990) points out, such an arrangement is not unusual for in "the majority of cases, Inuit children are raised in extended families with several members of the family involved in the caregiving and handling of the baby or toddler" (p. 74). Children are full members of the family, going everywhere the rest of the family goes from a very young age. They go to the store, to visit friends, to community meetings, to church, to fish and to pick berries. "An Inuk child is part of a richly woven fabric of kinship relations made up of blood relatives, adoptive relatives and fictive kin" (p. 74).

Jani's parents adopted her at birth; she is, in fact, the daughter of her mother's younger sister who has since left Labrador and moved to Montreal. Again, we see a difference between the values of the Inuit and those of their Canadian neighbors to the south. Crago (1990) noted that in the two communities she studied in Arctic Quebec, 40% of the children had been adopted into their families. "Inuit adoption, both traditionally and today, is a widely prevalent and socially valued practice which does not have the same value structure as adoption in southern Canada" (p. 74). Keeping with Inuit tradition, Jani's parents gave her the name of a recently deceased member of the community. The Inuit believe that when a child assumes another person's name, he or she also assumes certain attributes of the dead person's character. Moreover, people who share the same name share the same place in the familial structure. Thus, Jani, who was named after her grandmother, is addressed by her own mother as "Grandmother." The naming ritual helps children to learn the rather complicated kinship terminology of their language, a behavior that is highly valued in their society.

In school, Jani is perhaps more fortunate than many Native American and Native Canadian children. Her language is protected and valued in her school, a school that is officially and actually bilingual. Throughout the years of schooling, Jani will find that teachers implement the bilingual policy differently. In most cases, English is clearly the dominant language of instruction for most of the day, and the Inuktitut-speaking teacher provides support by way of instruction or explanation in the native language. In addition, there are formal lessons in Inuit language and culture designed to preserve native values in the younger generation. In most cases, English-speaking and Inuktitut-speaking co-teachers work together to ensure that children become literate in both languages and become knowledgeable about both cultures. More important than knowledge for the children is the valuing of their culture that occurs in classrooms such as hers.

Unfortunately, there is only limited data from which to reach conclusions about Jani's language learning. At this writing, Jani had not yet completed her kindergarten year. Carla Doyle reports that Jani's oral language grew impressively in the first few months. She was attentive, seemed to enjoy school and especially liked the books the teachers read to her. Carla reports that she has a slight accent when speaking English, but this may be misleading. Jani may simply have adopted the dialect of her own community, a dialect that differs markedly in pronunciation from Carla's more standard dialect. She can write her name and read a few words in both languages, more in Inuktitut than in English.

Currently, both Mag and Carla are optimistic about Jani's success in school. The indicators are mostly positive. The school that Jani attends typically achieves higher results (on the Canadian Test of Basic Skills or CTBS) than other schools in the Canadian north. Unfortunately, this is still below the Canadian average. Nevertheless, Jani is well on her way to becoming bilingual and to acquiring the education she will need to function in either or both cultures.

THE CONDITIONS FOR SUCCESSFUL SECOND LANGUAGE ACQUISITION

At the very least, Quy, Lucy and Jani teach us that children can become bilingual in either the home or the school setting. This is good news, particularly since much of the research reported in Chapter 4 suggested that the home provided the best situation for acquiring two languages. Lucy, in particular, teaches us that the school can be a good environment for second language learning *if* the language of the school is meaningful and purposeful and if it is spoken by other children and not just teachers. In daycare and preschool, Quy was not taught English but learned it in order to become a member of his peer group. In the kindergarten class, Lucy and Jani were not taught English either; it was simply there for the learning.

In taking a naturalistic approach in their classes, Colleen and Carla did not ignore the needs of their pupils. Both used non-intrusive methods of teaching the language. They used more repetition than they normally would, repetition of whole language events such as rereading and retelling certain stories as well as repetition of language units—structures, for example, and the words for common classroom objects and activities. Colleen paired native speakers (or very fluent non-native speakers such as Quy) with non-native speakers for many activities in the kindergarten. There were no native English speakers in Carla's class, but she paired stronger with weaker pupils and encouraged cooperative activities, a way of working very common in their culture. Carla and Colleen talked to the children about nearly everything that touched their lives—about the toys and other objects they brought to show her, about books, about family and community events, about fishing. She made the classroom such an exciting place to be that children were eager to share their observations and experiences. The children were highly motivated to learn enough English to participate. But even before they had much English to use, they had able teachers to help them out. The teacher was able to negotiate meaning even with beginners, as we see in Figure 5.6. The child, Tung, was a beginner in English who had been in Colleen MacKenna's class for two weeks when he stood up to tell this story in class.

Mrs. Mac: What have you got there, Tung?

Tung: (He holds up a painted wooden cup but doesn't speak.)

Mrs. M: What a pretty cup! Cup. Can all of you see Tung's cup? Isn't it a pretty one? (As the other children look at the cup and comment upon it, Mrs. MacKenna turns to Tung and speaks softly.) Can you say 'cup' Tung?

T: Kuh.

Mrs. M: Right! Where did you get your cup. Tung? Is it your Mummy's cup?

T: Mom kuh.

Mrs. M: (To everyone) This cup belongs to Tung's mother. What do you think she does with it?

Children: She drinks tea. Maybe put flowers in it. My mommy drink coffee.

Mrs. M: Those are good ideas. Tung, what does your mommy do with the cup? Drink tea? (She pantomimes drinking.)

T: (Shaking his head.) No.

Mrs. M: She doesn't drink from the cup?

T: No drink. Old.

Mrs. M: Oh, the cup is old? (Tung nods.) So she keeps it in a safe place to look at. (Tung nods again.)

Figure 5.6 Tung and Mrs. MacKenna telling a story

Although he used only seven words in the entire exchange, Tung managed to convey his message: His family owns an old, wooden cup which is not used for drinking but is decorative and kept in a safe place. Tung's rendering of his story is very revealing of the kind of language learning environment that the children in this kindergarten enjoyed. It is a small wonder that they learned so much English so rapidly given the amount of help and encouragement from their teacher!

There is another similarity in the three children's language learning that may not be immediately obvious but that is, I believe, essential to their success. I pointed out earlier that when Quy began kindergarten, he already had basic interpersonal communication skills in English. Lucy and Jani did not, but they did have them in their first languages. All three children might, then, have been able to build the more abstract kind of language of the school, cognitive academic language proficiency, on that base. But they did not have to. Colleen MacKenna and Carla Doyle encouraged the children to develop basic interpersonal skills in English first. By not *teaching* English and concentrating instead on communicating with the children, this teacher helped them to grow the foundational language on which they would later be able to build the more abstract language of the school.

This approach was especially helpful for beginning ESL learners such as Lucy and Jani. There are likely two reasons why it was so important. The first is that however easy children might make it seem, second language acquisition might not be as easy as adults think. In reporting their study of a two-and-a-half-year-old Japanese child learning English, Itoh and Hatch (1978) pointed out that the affectionate interaction with an adult produced the change in attitude toward learning a second language that contributed to his ultimate success (p. 77).

1. Focus on meaning rather than language.
2. Don't worry about interference from the first language.
3. Provide a positive and accepting environment.
4. Make sure ESL children have ample opportunity to interact with other children.

Figure 5.7   Four maxims for helping ESL children

The second reason is that a child's success in acquiring a second language in the school setting seems to be directly related to the *language interdependence hypothesis* (Cummins, 1980). The hypothesis holds that the

> cognitive-academic aspects of a first and second language are thought to be interdependent, and proficiency in a second language in a school setting is predicted to depend largely on previous learning of literacy-related functions of language.

> *(McLaughlin, 1981, p. 28)*

As noted earlier, there is a basic difference between the cognitive academic language required in most school situations and the more informal, natural interpersonal language that children learn outside. In second language learning, this means that the language children learn on their own outside school is usually very different from what is involved in most classroom learning. Colleen MacKenna's classroom was not most classrooms. Instead of beginning with the more abstract literacy related functions, she first helped the children to develop their informal language within the classroom. At the same time she prepared them for school language by reading them a minimum of two stories each day, by telling stories and talking about stories.

From the studies reviewed in Chapter 4 and from the experiences of Quy and Lucy in Colleen MacKenna's class and Jani in Carla Doyle's, we have begun to uncover some of the prerequisites for success in second language acquisition. We know, in short, that the conditions for success strongly resemble those for success in first language acquisition. The implications for the classroom are obvious and fairly easy to implement. They are based on four simple maxims, outlined in Figure 5.7.

Put into practice, these rules mandate a classroom that is friendly and accepting of the learner's language, in large part because they are based as much on common sense as they are on research and theory.

1. *Focus on meaning rather than language.*   All too often it is the case that the first lesson minority children learn is that what they say is less important than how they say it. This lesson does little to facilitate their learning. We will do well to recall the observation in Chapter 3 that adults facilitate children's language learning when they focus their attention and talk on whatever is occupying the child's attention. Quite simply, the best motivation for a child to learn a new language is the strong desire to talk about something or to someone in that language.

2. *Don't worry about initial language mixing or interference from the child's first language.*   Such mixing is probably more likely to occur when the focus is on communication for the simple reason that in trying to make themselves understood children may call upon whatever linguistic resources they have. Children are less likely to do so when attending to the form of what they say. Nevertheless, there seems to be a great deal of variation among children in the amount of mixing and the conditions under which it occurs. Both Colleen MacKenna and Carla Doyle report that among the children in their classes, even those of comparable backgrounds had very different patterns of language interference. Language mixing, therefore, should not be seen as evidence that there is anything amiss in the child's second language learning.

3. *Provide a positive and accepting environment.*   We saw in all three stories the importance of language environment. No teacher of young children needs to be reminded of the importance of the learning environment. For ESL learners, special care should be taken. Praise and encouragement are more effective than correction. Since young children make little use of correction anyway, it makes sense to replace it with support and reassurance. No doubt, some kinds of support are more effective than others. For instance, the teacher who makes a genuine attempt to negotiate meaning with children is offering better support than one who idly praises correct pronunciation.

A bilingual class provides a special and very nurturing kind of support for young children. There are a growing number of schools that provide such an environment, as we will see in Chapter 10. Such programs are relatively expensive, and where language groups are small or mixed, impractical. Teachers and parents should not worry, however, if their school is unable to provide a bilingual experience. A language-rich environment that provides incentives for children to learn and that values the culture they bring to the classroom will go a long way toward compensating for a monolingual environment.

4. *Make sure that ESL children have ample opportunity to interact with other children.*
Playing with children their own age provides second language learners with models of language appropriate to their needs and interests. Other children are better models of age- and situation-appropriate language than are adults. Besides, they provide the incentive for the second language learner to learn their language.

In the stories of the three children we met in this chapter, we saw that the conditions for success are varied but had certain commonalities. These four rules represent an attempt to define those commonalities. Following them will not guarantee that every ESL child becomes fully fluent in a short time, but it will help to make the task of learning a new language easier and more natural.

QUESTIONS FOR DISCUSSION

1. Can you think of additional ways of helping ESL children to gain Basic Interpersonal Communication Skills?

2. Often, older children arrive in an English-speaking country with knowledge of only written English and few if any oral skills. They may be placed into junior or senior

high school classes where the language demands are more academic than they are in the lower grades. Would a teacher be justified in assuming that the pupils have Basic Interpersonal Skills in the first language and moving directly into cognitive academic English?

3. Interview a bilingual adult and try to ascertain the key conditions that contributed to their bilingualism. Be sure to find out the age at which the second language was introduced and the environment (home or school) and any other factors that might have been relevant.

CHAPTER SIX

Theoretical Perspectives on Language Acquisition

We have seen in the previous chapters that children's accomplishment in learning language is very impressive. What we have not discovered is how they do it. At the end of this chapter, we still won't have an answer; the question is far too complex—or rather, the human learner is too complex—and our tools for studying children's language learning too rudimentary. It isn't that researchers, teachers, and parents have not tried to figure it out. Indeed, for much of human history, scholars have been studying children's language learning. In the 20th century alone, we find an immense volume of data. Ronjat, a French linguist, studied and published reports of the bilingual development of his son in 1913 and other major contributors in the first half of the century included Leopold (1939, 1947, 1948, 1949a, 1949b), Jakobson (1941, 1968), and Velten (1943).

Even more data have been collected in the second half of the century, particularly in the last 30 years. Raw data, however, are of interest only to the researchers themselves. In order to make sense to practitioners, and to be useful, especially, to educators trying to understand and plan for children's continued language learning, acquisition data must be viewed through the lens of a general theory. The relationship between research and theory is actually very straightforward. The data provide the materials from which a theory can be constructed and against which it can be tested. A coherent theory must account for all the facts of language acquisition found in the mass of data, but as we have seen, these facts come from a complex set of behaviors encompassed by human language. They come from phonology, morphology, syntax, semantics, and pragmatics; and it is thus not surprising that the task of constructing a general, comprehensive theory of language acquisition is a formidable one.

The task is complicated further by the fact that much of the data, gathered by different researchers under different conditions, seem contradictory. As an example, to understand how language develops in children, it is necessary to look at longitudinal data, that is, data gathered on the same children acquiring language over an extended period of time. Often, however, child language data are collected in cross-sectional studies, or studies of large numbers of children at different stages in their language development. These latter designs can produce a large amount of data very quickly and can give a good indication of what a large number of children know or can do at a particular age. If researchers collect data on a large number of children aged 2, 4 and 6, for example, they may be able to discern a pattern in the acquisition of whatever structure or behavior they are studying. But because these data capture only a moment in time, they may yield different results from longitudinal data. Since a theory of language acquisition must account for *both* development and language behavior at any point in that development, it is important to have both kinds of data to work with. The task is complicated, though, by the incongruities among the findings resulting from the various research designs. To date, then, there is no one theory which can do what a theory should do, namely to "organize the facts from these varied sources, generate testable and verifiable hypotheses, and provide an explanation of the acquisition process" (Gleason, 1989, p. 167).

As researchers continue to speculate about the nature of the underlying processes, they work within or through particular theoretical approaches. These approaches both guide their inquiry and help them to interpret their results. There are a number of competing theories of child language acquisition that linguists and educators categorize in various ways—as behaviorist, linguistic, cognitive, or interactionist, for example. The difficulty with such categorizations is that too frequently theories do not fit neatly into the assigned category. As an example, information processing, essentially a cognitive theory, relies on imitation, a notion usually associated with the behaviorists and also recognizes the role played by adults in the child's environment, the cornerstone of social interaction theory. This is true, in part, because no theory is ever conceived independent of the theories that preceded it. In any theory that enjoys any kind of academic respectability, there is almost always something salvageable that is carried over to the next, even one with a radically different outlook. It would be very unusual, then, to find a theory of language acquisition that bore no resemblance at all to its predecessors. Despite the non-exclusiveness of the categories, they are useful for distinguishing *broadly* between theories. In this chapter we will examine behaviorist, linguistic (or nativist), cognitive stage, information processing, and social interaction theories of language acquisition.

At a very basic level, what differentiates the first two types of theory are beliefs about the uniqueness of language learning. Behaviorist theories hold that there is nothing unique about language learning, that *all* human behavior, including language, has its basis in physical processes and can only be studied in terms of those processes. Linguistic theories, on the other hand, hold that language develops from structures and processes which are unique to language and which are present in the brain at birth. Cognitive theories (and information theory is a particular kind of cognitive theory) share with behaviorism the belief that language learning is not fundamentally different from other human learning. Interactionist theories, in contrast, assume that the course of language development is influenced by a myriad of factors—physical, linguistic, and social—and that these factors interact with one another, modify one another, and may produce different effects in different children. Both cognitive and interactionist approaches are generally less extreme than either behaviorist or linguistic theories.

In the next several pages, we will examine specific tenets of these four categories of theory. As we do so, we must keep in mind that no theory is as yet wholly satisfactory in accounting for everything we know from research and observation about children's language acquisition.

BEHAVIORIST THEORIES

What Behaviorists Believe

Behaviorism is well-rooted in North American psychological and linguistic traditions, but with regard to language acquisition, there were two major contributors, Leonard Bloomfield and B. F. Skinner. Leonard Bloomfield, in his book *Language* (1933) attempted to account for children's acquisition of early word meaning in behavioristic terms. He hypothesized five steps in the process, as shown in Figure 6.1.

The other major attempt to explain language acquisition through behaviorism was made by B. F. Skinner (1957). Skinner proposed an elaborate scheme of stimulus, reinforcement and association, and attempted to account for the acquisition of syntax as well as word meaning. Behaviorist theories focus on observable, measurable aspects of human language behavior. Anything that is not observable is *mentalistic*, and mentalistic explanations of language behavior are to be avoided in favor of processes that

1. Based on their innate capacity to vocalize, children make speech-like sounds. After repeatedly uttering a sound, they develop the "habit" of that sound.
2. An older speaker utters a sound which resembles one of the child's sounds. When the child hears the sound he/she utters the closest matching sound in the repertoire. This is the beginning of imitation.
3. The older speaker uses the word in the presence of the real object, for example, *ma* for *mama*. Mama's presence becomes a stimulus for saying *ma*.
4. The habit of saying *ma* gives rise to new habits. If, for instance, the child is accustomed to seeing her mother at bedtime, and then one night she fails to appear, she will say *ma* anyway. Assuming that the child is asking for her mother, the older speaker reinforces the behavior by responding. The child has thus begun to use the word when the stimulus is not present.
5. The child's speech improves as good attempts are reinforced and poor attempts lost through nonreinforcement or confusion.

(Adapted from *Language,* 1933, pp. 29–31)

Figure 6.1   Bloomfield's five steps in the acquisition of word meaning can be observed and measured. This is not to say that behaviorists eschew anything unobservable, for they readily acknowledge that language behavior has a physiological basis in the brain. What they reject outright is any claim that mental structures correspond to linguistic structures.

Behaviorism assumes two basic processes of learning—classical and operant conditioning. In language learning, classical conditioning is believed to account for receptive learning. For example, it would be assumed to work as follows. An infant sees the family dog every day and gradually comes to associate the word *dog* or the dog's name, say "Charlie," with the appearance of the dog. If the dog is not in the room and someone says "dog" or "Charlie" the child may look around, expecting to see the animal. Eventually, when the child wants to play with the dog, he or she will say "dog" or "Charlie." The dog itself is the unconditioned stimulus that provokes certain responses in the child, and the words *dog* and *Charlie* become conditioned stimuli which evoke essentially the same responses in the child as the living dog.

While classical conditioning is supposed to account for how children come to understand language, another set of principles is required to account for their productive learning—those of operant conditioning. In behaviorist psychology, operant conditioning is concerned with changes in voluntary, non-reflexive behavior that result from environmental consequences of that behavior, specifically reward and punishment. Behaviors that are rewarded are repeated while those that are punished are extinguished. In the case of early language, behavior would refer to the child's attempts to produce words, and those attempts that are rewarded are repeated and thus learned and those which are punished are abandoned. The assumption seems to be that those attempts that closely approximate the adult form will be rewarded, and those that do not will be punished. As the child grows more proficient, the adult modifies the practice of reinforcement, rewarding only those which conform to the adult standard. Behaviorists believe that both classical and operant conditioning continue to control learning into adulthood, but they are insufficient to account for the fast rate of language learning which occurs in the early childhood years.

The speed with which children acquire language suggests strongly that they do not learn every word and combination of words by going through the laborious processes described above. There simply has to be a faster route to mature behavior, and that route, according to behaviorists, is imitation. Imitation may be an exact replica of the modeled behavior or it may be an imperfect approximation; it may follow the modeled behavior immediately or it may follow a considerable delay. The concept can even be extended, as it has been by Whitehurst and Vasta (1975), to the acquisition of grammatical frames. They argue that children may reproduce grammatical structures they have heard but substituting their own words appropriate to their particular situation. Thus a child who has heard "Give me the teddy bear," may produce "Give me the cookie," or even, presumably, "Give her the book." It is assumed that successful imitation is followed by reinforcement, and thus the incentive to imitate is maintained.

Behaviorists contend, in summary, that infants begin as producers of random verbalizations. They become meaningful communicators through the simultaneous processes of classical conditioning, operant conditioning, and imitation, processes applied by others in their environment. Or, in David Ingram's (1989) words, "To explain language acquisition for the behaviorist, then, is to determine the set of environmental conditions that lead the child to identify and associate events with internal states" (p. 18).

This view of children as *objects* rather than *agents* in their own language learning is at odds with the views of theorists who consider children to be active participants in, even directors of, their own learning. Before considering their views, however, let us look briefly at some of the arguments against the behaviorist position.

The Case Against Behaviorism

As psychologists and linguists have gathered more and more data on children acquiring language, they have found many aspects of acquisition that behaviorism is at a loss to explain. The case against behaviorism is a strong one, based as it is both in research findings and in reason. The case has six basic components or arguments, including evidence of regression, the existence of novel forms, the absence or null effect of reinforcement, the early acquisition of abstract words, the uniformity of language acquisition in humans, and the species specificity of language.

1. *Evidence of Regression.*   Evidence of regression in language acquisition comes mainly from phonology and is of two types. The first occurs when a child apparently loses the ability to pronounce correctly a word which was previously correct. In her study of the acquisition of phonology, Lise Menn (1971) reported that the child Daniel's pronunciation of two words actually deteriorated. Where initially he had pronounced *down* as [dawn] and *stone* as [don], he subsequently began to pronounce *down* as [nawn] and *stone* as [non]. These changes occurred at a time when he was acquiring other nasal consonants in words such as *beans* which he pronounced as [menz] and *dance* which he pronounced as [naens].

The second type of regression involves the child's apparent inability to articulate a familiar sound in a new word. In other words, the learned sound may remain correct in known words but be deleted or substituted in new words. Menn used the example of Daniel's pronunciation of *hello* and *hi*, both early words and both pronounced with the initial consonant intact. As he learned other words beginning with the same sound, however, he pronounced them without the initial consonant. It would take considerable contortion of behaviorist theory to account for either type of regression, yet parents and others who have observed young children closely know that regression is a common occurrence in their language learning.

2. *Evidence of Novel Forms.*   The fact that children are able to produce novel forms of language, combinations of words and pronunciations they have never heard before, is another piece of evidence against behaviorism. It is true that the principles of imitation and analogy can account for some novel production, but they cannot be stretched to cover all. Consider, for example,

    a. Mikey gots no toys. (Mikey has no toys.)

    b. Want other one spoon, Daddy. (I want the other spoon, Daddy.)

    c. Me wants him all gone. (I want him to leave.)

These utterances are problematic for behaviorism on two grounds. First, children cannot imitate what, in all likelihood, they have not heard before. Second, it is difficult to imagine that any adult ever provided reinforcement for these forms. But then, this is the crux of another central difficulty with behaviorism, the fact that parents provide little feedback in matters of form.

3. *Absence or Null Effect of Reinforcement.*   The absence of reinforcement constitutes a major empirically justified argument against behaviorism. Brown (1973, quoted in McLaughlin, 1978) found that the basis for a parent's acceptance or rejection of a child's utterance is rarely structural. In response to the child who uttered "Mikey gots no toys," her mother responded "That's not true, dear. Mikey has a clown, and a truck and lots of other toys." She responded to the truth value of the statement and not to its grammaticality.

The second utterance was cited by Martin Braine (1971a); the entire dialogue went as follows:

Child: Want other one spoon, Daddy.
Father: You mean, you want the other spoon.
C: Yes, I want other one spoon, please Daddy.
D: Can you say 'the other spoon'?
C: Other . . . one . . . spoon.
F: Say "other."
C: Other.
F: "Spoon."
C: Spoon.
F: "Other . . . spoon."
C: Other . . . spoon. Now give me other one spoon. (pp. 160–161 quoted in McLaughlin, 1978, p. 24)

This example points to yet another dilemma in a theory that relies so heavily on reinforcement—that children do not attend to negative feedback about their linguistic forms. Even if parents try to turn children's attention to form and even if they succeed to some degree in getting them to mimic the correct form, children ignore the parent's teaching when left to their own devices. Furthermore, few parents try to interfere with infant pronunciations, being charmed instead by the baby talk, or perhaps understanding the futility of correction. Those who try usually find themselves frustrated as did the researchers who reported the fis phenomenon described in Chapter 1.

Actually, there is even more compelling evidence against the role of reinforcement in language learning. Katherine Nelson (1973, quoted in Reich, 1986, p. 321) conducted a study comparing language development in children whose mothers engaged in selective reinforcement with children at the one-word stage and mothers who did not. She found that the children whose mothers practiced reinforcement developed more slowly than the children whose mothers rarely or never practiced reinforcement for form. If language learning is dependent upon reinforcement, and reinforcement does not occur, then learning cannot occur. But learning does occur in the absence of reinforcement. And so if positive reinforcement of grammatical forms actually *impedes* language development, then we have even more reason to question the theory.

4. *Learning of Abstract Words.* Another piece of evidence against behaviorism comes from children's learning of words with abstract meanings. It *might* be possible to account for children's learning of their first words via a behaviorist notion of conditioning, as indicated in the example of the dog's name, Charlie, above. This explanation is not altogether untenable for concrete words like *dog, milk, bottle, juice, mama, daddy, water,* and so on. It is far less tenable for words such as *more, big,* and *little* which do not have concrete referents. Yet these words, and other abstract words, are acquired early, indicating that a more sophisticated explanation is required. So far the argument against behaviorism has been based in research and observation of children's actual language learning. The last two pieces of evidence concern language in the human species.

5. *The Uniformity of Language Learning.* A highly compelling argument against behaviorism is the uniformity with which children around the world learn language. Not only do almost all children acquire language, but there is evidence that they do so in a manner that is remarkably consistent. Both Brown (1973) and Slobin (1979) have reported that at the two-word stage children across many different languages exhibit remarkably similar language learning behavior. They express essentially the same kinds of meaning and intent in highly similar utterances. Parents of young children know that they learn very early to say "no" as in ("no nap" or "no go") and to ask for more ("more juice" or "more cookie").

This uniformity of intent and language has important implications for behaviorism. Specifically, it would be reasonable to expect that if the behaviorists were correct and language were merely a result of environmental shaping of an organism with an innate capacity for general learning, then there would be a great deal of variation among language learners. Given such variability in societies and individuals, it would be reasonable to expect that some children would never acquire language at all. Yet this is not the case. Because nearly all children on the planet learn language and because there is so much uniformity in the way they do so, we must again question the assumptions on which the behaviorist model is built.

6. *Language is Uniquely Human.* The final argument against behaviorism is also related to language and the human species and goes like this: If language learning were simply a matter of conditioning and imitation as described earlier, then it would be expected that animals other than humans could learn language. Before we can sensibly address the question of animal language, however, we need some clear definition of language. Otherwise, we do not know whether the waggle dance of bees and the courting calls of jackdaws qualify as language. Clearly each is a communicative system of some sort, but does either constitute language?

Human language, most researchers argue, has characteristics not found in any other form of animal communication. Although they have produced several different lists of attributes which mark human language, most researchers would likely agree that language has three essential attributes. First, it is productive, meaning that speakers can understand and produce utterances which they have never heard before and they can also create new utterances by recombining elements they already know. Second, language has the capacity to represent ideas, objects, and events with symbols. This property is termed *semanticity*. Third, true language has the capacity of displacement, meaning that it can be used to create messages which are not tied to the immediate environment. Bees and jackdaws both fall short of establishing these criteria.

In Chapter 1, we saw that bees use the waggle dance to communicate information to other bees about the distance and direction of the nectar-filled flowers. The point made there that is crucial to the current argument is that the information is iconic, that is, the information is physically represented by the movement of the bees. For this reason, dancing bees cannot lie about the direction. Nor can they comment on any aspect of their experience of locating the honey nor the quality of what they found. Because the message is iconic and limited to the context of gathering nectar, it fails on both productivity and displacement criteria.

Jackdaws, relatives of the crow, have courting (or mating) calls, calls used when they fly away, and warning calls which they use before attacking any creature carrying a dangling black object. Like the dance of the bees, this communication system has meaning to its users and thus might be considered to have semanticity. But also like the dance of the bees, it is very strictly bound to the context of the present. It thus fails on the criteria of displacement and productivity.

Bees and jackdaws are not the only animals which have communication systems. Whales, dolphins, sticklebacks (a small fish), gibbons, and meadowlarks have also been found to possess intricate ways of communicating. But none meets the three basic criteria which define human language. It might be argued, however, that it is unfair to compare communication systems of animals which are such a great evolutionary distance from humans. Perhaps it is fairer to consider only the linguistic abilities of the other primates, and it is certainly easy to do so because a number of attempts have been made to study primate language.

Earlier in this century, there were attempts to teach chimpanzees to talk. These early attempts failed because chimpanzees do not have a vocal apparatus which compares with the human's. Later researchers abandoned the notion of speech and concentrated on the symbolic nature of language, sign language in the case of Washoe, Moja, Pili (Gardner & Gardner, 1975) and Nim Chimpsky (Terrace, 1980), and a form of written language involving plastic tokens in the case of Sarah (Premack & Premack, 1983).

Results of these studies have shown chimpanzees to have a very limited capacity for symbolic representation. There does seem to be some evidence, although not overwhelming at this point, that chimpanzees can be taught to communicate, and that the system they use for doing so has some degree of semanticity. There is serious doubt, however, about the chimps' capacity for productivity and displacement. Studying video-tapes of Nim Chimpsky, Terrace (1980) found that most of the chimp's signing was prompted by his teacher, that is, he did not initiate conversation and that Nim's utterances mostly consisted of elements in his teacher's prior utterances. This brings to mind the story of Clever Hans, the horse who could do arithmetic problems; it was found that the trainer was unconsciously signaling the correct number of pawing movements.

Perhaps the most concise way of distinguishing between human language and animal communication is by invoking Vygotsky's notions of signs and tools, or internalized representations and physical objects for dealing with the external world. As Pflaum (1986) writes,

> Primates have the ability to signal (to warn of danger, for example), and they use tools. (Van Lawick-Goodall [1971] described chimps' use of narrow sticks to get ants to eat.) Their inability to integrate tools into signs and to generate signs for new situations marks the difference between them and humans and explains their inability to acquire language naturally. (p. 10)

The linguistic accomplishments of non-human primates have so far failed to mount any serious challenge to the position that language is uniquely human. Research which is currently being carried out with pygmy chimpanzees from the rain forests of Zaire (now the Democratic Republic of the Congo) may produce different and more convincing results, since these rare chimps are considered to be more social and more intelligent than the larger common chimpanzees which have been the subjects of prior investigations. For now, it is safe to say that humans alone have language. This argument is viewed by some as evidence for linguistic, or nativist, theories.

LINGUISTIC NATIVISM

What Nativists Believe

As might be expected, the bias of linguistic approaches is toward language structure and the child's ability to learn it. Nativists begin with two assumptions, that there is structure in language which exists independent of language use and that children are endowed with dedicated ability to acquire that structure. They assume, in other words, that language learning differs from all other human learning.

This specialized ability is attributed to an innate capacity for language learning. This dedicated capacity (which Chomsky, 1965, called the *Language Acquisition Device* or LAD) is what prepares the child to make sense of language, to discover the structure and the meaning-making potential of language. How the LAD is actually constructed is the subject of heated debate among linguists. Some argue that it consists essentially of a set of linguistic universals, such things as the existence and possible functions of word order, word classes, and the existence and function of sentences. These universals serve to constrain the possible hypotheses children make about the structure of the language they hear. They also compensate for the "poverty of the stimulus," a phrase which refers to the Chomskyan claim that the language to which children are exposed is limited in both quality and quantity. It provides, in other words, a database which is much too impoverished to allow for children to work out complex linguistic rules.

Others contend that the LAD simply endows children with a set of "general procedures for discovering how language is to be learned" (Crystal 1987, p. 234).

Although this is a weaker interpretation of what a language acquisition device might be, it should be noted that the general procedures are *not* general cognitive procedures for making sense of the world but procedures dedicated to the task of making sense of language. Proponents of linguistically based theories of language acquisition would not deny the importance of the environment in language learning, but they would minimize its impact. Rather than seeing the environment as shaping a child's language development, they view its function largely as one of activating the innate, physiologically based system.

Linguistically based theories hold a certain appeal. Clearly the learning of structure is an important part of language learning, and the speed with which the child learns so much complex grammar is impressive enough to warrant our consideration of an innate device. Moreover, the job of explaining language acquisition is made easier if theorists can assume that certain parts of the learning mechanism are innate. But what is the evidence?

Essentially there are two types. One is research evidence on children's learning of structural rules, and the other relies on the argument that humans must possess innate linguistic capabilities. A number of studies strongly indicate that children learn grammatical rules. Slobin (1971) asserts, for example, that the basic organization of language emerges from the time children begin putting two words together. At this stage and very clearly by the time they begin to produce sentences longer than two words, children use principles of hierarchical structure to form their utterances. Moreover, early awareness of syntactic rules has been documented not only in children learning English but also in children learning a number of different languages (e.g., Braine, 1963, 1976).

Many researchers have focused on the phenomenon of overgeneralization (or overregularization) as evidence for rule learning. When children who have previously produced forms such as *made* and *went* suddenly begin to produce *maked* and *goed* (which they are unlikely to have heard before), researchers take it as evidence that they are in the process of learning the regular past tense rule. They have overgeneralized the application of their newly acquired rule to irregular (and previously learned) as well as regular verbs. The phenomenon of overgeneralization has been observed in children acquiring a great many different languages including Spanish, Japanese, Hebrew, Russian, Finnish, Turkish, and English.

Children's knowledge of rules has been studied not only in natural observations of children but in laboratory studies as well. One of the best known of these was devised by Jean Berko (1958) to investigate children's knowledge of plurals and other grammatical morphemes. She showed children pictures of creatures and objects which she gave nonsense labels and asked children to produce alternate forms. For example, she showed a picture of a fat, birdlike creature and gave the following prompt: "This is a wug. Now there is another one. There are two of them. There are two _____." This procedure has undergone adaptation and been replicated many times. Although investigators have sometimes disagreed on the precise nature of the rules children acquired, most are in agreement that the evidence strongly indicates that children's language is rule-governed.

The second type of argument in support of innatist theories is biological, and there are a number of observations which support the view that children are born with special biological equipment which, when triggered, results in language acquisition. For example, a number of studies have shown that very young infants have the ability to perceive relatively fine acoustic distinctions in speech sounds and to respond differently to speech and non-speech sounds. The fact that they can do so at such a young age argues for an innate predisposition to language learning.

The similarity of the course of early language development in children both within a culture and from different languages and cultures argues for biological innateness. A number of researchers have studied the order in which children acquire the grammatical morphemes of English and have found remarkable consistency. Cazden (1968), Brown (1973), and deVilliers and deVilliers (1973), in their Morpheme Acquisition Order (MAO) studies established that English-speaking children acquire 14 grammatical morphemes (10 inflections, 2 articles, and 2 prepositions) in a highly similar order. Although there are many studies of children's morphological development in other languages, there are none which are directly comparable with the MAO studies and thus we cannot yet confirm the finding from English. It does seem to be the case, however, that "morphology in all languages appears to be acquired in similar ways and at similar stages of development" (Tager-Flusberg, 1989, p. 149).

There also seems to be remarkable consistency in the order in which children acquire larger syntactic structures. There is evidence, for example, that children acquire *wh-* questions (those beginning with what, where, who, when, how, and why) in a particular order (Wootten, et al., 1979, cited in Tager-Flusberg, 1989). Slobin (1982) observed that young children from a number of different language backgrounds used Subject-Object word order regardless of the order used by adult speakers of the same language. This ability might be attributed to some sort of innate predisposition toward language, a component of the LAD which knows or expects that grammatical classes exist.

On the other hand, it is likely that children produce Subject-Object structures in response to particular semantic relationships which they find in their worlds. At the two- and three-word stage, most of the sentences which children produce have semantic agents as subjects. This fact gives children a leg up on working out more abstract syntactic relationships in more complex sentences (Tager-Flusberg, 1989, p. 143). The fact that children prefer Subject-Object order, then, does not necessarily argue for the existence of a language acquisition device; it may be evidence only for a generalized cognitive ability to figure things out, among them the fact that agents act upon objects. It is fortuitous for English-speaking children that their language happens to express these relationships in the same syntactic order as they initially expressed them.

A final argument for linguistic nativism takes the form of evidence for a biological critical period during which language must be acquired if it is to be acquired fully. The notion of critical period comes from the study of behavior among goslings, rats, sparrows, and other non-human animals. Specifically, there seem to be certain periods of development during which a certain stimulus has to be present if young animals are to develop normal behavior. One case which is somewhat analogous to the human is that of the white-crowned sparrow. Reich (1986) relates Marler's (1970) observation that this bird learns its own song if and only if it hears the song during a critical period of its development. It does not acquire its song if raised in isolation nor does it acquire the song of other birds even if exposed during the critical period. Apparently, the fact that it does not acquire the songs of other birds cannot be attributed to its inability to produce other songs since it can acquire any of a number of different dialects present among members of the species. Marler argues that these birds appear to be born with a template which rejects all but their own song, an argument which seems analogous to Chomsky's case for humans (Marler, 1977, cited in Reich, 1986, p. 291).

The case for a critical period related to language was first made by Wilder Penfield (Penfield & Roberts, 1959) who based his argument on observations that brain-damaged children have better recovery potential than adults with similar damage. The argument for a critical period was further advanced by Eric Lenneberg (1967) who asserted that all that is required for a child to acquire language between the ages of 2 and puberty is adequate exposure to language. He also relied on the experiences of brain-damaged children and adults, arguing that if adults experienced injury to the left hemisphere, believed to be the dominant hemisphere for language processing, and failed to recover within a few months, they would never recover fully. Children, on the other hand, were capable of a complete recovery of language functions if the left hemisphere damage occurred when they were very young. Based largely on Basser's (1962) survey of the literature on hemispherectomies, Lenneberg went on to conclude that children experienced no speech disorders following surgery (except where aphasia had occurred before the operation) while adults experienced a variety of language disorders and were unable to recover language function fully.

Later, Krashen (1973) reexamined Basser's data and found that all the children who had their left hemispheres removed were under 5 years of age at the time of the operation. This fact suggested that if Lenneberg and Penfield were right about a critical period, that it must occur before the age of 5 and not 9, as Penfield suggested, or 13, as Lenneberg suggested. Yet it is the case that a great deal of language learning occurs after age 5 (and, indeed, some occurs after age 13), and so it would seem that a critical period for language acquisition might be critical only for the triggering of language acquisition. That is, a weakened version of the critical period hypothesis would claim that if language acquisition is to occur it must begin during a critical period.

But what if it does not? The case of Genie suggests that language learning *can* occur even when it is begun much later than the age of 5. In Los Angeles in 1970, a girl of 13 years and 9 months was discovered after having been kept in physical and social isolation from the age of 20 months. Genie had been kept in a small, closed room where she was physically punished for making any noise and was never spoken to. Her father and brother sometimes made barking noises at her, and her mother was forbidden all but minimal contact at feeding time. There was neither radio nor television in the house. Not surprisingly, Genie's condition was such when she was found that she required hospitalization and she remained in the hospital for almost a year until she was placed with a foster family.

Medical examinations conducted during that time found no evidence of neurological disease or brain damage although functionally the girl was severely retarded (McLaughlin, 1984a, p. 51). It appeared that she was healthy apart from suffering the devastating effects of complete social isolation. Having been denied exposure to language from the age of 20 months, Genie seemed to be an ideal test case for the critical period hypothesis. Needless to say, linguists were very interested in Genie and her language development has been carefully charted. While she has acquired a great deal of proficiency in English, analysis of her development has revealed a number of abnormalities. The gap between her ability to produce and comprehend speech was found to be wider than normal, she had difficulty in acquiring certain syntactic skills, and her overall rate of development was abnormally slow (Curtiss, 1977). If Genie had acquired no language, her case would have provided very strong evidence for Lenneberg's version of the critical period hypothesis. But despite the fact that she had a difficult time of it, she did acquire a great deal of language, particularly vocabulary, and she did so after the age of puberty. It would seem, then, that her accomplishment offers no clear evidence either for or against the critical period hypothesis.

Genie is not the only child to grow up in social isolation. Crystal lists 48 such children either reared in the wild by animals or in isolation from human contact. Most of the reports of these children are sparse and only a few contain any information about the children's language ability. According to Crystal, what information exists is clear: "none could speak at all, and most had no comprehension of speech. Most attempts to teach them to speak failed" (Crystal, 1987, p. 289). The difficulty in considering these children as evidence in favor of a critical period is the confounding factor of profound social deprivation. In other words, in accounting for these children's failure to acquire language, it is impossible to separate the effects of growing up isolated from normal human society from possible biological effects.

On the matter of a critical period for language acquisition, then, the jury is still out. The evidence is controversial and the conclusions tentative. It does seem that a first language is harder to learn after puberty than before, but since no one would be acquiring a first language at this age except in abnormal circumstances, the import of this fact is dubious. As we shall find later, however, a great deal of second language learning is accomplished by adults. It may be the case that language learning which occurs after puberty requires a different kind of cognitive activity than early language learning. It is impossible to tell, given our present state of knowledge, whether this difference is biologically or environmentally determined or both. The critical period question will undoubtedly remain an important one for researchers in neurology and linguistics for decades to come.

The Case Against Linguistic Nativism

Appealing as nativism might be in comparison to behaviorism, there are arguments against it. Here we will consider five.

1. *Occam's Razor.* One argument against linguistically based acquisition theories, and one which lends some credence to behaviorism, is a philosophical one based on a principle of science known as Occam's Razor. Occam was a 12th century philosopher who articulated what is essentially a simplicity criterion for evaluating theories. Specifically, the principle was that entities should not be multiplied beyond necessity. Applied to language acquisition theories, the principle would lead us to select a general learning theory over a language-specific learning theory, that is, one which accorded language learning special status. It would, then, be "incumbent upon Chomsky and other advocates of special learning principles for language to argue that language is a special case" (Reich, 1986, p. 284). As Reich points out, advocates of this position often depend upon this kind of philosophical argument and put little stock in research evidence, especially if it is not consistent with their views (p. 291).

2. *Critical Period.*   A second argument against nativism concerns the critical period. A cornerstone of linguistic theories of acquisition is the speed of acquisition argument which assumes that because children learn so much complex language structure in such a short time, they must have a biological advantage. We have already seen, however, that the notion of a critical period for language acquisition remains highly controversial. Certainly there is no known neurological basis for such a claim.

3. *TG Grammars.*   A more damaging argument against linguistic theories has to do with the nature of the grammars written by Chomskyan linguists of the sixties and seventies. Transformational-generative grammar, which was considered revolutionary at the time, was the backbone of nativist theories. There is no doubt that TG grammars were impressive in their ability to account for the regularities and the variety of English sentences. But to do so, they were necessarily complex and abstract, consisting, for example, of abstract categories which were far removed from the surface forms and meanings of real sentences uttered by real speakers in real time (Bohannon & Warren-Leubecker, 1989, p. 197). Language acquisition researchers were troubled by the fact that such grammars were so far removed from the experience of the child acquiring language. If linguistic rules were to be psychologically real, that is, if they were to represent somehow speakers' knowledge of their language, they argued, the rules had to be learnable. The farther the formulation of the rule was from the reality of the sentence or what native speakers would perceive as the reality of the sentence, the harder it would be to explain how the child could come to know the rule. As Bohannon and Warren-Leubecker point out, the complexity and abstractness of grammars "becomes an especially damaging flaw in the traditional linguistic approach" as evidence mounts "that the major part of language acquisition involves semantic, not just syntactic, processes . . ." (Bohannon & Warren-Leubecker, 1989, p. 197).

4. *Negative Linguistic Evidence.*   Perhaps even more damaging to nativist theories than the complexity and abstractness of the grammars to be acquired is the issue of negative evidence. Central to the nativist approach is the belief that children are not generally provided with negative linguistic evidence and that when they are, they tend to ignore it. This being the case, they must have an innate mechanism by which to discover the rules. Otherwise, the poverty of the stimulus with regard to positive and negative information about structure would make it impossible for them to learn the rules of language. If it were the case, however, that children received information about the acceptability of language structure, then the nativists' arguments about learnability would begin to crumble. In fact, a number of studies have suggested that children *do* receive such information.

While parents and other caregivers do not negatively reinforce, in the behaviorist sense, utterances that do not conform with adult structure, there is evidence that they react differently to poorly formed and well-formed utterances. Several studies have been reported suggesting that parents do not ignore the grammatical errors of their young children. They may not correct the error overtly, but they repeat sentences with errors less frequently than they repeat well-formed ones (Hirsh-Pashek, Treiman, & Schneiderman, 1984). When they do repeat poorly formed sentences, they usually rephrase them. Parents are more likely to expand their children's ungrammatical sentences and to question children when their previous utterance contains a grammatical error than when it is error-free (Demetras, Post, & Snow, 1986; Penner, 1987). Moreover, Bohannon and Stanowicz (1988) report that "children are more likely to imitate expansions and recasts than any other utterances" (cited in Bohannon and Warren-Leubecker, 1989, p. 198).

It would seem, then, that adults do provide negative information about language structure and that children respond to it. While a great deal more research must be done before we can speak with any clarity on the role of negative information in language acquisition, it certainly cannot be ruled out as a contributing factor. This being the case, one of the foundations of linguistic theories of acquisition is weakened.

5. *Environment.*   A final argument in the case against nativism concerns environment. For fairly obvious reasons, nativists have never considered environment, beyond some very basic level of exposure to human interaction, as playing a central role in language acquisition. Yet teachers know that environment plays a major role in children's language development during the school years. In the next chapter, we will see how one child struggled to learn language after the age of 5. His was not a case of social isolation but of linguistic deprivation to the degree that when he began school, he had very limited language exposure. Other research tells us that children whose only exposure to language is television acquire little speech (Bohannon & Warren-Leubecker, 1989, p. 199).

COGNITIVE THEORIES

Cognitive theories of language consider language acquisition as part of children's more general cognitive development. There are many kinds of cognitive theory, but two are of particular interest to understanding language acquisition. The first are theories which postulate stages of cognitive development that have parallels in linguistic achievement. The second are based upon information processing theory and postulate no particular innate mechanism. In the following pages, we will look at Piaget's theory of cognitive development and, very briefly, at Luria's and Bruner's.

Piaget's Cognitive Theory

Piaget, of course, was a biologist with a particular interest in how humans acquire knowledge. His theory of cognition is general and not applied specifically to language acquisition. It holds that language is an aspect of general cognitive development. Although it shares certain beliefs with both behaviorism and nativism, it differs fundamentally from both. Piagetian theory shares with behaviorism the view that language learning is accomplished in much the same way as all human learning, but the two differ dramatically on how that learning is accomplished. Here Piagetian theory resembles nativism because it relies on the notion of innate structures which function globally in the development of thought. The difference between Chomskyan nativism and Piagetian nativism is obvious. Chomsky postulates an innate device dedicated to language learning while Piaget believes in an interdependence of language and cognition, that language development has its foundation in the more fundamental development in cognition.

Piaget, however, does not view language as central to cognitive development but rather as an outside agent. As the child "comes to understand language, he has to assimilate and then accommodate the lingual signs to his thought structures, but if he is to find his own meaning, the symbolic structuring must come first and not be confused by adult language structures" (Smith, Goodman, & Meredith, 1970, p. 133). In other words, according to Piaget, conceptualization precedes language. This is not to say that language does not play an important role in development. Language is a key element in children's social interaction with adults and other children, and this interaction is crucial in order for children to move away from the egocentric point of view. The most useful way of thinking about Piaget and language is as an explanation of the cognitive foundations of language learning.

Support for the Piagetian view of language development would consist of evidence showing links between cognitive development and language structures. Crystal uses the example of the comparative. Before children can express a sentence such as *This car is bigger than that*, they must first have the conceptual ability to judge the relative sizes of two objects (Crystal, 1987, p. 234). There is research evidence to support the view that early language correlates with certain kinds of conceptual development. For example, a concept that children acquire early, during the sensorimotor stage, is object permanence. At about the same time, they also acquire the *disappearance* words such as "allgone" (Bohannon & Warren-Leubecker, 1989, p. 200). On the other hand, it would seem that the concept of object permanence should be in place before the emergence of the first words which frequently label those objects, but this does not seem to be the case. What does seem to be the case is that the first words appear once children understand that other people may act as agents for actions (Bates, 1976).

Researchers have also demonstrated correlations between later linguistic and non-linguistic development. One of the issues they addressed is the relationship between certain inflectional morphemes and the concepts that they express—plurality or past time, for example. It would be highly unlikely if children were to acquire and use the past tense form, for example, before they had acquired the basic concept of object permanence—past tense is used largely to talk about things that are not currently in the immediate environment. And they do not, according to work done by Slobin (1979) and by Block and Kessel (1980). Following this reasoning, it is not surprising that children generally acquire the plural and the progressive marker, *-ing*, before morphemes such as the past tense marker or the third person singular marker. These are attached to nouns and verbs; objects and their movements are highly significant in young children's lives, and particularly to their achievement of the concept of object permanence. Language acquisition, then, as seen from the Piagetian perspective, is not distinct from other human cognitive activity but runs a parallel course with and at the same time depends upon maturation of the child's cognitive system.

Luria and Bruner

There are, of course, other cognitively based views of language acquisition which, like Piaget's, are particularly concerned with developmental sequences, or stages. Among them are Luria's (Luria & Yudovich, 1971) and Bruner's (1983, 1984, 1986). The difference between Luria and Piaget is fundamental: Piaget believes that language, while not completely peripheral to cognitive development, is secondary in importance to "learning through operations." Luria, on the other hand, is saying that development in thinking is achieved through the use of language to structure and control behavior. (Stringer et al., 1973, p. 93). Bruner has taken neither view but has offered something of a compromise by suggesting "that in the course of evolution, man has developed three important skills of representation: enactive, iconic and symbolic" (Stringer et al., 1973, p. 93). Enactive representation is the representation of behavior in motor terms such as the ability to roller-skate. Iconic representation is representation through images, that is, the use of a mental picture to guide our activity, and symbolic representation occurs when images become symbols. According to Bruner, these are cognitive tools which develop successively but which also overlap to some degree. Moreover, individuals may vary in their use of these tools, depending on a variety of factors including their age, education and cultural environment.

The cognitive theories discussed so far describe development in terms of stages. These are not discrete stages but rather cumulative ones in the sense that what is learned in one stage is carried forward and integrated into the next. Learning in any stage is never discarded but becomes part of the mechanism by which the child learns in the next. Not all cognitive theories of language acquisition are stage based, however. Information processing is one such theory.

Information Processing

Psychologists and psycholinguists use the term *information processing* to refer to the processes humans use to identify and understand meanings in spoken and written communication as well as the processes by which they store, organize and retrieve those meanings (Richards, Platt, & Weber, 1985, p. 140). Although interest in this area has traditionally been directed toward understanding the processes involved in comprehension of both written and spoken meaning, the paradigm has recently gained favor as one for investigating and understanding language acquisition. Those who work within this paradigm begin with a model representing their best understanding of how mature speakers process speech and then work backward to unravel how they developed their mature language systems. The connection between the comprehension strategies of mature speakers and the acquisition strategies of infants may not be immediately obvious. Certainly making such connections requires that we view children as being similar to adults in important ways. Whether or not they are, a growing number of researchers are trying to understand language learning by beginning with a model of the adult language user's system and then working backward to discover how it might have been created (Gleitman & Wanner, 1982).

Information processing models of language acquisition are highly technical and beyond the scope of this chapter. Briefly, however, they are based on the principles of parallel distributed processing (PDP) and presuppose no innate structures other than a *processor* or learning mechanism. PDP refers to the brain's ability to process a multitude of stimuli simultaneously rather than sequentially, but the processing is not mere stimulus-response association. One model of information processing, the competition model (Bates & MacWhinney, 1987), assumes that a number of language forms may compete as stimuli to represent a particular meaning. For instance, both *went* and *goed* would be possible representatives of the meaning of the verb *go* in the past tense. Children eventually learn *went* because they hear it more frequently; it matches the adult form. Children thus learn the language they hear. The correct forms are the ones they hear most often and thus win in the competition between adult and immature forms. This model of acquisition requires the child to have no innate mechanism in order to learn to process language.

A full evaluation of this theory cannot be made here for two reasons. In the first place, information processing and parallel distributed processing models on which it is based are extremely complicated. In the second place, they are as yet of little use to teachers because there are insufficient data gathered and analyzed from this perspective. It would seem, however, that the strength of this theory lies partly in the strong bond it postulates between children's cognitive development and the language environment in which they learn. It differs from nativist linguistic and Piagetian cognitive theories in that it assumes no innate mechanisms but shares with the latter the assumption that language learning is part of more general cognitive development. The difficulty with it is its assumption that children are qualitatively similar to adults when it comes to language processing.

The Case Against Cognitive Theories

Cognitive theories are appealing for a number of reasons. One is that because they do not postulate a unique status for language acquisition within cognitive development, neither do they violate the simplicity criterion known as Occam's Razor and described earlier in this chapter. They also appeal to teachers who have observed strong correlations between children's language development and other cognitive and academic growth.

Unfortunately, it is this notion of correlation that identifies a central piece of evidence in the case against Piaget. To be more precise, establishing a correlation between any particular language behavior and an aspect of nonlinguistic development does not mean that either caused or even contributed to the other. There are necessarily a number of developmental milestones which occur at about the same time as others. The loss of baby teeth, for example, is predictable but probably not related to concurrent language behavior (with the possible exception of trouble with sibilants). On the other hand, if researchers were able to isolate particular cognitive accomplishments which *always* preceded particular language achievements, and further, that the language behavior failed to appear *unless* the nonlinguistic behavior appeared first, then they would be able to make a better case for a cognitive acquisition theory. So far, they have been unable to do so. Additional damage to cognitive language theory comes from the work of researchers who have found that children with Turner's syndrome score poorly on tests of cognitive ability yet appear to have normal language ability (Curtiss, 1977, 1981; Curtiss & Yamada, 1978; Curtiss, Yamada, & Fromkin, 1979). If it is the case that cognitive and language skills are indeed separable, then the cognitive language theorists will have to reconsider their position on their interdependence. To be fair, however, we cannot dismiss cognitive language theory so easily because "the broad assertion that cognitive development determines language development remains virtually untested at this time" (Bohannon & Warren-Leubecker, 1989, p. 202).

SOCIAL INTERACTION THEORY

What Social Interactionists Believe

Social interaction theory has been described as a middle-of-the-road compromise in the great debate between behaviorism and nativism (Hulit & Howard, 1993, p. 33). Certainly it bears some resemblance to both of these as well as to cognitive theories, but, of course, it has its unique defining traits. Essentially, social interactionists believe that human speech emerged and its forms have their bases in the social role that language plays in human interaction. As children grow older, they begin to interact with adults in more mature ways. They are faced with more complex communication tasks, and adult caregivers help them to meet these tasks by providing appropriate language. With more sophisticated language skills, children are able to engage in even more complex social interactions for which the caregivers provide language assistance, and the cycle continues.

Social interactionists, like behaviorists, believe that environment plays a central role in the growth of language. Both see parents as crucial to the process, but there is a major difference. Behaviorists tend to view children as passive vessels into which language is poured while social interactionists believe that children are active participants through their interaction with their parents. Like nativists, social interactionists hold that language behavior, and, thus, language learning, are unique from other behavior and learning. Both are concerned with universals, or those structures common to all languages. Social interactionists do not, however, focus on structure to the same degree that nativists do. Rather, they are interested in how structure helps the child to function socially with language and thus learn more of it. They would also concede that children come to the task of language acquisition with some innate predisposition to succeed, but they would argue that the innate ability is of less importance than the social environment.

Social interactionists agree with cognitivists that language learning is a complex accomplishment that involves the child's active participation. They would also agree that children cannot acquire language until they have reached a certain level of cognitive maturity. On the other hand, they emphasize that "the environment is the place to look for the emergence of language" (Berko-Gleason, 1993, p. 274). Social interaction theory assumes that a child's acquisition of language is influenced by the interaction of a number of factors that are physical, linguistic, and social in nature. Because children differ in physical and cognitive abilities as well as in the social environment in which they live, this interaction may produce different effects in different children.

The previous paragraph suggests that there is a single theory called the social interactive theory. This is not quite the case. Just as cognitivism encompasses a wide variety of different theories, so is social interaction theory an umbrella for a number of different perspectives.

There are a great many advocates for the role of the environment in language acquisition. One of them was Vygotsky, a Soviet psychologist who died in 1934. While his work might rightly be considered in the section on cognitive theories of language acquisition, I have placed it in this section because of the emphasis he placed on the role played by interaction with the environment, and particularly with older children and adults.

> Language is a major stimulant for conceptual growth, and conceptual growth is also dependent on interaction with objects in the environment. Moreover, adults (and older children) have a role in stimulating language growth through a variety of means. (Pflaum, 1986, p. 11)

This stimulation, he believed, should occur within the zone of proximal development, which Vygotsky defined as the distance between a child's actual level of development and the level at which she could function with adult assistance. This emphasis on the role of the adult, whether parent, teacher, or friend, in the child's conceptual and linguistic development sets Vygotsky apart from Piaget and puts him in line with current theorists who emphasize the mother's (or other caregiver's) contribution to the child's language learning.

In the past two decades, there has been a growing interest in the part this input plays in the child's linguistic accomplishments, and one of the central findings has been that mothers' talk to their children is by no means as impoverished as nativist linguistic theory assumed it to be. Despite the fact that some parents talk to their children differently from the way they talk to other adults, research has shown that the adaptations they make facilitate rather than hinder language learning. Even baby talk, that unusual vocal behavior which characterizes some adult's speech with infants, seems to help. Field and colleagues (1982) hypothesize that children learn to control their vocal apparatus by watching their mothers make the exaggerated speech sounds of baby talk. Other researchers postulate that the talk and play that occurs between parents and young children forms the basis for later patterns of turn-taking in conversations (Stern, Beebe, Jaffe, & Bennet, 1977).

The question that is of primary interest in language acquisition theory is how children acquire the ability to express their intentions or meanings in language. Interactionists believe that they do so through a process of negotiation with their mothers or principal caregivers. This negotiation occurs partly as a result of mothers treating children's speech, even if it is babbling, as meaningful and intentional. Gradually, as mothers persist in trying to make sense of children's speech, they also begin to negotiate meaning and intent with their children. It is easy to demonstrate how such negotiation takes place.

> Christopher, age 13 months, is sitting on the living room floor, barefoot, playing with his older brother Kerry (2;0) and their mother.

Christopher: Want du!
Mum: You want your shoes?
C: (He looks puzzled.) Du. Du.
M: (She looks around for something else he might be asking for and holds up a stuffed bear.) You want Gurgles?
C: No. Want du.
M: (To her other son.) Do you know what Chris wants?
K: He want this. (He holds up the wooden car he is playing with.)
C: (Showing no interest in the car.) Du peez. At this point, he gets up and starts toward the kitchen.
M: Oh, you want juice!
C: Yeah. Du.

Here, Chris's mother does not give up easily on understanding him. There is evidence that mothers of even younger children behave in a similar manner and may, in fact, teach the child language in what Golinkoff (1983) has called "conversational bouts." Certainly they actively teach children the social routines of greetings, leave-takings, and politeness. Whether they engage in any other active teaching and whether it does anything to facilitate language acquisition are questions yet to be answered, although we do know how little effect the teaching of structure usually has.

Halliday (1975) saw language acquisition as being heavily reliant on communicative interaction. Taking a functional view, he believed that the language structures necessary for realizing the various language functions are learned, along with the functions themselves, through learning to communicate. Obviously, the child does not do this alone. It seems, however, that environment may play a different kind of role in children's learning of grammar. Specifically, if we assume that children figure out which forms are grammatical from being consistently exposed to correct forms, then the language which children hear plays a significant role in the acquisition process. Parents play an important role in matching the language *input* to the appropriate level of cognitive and language development of their children. Speech to the very young is much simpler than it is to older children. For example, sentences spoken to young children are shorter and not as varied in structure as those presented to older children. It is probably not the case that adults consciously make such adjustments to their speech; what is more likely is that in their attempts to communicate with children, they unconsciously match their language to the appropriate cognitive and linguistic level for the child.

There is another way in which parents or other caregivers likely contribute to children's language acquisition, and that is by talking with them about and focusing their attention upon things which are in the immediate environment. One of the central tasks in learning language is to match language with meaning, a task that parents facilitate by focusing their talk on whatever is holding the child's attention. If the child is chasing the family cat, the cat is what they all talk about. The child thus comes to understand what the word *cat* means.

It may also be the case, as Bohannon and Warren-Leubecker (1989) point out, that the same process may lead children to notice the difference between their own expressions and the more mature ones of the older speakers around them (p. 190). We saw earlier that parents are more likely to expand and extend their children's imperfectly formed utterances. When an expanded, correct utterance immediately follows an immature one, children may note the difference and, gradually, make changes to approximate the adult form more closely. It may be, then, that imitation *does* play a role in language acquisition, but social interactionists would see this role as qualitatively different and as less central to overall language development than would behaviorists.

One of the interesting and compelling aspects of social interaction approaches is that they come down on neither side of the nature/nurture controversy. On the one hand, social interactionists admit to the likelihood that children possess an innate predisposition to learn language. On the other, they believe that while environment alone cannot account for the acquisition process, it serves as more than a trigger for acquisition. It serves, instead, to provide a rich source of data from which children form and test hypotheses about language structures. The relationship between language acquisition and social interaction is symbiotic: Social interaction provides essential experience with language and language affords children opportunities for expanding their social interactions.

The Case Against Social Interaction Theories

As intuitively reasonable as the social interaction approaches may seem, particularly to teachers, they are by no means widely accepted. There are several counterarguments, three of which are worth noting here.

1. *Caretaker Speech.*   The first argument against social interaction challenges the role of caretaker speech. Some researchers claim that although caretaker speech may be simplified in comparison to speech with other adults, it is by no means simple. In other words, the caretaker speech may be different and to some degree simpler, but it retains a great deal of linguistic complexity. Others point out that researchers have failed to show correlations between the simplified input language and the parallel forms which subsequently appear in the child's speech. Bohannon and Warren-Leubecker (1989) report studies (cf. Hoff-Ginsburg, 1986; Newport, 1976) showing "the complexity of maternal speech addressed to the children to be unrelated to the children's language gains" (p. 207).

2. *How Adjustments Facilitate Learning.* The second argument goes like this: Social interaction theory assumes that caretakers adjust their speech to provide input that is both comprehensible and useful to children in making and testing hypotheses about language structure. Even given that this is true (and as we noted, it is not by any means universally accepted that it is), theorists must specify just how such adaptations facilitate language acquisition. They have yet to do so.

3. *Universality.* Perhaps the most persuasive counterargument concerns universality. As Susanna Pflaum has pointed out, if the dialogue between parent and child is the critical mechanism for language learning, then such dialogues would be found in the language learning of all children everywhere. A number of researchers have demonstrated that this is not the case. Heath (1983, 1986), Schieffelin and Ochs (1983) and others have described very different adult-child exchanges in different cultural groups. In one community studied by Heath, for example, it appears that baby talk does not exist; and if children wish to participate in the talk of the group, they have to interrupt to do so. In Chipewyan communities, parents do not expect their children to speak until sometime around the age of 5 (Scollon & Scollon, 1981). Nevertheless, these children and children in all cultural groups learn language.

We must remember in considering the case against social interaction that because it is a relatively new theory, many of its explanations for acquisition phenomena have not been subjected to empirical verification. But this also means that the argument against social interaction theory is speculative as well.

WHAT THEORY HAS TO SAY ABOUT LANGUAGE LEARNING AND ENVIRONMENT

The theories discussed in this chapter take different views on the contribution the child's environment makes to language acquisition. With the exception of the strict, or strong-position nativists, most agree that some kind of interaction is necessary but disagree about the degree or kind of interaction children need to acquire language. Research has not yet resolved the issue, and I would suggest three reasons why this is the case. The first, and most obvious, is that research is never neutral. The hypotheses with which investigators begin, the observations they make, and the methods they use are all biased by their theoretical perspectives. Research cannot be neutral. In a real sense, theory serves as the lens which we point at and through which we see research data. It would be expected, then, that research findings would be somewhat contradictory.

The second reason is methodological. Our tools for evaluating social interaction and its impact on language acquisition still need refining. Because they have not been extensively used yet and because their use has been mostly confined to studies of children in the majority culture in North America, they are still relatively clumsy and largely untested. The third reason is that we still have too few studies of interaction patterns in other languages and cultures—studies of the caliber of those conducted by Shirley Brice Heath, for example. Only when we understand how a variety of peoples interact with their children can we be begin to understand how that interaction influences language acquisition.

Still, we must hold on to the fact that no research to date has suggested that interaction plays no role. Even Heath's finding, cited earlier that baby talk does not exist in some communities, should not be taken to mean that *no* social interaction occurs. It means only that parent-child interaction as we know it in the dominant white culture does not exist in this community, and yet the children learn language. It also suggests that we need to look further to try to understand social interaction patterns in other cultures before we can really assess the role they play in language acquisition.

CONCLUSION

In Chapter 3, we traced the course of language development from infancy through the preschool and early school years. We saw how children grew from infants with amazing powers of linguistic perception but little productive ability to school-aged children capable of producing complex sentences and sophisticated meanings. In this chapter, we examined several different theories of how they did so. None of these theories stands alone either in the position it takes—we have seen how certain beliefs are shared by different theories—nor in its ability to tell us how children acquire language—we have seen that there are cases to be made against each one. Indeed, if anyone could tell us with any certainty how children do accomplish what they do in language learning, we would not need this lengthy description of theory for we would have entered into the realm of fact.

Teachers and students of language are sometimes uncomfortable with the uncertainty inherent in theory. Faced with the reality of teaching children and all the decisions that entails, they prefer hard truths. Unfortunately, the hard truth is hard to come by in this field, and so for the time being we must settle for something less. Yet we are not working entirely in the dark. We have the benefit of an abundance of quality data about children learning language and we have the privilege and the ability to consider those data and the theories which they either support or refute within our own observations and experiences as teachers of young children.

My own bias, based on my experience as a teacher, linguist, and researcher, is toward the social interactive view of language. I have witnessed the growth of oral and written language in children in schools, growth directly attributable to the interaction among children and between children and teachers. Nowhere is the importance of social interaction more obvious than in the ESL children. Social interaction is, in brief, a theory through which we can usefully view children's language growth in the school years.

QUESTIONS FOR DISCUSSION

1. The information processing approach bears a striking resemblance to models of computer processing. Computer languages have existed since the invention of

computers. Computer-generated speech has been with us for years. What are the essential differences between computer languages, computer-generated speech and human language?

2. How would social interactionists account for the normal language acquisition of a hearing child brought up by deaf parents?

3. Keeping in mind that a theory must account for all the data of language acquisition, can you think of language data that any of the theories identified in this chapter would have difficulty accounting for?

4. What is the problem faced by behaviorism's attempt to explain the acquisition of meaning in terms of classical conditioning?

5. What is the relevance of the distinction between deep and surface structure to the nativist theory of language acquisition?

6. Which, if any, of these theories would seem most easily generalizable to second language learning?

7. Does the case of Genie offer evidence for or against the social interactionist theory?

CHAPTER SEVEN

Michael's Miracle

LANGUAGE DISORDERS IN MONOLINGUAL AND BILINGUAL CHILDREN

Children such as Quy, Lucy, and Jani are in a real sense linguistically blessed. By the time they are a few years into their schooling, they have two languages, and as we have seen there is no reason why their bilingualism should be anything but an asset in the educational process. Unfortunately, not all children are blessed in this way. Some are born with or acquire disorders that inhibit their ability to learn or to function in language. Children may have physical disabilities that impair their language ability in varying degrees, and others have emotional or learning disorders that make language learning especially challenging. A complete description of the disabilities and disorders that may have an impact on language and learning is beyond the scope of this book. Besides, there are excellent ones devoted entirely to the topic. Some familiarity with the nature of language disorders is, however, necessary for teachers and anyone else interested in children's language and learning. In this chapter, we will focus on the more common communicative disorders that teachers may encounter.

We begin with an overview of four broad categories of language disorders and conclude the chapter with the story of a child with a somewhat unusual language disorder. Michael is a child with what might be called induced language delay. His is a type of disorder that affects a small number of bilingual children whose parents are not part of the dominant language and culture. In attempting to understand Michael's language development, we come to an even greater appreciation of the importance of environment. The final section of the chapter will consist of a brief discussion of the problems associated with diagnosing language disorders, particularly in bilingual children.

There are a number of ways to organize a discussion of language disorder or disability. The two most common classifications are according to apparent cause and according to effect on the language output of the child. The first entails an examination of the language problems encountered by children with particular disorders—hearing impairment, for example, or cognitive disabilities. The second entails an examination of aspects of the language produced—voice quality, for example, or problems with the rate or rhythm of speech. However we structure our discussion, we are really talking about a continuum of dysfunction, from severe disorders resulting in total non-communication to relatively mild disorders such as hoarseness of voice or an inability to produce sibilants.

Few disorders are linked to a single cause. Although certain disabilities tend to result in certain language dysfunctions, the same problem, or symptom, occurring in two children may have entirely different and unrelated causes. For these reasons, I have chosen to organize the discussion around descriptions of particular language disorders. Before doing so, however, it is important to mark an important distinction between communicative disorders and communicative differences.

Disorder or Difference?

Communicative disorders result in speech that is so defective that it interferes with one's ability to convey messages clearly and effectively during interactions with community members who speak the same language and dialect (Mattes & Omark, 1984, p. 2). Children with communicative disorders should receive remedial assistance, but children with communicative differences do not require, and in fact could be adversely affected by, attempts at remediation. Communicative differences are variations from the language norm of the community that arise out of dialect or language differences. Obviously, where the norm of the community is a particular dialect or a particular language, communicative differences are likely to appear in bilingual, bicultural children. We have already seen that the phonology of children's first language may temporarily influence their pronunciation of the second. Indeed, certain pronunciations are expected and almost legendary, such as the l/r confusion experienced by many Asian learners of English. But we also find language differences among speakers of the same language. There is, or should be, a wide range of acceptability that permits certain of these differences—such as both the British and the American pronunciation of *erudite*. We must not label as *disorder* those things that are only *different*, for the latter

1. may be developmental and will change as the child becomes more proficient in the language, or
2. may not need to be changed.

Certainly, dialect should not be confused with disorder. If children demonstrate any speech behavior or language use that others in their peer group or ethnic community also demonstrate, then it is obvious that their language is not disordered but different. Theirs is a legitimate means of expression and not in need of remediation. The child,

Bob, whom we encounter in Chapter 10, is a good example of a child whose English, though not standard, is the English of his community. He is confused by attempts at correction. Different language should, in other words, be left alone.

The distinction between disorder and difference may seem obvious, but it is not one that is always made. Bilingual children with imperfect command of English (i.e., the language of the school) are too often counted as functionally handicapped because their communicative ability is "impaired." That this impairment is really only a developmental stage escapes the notice of some educators who send these children to speech or language pathologists for remediation. Of course, bilingual children may have language disorders, but they are no more prevalent in the bilingual than in the monolingual population (although non-mainstream children are more often referred for intervention) and especial care must be taken in diagnosing language dysfunction in bilingual children.

Four Types of Communicative Disorder

The most common communicative disorders that a teacher is likely to encounter are related to:

1. voice production,
2. fluency,
3. articulation of particular sounds, and
4. language processing.

Each type may occur with varying degrees of severity and in both monolingual and bilingual children. We will consider each in turn.

Voice Disorders

Any non-temporary affliction that affects the quality of the voice is considered a voice disorder. Conditions such as chronic hoarseness not caused by colds or laryngitis, extreme breathiness or hypernasality *may* be classified as voice disorders. In severe cases, the pitch, volume, and timbre of the voice may be so distorted that the speaker is unintelligible. In milder cases, the vocal quality may simply be inappropriate to the speaker's age or sex or to the situation but impede intelligibility only slightly.

Essentially, there are two types of vocal disorder: those associated with phonation, or abnormalities in the vibration of the vocal folds, and those associated with resonance, or abnormalities in the modification of the sound as it passes through the vocal tract. Excessive breathiness and hoarseness would be examples of phonation problems while excessive nasality would be a resonance disorder. There are a number of causes of vocal disorders, but only about one-third of them anatomical or neurophysiological. Most have other causes such as emotional stress or abuse of the vocal apparatus caused by excessive use of the voice, in singing, speaking, or shouting. Such abuse may result in a temporary physical disorder such as nodules or ulcers on the vocal folds, but treatment other than rest is not usually required.

Teachers need not worry about the accurate diagnosis of a vocal disorder, because there are competent professionals to do that. Their main concern is in detecting that a vocal disorder might exist, a task that might not be as straightforward as it sounds. As Mattes and Omark caution, even vocal disorders come with cultural values and biases attached. Cultures vary, for instance, in the degree of breathiness or nasality they consider normal or acceptable in speech. For this reason, educators should exercise some caution in deciding which conditions should be remediated. A sensible guideline is to refer those conditions which result in reduced intelligibility or which are esthetically displeasing to the others in the child's own culture (1984, p. 2). It would not be possible, then, for a teacher who is a member of the dominant culture to determine the effect on members of the child's culture. Whenever possible, bilingual children should be tested for vocal disorders in their first language. Otherwise, it may not be possible to distinguish certain normal first language vocal behaviors from those that may indicate a disorder. In general, classroom teachers need not worry about making an accurate diagnosis of vocal disorder. If there is something unusual about a child's vocal quality which persists and which is not apparent in others of the child's peer group, then the child should be referred to a speech or language pathologist or the family physician. A true voice disorder should affect both languages, but since teachers cannot be sure whether the child is transferring first language vocal habits to English, they should make every effort to have an assessment done in the child's native language.

Fluency Disorders

Children with fluency disorders have difficulty in speaking rapidly and continuously. They usually speak with an abnormal rate, rhythm, or both. The best known of the fluency disorders is stuttering, but there are others which impede the comprehensibility of speech. One of these is cluttering, a less common disorder involving the excessively rapid production of speech. Children with this disorder are "unable to control their speech rate, and as a result introduce distortions of rhythm and articulation into their speech" (Crystal, 1987, p. 278). Unlike stutterers, they also seem largely unaware that their speech is either partly or totally unintelligible to the listener.

There are a great many theories, but at this time there is no consensus about the cause of fluency disorders. Physical origins have been suggested as have psychological and neurological ones. Fortunately, treatment programs are in advance of theory; a great many programs and methods exist for the treatment of stuttering, in particular. For the classroom teacher, the most important issue is not the treatment of fluency disorders but referring children who require it.

Children learning their first language frequently experience a temporary fluency dysfunction. The most common symptom is lengthy hesitation and it occurs typically in children around the age of 3, although it can affect speakers of any age. Most people, when speaking under pressure, will find themselves pausing as they search for an elusive word or repeating themselves unnecessarily. Care must be taken to distinguish both developmental and temporary stress-induced disfluency from the type which may be a true pathology.

Care must also be taken, as in the diagnosis of voice disorders, to assure that bilingual children are correctly diagnosed. Once again, there is the possibility that what appears to be a dysfunction may be only a difference caused by either the transfer of first language speech and cultural patterns to the new language or by limited proficiency in English. While neither severe stuttering nor cluttering are culturally induced, it is the case that not all cultures take the view of stuttering that we do. Mattes and Omark report that cultures differ in their views about what should be remediated. North American Cowichans sometimes view stuttering as supernatural, for example, and some other cultures are far more accepting of fluency differences (Mattes & Omark 1984, p. 4).

A more common diagnostic problem occurs with bilingual children. Children learning English as a second language, for instance, may speak with hesitations, false starts, and frequent repetitions that impede the easy flow of speech. These occur when the child has difficulty in thinking of the appropriate word in English, or perhaps doesn't know it, or when the child is in any way unsure of the language. It would be a mistake to classify these developmental differences as fluency disorders; they will in all likelihood disappear as the child learns more of the language.

Articulation Disorders

Articulation disorders comprise a wide range of problems. At one end of the spectrum are difficulties with the pronunciation of a particular sound that have little impact on intelligibility. Lisping is an example of one of these milder disorders. At the other end are phonological systems that are so severely impaired that speech is totally incomprehensible. Sometimes these disorders result from serious injury to the brain. Children with disorders of this magnitude are easily identified and referred for treatment. The more problematic case for classroom teachers is children whose misarticulations are minor and may not need remediation because they are developmental.

As we saw in Chapter 3, although the phonological system is largely in place by the time a child is school aged, there may be certain distinctions still to be worked out. A few children may still produce [w] for [l], for [r], or for both even after they have begun school. Usually, these three sounds are acquired by the age of 4, but occasionally the distinction is not worked out until a year or so later even though speech is normal in all other ways. As Crystal (1987) has noted, "many of the pronunciation problems that cause parental concern are due to a general delay in the ability to control movements" (p. 277). Delay is not the same as deviance. If we find that a child's pronunciation is different from her peers', then there are two possibilities. If the school-aged child's phonological system appears to be essentially the same as that of a younger normal child, then it is not deviant but simply delayed. It is simply a matter of slower development than is usual. But if there are "patterns of acquisition that never appear in a young normal child," then "we can say the child has a deviant system" (Ingram, 1976, p. 98). In the case of phonological deviance, the child should be referred for remediation. The speech therapist or language pathologist will be able to distinguish delayed from deviant speech if the teacher is in doubt about the cause of a child's mispronunciation.

Bilingual children may present particular diagnostic problems. Because articulation disorders may result from regular but different phonological processes, there is a possibility that a bilingual child will experience interference between the sound systems of the first and the second languages. This is one reason that some children learning English as their second language pronounce words differently from monolingual English speakers. It has been observed, for example, that French children sometimes substitute [d] or [t] for the *th-* sounds in English. It is thought that this is because French has no *th-* sound. Spanish and many other Romance languages simply have fewer consonant and vowel sounds than English, and thus speakers of these learning English must learn additional sounds. While they are doing so, they may substitute related sounds, either from English or from their own language, for a time. Another type of phonological difference can occur when two languages have the same sound or sounds but produce them slightly differently. Portuguese, for example, has the [p] sound, but it is not aspirated as it is at the beginning of English words. When a Portuguese speaker produces a [p] in the manner of Portuguese, it may sound more like a [b] to an English speaker.

The distribution of sounds in words differs between languages and contributes to some of the articulation problems experienced by non-native speakers. In Mandarin, for example, the only consonants occurring in word-final position are nasals. Chinese children may, thus, leave off final consonants that are not nasal. The important point for the teacher to remember is that in children, these articulation problems are developmental and will be overcome as the child becomes more proficient in the language. Although certain techniques that speech therapists use *may* be useful with ESL learners whose developmental errors persist, these children should not, as a rule, be referred for therapy.

The question arises, then, of how the classroom teacher knows which pronunciation problems are indicative of an articulation disorder. We return to the criteria discussed above. Bilingual children should be assessed in their native language and referred for therapy only if an articulation disorder is present in that language. If first-language assessment is not possible (if, for example, one cannot find a Cowichan speaker in Boston), then the teacher should proceed under the assumption that there is no articulation disorder. If the child's pronunciation remains heavily distorted over an extended period (more than a year for a child in kindergarten, Grade 1, or 2 or more than 2 years if the child is older), a speech therapist might be able to do a complete profile of the child's English phonology and make some reasonable guess about the causes of the pronunciation problems. Happily, young children tend to acquire native-like pronunciation fairly easily. Bilingual children may have difficulty with English pronunciation because they have had relatively less exposure and opportunity to practice it, but they are no more prone to articulation disorders than the monolingual population.

Language Disorders

Also known as language disability, language disorder refers to "any systematic deviation in the way people speak, listen, read, write, or sign that interferes with their ability to communicate with their peers" (Crystal, 1987, p. 264). As with voice, fluency and articulation disorders, language disability covers a wide spectrum of dysfunction and may affect the structure, content, or use of language. The causes are varied, but in a large proportion of cases, there are clearly physical origins. Brain damage, causing mental or physical disability that may have a serious effect on language skills, and deafness are the two principal physical impairments underlying language disorders.

The disorders themselves vary in severity and in the level of language they affect. Language impairments that result from specific brain damage are collectively called aphasias. Aphasia refers to the loss of ability to use and understand language and excludes language disorders associated with other physical conditions such as deafness. Although there are a number of different kinds of aphasia corresponding to the particular area of the brain that is damaged, they can be broadly classified into *receptive*, *expressive*, and *global aphasias.*

Receptive aphasia, also called *sensory aphasia* or *Wernicke's aphasia*, results from a lesion to a region in the upper back part of the temporal lobe of the brain called Wernicke's area. People suffering from this type of aphasia typically exhibit no articulation difficulty or disfluency. In fact, their language may be characterized by excessive fluency. What is affected is comprehension, and as a result, speech may be marked by repeated patterns or formulaic phrases, by unintelligible sequences of words, or odd combinations of words or even phonemes. Sufferers of receptive aphasia may also experience problems in retrieving words from memory (Crystal, 1987, p. 271).

Expressive aphasia is also known as *motor aphasia* and as *Broca's aphasia*, after the French neurologist who found that damage to the lower back part of the frontal lobe interferes with speaking ability. Patients with expressive aphasia suffer severe impairment to their articulation and fluency. Speech is often very slow and labored, with many hesitations and disturbances in the individual sounds and in the prosodic features of the utterance. Sentences tend to be very short and telegraphic in structure, composed of few words with little attention to the requirements of grammar. In contrast to receptive aphasics, expressive aphasics have little difficulty with comprehension.

In patients with global aphasia, the symptoms of expressive and receptive aphasia are combined. They have minimal speech capability and their comprehension is also very limited. Because the prognosis for recovery, or even for significant improvement, is poor, this type of aphasia is sometimes known as "irreversible aphasia syndrome" (Crystal, 1987, p. 271).

The diagnosis and treatment of aphasic children rests beyond the expertise and responsibility of classroom teachers. Most school systems provide specialists to whom children can be referred in the unlikely case that they have not been identified before they reach school age. It would not be unlikely, on the other hand, for teachers to encounter children with some degree of hearing impairment, since an estimated 6–7% of the population suffers some degree of hearing loss. Again, there are specially trained speech and language pathologists available in most districts to provide advice, but some knowledge of developmental trends in deaf children's language is useful for all teachers.

We saw in earlier chapters that the language environment is essential to language acquisition. Children need to hear language and have opportunities to use it. Hearing impaired children have been deprived, in varying degrees depending on the severity of their hearing loss, of the sensory input of language. Without that input, they will not develop speech.

Children who are born with hearing impairment that limits their perception of sounds to those exceeding 60 decibels (dB), or about the intensity level of a baby's cry, generally will not be able to develop spontaneous oral language that approximates that of hearing children. Children born with losses exceeding 90 dB are considered deaf and will not develop speech and language skills spontaneously (without educational and therapeutic intervention) (Ratner, 1989, p. 370).

In general, there is a correspondence between the severity of the loss and the degree of language disability. In other words, when children can hear only a limited range of the sounds produced in normal speech, they will likely develop speech that is difficult to understand. The greater the degree of deafness, the more distorted the pronunciation. If the hearing loss is only minor, though, children will benefit from most of the language around them. They may not hear whispering or softly spoken language from a distance or outside their line of vision, but in most ways their language will develop more or less normally.

As Ratner points out, an articulatory disability is less influential on children's school success than are disabilities in syntax and semantics that directly influence their ability to develop proficiency in reading and writing. "Over the years, repeated surveys of the reading abilities of older deaf children and adults suggest that their reading ability may never surpass that of 4th- to 5th- grade hearing children (Hammermeister, 1972; Trybus & Karchmer, 1977)" (cited in Ratner, 1989, pp. 373–374). Other studies point to an incomplete grasp of syntax as the reason underlying the reading problem. Some of the syntactic problems that deaf children have are similar to those experienced by normally-developing hearing children. But they also have particular problems with the verb phrase—in particular, modals and other auxiliary verbs as well as infinitives (e.g., *To see is to believe*) and gerunds (e.g., *Seeing is believing*). Other syntactic structures that cause problems in comprehension include negation, question formation, relativization and complementation (structures such as *Mother went shopping* or *She saw the man driving*). Deaf children are more likely to produce sentences such as:

Sheila take the cat no. (negation)

Who the girl take the cat? (question formation)

I saw the girl that the girl took it. (relativization)

Mommy goes to shopping. (complementation).

Because language disorders of this severity are caused by a dysfunction in the process underlying the surface production of *any* language, children with more than one language will have all their languages affected. It is not possible for a systemic language disorder of this fourth type to affect only one of a bilingual's languages. It is, thus, important for teachers who suspect systemic disorders in bilingual children to have their language evaluated in both languages.

Language Problems of Bilingual Children

When bilingual children were studied earlier in this century, researchers were mainly interested in how bilingualism facilitated or interfered with language development. Many of these studies concluded that monolinguals performed better than bilinguals on measures with one language only. Bilingual French/English children would, for example, perform worse on tests of either English or French than would monolingual children taking language-appropriate tests. Bilinguals were found to have smaller vocabularies (Saer, 1922; Grabo, 1931; Barke & Parry-Williams, 1938) and to make more grammatical errors (Carrow, 1957; Smith, 1933, 1935 all cited in Abudarham, 1980, p. 236). The flaw in these studies was that most of them considered only one of the bilingual's languages or each language separately. They did not consider the totality of the language system of the bilingual, that is, the full communicative capacity provided by the two languages (Abudarham, 1980, p. 236). Yet researchers all too often reached the conclusion that bilingualism was a disadvantage to the child. As Macnamara wrote, "there is some firmly grounded evidence indicating that the bilinguals have a weaker grasp of language than monoglots" (Macnamara, 1966, cited in Abudarham, 1980, p. 236). More recent research has attempted to correct this flaw by testing bilinguals' proficiency in both their languages. These studies have been useful in affirming the linguistic normality of bilinguals, but they have not provided specific measures to be used to diagnose language disorders in bilingual children.

Any language disability which can affect monolingual children can also affect bilinguals. On the other hand, educators have identified certain language problems associated *only* with bilingual children. It has been noted, for example, that children being educated in a second language are usually successful when their native language is the dominant language of the community (Cummins, 1979a). This is the case, for example, with English-speaking children in French immersion programs. In contrast, children whose native language is a minority language fare less well in school. It has also been noted that some children seem to enjoy cognitive advantages tied to their bilingualism while others do not (Peal & Lambert 1962 cited in Edelsky et al., 1983) and that older children being educated in a non-native setting are generally more successful than younger ones (Toukomaa & Skutnabb-Kangas, 1977, cited in Edelsky et al., 1983).

To explain these somewhat contradictory observations, Canadian researchers Jim Cummins and Merrill Swain proposed the distinction between cognitive academic language and language used for most interpersonal communication. They suggested that school success is more closely related to children's cognitive academic language proficiency (CALP) than to their proficiency with the language used for social interaction (tested for by the BICS). Cummins also developed two hypotheses, the threshold hypothesis and the developmental interdependence hypothesis which, along with BICS and CALP, were intended to account for the differences in school success among bilingual children. According to the threshold hypothesis, a second language learner must attain "a certain 'threshold' level of proficiency . . . in that language before the learner can benefit from the use of the language as a medium of instruction in school" (Richards, Platt, & Weber, 1985, p. 293). Cummins also asserts that the level of proficiency children attain in the second language "depends upon the level of proficiency the child learner has reached in the first language at the time when extensive exposure begins" (Richards, Platt, & Weber, 1985, p. 293). This is the interdependence hypothesis.

Minority children who come to school without having attained cognitive academic language proficiency in at least one of their languages are supposedly educationally at risk. Children who begin school with neither CALP nor BICS are sometimes labeled as semilingual. Although the term is no longer widely used in North America, semilingual is used in Europe, principally in Scandinavia, to refer to bilingual children who have not mastered either of their languages "well enough to handle 'abstract cognitive/language' tasks involving 'meanings for abstract concepts, synonyms, etc. as well as vocabulary" (Skutnabb-Kangas & Toukomaa, cited in Cummins 1979a, p. 231).

Researchers such as Carole Edelsky and her colleagues (1983) and Martin-Jones and Romaine (1986) have pointed out, however, that the BICS and CALP distinction, the threshold hypothesis, the interdependence hypothesis and the assumption of semilingualism are dangerous and wrong. They are dangerous because they essentially constitute a "blame-the-victim" theory: bilingual children have trouble in school because of something they did not bring, namely the degree of proficiency in English which the school deems necessary. This view fails to recognize and to take advantage of the totality of the language that these children *do* bring. The two hypotheses and the label semilingual are often wrong because they rely on data from tests and test settings which are inadequate to assess children's language competence.

In general, school personnel test those aspects of language that they know how to test. These include pronunciation and vocabulary, frequently measured by worksheets and standardized tests. These fragments of language are quantified "without regard for their interrelationship with other levels of linguistic organization" (Martin-Jones & Romaine, 1986, p. 29), and in such a way that they tell us more about what children do *not* know than what they *do* know about language. Basing his claim on his own clinical experience in Britain, Abudarham (1980) asserts that standardized tests such as the Peabody Picture Vocabulary Test (PPVT) have "little, if any, diagnostic or prognostic value" with dual language children (pp. 231–232), in large part because they reveal deficits in the second language without tapping children's native language resources. The fact that such measures tell us little about what children know about language or what they can do with language does not deter well-intentioned educators from using them nor from reaching conclusions about bilingual children which may be faulty. As Martin-Jones and Romaine point out, most language tests given in schools "are only indirectly related to common sense notions of what it means to be a competent language user" (1986, p. 29). This being the case, it is easy to see the potential for abuse. As the authors point out, when notions like "the ability to extract meaning" become operationalized as scores on, for example, reading tests, a child who fails is then labeled as one who is "unable to extract meaning." Similarly, when the cognitive aspects of language are tested in terms of, say, being able to produce synonyms, then the child who can't is branded as "lacking in the cognitive aspects of language development" (Martin-Jones & Romaine, 1986, p. 29).

Once educators who make decisions on behalf of bilingual children get it into their heads that such things as mastering complex syntactic structures, providing synonyms on vocabulary lists and even correct spelling are valid indicators of language proficiency, they cease to question the real nature of language ability and how it might or might not be revealed by such measures. In a real sense, then, the explanation attempted by the BICS and CALP distinction and by the threshold and the interdependence hypotheses constitute a deficit theory. In other words, bilingual children's lack of success in the majority language and in school is attributed to that which they do *not* bring to school and not to any deficiency in the school's assessment of such children or in their curriculum for or teaching of bilingual children. With Native American and Inuit children, the problem may be especially acute.

Martha Crago (1990) points out that teachers and speech-language pathologists run the risk of misdiagnosing Inuit children because they fail to understand the role of cultural context in assessing children's communication with their caregivers. It is more important to understand the nature of this interaction than it is to measure their linguistic accomplishments in English before reaching any conclusion about the need for remediation. Studying the communicative interaction patterns of Inuit children and caregivers in northern Quebec, Crago found that three main themes described the accommodation adults made in communicating with young children. They included

1. child-centred accommodation . . . or "softening the world for the child,"
2. situation-centred accommodation or "strengthening the child for the world," and
3. the co-construction of communication without talk or "not always in words." (Crago, 1990, p. 78)

The third point is especially important when we compare Inuit accommodation with that of the dominant white culture. In the dominant culture, we tend to judge children's linguistic ability on production measures—how much they talk, the length of utterances, etc. In Inuit, the judgment is made on the basis of what children understand. "The ability to understand and to do what is asked is valued behavior. Inuit children are socialized in their society by encouraging them to follow directives" (Crago, 1990, p. 78).

Another significant difference that Crago noted between Inuit communicative behavior and that of the dominant culture is related to asking and answering questions. Studying two older and two younger mothers, she noted that on 80 hours of videotape there were few questions asked of the children. The older mothers, in fact, asked only one type of question, and that was "What's the matter?" asked only when their children cried. The younger mothers, perhaps reflecting more influence from the dominant culture, asked a wider range of questions, "test" questions such as "What's this?" and "How old are you?" This finding is significant for teachers because it means that the kinds of questions routinely asked in school by dominant culture teachers will be unfamiliar to many of the Inuit children (p. 80).

Crago offers four concrete suggestions for teachers or speech-language pathologists to use when developing a strategy for dealing with other cultures. The following are based on her research in Inuit communities but generalizable to other minority groups.

1. Language disorders in children need to be defined according to the norms of their community. For example, verbal expressive behavior in Inuit children has a different role than it does in white middle-class North American culture. Appropriate comprehension and listening skills are as important to Inuit children as appropriate talking is. In language and speech assessments and in intervention, task formats that involve comprehension and repetition are likely to work well. In addition, since children are not expected to be involved in extended conversation with adults, language samples that are elicited by an adult may not be representative of a child's abilities. Better results might be obtained from sampling children's language in situations where they talk and play with each other.

2. It is strongly recommended that community personnel be trained to do assessments and intervention. Such training should take the form of resource collaboration with both professional speech-language pathologists and native speakers sharing their knowledge and experience with each other.

3. Intervention strategies must be designed to fit the cultural patterns of the community. This is particularly true in training caretakers. In many cultures, siblings, maternal grandmothers or others may be as important to the intervention process as the parents. The communicative interactional content of intervention also needs to stress when not to talk as well as when and how to talk. Intervention and assessments involving such practices as labelling, answering test questions, making event-cases, and learning to question do not appear to be culturally appropriate.

4. Clinical intervention with children must be based on a clear understanding of the kind of children parents are trying to raise and appreciation for why they are doing so. The socialization of children to their culture is an important and delicate process into which language is tightly interwoven. The violation of native people's cultural and socialization practices by a lack of acceptance of the importance of this relationship prevents the formulation of appropriate intervention and assessment strategies. Practitioners of speech-language pathology need to address this issue forthrightly by actively seeking information on the cultures that they serve. (Crago, 1990, p. 82)

Although she does not make the claim directly, Crago's research leads to the conclusion that there is a higher risk that Inuit children, indeed all bilingual children, will be misdiagnosed as having some kind of communicative or speech disorder than their monolingual dominant-cultural peers.

Nevertheless, from time to time a bilingual child will enter school with a particular language disability that is related to decisions made in the home. Such a child has severe and obvious difficulty communicating in *either* language and, in the past, would have been labeled as semilingual. Today, however, the term has such negative connotations that it has largely been abandoned in North America. Michael is such a child, and the story of his language development is revealing for what it says about the importance of language environment.

MICHAEL'S LANGUAGE DEVELOPMENT

Michael was in the same kindergarten class as Lucy, the child we met earlier. I first met him when I visited the class in September, about 2 weeks after the beginning of the school year. He was sitting on the floor with the other children listening as the teacher read "The Three Bears." He seemed to be engrossed in the activity and watched the teacher intently as he listened. He laughed when the other children laughed but otherwise remained silent. Many of the other children, in contrast, would respond to the teacher's occasional questions by calling out answers—"Goldilocks!"— or would comment on the familiar story. During that visit to the classroom, I met with the children individually to try to determine their level of English language proficiency. I sat at a table in the back of the classroom and called the children to me one at a time. When I called Michael's name, he looked up but did not move. Nor did he respond to my request to join me, although when I called his name a second time and motioned to him, he did come to the back of the room.

He sat quietly at the table, following my eyes with his as I talked to him. The only response he made to any of my questions was to give his name when I asked. I tried asking him the names of various objects—shoes, a book, his nose, his shirt, a picture of a bird—but he merely looked at me. I then tried to get him to repeat the names of these same objects. When he appeared not to understand the task, I demonstrated with another child. His repetitions were mostly highly nasalized monosyllables which sounded alike, something like "muh."

At the end of the day, I talked with the kindergarten teacher to try to learn something about Michael's background. Unfortunately, the ESL consultant who usually visited the homes of new pupils had not yet visited Michael's home and the kindergarten teacher knew very little about him. She thought it likely, given his last name, that his family spoke Italian at home but she had not been able to verify this. His registration card was only partly complete, and she was able to ascertain only that he was 4;5 and that he had one older sibling who was not in school. She reported that Michael seemed to enjoy coming to school, caused no problems in class, but had not spoken except to say his name when asked. He seemed very attentive and often smiled or laughed at the actions of the other children. Neither the teacher nor I was particularly concerned about his silence; we assumed that he was a beginner in English and we both knew that an extended silent period is quite normal in young second language learners.

Michael was absent during my next visit to the class, and it was nearly 3 weeks later when I saw him again. I could tell by the expression on his face that he remembered me and came immediately to my table when I called him. Once again he watched me closely and he seemed to understand more of what I said. He responded correctly when asked to name pictures of a house, a bear and a bed from "The Three Bears." He also responded "I don't know" when I asked him what a picture of a tree was and again when I showed him a picture of a bird and asked what it was. To the other questions he gave no response at all. In all his utterances, his pronunciation remained badly distorted. His teacher had learned nothing more about his background but told me that he was an even-tempered child who seemed to enjoy school, but as a watcher rather than a joiner. He seldom participated in his classmates' activities and waited patiently for crayons or toys to become available. He was still silent, speaking only when he was alone with his teacher and then only repeating the names of objects after her. She could recall no instance of his initiating speech.

Although I visited the class on a number of occasions during the next month, it was not until late November that I learned anything more about Michael. The ESL consultant had visited his home and had met both his father and mother whose native language was indeed Italian. The parents, she reported, spoke very limited English, but the father seemed to understand most of what she explained about the school's kindergarten and ESL programs. She also learned that Michael's grandmother lived with the family and that Michael had a teenaged sister who did not live at home. In short, she was able to learn very little more about Michael.

Michael's teacher, however, had happened to meet his sister and had learned from her more about Michael's background. His sister had been born in Italy and had moved with her family to Canada when she was 9 years old, 6 years before Michael was born. She said that she had found it very difficult to learn English, although it was the impression of the teacher that she spoke fluently and with no foreign accent. She struggled through school, a fact which caused her parents a great deal of anxiety, but eventually completed high school. At that point, when Michael was approximately 2;6, she left home and had only infrequent contact—perhaps once a week—with her younger brother. Before she left and occasionally when she returned to visit the family, she would read aloud to Michael, although infrequently, and sometimes played children's records for him. When the teacher asked her which language she used in communicating with Michael, she gave an answer that was extremely revealing. English, she said, was the only language that her parents permitted to be used with Michael.

Convinced that their daughter's problems in school were a result of her limited English proficiency, his parents had determined that Michael would learn *only* English. Unfortunately, they spoke very little English themselves and his contact with his sister and her English-speaking friends was minimal. According to his sister, Michael understood Italian and spoke a few words, but his parents discouraged conversation in that language and Michael seemed content to listen. They did not read to him in Italian and could not read to him in English, although they did provide a number of English-language children's books and records for him. Michael's teacher found this last observation especially interesting because she had observed that he seemed to be familiar with some of the songs played or sung in class even though he never joined in singing them.

To complicate Michael's learning of English even further, both his parents worked outside the home and he was left in the care of his paternal grandmother who spoke no English at all. She had been instructed not to speak Italian to Michael because the parents were adamant that Michael not learn Italian. Very likely, she did speak some Italian to the child, for it is hard to imagine that she would love and care for him in total silence. But whatever communication occurred between grandmother and grandson was not sufficient for him to acquire a functional first language, at least so far as we were able to determine.

From this time in November until the end of the school year, I took especial care to observe and to document Michael's language learning. During that time, there were many occasions on which I was disheartened, convinced that Michael was making no progress at all. He was always attentive in class and in conversation with me, but he rarely spoke except in private conversation with his teacher or with me. At various points in the year, when I compared his language development with that of the other ESL children in the class, I could see that Michael's vocabulary was extremely limited, his sentences short and filled with errors which the other children had either not made or had long since stopped making, and his pronunciation, though improved, still greatly distorted. At the end of the school year, his teacher, the ESL consultant and I agreed that Michael was not ready to go into Grade 1 in the coming term. His oral language development lagged so far behind that of his peers that it seemed highly unlikely that he would be ready to cope with the demands of literacy in 3 short months, particularly if he had little practice in English in the summer months. Unfortunately, the ESL consultant had made little headway in convincing Michael's parents to speak and read Italian to him, so it seemed likely that Michael's exposure to *any* language would be curtailed during the school break.

When the school year ended, then, my assessment of Michael's language learning and my prognosis for future language development was not a positive one. As I began to listen to the tape recordings and read the transcripts from the previous 9 months, however, my assessment of his progress changed. At the end of May, Michael's language, when compared with other children in the class, seemed painfully underdeveloped. But as I retraced his growth during the year by listening to the tapes and reading the transcripts, I realized that he had made a great deal of progress. His rate of development and the degree of fluency he had attained by June were well below those of any other child in the class, but when I considered his language on its own merits, I could see growth. His pronunciation, which in the fall had been almost unintelligible, retained some distortion but was intelligible and showed improvement every month. Even at the end of the school year, when he added a new word to his vocabulary, the pronunciation would initially be highly distorted but would soon improve. In other areas of language, Michael showed more impressive growth. His comprehension, accuracy (both in syntax and in choice of words), fluency, and communicative competence all improved dramatically over the school year.

Comprehension

For kindergarten-aged children, comprehension refers only to the understanding of oral language and not written language. It is usually gauged by assessing their verbal and non-verbal responses to the language they hear. Throughout the school year, Michael's teacher had administered the Bilingual Syntax Measure (BSM). The BSM is a test sometimes used to assess English language proficiency in children from about kindergarten through about Grade 3. It consists of a set of simple, brightly colored pictures and questions designed to elicit certain grammatical structures such as tense markers, plurals, and possessives, as well as more complex forms such as the present perfect and conditionals. While this is not a test designed to measure comprehension, it was very clear in the early attempts to administer the test to Michael that he did not understand the questions. For example, in January, his response to the question, "What is the mommy bird going to do with the worm?" was "Eat it." But the picture makes it abundantly clear that she is going to give it to her baby birds. Thinking that he may have meant that the baby birds were going to eat the worm, I asked him "Who will eat the worm?" to which he replied by pointing to the mother bird. In March, however, and again in June, his responses, "She's give them food" and "Give it to babies," indicated that he had understood the question.

The same pattern appeared in his responses to the question "Why is the dog looking at the king?" the expected answer to which is "Because he's hungry" (the dog, that is). In November, Michael responded "Doggy looking that turkey." In January, he responded "Cause he eat, him eat," which may have indicated correct comprehension and problems with sentence formation. But it was clear in March that he could both understand the question and produce the appropriate response: "Because him hungry."

The evidence from the BSM would not be adequate for assessing Michael's level of comprehension. In Michael's case, however, his difficulty in comprehension was apparent for several months in much of the interaction between Michael and me and between Michael and his teacher. But the same improvement which appeared in his performance on the BSM was also evident in other situations of language use. While it is sometimes difficult to distinguish comprehension errors from production errors—in other words, to know whether a child hasn't understood what is said or does not know how to respond appropriately—it is certain that no language development would have taken place over the school year unless he had first experienced improved comprehension. Learners' ability to speak a second language nearly always lags behind their understanding of it.

Accuracy

One of the problems in evaluating how much a child's accuracy in using the language has improved is this confounding of accuracy with comprehension. With the BSM, however, this problem is minimized through the use of simple, unambiguous pictures and by the teacher's assuring before beginning the procedure that the child knows the names for the objects and the actions portrayed. In assessing Michael's accuracy in answering the BSM questions, once it was clear that he understood them, it was obvious that he responded with semantic accuracy long before he had mastered syntactic accuracy. The excerpts in Table 7.1 illustrate this point.

All of Michael's talk with adults and his infrequent spontaneous speech were marked by the same kinds of grammatical errors as his responses to the BSM. What is more interesting, however, is the fact that his grammatical system at any one time seemed to be mostly consistent. It would be surprising if a child acquiring a second language were to manifest a completely stable grammar, especially for an extended period of time. As language learners are exposed to more and more language, they figure out the rules more accurately and their grammars undergo changes. This is the central claim of the interlanguage hypothesis that we examined in Chapter 4, and it is certainly true for Michael. We can see an example of his grammar in transition in two of

Table 7.1   Selected Answers and Responses to BSM by Michael

Question	Response
What is the mommy bird going to do with the worm?	She's give them food. (March)
Why's he so fat?	Because him eat too lots. (June)
And why's he so skinny?	Because he was eating. (March)
	Because he's not eating. (June)
Why are their eyes closed?	Because them go bed. (March)
Why do you think she's so happy?	Her like it outside. (June)
Why do you think this man lives in this house?	Because him house is fat. (March)

the answers in Table 7.1. He says at one point "Because him eats too lots" and a few minutes later, "Because he's not eating." The third person subject pronoun is an unstable form for Michael at this time, most likely because he was in the process of modifying his previous grammar, which used "him" and "her" in subject position. This is a process which began earlier and which was well underway by June. The following September, I went back to the school to find out whether a number of the observations and predictions I had made about Michael's language growth had been accurate. I found out that when he returned to school in September, he had sorted out the distinction for both the masculine and feminine pronouns.

Fluency

In second language acquisition, fluency refers to the ability to produce language with relative ease and to communicate ideas effectively. Fluency has little to do with either grammatical accuracy or correct pronunciation unless severe deficiency in either impedes the flow of language. There are a number of ways of measuring fluency, including the number of times a child initiates speech. We have already seen why this might provide us with faulty information with certain minority groups. With Michael, this measure would indicate no fluency at all. In his case, a rough indication was obtained simply by counting and comparing the number of words produced in response to the same set of questions over time. In November, the 21 questions of the BSM elicited 28 words in response, or an average of 1.33 words per response. By January, the number of words jumped to 52, or an average of 2.48, and by June there was an increase to 69 for an average of 3.29. During the school year, then, there was an appreciable increase in fluency as indicated by the number of words produced in this highly controlled situation. With a great deal of prompting and the use of a picture book, Michael was able to tell me the story of "The Three Bears."

Terry Piper: Will you tell me a story Michael? What do you see?
Michael: The girl leaving in . . . (long pause)
T: What is the girl doing?
M: Leaving in bear bed.
T: What's she doing now?

M: Look in kitchen.
T: And what's she doing here?
M: Her (unintelligible) chair.
T: What did she do to the chair?
M: Wreck chair.
T: Right! And now what's she doing?
M: Sleepin' in bed now.
T: Yes?
M: That's the end.
T: No, not yet. What are these?
M: Those are bear.
T: What are they doing?
M: Them, them, this—the girl eat them.
T: What's this bear doing?
M: Him (unintelligible)
T: What?
M: That girl eat again.
T: What's happening here?
M: That bear—her sleeping on her bed.
T: And now what's the girl doing?
M: (unintelligible) out window.
T: Yes. And what are the bears doing?
M: Lookin' out. (long pause)
T: Is that the end?
M: Yeah.

Michael's telling of the story took a great deal of effort both for him and for me, but eventually he more or less got it told. This is not by any means a fluent telling for a child at the end of the kindergarten year, but when we recall that Michael did not speak at all in September, we have to count his hesitant retelling of "The Three Bears" as significant progress. Nevertheless, as a comparison, it is useful to read Lucy's retelling of the same story at approximately the same time (p. 133).

We find much more fluency in Lucy's rendering of the story. Where Michael had to be prompted into speech that came haltingly and in small quantity, the language seemed to pour from Lucy. Her telling also had flawed syntax but once she got involved in her narrative, she told it coherently, using adverbial connectives to maintain continuity.

Other samples of Michael's speech showed the same pattern and rate of growth in fluency—steady but very, very slow. Improved fluency results from improved comprehension and productive ability, but it is also related to a somewhat amorphous aspect of language ability, namely communicative competence. We have seen that language acquisition has its roots in the child's wish to make meaning, to communicate. As a child's need and desire to communicate grows, language learning takes place. The most important index of language learning, then, is the overall growth in communicative competence.

Communicative Competence

The ability to communicate competently involves more than the ability to form grammatically correct utterances. It includes knowing the rules of speaking, how to use and respond to requests, apologies, invitations, thanks, etc., and how to use language appropriately. Communicative competence is difficult to measure, but it is not difficult for a teacher or other observer with extensive opportunity to observe a child to reach a fairly accurate and useful conclusion about the child's level of communicative competence.

In Michael's case, there was little spontaneous speech from which to judge his communicative ability. Over the course of the school year, there was some growth. In March, the following dialogue was recorded.

Terry Piper: What are these children doing, Michael?
Michael: I need big dog.
T: Do you? Why?
M: 'Cause, mm, I leave my mom.
T: You need the dog when you leave your mom?
M: Yeah. Dog, mm, dog go school.
T: The dog would go to school with you?
M: Yeah.

As brief as it was, the exchange provided some evidence that Michael was increasing his repertoire of language functions. Michael declined to talk about the topic I introduced but used language instead to say something that he wanted to say. He was obviously trying to tell me about his wish for a dog and what that dog would do. The fact that he rarely initiated speech is not in itself an indication of poor communicative ability. We have already seen that there are many cultures in which such behavior is discouraged. It does suggest, however, that Michael was using only a limited number of the possible functions to which language can be put. The transcripts revealed a small number of spontaneous utterances, of Michael's using language to express his own meanings. As before, comparison with other second language learners in the class made Michael seem extremely reticent. Late in the year, however, an exchange took place with another child that suggested that he was beginning to use language for his own purposes. Three children, Rapinder, Jenny, and Michael were sitting together at a table during snack time. Jenny had brought a mandarin orange for her snack and Michael clearly craved it.

Michael: What dat?
Jenny: It's a mandarin. My mommy gave it to me.
Rapinder: I got apple.
M: Me too. You want? (offering it to Jenny)
J: No, I want this.
M: Me too. You take. (offering the apple again)
J: No. I want mandarin. (She begins to peel it.)

R: Michael want to trade.

M: Yeah. Want trade.

J: No. I give you one piece. (She continues to peel the mandarin and hands Michael a piece.)

M: Thank you.

It would be presumptuous and likely wrong to label Michael as a semilingual if for no other reason than we had no accurate indication of his proficiency in Italian. Moreover, his English was growing—very slowly, but growing. Nevertheless, Michael was obviously a child at risk in the educational system. Bilingual children with similar but usually less severe language problems do appear in elementary schools from time to time. It may be frustrating for educators who have no appropriate label for them to plan for their education, but it is possible and does not require administering sophisticated tests. In Michael's case, no standardized tests were attempted, and the only test administered was the Bilingual Syntax Measure. Even with this test, the results were not used to label, place, or plan instruction for the child. Rather, the teacher relied on information gathered from the parents, on her own experience of other children of the same age, on her direct observation of and conversation with the child, and on her professional common sense in planning language experiences for Michael. In the case of bilingual children, and particularly since language tests are of questionable validity anyway, it is perhaps a blessing that formal diagnostic tests do not exist. There is little doubt that if they did, a great many bilingual children would be wrongly diagnosed as having a language impairment when, in fact, their problems with language were merely developmental.

PRINCIPLES AND GUIDELINES FOR ASSESSING BILINGUAL CHILDREN

What Crago and other researchers have learned from their ethnographic research, Michael's teacher learned in her own classroom. She adopted and applied a principle that is very basic in assessing the language of bilingual children: No decision about a language disorder can be made without first assessing the child's entire linguistic repertoire. In bilingual children, this includes both languages and, in some children, the merger of the two. In Michael's case, it would have been impossible to begin to understand his language problems in school without benefit of the additional information about his situation at home. We saw that Michael suffered from delayed development in his first language, and it was not, therefore, surprising that he had a problem learning English as a second language. But we must also keep in mind the bilingual child who has normal first language development, which brings us to the second principle in assessing language disorders in bilingual children: If a child does not have a language disorder in the native language, then whatever communicative disorders which may be manifested in the second language cannot be a language disorder.

Once again, we see that assessment in the child's native language is important. But is it possible? There have been efforts to create language proficiency tests that can be standardized in two languages. In the United States, the Test of Auditory Comprehension of Language is standardized on a bilingual population in both English and Spanish. The problem with such a test, however, is that it measures the child's performance in each language independently and does not thus provide any indication of the child's overall language ability. As Abudarham (1980) points out, "If a child knows the correct response in the language not being currently tested, he is not credited with a positive score" (p. 239). Abudarham identifies another problem with most language tests used with bilingual learners. Because most language tests assume a developmental sequence, earlier test items are likely to use and test vocabulary appropriate to early childhood and later items will require vocabulary appropriate to older children, etc. For bilingual children who may have acquired their second language after early childhood, any early childhood words which appear on the test may be unfamiliar. They may well know other words, and they may also know words appropriate to their age at the time of testing, but their test results once again fail to reveal what they *do know.*

School personnel use tests because they are available, but also because they do not know of alternatives. Yet, if the tests are not providing reliable data, then they must be abandoned. But what is the alternative? We saw already how one teacher gathered information about the language background of one of the children in her class. Of course, not all teachers have access to such information. The following guidelines are intended to help educators in identifying language disorders in bilingual children.

1. Gather all possible information about the child's language background. Without intruding on the family's privacy, try to find out whether the child is a talker or is especially reticent, whether he or she has been read to and enjoys books, and the parents' attitude toward school. It is also useful to know whether the child has siblings and what languages are spoken by the child's playmates. Enlist a bilingual adult, ideally another teacher, or an older child if necessary.

2. Be careful in how you use the information you gather. Care should be taken not only to ensure the confidentiality of anything you learn about the child and family but also to interpret your findings fairly. This latter point is especially important. If you learn, for example, that the child says very little, do not jump to the conclusion that he or she doesn't have adequate knowledge of language. It may be that such behavior is normal within the child's cultural group, which brings us to the next point.

3. Whatever language behavior you observe should be compared to that of other bilingual children with similar cultural and language background. If you find even one other child who manifests the same or a similar phenomenon, then it is unlikely that you have uncovered a true disorder.

4. Expect second language learners to make grammatical errors. These may resemble errors made by first language learners at an earlier age or they may be unique to second language learners. In acquiring the system of the second language, learners often make generalizations about that system which are only partly true, but these do not constitute evidence of a language disorder. As an example, many Southeast Asians produce the tag "isn't it" in sentences such as

a. It is a beautiful day, isn't it?
b. It is time to go, isn't it?
c. She looks very beautiful, isn't it?

They have obviously made an error in their hypothesis about how tag questions are formed in English, but it is a common error among non-native learners of English. It is not evidence of a language disorder.

5. Under some circumstances, children may lose proficiency in their first language. It is not exposure to the second per se which leads to this loss. Rather, children who lose opportunities to use their first language may lose ground in that language. If, for example, a young Cree-speaking child moves with her family to the city and loses the extended family and Cree community, her Cree language *may* suffer. Surrounded by English, she no longer has the opportunities to use her own language that she once had. There is also pressure from the school to learn English. If school personnel manage to test her in the Cree language, especially after she has been away from the Cree community for a year or more, they may find that her language seems to be underdeveloped. But the school has failed once again, not only in their assumption of abnormal first language ability but in not measuring the *total* of the child's linguistic capability, that is, in Cree *and* English.

6. Remember that it is normal for some children to use *both* languages to communicate. Mattes and Omark (1984) differentiate between linguistic borrowing and code switching. The former occurs when speakers incorporate elements of one language into another, particularly words. An example of borrowing would be the use of a single word from one language in the sentence of another, and is especially common when the speaker does not know the word in the other language. The latter involves switching back and forth between languages but is not limited to individual words. A speaker may begin a sentence in one language and switch to another for a phrase and then back to the original. Both borrowing and code switching are normal phenomena in bilinguals. They represent a legitimate means of communication and should not be taken as evidence of a language disorder.

7. Look for possible cultural and language bias in any test or other instrument used to make decisions about bilingual children. In order to do this, it will be necessary to

8. Learn as much as possible about the traditional and contemporary lifestyles of the cultures that you encounter in your community. Try to understand, for example, the different patterns of human development within different cultures as well as their value systems and beliefs and assumptions about education. Remember, however, that

9. Each child is an individual whose own linguistic and cultural experiences will be to some degree unique. Do not assume that what you have learned about one child will always pertain to others from the same or similar background.

10. Finally, learn to trust your own judgment based on your experience with children of the same age. When there is a doubt about the child's language, adopt a wait-and-see attitude. Many patterns of second language learning are normal and it would be a mistake not to give a child adequate opportunity to learn with a friendly and facilitative classroom environment.

CONCLUSION

Children's need and wish to communicate is so great that they are frequently able to overcome severe disabilities to acquire language. In this chapter, we have looked briefly at some of the more common negative influences on language growth. We have also examined the case of a kindergarten child who was, as his teacher put it, "not quite as bilingual as he should be." The factors that had such a damaging effect on Michael's language serve as yet another reminder to us about the importance of the language environment. Tulips don't grow on rocks and language doesn't grow in the absence of language.

There is a danger that reading about Michael and the apparent causes of his problems will lead educators to the conclusion that bilingualism has the potential for causing severe language disorders. This is not the case, and to think of Michael's case as a warning is to miss the point. That point is, quite simply, that against the odds, and when judged in terms of what he *could* do with language rather than what he could *not* do, Michael made impressive gains in learning English.

The chapter concludes with a set of guidelines intended to help those who come into contact with bilingual children to make intelligent decisions about them and to treat them fairly. The guidelines are not intended as a program of intervention but rather as thought-provoking prerequisites to our educational planning.

QUESTIONS FOR DISCUSSION

1. The author writes that as a rule ESL children having pronunciation difficulty should not be referred for therapy. Why do you think this is true?

2. In her ethnographic study of how caregivers and children interact with one another in the Inuit culture, Martha Crago not only observed interactions but interviewed mothers. What kind of information could they provide that would be useful to teachers or language pathologists?

3. In the school in which Crago carried out her study, Inuktitut is the language of the school for the first 3 years (kindergarten through Grade 2). If there were suddenly an increase in the number of referrals to the language pathologist in Grade 3, what would you think was the cause?

4. Why do you think it is so prevalent for teachers to think of second language learners in terms of deficits, or what the students do *not* know about the language? Is there any real danger to teachers' holding that view?

5. According to British estimates in the early 1970s, between 2% and 3% of the total population of children require some sort of speech therapy. These figures include

preschool, ordinary, educationally sub-normal in both moderate and severe categories as well as children who are physically disabled. See Crystal, 1987, pp. 264–281 for further information. In an area of Canada with two significant minority populations, the number is approximately 15%. What possible reasons exist for such a deviation from the norm?

Post Script: Michael is in his early twenties today. He is working in the fisheries in northern British Columbia, having dropped out of school at the end of his Grade 10 year. His parents returned to Italy after Michael left school.

CHAPTER EIGHT

Language and the Society of Home and School

We concluded Chapter 6 by examining social interaction theories that emphasize the importance of environment and children's interaction with the people in their environment. One way of thinking about language development is to conceive of the child's social circle as an ever-widening one, starting with the mother and moving outward to encompass first the immediate and extended family, then other relatives and playmates, neighbors, shopkeepers, friends of siblings, and eventually, when the child reaches school age, teachers and all the other folk who populate schools. As that circle widens, so do the opportunities for and the demands on language.

Language develops within a social, interactional, and in the dominant English-speaking culture, conversational milieu. Few people would argue about the centrality of social situations in the acquisition of language, but if evidence were needed, we have only to look to autism. Autistic children seldom acquire speech even though many have normal intelligence. Suffering from a social interaction deficit, these children, to be blunt about it, have no reason to talk, and they do not. Children learn to talk because they live in a community of talkers in which membership to a large degree depends upon the ability to function with language.

As they learn language, children learn at the same time the social rules of language and how to manipulate or modify the use of these rules to fit the situation. In fact, it can be argued that outside literacy, the most dramatic language development of the school years is in pragmatics, or the appropriate use of language. Although, as we will see below, children begin school having developed at least some facility with all the functions of language, they are still rather limited in their conversational abilities. Through the school years and beyond, one of the principal tasks of language learning is learning the art of effective communication for a large variety of purposes and in many different situations. In this chapter, we will take a broad look at pragmatics, or how children learn the complex interaction of language and social situation. We will then look at sociolinguistic interaction within a defined set of language functions.

PRAGMATICS IN THE SCHOOL YEARS

Broadly speaking, the tasks facing children in the school years are to build conversational competence, to master the art of the narrative, and to meet the new cognitive demands of schooling. In the next chapter, we will look more closely at the cognitive demands of schooling. Here we will look primarily at the more social aspects of language learning in the school years, beginning with conversation. Building conversational competence involves learning to take into account the listener's perspective, becoming sensitive to relevance, learning to make conversational repairs, making indirect requests, and becoming socialized to gender-based linguistic differences.

Building Conversational Skills

Becoming sensitive to the listener's perspective is a prerequisite to effective conversation. Unless a speaker is aware of the listener's attention and comprehension, he is unable to structure his narrative or information in a way that makes sense to the listener. I was once traveling in China with a friend who did not have, as I had, experience teaching English as a second language. We got into a taxi outside our hotel one morning, and he gave directions to the taxi driver in English. The taxi driver obviously didn't understand, and we secured the assistance of the doorman. The driver, he said, had understood where we wanted to go; he just didn't know where it was. My companion responded that it was near and that he would direct. He proceeded to do so, rather offhandedly, in the manner of "Take a left at the second light." Some time later, he interrupted his conversation with me to observe that the driver should have turned at the previous light as he had been told. I couldn't resist pointing out that he had not done any comprehension checks to determine that the driver had understood his directions. The point for our discussion here is that effective communication depends upon being able to put oneself to some degree in the role of the listener. As children move out of the egocentric stage, their awareness of those around them increases, and this awareness leads to an increasing awareness of their needs as listeners.

Another aspect of effective conversation concerns what children know and the language they have available for talking about them. As Hulit and Howard (1993) point out, "It is difficult for any speaker to provide information to his listener if his own understanding is lacking" (p. 242). The school-age child knows more about the world than the preschool child and has more language to express it. Throughout the school years, children continue to add to their store of general knowledge about the world. This, combined with their improved cognitive abilities and language competence, makes them much more effective conversationalists.

The ability to make conversational repairs is related to sensitivity to listeners. If the listener does not understand what the speaker has said and the speaker is aware of that, he will attempt to correct the conversational breakdown. Becoming competent with this facet of conversation entails the ability to request clarification, the ability to perceive when clarification is required, and the ability to provide clarification. These are skills that children must acquire during the school years to become effective communicators. Preschool children will attempt to repair a wayward or broken conversation if asked to do so, but they will not be terribly successful. They will only rarely perceive the need to repair the conversation without being asked directly, but they are more successful with requesting clarification, although their methods may differ from adults'.

Sometimes, when the first attempt at repair fails, subsequent repairs are attempted. These are called *stacked repairs*. These can occur with nearly any topic and are most frequent when one conversationalist has more knowledge about the subject than another or when the primary context for certain lexical items differs for the speakers. The following exchange occurred between my friend Bernadette and me last summer.

Terry Piper: You'll never guess what I did this weekend.
Bernadette: I'm afraid to.
TP: I went shopping.
BP: Oh, oh. Sweetn's? (a local boutique)
TP: No. I bought a Suzuki.
BP: A what?
TP: A Suzuki X-90. Actually, I leased it.
BP: Why?
TP: Well, I thought it was about time. And I got a really good deal on it.
BP: (Looking thoroughly bewildered.) But, Terry, what are you going to *do* with it?
TP: (Finally catching on that we're talking about different things.) Bernadette, I'm not talking about a motorcycle!
BP: I didn't think you were. I thought you meant a violin.

The repair was left so late in the conversation not because I was not unaware of her response, but that I attributed it to the wrong reasons. I assumed that she was surprised by the size of the financial commitment or that I'd actually bought a car after depending on public transport for so long. In fact, her main context for *Suzuki* was violin and not vehicle.

Becoming sensitive to relevance is a task a child must accomplish on two levels. The first is topic relevance. During the school years, the child becomes increasingly aware that adults and older children will be more interested in a conversation whose topic is timely, pertinent, or useful. They will engage for only so long if they perceive the topic to be of no interest to them. The second kind of relevance is intraconversational relevance. Part of successful conversation is contributing useful, relevant commentary, and this is something that the child must learn, as with most language, without actually being taught. A further lesson is that the child alone will not be the arbiter of what is relevant. Preschool children (and some adults!) sometimes engage in parallel monologues, primarily because they have not mastered the notion of relevance. The following is an example.

Janie: I don't want to play checkers.
Doug: I don't want to play dolls.
J: Checkers is boring.
D: Dolls is *more* boring.
J: Mom wouldn't let me go to the party with Candace.
D: My dog had to go to the doctor.
J: It's not fair.
D: But he's sick.
J: What? Who's sick?

The ability to make indirect requests is acquired during the school years. Learning to say "It's dark in here" or "Don't you think it's a little dark in here?" as a way of getting the lights turned on will make the child more popular with the adult community than "Turn on the lights." At age 4 or 5, a child will understand "Don't you think it's a little dark in here?" not as a request to turn the lights on but as a question asking for an opinion. Learning to make and to respond to indirect requests is mastered in the early school years. According to Ervin-Tripp and Gordon (1986), the child uses two simple rules: be brief and be creative enough not to seem demanding. Learning the rules of politeness—whom to interrupt and when, the necessity of being more polite when trying to win favor, and the degree of politeness that must be evident to make a very large request as opposed to a small one are all aspects of learning to deal with indirect requests.

Acquiring gender-based language differences is an important aspect of sociolinguistic competence. There is little doubt that these differences are a result of socialization, a process that begins at home and continues in school. Males and females differ both in the vocabulary they use and in their style of speech (and perhaps writing, although that may be more difficult to detect except in any but personal writing). It will be interesting to see in the next several decades whether closing the gender gap in education, employment, and politics will eventually narrow or close the gender gap in language as well. Some of the differences children will eventually manifest if this gap does not close include the following.

1. Men tend to talk more than women do. Their conversations are longer with other men than they are with women (Swacher, 1975).

2. Men interrupt more, and they are more likely to interrupt women than other men (Parlee, 1979).

3. Women are more likely to interrupt women than men (Willis & Williams, 1976 reported in Hulit & Howard, 1993).

4. Women more readily surrender the topic of conversation as well as their turns.

5. In conversations in which both men and women participate, only about one third of the topics introduced by women into conversation are sustained while nearly all topics introduced by men are sustained (Adapted from Ehrenreich, 1981).

By the time they reach school age, children in the dominant culture have begun to use gender-appropriate language. From the time they are about 4, their topics of talk are differentiated along the same lines as adult male/female talk. Moreover, according to research done by Carol Edelsky (1977), when they begin school, children are already able to distinguish between male and female speakers on the basis of vocabulary used in emotional expressions. Early socialization into these roles occurs, of course, in the home. Research has shown that caregivers talk differently to boys and girls. For example, while mothers are likely to use nicknames for either sons or daughters, the kinds of nicknames differ. Fathers are more likely to use nicknames for their daughters and typically choose terms of endearment or food terms (*Daddy's sweetheart, cupcake, pumpkin*). When they do adopt nicknames for their sons, they choose names such as *ding-a-ling* (Berko-Gleason & Greif, 1983), *sport*, or *champ*.

Conversation, of course, is but one of the language skills that children master during the school years. Another one, perhaps even more important to school success than conversation, is the ability to tell a coherent tale, that is, to construct a narrative.

Learning to Construct Narrative

Certainly, conversation can entail narrative, but generally conversation is characterized more by turn taking than by narrative monologue (although some people appear not to know the difference). The differences are obvious—a narrative involves one person telling a story to one or more other people. It is largely uninterrupted (when it is, it becomes a conversation), and the full burden falls on the speaker. Learning how narratives are constructed is important to reading comprehension, writing, and oral language development. What children have to learn about narrative includes the various components of the narrative as well as the structure of the narrative.

Before they reach school, most children begin to create their own stories that include devices that they will later encounter in print. A narrative consists of a setting that provides information about the location, the characters, and any relevant background information to the episode. The episode is the heart of the narrative and contains information about the event that caused the main character to act, the character's action, and success or lack of success in carrying out the action and the consequences of the plan. It might also include the character's own feelings about the action. When a hearer (or reader) complains about not being able to understand a narrative, it is usually because critical elements of the episode are missing.

Children acquire the ability to narrate in regular stages related to both age and culture. Primitive narrative structures begin to appear sometime after the age of 3. These first attempts lack setting and organization. Little information is provided, and the child depends on prosodic devices to convey much of the tale. Gradually, the child starts to organize the narrative temporally. These narratives will have a discernible beginning, middle, and end, but there will be little information provided about motivation, and the plot will be thin or non-existent. By the end of the first or second year of school, plots begin to emerge, and, partly as a result of increased exposure to printed stories, the devices for carrying the plot forward become more sophisticated. This pattern of development applies to English speakers.

Dickinson, Wolf, and Stotsky (1993) point out that culture plays a major role in the development of narrative. "The narratives of African-American [girls especially] tend to have a structure distinct from that of middle-class white children. They use an approach referred to as **topic-associating,** which juxtaposes thematically related incidents to make a point implicitly" (p. 373). To those unfamiliar with this narrative structure, the resulting stories are difficult to follow because they lack the familiar explicit indicators of shifts in time, character, or setting. Japanese children's narratives also have a distinct character. They tend to be succinct and, consistent with the Japanese *haiku*, told in sets of three episodes (Dickinson et al., 1993, p. 373).

Whatever their previous cultural experience of narrative, when they get to school, children will face the task of linking oral and written language. Narrative is the principal link between the two. There are two kinds of evidence that this is an extremely important link. The first is that children with moderate to severe reading problems frequently have deficient narrative skills. The second is the evidence that in kindergarten children, there is a significant and positive correlation between the ability to name letters and to write and the ability to understand stories (Dickinson & Snow, 1987; Dickinson et al., 1993).

LANGUAGE FUNCTIONS

A very concrete way of categorizing children's language development within a social interaction theoretical framework is to define the different functions that language serves in their lives. Thinking about language growth as a child's expanding the number of functions language plays and the quality of interaction within each function also helps us to evaluate the quality of language in the classroom. It would be possible, of course, to theorize about language acquisition from the perspective of language function, as Halliday (1975, 1978) did. A purely functional analysis of language acquisition is somewhat problematic, however.

D. Piper (1992) identifies three problems with a purely functional analysis. The first has to do with intent. Using the example of a doctor lecturing a patient on the likely consequences of overeating and smoking, Piper points out that the doctor might not consciously conceive of her diatribe as a warning but might view it as a "dispassionate description of facts" (p. 244). Similarly, a mother, worried about her child being late getting home, might, upon the child's tardy arrival, demand "Just where do you think you've been?" She might believe that she is asking the child for an explanation (as she probably is) and not recognize the further function of the question—to express her fear and perhaps a warning to the child.

The second problem also relates to intent, and that is that it is often difficult for a researcher (or a teacher) to determine just what *was* intended. A full understanding of the situation, and perhaps a personal history of the speakers, would be required to get the correct meaning from a sentence such as those in the paragraph above. A final problem exists even if we are able to solve the first two. This is the problem of "polyphony" in adult speech and, thus, to some degree in children's speech. In other words, utterances have many functions, intended and not, and some of these might actually change during the course of the utterance as a result of situational feedback.

These problems with functional analysis are significant not only to the researcher but to the teacher because they point to the difficulty of assessing a child's functional competence. The importance of understanding about the multitude of functions language serves in children's lives, however, is not to assess them but to ensure that children's experience of language in school is as functionally rich as it was at home. Besides, one thing is clear. Language learning is indistinct from learning to use language in functional ways. Common sense tells us that this is true. How could we, after all, claim that we had mastered a language if we had mastered the grammar and phonology and knew many thousands of words, and yet could not use it in any social setting, to any practical use?

In the next pages, I will attempt to characterize the roles language plays in the lives of preschool children so that later we may compare this early experience with the typical school experience of language and learning. We will begin by looking at the uses to which children put language as they learn it.

THE FUNCTIONS OF LANGUAGE IN CHILDREN'S LIVES

We saw in earlier chapters that linguists and others interested in language acquisition may study it from a number of vantage points. For teachers, whose interest is in working with children to provide language-rich environments in which their language can continue to flourish, a particularly useful way of thinking about language acquisition is in functional terms. A number of researchers have examined language acquisition and language use from that perspective. Because their purposes and methods differed, each researcher came up with a distinct set of functional categories. We will not consider here all the functional schemes proposed by researchers, but will concentrate on four, those of Halliday (1975, 1978), Shacter et al. (1974), Tough (1977, 1979), and Shafer et al. (1983).

Four Perspectives on Language Function

One of the first and most influential researchers to use a functional analysis was M. A. K. Halliday, a British linguist who employed the notion of function in describing his son Nigel's early language acquisition. He identified seven early functions that accounted for all the uses to which Nigel put the words he was learning. In order to classify Nigel's early words in this manner, Halliday had to make judgments about what meaning his son intended—what he was trying to accomplish with each utterance.

Ingram (1989, p. 171) has pointed out that Halliday provides no operational procedures for researchers to follow in making such judgments, making it difficult for them to apply his method to the analysis of other children's speech in order to discover how universal the functions truly are. Ingram may be right, but he is writing as a linguist with particular goals in studying language acquisition and with rigorous standards for accomplishing them. Parents and teachers, in contrast, are accustomed to making precisely these kinds of judgments about children's intentions. Doubtless they are sometimes wrong, but even then there is opportunity for unraveling intent and recreating the fabric of meaningful discourse. Focused as they are on communicating with children, they find sense in a functional analysis.

The functions Halliday identified included the instrumental, regulatory, personal, interactional, heuristic, imaginative, and informative functions. All these were present in the child's language before the age of 2. Later, he postulated, children make a transition to the more abstract uses of language that characterize adult speech. He therefore added four functional categories to account for the more mature uses to which children put language. These included the interpretive, the logical, the participatory, and the organizing functions (Halliday, 1978).

Schacter et al. (1974) proposed nine functional categories that were also based on the analysis of young children's speech. They recorded 6,000 utterances made by children playing in nursery schools and then classified them according to how the investigators perceived the intent of each utterance. The nine categories these researchers identified included: expressive, desire implementing, possession-rights-implementing, ego-enhancing, self-referring-including, joining, collaborative, learning-implementing, and reporting. Notice that while most of these functions demonstrate the highly egocentric nature of preschool children, they also use language for social purposes (the joining and collaborative functions) and for learning (the learning-implementing and reporting functions).

Based on her own and on the work of previous work of Halliday, Vygotsky, Luria, Bruner and others, Joan Tough established her own theory of language functions. According to her analysis of preschool children's language, Tough (1977, 1979) concluded that four functions account for their language use: directive, interpretive, projective, and relational. She went further to describe specific uses which children make of language within each function and also identified specific strategies they use to accomplish each use. Finally, Shafer, Staab, and Smith (1983) condensed Tough's categories to a set of five, which they used for their book on developing children's language functions in school. The four different systems are shown in Table 8.1. This shows the four different sets of functional categories proposed by the different researchers together with a description of each category.

The most comprehensive of the functional systems is Halliday's, which postulates seven early functional categories and four later ones. The least inclusive is Tough's with four, but she covers the same language use by developing an elaborate network of uses and strategies for implementing the uses for each function. Whichever system we might choose to follow, it is clear that children's capacity to function in language is rich and varied. Although I will refer occasionally to some of the early functions in Halliday's system, for the purpose of discussion henceforth I will use the functional

Table 8.1 Rough Equivalents of Four Functional Systems

Description	Halliday	Tough	Schacter et al.	Shafer, Staab, & Smith
Early Functions				
Satisfy needs; get things done	Instrumental	Directive	Desire implementing	Social needs
Control behavior of others	Regulatory	Directive	Possession-rights; implementing	Controlling
Tell about self	Personal	Relational	Ego-enhancing	Social needs
Get along with others	Interactional		Joining; collaborative	Social need; projecting
Find out and learn	Heuristic		Learning-implementing	
Pretend, make believe	Imaginative	Projective		
Communicate information to others	Informative		Reporting	Informing
Later Functions				
Interpret whole of experience	Interpretive	Interpretive		Forecasting and reasoning; projecting
Express logical relations	Logical	Interpretive		Forecasting and reasoning
Express wishes, feelings, attitudes, judgments	Participatory	Relational	Possession-needs-implementing; self-referring-including	Social needs
Organize discourse	Organizing			Forecasting and reasoning; projecting

scheme suggested by Shafer, Staab, and Smith (1983), not because it is more comprehensive than the others but because it was created with the stated purpose of helping "teachers to develop various language functions with children in order for them to succeed in school and throughout life" (p. 20).

Five Functions of Language

1. *Children use language to assert and maintain social needs.*   When very young children make a demand (*Want juice!*), they are asserting a need. When they lay claim to a favorite toy (*That mine!*), they are asserting their personal right to have the toy. This function has several subfunctions. Shafer, Staab, and Smith identify five. A 6-year-old who warns a playmate, *I'm gonna tell!* is using language to threaten. The same child who contends that *It's not fair,* or who argues that *It is* not *your truck!* is asserting herself in

different but related ways, to give a negative opinion in the first instance and to argue in the second. When 5-year-old Janet complained that Matthew's drawing was "like a baby's," she was using language to criticize.

Children are also using this function when they assert positive expressions (*That looks pretty, Mom*) or when they ask an opinion (*Do you like this one?*). Incidental expressions such as *Oh, No!* are considered to belong to the same function. All exemplify all ways in which young children assert their rights and their identities as individuals. This is an early function to appear in their language because young children are egocentric, and it continues to develop well into the school years. As they approach school age, children's ways of expressing their personal rights and needs will conform more to the socially accepted forms of the adult world. Also as they grow older, they hear and learn to ask others' opinions, which has the effect of clarifying their personal needs but may also serve to keep the conversation going. Incidental expressions such as *Oh yes?* or *That's right* serve a similar function of moving the discourse along. Children will become increasingly able to voice agreement with and compliments of others, which contributes significantly to their ability to use language to maintain social relationships. This function is comparable to Halliday's instrumental function and is one of the earliest to develop.

2. *Children use language to project into novel situations.*   Play is very important in children's lives, and language is an important part of much of that play. When children enter into make-believe worlds and roles, they use language to project themselves into the part. Most of us have heard a young child at play alone, playing two or more parts in an imaginary situation. The child will use a different pitch and manner of speaking for the various characters. "Projecting is the function of reaching out into other person's experiences or into novel circumstances that we have not actually encountered ourselves" (Shafer et al., 1983, p. 103). This may be real or imagined. Because they are egocentric, young children's use of projecting language for real situations may be somewhat limited until they approach school age. It is difficult for them to assume another person's perspective. Still, there are circumstances that demonstrate that even very young children have the capacity to project themselves into the identities or experiences of others.

When children engage in make-believe, they are reaching outside their identities into another experience. When they engage in dialogues such as the following, they are using projecting language.

Amy and Martha, both 4, are playing house.

Martha: I'm the mommy and you can be the neighbor.

Amy: No, I want to be the mommy.

M: I'll let you wear my Mommy's pretty scarf.

A: Okay. But Sally (a doll) is *my* baby. She wants to be my baby. Jilly wants to be yours. See, she's nodding her head.

This is clearly an example of projecting language being used in an imaginative context, but it demonstrates Amy's ability to express her own views as if they belonged to the dolls. This is the type of projecting that young children are likely to do. As they become older and less ego-centered, they will become increasingly able to use projecting language to project completely outside their own experience. In preschool children, the projecting function includes projecting into the feelings, reactions and experiences of others, both real and imaginative.

3. *Children use language for controlling the self and others.*   This is the language of getting the job done. It is akin to Halliday's instrumental function and to his regulatory function. It is the use children make of language when they direct others' actions or their own in expressions such as *Give me that truck* or *Look at this*. It is also the language used for requesting directions in utterances such as *What do you want me to do with this cup?* or *Where should we stick the red star?* and for seeking others' attention in commands like *Watch me!* or *Look at this!* Sometimes this function is directed toward the child's own behavior. A child playing alone, or with other children, might be heard saying *This goes here and now it's done*. The comment is not directed to another speaker but serves the purpose of monitoring the child's own activity, much as adults talk themselves through complex or multifaceted tasks.

Shafer et al. (1983) point out that controlling language may consist either of very explicit statements such as *Shut the window*, or of implicit statements, such as *I think the plant looks dry*, which, if spoken with the intent of getting someone to water the plant, is equally controlling in function (p. 65).

Not only is the controlling function of language used to get things done, a very important function in the lives of young children, it also plays an important role in learning. When it is used to instruct the self or direct others in ways that facilitate understanding, it is helping children to make sense of the world around them and is thus related to Halliday's heuristic function, which is a valuable tool for their early learning.

4. *Children use language to inform.*   Children no doubt hear a great deal of this type of language both before and after they begin school. It is the language for commenting on events past and present (*That's a fat frog; I saw one like it in the park*), for labeling (*That's a bus*), for talking about sequences of events (*You should wait to do that after we put the paint on*), and for talking about details (*It's not brown exactly, more like a funny red*). Other subfunctions include the language of comparison (*This blue is better than that one*), the language for making generalizations on the basis of specific events or details (*See the way it's smashed? Someone must have hit it*), and for requesting information (*What do you call this? What color was it before?*).

In the very earliest stages of language acquisition, children begin by labeling the objects in their environment—*Mummy, Ginger cat, truck, boat, juice*. Very soon, they expand this function. Any parent of a toddler knows, for example, that requesting information is one of the first types of informing language which children acquire. Children ask questions to sort out the workings of the world, and when parents answer their questions, they are exposing their children to even more informing language. We can see that this function of language serves children in some of the same ways as Halliday's heuristic function. Because it is the language used to discover, to test whether things are as they appear to be, to question the world, informative language is an extremely important function for children to develop if they are to succeed in school.

5. *Children use language to forecast and reason.*   As we have seen, children put both controlling and informing language to uses that enhance their learning. The principal language function they employ in the business of learning, however, is the language of forecasting and reasoning, the language Halliday identified as heuristic. It is the language that expresses their curiosity and allows them to find out about the world. It is used with extreme frequency by toddlers asking *Why can't I?* or *Why does the wheel go around?* Subfunctions other than the requesting of information include predicting an event and forecasting or reasoning about causal relationships. Shafer et al. (1983) point out that the predicting of an event may be based on obvious reasons, either stated or not, or it may have reasons that are neither stated nor immediately apparent. Their example is of a child who looks out the window at a threatening sky and observes, *I think it's going to rain.* In this case, it is clear that the reason for the statement is the darkness of the sky. Another child, however, might look into a sunny sky and make the same prediction. In this case, there is no obvious reason for the speculation (p. 93). In the first instance, parents will usually respond by agreeing that the child's prediction is likely. In the second, they will usually try to draw out a reason for the child's gloomy forecast. In questioning the child and offering possible reasons or alternative conclusions, they engage the child in reasoning about an event and provide representative language for doing so.

While all the language functions provide a window on children's cognitive development, the forecasting and reasoning function of language is especially revealing. By carefully observing children's use of language to forecast and reason, we gain valuable insights into the growth in their reasoning. The following two dialogues illustrate this point.

> Amy, age 4, is in trouble with her 12-year-old sister Sara.
> **Sara:** I told you to stay out of my things. Look what you did!
> **Amy:** No.
> **S:** What do you mean, no? Don't tell me you weren't playing with my nail polish.
>   You got it all over the vanity. Mom's going to kill us both. And it's all your fault.
> **A:** I didn't.
> **S:** Then who did?
> **A:** (Thinking for a minute.) Sam was here. I guess he—
> **S:** Oh right. So when did Sam start polishing his nails with bright pink paint?
> **A:** I don't know.
> **S:** Well, will you at least help me clean it up?
> **A:** (Relieved) Okay. We won't get in trouble, right?
> **S:** Well, not if we get it all off. Go in the kitchen and get me a whole lot of paper
>   towels.

Six-year-old Danny and his mother are having a discussion about his afternoon plans. Danny wants to go to a showing of a children's film at the local library, something he usually does once a week.

> **Danny:** Why can't I go? James gets to go.
> **Mother:** I explained already. You can't go because I have to work tonight and I won't
>   be able to pick you up. And Daddy's car is in the shop.

D: Why can't I ride with James?

M: Usually, you can, but today James' mother is dropping him off and then his Dad's picking him up—

D: I can ride with his Dad.

M: Not today because they're not going home afterward. They're going to James's grandmother's house.

D: I can go there, too!

M: No, you can't. You weren't invited this time. But I'm sure James will invite you another time.

We see in the first dialogue that Amy is able to understand her sister's reasoning, helped along by the somewhat perilous situation in which she finds herself, far better than she is able to reason herself. Nevertheless, we see evidence that she is capable of causal reasoning in her *We won't get in trouble, right?* This question implies her understanding of the contingency—if they clean up the mess, they will avoid trouble. We also see her reasoning that because Sam was also in the house, the blame might be laid at his feet, a slightly different type of causal reasoning.

In Danny, we find a child with much better developed reasoning skills. As he makes his case for going to the film, we see an implied justification in his pointing out that James is being allowed to go. We find, too, that he is able to understand his mother's rather complex explanation of the reasons why he cannot go with James. Even though he doesn't accept the argument, he clearly understands it. The 2 years' difference in the ages of Amy and Danny makes a world of difference in their verbal reasoning abilities.

Language Functions Across Cultures

The examples used in our discussion so far have been from English-speaking children learning their native language. While it is certainly possible to examine the language growth of non-native speakers in terms of language function, care must be taken not to make faulty assumptions. We have already seen how difficult it is to be certain that we have identified the speaker's intent correctly. We know that language functions are related to situations. People in different cultures react to situations differently, and the language that is appropriate for situations differs as well. We learned earlier that in Inuit culture children are deemed to have acquired their native language when they demonstrate their understanding by doing as they are told. Inuit children might use different expressions from native-English speakers to serve the same function or might appear not to have acquired the function at all. But when we are dealing cross-culturally, we have to be especially careful not to assume too much from what a child does *not* say. In judging a child's language attainment, remember that understanding of the function is just as important as producing it. Remember, too, that some functions are extremely difficult to observe, but that failure to observe a function does not mean absence of the function in the child's repertoire.

CONCLUSION

The purpose of this chapter was to look more carefully at the social aspects of language in children's lives. We began with looking at the development of pragmatics in school-aged children and concluded with a categorical analysis of language functions, or the uses to which children normally put language. The purpose was not only to shed greater light on the accomplishment of language learning, but to establish linkages between the home experience and the school experience of language learning. In the next chapter, we see more linkages as we explore the relationship between language and cognitive growth. In our discussion of language functions in early childhood, we have considered the relationship from the perspective of language. In the next chapter, we will turn the mirror around and view the relationship from the perspective of cognitive growth. The two are not, of course, independent, but we gain a greater understanding of the relationship by viewing it from both perspectives.

EXERCISES AND QUESTIONS FOR DISCUSSION

1. Both men and women develop the full range of language functions, but some writers have observed differences in the ways in which such functions are expressed. Consider each of the following questions and determine whether men and women might use them to express different functions.
   a. Do we have any tea?
   b. Where's the butter?
   c. Aren't you ready yet?
   d. Are you watching that program (on television)?

2. Try to think of as many possible functions as you can for each of the following utterances. Be sure to provide the context for each.
   a. So, what do you think of the Yankees' chances this year?
   b. Is it midnight already?

3. What has the child had to learn to understand why the first request might be permissible and the second not.
   a. If you've finished with that section of the paper, could I have a look at it?
   b. If you're not doing anything this weekend, would you mind driving me to New Jersey? (assuming the speaker lives in Virginia).

4. Consider the following conversation.

   Max: The weather report says rain for tomorrow.
   Mim: Let's have pot roast.
   Max: No point in mowing the lawn today.
   Mim: We could barbecue a chicken, I guess. Or go out.
   Max: Tomorrow?
   Mim: No, today.
   Max: I was talking about tomorrow.
   Mim: I was talking about supper.

What is the topic of the conversation? How old do you think the speakers are? What do they have to learn about conversation?

5. How does conversation differ from narrative discourse?

6. Collect two samples of conversation. Remove all names and personal pronouns and share them with a classmate. See whether the classmate can identify the sex of the participants.

7. Think about your own language use during the course of the past day. Did you use all the functions identified in this chapter? Which were most frequently used?

8. To what degree do you believe the differences between male and female language are socially induced? What evidence can you bring to support your position?

CHAPTER NINE

Language and Cognitive Growth

In Chapter 1, I made the claim that language is special in the life of the child. Later, I claimed that language development is unique and based in social interaction, but this in no way implies that it happens independent of cognitive development. Language and cognition develop in tandem. Or, as Alice Yardley (1973) puts it,

> ... there is a close connection between words and thought, and at all stages language development is crucial to thought activity. The two are not identical, but they are interdependent, and the context within which the child acquires language has a permanent influence over the way he learns to think. (p. 13)

It is now time to talk in greater detail about language and its special relationship to learning. The purpose of this chapter is to attempt to characterize the role language plays in the learning of preschool children so that in Chapter 10 we may compare this early experience with the typical school experience of language and learning.

Although language and cognition are related processes, the relationship is not well understood. It is still a matter of intense inquiry among psychologists and linguists, but it seems to be the case that neither depends upon the other. As Ratner (1993) points out, "... it is not clear that language development is contingent upon mastery of any specific subset of cognitive abilities .... It is more likely that linguistic and cognitive development may progress in parallel" (p. 335). It does seem to be the case, however, that language does influence cognitive growth in a variety of ways. In the pages that follow, we will look at those cognitive processes that appear to be most intricately connected to language.

Cognition is not a monolithic process. We cannot, therefore, talk about children's cognitive growth as though it consisted of a single process of change. In fact, what we commonly call cognitive development actually involves changes in a number of different capacities including perception, memory, conceptualization, and academic skills. We will not talk at length here about perception, because even though there is little doubt that language plays an important part in human perception, the most interesting aspects of perceptual development occur in the first 6 months of life, before the onset of language. Rather, we will concern ourselves with the relationship of language to memory and conceptualization and to the child's achievement in academic thinking.

THE ROLE OF LANGUAGE IN MEMORY DEVELOPMENT

Not all memory is language-based. A person who misses a step on a stairway, for example, will often say, "There's one more than I thought," when, in fact, the memory of the number of stairs had likely never been thought of, much less articulated in language. Nevertheless, memory and language are usually linked. A simple experiment reported by Carmichael, Hogan, and Walter (1932) demonstrated how inextricable that link can be. In reproducing line drawings they had been asked to remember, subjects in the study routinely distorted them consistent with additional *verbal* information they had received. Language provides not only a means of encoding experience but influences the recall of that experience. In other words, they allowed what they were told to override what they had seen.

The simple fact of memory development is that as children grow older, their memories improve. But why? What makes this growth possible? Siegler (1991) offers four possible explanations. One is that as children mature, their basic capacity increases. In other words, the physical and physiological mechanisms responsible for memories expand. Another possibility is that children's memory strategies improve; through practice they get better at the procedures involved in storage and retrieval. A third explanation is that as children grow older they learn more about memory and how it works, and they use this knowledge to manage their own memories. Finally, it could be the case that because older children have greater prior knowledge of the content they need to remember, they have a sounder basis on which to remember new material (pp.173-175).

It is likely, in fact, that all four explanations have some basis in reality, that is, that increased capacity, greater sophistication in using strategies, metamemory, and other experience all contribute to memory development. For our purpose, however, the question is not the degree to which any one contributes to cognitive growth but how language is involved in each.

Basic Capacities

Basic capacities include those frequently used components of memory that form the foundations for cognitive activity. Such processes as recognition, association, storage, and retrieval are prerequisites to all thinking. How language is involved may not be immediately obvious, but if we consider just what constitutes development of some of these processes, the relationship becomes clearer.

Recognition is at the heart of memory; cognitive development could not proceed without it. With regard to language, however, recognition is not an especially interesting phenomenon because the ability is amazingly well developed even in newborns. What role language plays in auditory recognition is unclear. We saw in an earlier chapter that very young infants are capable not only of recognizing human speech sounds but also of recognizing subtle differences between speech sounds. One interesting piece of research does, however, shed light on the nature of the interaction between language and early recognitory behavior.

We saw in Chapter 3 that infants as young as 1 month are able to discriminate between certain speech sounds such as voiced and voiceless consonants. Infants seem to be able to mark these and certain other speech distinctions no matter what language is being spoken around them. This very early ability would suggest that some innate mechanism is operating. The question that arises is at what point the infant's recognitory ability becomes attuned to a particular language. Two studies, reported by Reich (1986, p. 25), shed some light on this question. Researchers in one study found that infants in the first 6 months were unable to recognize certain acoustic distinctions that their Spanish-speaking parents recognized (Lasky et al., 1975). A second study of children who were 7 months old showed that children of Spanish-speaking parents could recognize the Spanish distinction better than children of the same age exposed to the English language (Eilers et al., 1979). It would seem, then, that around 7 months is the age at which children begin to recognize the distinctions appropriate to the language around them.

Another aspect of basic memory capacity that is present at birth but which increases with age is association. It also changes in character. Infants are capable of associating certain stimuli with certain responses. In one experiment with 3-month-olds, researchers attached a string from their ankles to a mobile. The babies quickly learned that kicking their legs caused the mobile to move. Another study showed that they could remember what they had learned as long as 8 days later (Sullivan, Rovee-Collier, & Tynes, 1979, cited in Siegler, 1986). As children get older and acquire language, they are able to make an entirely new set of associations, verbal associations, and their memory and learning capacities thus increase.

Further evidence that language is important in the development of memory is found in the phenomenon of infant amnesia. Adults have very long memories. Most of us can recall events that occurred or recognize people that we knew decades ago. Even young children are very good at recognizing pictures they have seen even though a considerable time has passed. Yet few adults have any memories of infancy. Those who claim to recall an occurrence from early infancy are usually found to be remembering someone else's account of those events. The passage of time alone cannot account for our inability to recall the first months of life. What likely does account for it is a difference in the way in which infants encode events and the way older children and adults encode events. As Siegler (1991) points out,

> Whether people can remember depends critically on the fit between the way in which they earlier encoded the information and the way in which they later attempt to retrieve it. The better able the person is to reconstruct the perspective from which the material was encoded, the more likely that recall will be successful. (p. 178)

And this is where language comes in. Older children have language as part of the context of experience and thus available as a means of encoding while infants do not. It seems probable that the onset of language represents an important device for increasing basic memory capacity. It also provides the child with a valuable memory strategy. We have all had the experience of repeating over and over something that we wanted to remember later. This strategy of rehearsal is one of several which are central to the development of memory.

Memory Strategies

Those conscious activities which we engage in with the hope of improving our chances of remembering are called memory strategies. They occur at some time between the event or experience to be recalled and the act of recalling. Rehearsal is one such strategy and language is crucial to it. Research has established clearly that the strategy of rehearsal plays an important role in memory improvement. Children who verbally rehearse the names of pictures can recall more pictures than children who do not rehearse the names. Without language, of course, they would be unable to do so.

A second strategy involves organization. Children 5 and 6 years old make less use of categories than do children of 9 or older. That language plays a central role in our ability to categorize is easily demonstrated by an experiment commonly done in psychology classes. Consider the following list of words:

desk	dog
computer	hamster
telephone	tomato
bookshelf	lettuce
cat	radish
bird	cabbage

If you try to remember the list as a list of unrelated words, you may remember as many as half the items. If, on the other hand, you mentally organize the list into three categories, office equipment, animals, and vegetables, you will do much better. If you go even further and sub-categorize the latter two as household pets and salad ingredients, you will do better still. The ability to categorize is closely associated with language; it is impossible to do it effectively without the verbal labels for classification.

One additional strategy for improving memory deserves mention because it is closely related to linguistic development. Elaboration can be similar to organization in that it involves making connections between items or events, but it differs in that it can occur even when no categorical relations exist between them. Elaborations can be images, as when a girl trying to remember to buy an umbrella, a bottle of ink, and shampoo forms a mental picture of herself holding the umbrella to protect her clean hair and the bottle of ink she is carrying, or they can be verbal. *Mnemonics* are common verbal elaborations. Many of us can recall learning the names of the lines of the treble clef (e, g, b, d, f) by using the phrase Every Good Boy Does Fine, and the spaces by spelling FACE. There is evidence that children 4 years of age can be taught to form verbal elaborations for remembering two terms and use them successfully in recall. Attempts to teach them to form visual images are less successful. Language is clearly involved, then, in the strategies children employ to store and to retrieve experience. It is also involved in the improvement of metamemory.

Metamemory

A component of metacognition, metamemory refers to the knowledge children have about how memory works. It is not hard to find examples of metamemory being called upon. Take the adult who is watching a television drama and reading the newspaper at the same time. She goes back and forth, sampling information from the television screen and the newspaper page in turn. The procedure goes smoothly enough until she discovers she has missed something, say in the television program, and what is happening no longer makes sense. What she will do in such a case is to abandon the paper and pay close attention to the television, hoping to find clues to what she has missed. Usually in television, this strategy works, but it is the decision to employ the strategy which constitutes metamemory. As children grow older, they learn about the limitations and the fallibility of memory, and this knowledge directs them to develop a feeling for what is hard to remember as well as strategies for remembering those things.

At the very heart of metamemory is the act of monitoring, and an experiment conducted by Markman (1979) sheds light on the nature of monitoring growth in young children and on its relationship to language. Children between 8 and 11 years were read a short passage on the making of Baked Alaska. In the second sentence of the passage they heard that the ice cream melts in the hot oven. Two sentences later, they heard that the ice cream stays hard and does not melt. Nearly half the subjects in the study failed to identify the contradiction even when they had been warned that the story was problematic. The children who did not notice the disparity seemed to be concentrating on the soundness of each individual statement rather than on the sense they made in total (Markman, 1979, cited in Siegler, 1986, pp. 242–243). Their monitoring of their own understanding differed in kind from that of older children and adults. But how does monitoring relate to language? From about 2 years, children are able to correct their own language errors indicating use of a language monitor which compares their utterances to what they know of language. They apply this monitor to their own pronunciation, vocabulary choices, and grammar. As we also saw in Chapter 3, they monitor what they hear, rejecting adults' infantile pronunciations when they fail to correspond to those stored in memory. Once children begin school, they begin to apply the same kinds of monitoring to their reading, eventually learning to monitor their comprehension of what they are reading and to intervene, much as our television watcher above, when it is found wanting. In general, the ability to monitor one's own comprehension marks an important distinction between good and poor readers. More mature and better readers do frequent comprehension checks and go back and read again if they find their understanding wanting. Ironically, less able readers, who could benefit most from such rereading, seldom do so.

Finally, we come to the place of content knowledge in memory development and its relationship to language. The more children know about the world, the easier it is to find conceptual pegs for new information. Actually, content knowledge influences memory in at least two ways. It affects the amount of information recalled as well as what is recalled. Take, for example, two women attending a cat show together. Both have seen cats, of course, but one has never been to a cat show before, never owned a cat, and prefers dogs. The second woman has two cats of her own, has always had at least one cat, and has attended many cat shows. The second woman will be able to recall more about what she has seen and different information from the first. While the first woman might report going to a cat show and seeing a lot of cats, some with long hair and some with short, some white, some black and some striped; the second woman is more likely to recall seeing a prize-winning flame-pointed Himalayan and a lilac-pointed Siamese and the fact that there were only three Burmese when normally she would expect to see at least a dozen. The content knowledge that the second woman has about cats has provided an organizational framework to facilitate her storage and recall of the information surrounding the cat show.

The availability of background content knowledge sometimes leads to the recall of details which, although plausible, never in fact occurred. In the act of reconstructing a sequence of events surrounding a baseball game, a person knowledgeable about baseball may recall that there were four batters in the third inning and that the first one struck out. In attempting to explain the remainder of the inning, she may report that the second batter was walked and the next two struck out when, in fact, the second and third *both* walked and the fourth hit into a double play. Either sequence of events is plausible, and because she has the framework of the rules of baseball and prior experience watching the game, she constructs a perfectly conceivable but inaccurate account. A person unfamiliar with baseball would not make such a mistake; neither would she recall as much about the game.

The role that language plays in content knowledge is twofold. First, it is the medium through which children acquire much of their knowledge about the world. Second, it facilitates the formation of organizational networks which not only make this knowledge more readily available but which make possible the integration of new, related items. We have already seen in our discussion of memory strategies that language plays a central role in categorization. The ability to categorize makes it possible to store and retrieve *more* information, thus improving memory.

Language, Memory, and the Child's Perspective

In the previous section, the questions under discussion were What capacities change in the process of memory development? and What is the role of language in those changes? These are adult interpretations of the issues, not child interpretations. Indeed, infants would be quite surprised to learn that at such a tender age they are engaging in such esoteric activities. It is likely impossible that we will ever know just what children's perspective is on any aspect of growth in the very early years. But it is important that we try to understand what actually happens from the child's perspective while these important changes are taking place.

Put another way, the question is: What are children doing while the basic capacities, memory strategies, and metamemory develop and how does what they're doing contribute to that development? Children's auditory discrimination becomes attuned to the native language at around 6 or 7 months of age. It is unlikely that they are conducting acoustic experiments on themselves. Rather, they are engaging their mothers, fathers, or others in a variety of language activities. A recording of Janet's mother talking to her when she was not quite 6 months old illustrates the kinds of language experience which an infant has.

> And what would our princess like to wear this morning? How about this purple jumpsuit? Do you like purple? Yes. This is definitely purple, isn't it? Okay. You'd rather play with that one. Okay, why not? You play with it and I'll put this yellow one on you instead. That's Daddy's favorite color. Daddy? You like Daddy don't you? Well, he'll really like this outfit, won't he? You sure are happy this morning. What's making you so happy? (She picks up Janet's stuffed mouse named Mealey.) Is Mealey happy, too? Why do you think Mealey's so happy? 'Cause he loves Janet.

In many of these sorts of interactions since birth, Janet has come to realize that the language noises she hears are purposeful, communicative and that they are associated with pleasurable events, particularly the society of other people.

Similarly, what concerns children as they make associations between objects and labels is not the increased memory capacity nor even the enlarged vocabulary that will result. They are consumed, instead, with a lively and eager curiosity. They want to know what the things in their world are called, and when they find out, they rehearse or practice them until they can remember them. Most likely, they practice not in a conscious effort to remember, but because playing with language in this way is fun. They engage in rhyming word play because it is fun to do and as a way of actively exploring the characteristics of the language they are beginning to learn. That they are also developing verbal elaboration strategies that will increase memory is of no consequence to them. At this very young age—even before the first birthday—children are already taking charge of their own learning.

They are still in charge as their vocabulary grows and they begin to mark meaning distinctions. As they learn that some furry four-legged creatures are cats and others dogs and that certain features distinguish them, children are not aware that they are also developing another memory strategy. They are learning which distinctions matter in their world. Acquiring content knowledge helps them to organize their experience and to retrieve it more easily, but they don't do it for that reason. In organizing their experience, they are trying to discern meaningful order in their worlds. Their curiosity and need to understand the world lead them to work out the distinctions that are relevant to it. Language, then, is central to the growth of memory, which, in turn, is central to children's cognitive development. From children's perspective, language is a principal means by which they come to understand and to organize their experience, in play and in all sorts of social interaction. The desire to learn and the desire to learn language are rooted in a common ground—children's active attempts to understand and make sense of the world in which they live.

THE ROLE OF LANGUAGE IN CONCEPTUAL DEVELOPMENT

Anyone interested in children's learning must also be interested in conceptual growth and in theories of conceptual development. After all, what we believe about the nature of concepts shapes our beliefs about human learning.

> . . . Different views of the nature of concepts lead to different expectations about the order in which children will learn particular concepts, to different explanations of why some concepts are difficult for them to learn, and to different implications about how children should be taught new concepts. (Siegler, 1986, pp. 260–261)

There is no universal agreement among philosophers, psychologists, and educators as to the definition of concept, although at a very basic level most would agree that a concept consists of a grouping of objects, events, ideas, people, or attributes that share some similarities. Conceptualization seems to serve two functions in human cognition. First, as we have already seen, categorization, which is at the heart of conceptualization, is important to the development of memory. Second, concepts allow us to take our understanding beyond the bounds of our own experience. As an example, the woman in our earlier example who has never seen a Blue Point will immediately know something about the animal if she is told that it is a cat, and more still if she learned anything at all at the cat show, if she is told that it is a Siamese cat.

Psychologists' and Linguists' Views Compared

Nowhere is the importance of language to cognitive development more obvious than in conceptualization. We have only to compare psychologists' theories of concept formation with theories of semantic development to see the connections. Take, for example, Pease, Gleason, and Pan, writing on the categorical or semantic feature theory of semantic development.

> One explanation of early semantic development is that children acquire categorical concepts and that categories are defined by certain features. For instance, the word dog refers to a category of animals with a set of distinguishing features: they are alive and warm-blooded, have four legs, bark, and are covered with hair. According to Eve Clark (1974), when a child learns a new word, it is in the context of a specific situation: the word dog may at first be understood to apply only to the child's own dog. Only later comes the understanding that other creatures may also be called dog as long as they share the small set of critical features that uniquely define the category. (1989, p. 105)

Their example of how semantic feature theory might work bears a striking resemblance to Siegler's (1991) description of a theory of conceptual development known as defining-features representations.

> Defining-features representations are like the simplest and most straightforward dictionary definitions. They include only the necessary and sufficient features that determine whether an example is or is not an instance of the concept. (p. 213)

These authors, though writing from different perspectives, are describing the same thing; the first is merely focusing on language as the medium by which concepts are represented. It should be noted, however, that although many linguists and psychologists have written about children's representing concepts in terms of defining features, there is no universal agreement that very young children are capable of representing concepts in this way. Piaget was one theorist who believed that young children categorize on the basis of themes—a dog and a bone might be put into the same conceptual category because dogs eat bones—and that the nature of conceptual development lies in their learning to conceptualize on the basis of shared characteristics. An analogous parallel occurs between aspects of probabilistic representations in conceptualization theory and prototypes in language acquisition theory. In conceptualization theory, the probabilistic view holds that some objects may be perceived as better examples of a particular conceptual category than others. People may view Persians as better examples of cats than Manxes, apples as better examples of fruits than raisins, and steak as a better example of meat than chopped liver. The reasons why they have these preferences is that they consider the properties required for an object to belong to a certain conceptual category and choose as best the one which has the most. Thus, a Persian might be considered a better example of cat on the basis of its length of hair and length of tail; on the basis of these features, the probability is higher that the Persian is a cat than the Manx.

There is an echo of this reasoning in the description of the prototype theory of semantic development, "Yet another theory suggests that we first acquire concepts that are protypical, or the best examples of the categories we are learning" (Rosch & Mervis, 1975). Rosch and her colleagues have shown that we all share the view that some members of a category are much better representatives, or exemplars, than others. A German shepherd is a better dog than a Chihuahua; a robin is a better bird than a chicken. According to prototype theory, children acquire these core concepts when they acquire meaning and only later come to recognize members of that category that are distant from the prototypes (Pease, Gleason, & Pan, 1989, p. 105).

There is also a parallel between the nature of children's development as it is seen within an exemplar-based representational view of conceptualization and language growth which proceeds from lexical to rule learning. Those who believe in exemplar-based representation believe that children store numerous examples of objects and events as they occur in life. When they encounter a new object or event, they compare it to other examples in memory to determine whether the new object or event matches stored examples or the exemplar-based representations they may have created from stored examples. Under this view, development would consist of moving from exemplar-based representations to the learning of rules or regularities. Indeed, research has shown that 7-year-olds learn more effectively under conditions which encouraged them to pay careful attention to particular examples and 10-year-olds learned equally well under this condition and under the condition which promoted rule learning (Kossan, 1981).

Both linguistic and interactionist theories of language acquisition would claim that while children may begin by learning individual words and their meanings and, possibly, that early sentences are learned as wholes, language acquisition cannot progress until the child begins to learn the rules for putting words into sentences. They would cite as evidence the fact that the number of potential sentences which can be understood and produced is infinite and that no one can learn every exemplar sentence in a language. The similarity between theories of concept formation and those of semantic development is not merely serendipitous. The first words that children acquire and the use to which they put them provide a mirror on the concepts they are acquiring. More likely than not, language influences those concepts. Certainly there is evidence that people "find it easier to make a conceptual distinction if it neatly corresponds to words available in their language" (Crystal, 1987, p. 15). It would follow, then, that children's increasing facility with conceptualization corresponds to their increasing facility with language.

Language and Conceptualization from the Child's Perspective

In the lives of children, language and the ability to conceptualize provide a means for them to extend their understanding beyond the bounds of their own experience. Although it is possible to understand an idea or a concept without being able to put it into words, it is the very act of putting it into words that clarifies and makes understanding precise. Attempting to verbalize a "fuzzy" idea serves to crystalize both what we know and what we do not—our understanding and our ignorance. Most of us are aware of the former—Donald Murray has often said that he writes to find out what he knows. The latter notion of revealing ignorance is, perhaps, less familiar. Yet learning involves, in Margaret Donaldson's (1978) words, "a simple realization of ignorance" (p. 76). Implicit in the notion of wanting to know is the awareness that we do not. There is no better way of capturing that awareness than to try to put into words an idea or a concept of which we have imperfect understanding. In a real sense, then, children talk their way to understanding. This is true of learning in general and of language learning in particular. Children begin to talk long before they are masters of the language and it is through talk that they acquire the skills to *become* masters. In their early talk, we find not only evidence that they practice or rehearse the language they are learning but evidence that they are actively engaged in the figuring out of the system that is language. A dialogue between Shelly, a child of 3;6, and her mother illustrates:

Mother: It's cold outside. Let's put on your pants.
Shelly: Where?
M: There, on your bed.
S: Pants? No, only pant. One.
M: Oh, I see. No, these are called pants even though there's only one of them.
S: Why?
M: I don't know. Maybe 'cause there are two legs.
S: Oh. Pantlegs.
M: Very good!

In this exchange, we see that Shelly has acquired both the concept and the language to express the plural. But her understanding is not perfect, and so she assumes, quite reasonably, that because pants *sounds* plural, it must *be* plural. She is initially unaware of her ignorance but once her mother explains the error, she readily incorporates the explanation into her vocabulary and to her comprehension of the rules for plural formation. Perhaps the most important point to be made here is that Shelly does not wait for someone to instruct her in the ways of language; she gets on with the business of learning it as she learns about the world around her.

THE ROLE OF LANGUAGE IN THE DEVELOPMENT OF ACADEMIC SKILLS

Although a great deal of children's academic thinking develops during the school years, it has been estimated that 33% of a child's academic skills are attained before age 6 (Yardley, 1973). How language serves to shape children's academic thinking is thus of utmost concern since this is the time during which the foundations for their future success in school are laid. Before they begin formal schooling, children have a great deal of experience in learning. In fact, in some ways, very young children may be at an advantage. As Alice Yardley (1973) observed, "The pre-speech child has a distinct advantage in that because he has no words, he is protected from being told what to learn and how to learn it, and how to solve his problems" (p. 16). Wise parents refrain from providing too much help and thus depriving the child of the rewarding experience of finding a solution independently. Whether the problem is putting the shoe on the appropriate foot, fitting a round puzzle piece into its proper space, or figuring out the mechanics of a zipper, the parent who insists on telling the child how to solve the problem, or worse, solving it for him, takes away the experience of learning. Fortunately, childhood abounds with such opportunities and even children with over-helpful parents will find a great deal to learn and will develop a great many strategies for doing so. Much of this learning is related to the subjects they later encounter in school, because their parents have actively taught them, because they have watched educational television programs such as *Sesame Street* and *The Electric Company*, or in some instances, because they have found their own resources for learning. Three areas in which they have learned a great deal about how to learn are reading, writing, and arithmetic.

Early Learning of Mathematics

Most of today's children know how to solve addition problems with sums lower than 10 before they enter school. One of the strategies which preschool children use is to choose the larger of the two numbers to be added and count upward from it the number of times indicated by the smaller number. Thus a child adding three and five would begin with five and count up three—five, *six, seven, eight*. Notice that the ability to apply this strategy rests in memory and in language. The child has to be able to remember the strategy and then, in essence, rename one as six, two as seven, and three as eight. This is not the only approach children use, however. Sometimes they simply put up their fingers and count on them and other times they simply recall the answer from memory.

Children also use counting strategies in solving subtraction problems, counting either up from the lower number to the higher or down from the higher number to the number indicated by the lower. Which of the two strategies they use seems to depend on which requires the fewer counts. For the problem, $6 - 2$, for example, children would likely count backward from six, two counts since this is easier than counting upward from two to six, which would require four counts. For our purpose, what is interesting about these early strategies is that they all require the child to count and counting is not possible without language. It is not unwarranted to claim, then, that children's early mathematics ability resides in language.

What kinds of experiences do preschool children have with learning mathematics? During the latter years of the 1980s, there were a number of disturbing reports in the press of Yuppie parents who transferred their own ambition to their children and enrolled them in high pressure academic preschools or engaged them at a tender age in such questionable educational practices as superlearning. While it may turn out that these early enrichment programs did in fact produce children who achieved superior marks in school and entrance to Harvard or Oxford, we have to wonder about the cost to the child of a lost childhood. Happily, such high pressure programs are not necessary; the child in the course of a normal childhood develops a natural interest in numbers. From the time the infant notices that the cookies have been eaten and observes *No more* or *All gone*, the foundations for numeracy are established. Later, the addition or subtraction of objects within their own worlds of experience—blocks, small wooden people and animals, finger puppets—propel children along the path of counting, which leads eventually to addition and subtraction. Parents need not teach basic arithmetic to their children—for example, drill the sums, requiring children to memorize one plus one is two, two plus two is four, etc. In fact, they may impede the child's own problem-solving skills by doing so. All they need do is to encourage their children's natural curiosity and, possibly, to play counting and rhyming games with their children. By doing so they will be, in a real sense, laying the foundations on which later success in school mathematics will be based. Mathematics is not the only academic skill which children begin to acquire before they start school. It is only one of the three Rs which our society normally considers to be the rudiments of academic learning. Reading and writing are rudimentary not only as subjects in their own right but because they are essential to success in almost all subjects children encounter during their 12 or 13 years of formal schooling. A number of researchers have established clearly that children learn a great deal about both before they get to school.

Early Learning Associated with Reading

Learning to read can be thought of as an evolutionary process that begins shortly after birth:

> Children first construct concepts about books and how print works, and then begin to attend to aspects of the print that surrounds them. This is followed by growth of phonemic awareness and acquisition of phoneme-grapheme knowledge. As children construct knowledge about print and the relationship between print and speech, they also are building oral language skills that support their progress as they encounter the demands of first grade and begin to move into conventional forms of reading and writing. (Dickinson et al., 1993, p. 376)

The question we have been asking about the role language plays in early learning is more simply put: What is the role of *speech* in children's early reading? Shortly we will see that it does play an important role. But we also need to have a broader understanding of the reading process. To understand the nature of children's early knowledge of and about reading, we could take one of two broad approaches. We could attempt to describe the roughly chronological stages of the reading process, that is, what children typically know and do at a particular age. Or we could break the reading process down into a number of component skills and describe the learning associated with each. For our purpose, it is most revealing to do the latter, focusing in particular on letter perception, phonemic awareness, word identification, and the processes involved in the comprehension of larger prose units. The question before us, then, is what is the nature of children's knowledge of these components of reading before they begin school and how did they come by it?

To begin with, a great many children do learn to read before they begin school. By reading I mean not only word identification of the type they learn on *Sesame Street* but also the ability to recreate meaning from printed text whether that text be a sign in a grocery store, a toy advertisement, or a children's book. My elder son began to identify individual words well before his third birthday. Noticing his interest in the words on *Sesame Street*, I placed large-print labels on many of the more common objects in the house but made no further effort to teach him to read. He learned the associations very quickly and by the time he was just past 3 was sounding out the words in his own books that I had been reading to him for some time. He already knew the stories the books told and had learned from *Sesame Street* that letters had sound equivalents and had put the two kinds of knowledge together. He had, in essence, taught himself to read. My experience with my son is consistent with what research has to say about early readers. The factors that determine whether a child will learn to read before schooling are the degree of interest the child has in reading and the degree of interest the parents have in reading as demonstrated by their reading to the child, reading for pleasure themselves, and having plenty of reading materials available in the home (Durkin, 1966).

Even children who do not learn to read text before they begin school know a great deal about the process of reading. It is as though they have been getting ready to learn to read since birth. They have acquired certain abilities that are necessary to reading ability. These cognitive correlates of early reading ability include the perception of letters as being distinct from other kinds of marks, drawings, and squiggles that one might encounter in the world and as being distinct from one another. Marking these kinds of discriminations is a complex perceptual task, requiring children to learn which curved, horizontal, vertical, and diagonal lines are meaningful and which only incidental. Both parents and educators have pondered the question of whether teaching children the names of the letters helps the children learn to read. The research evidence is not clear on the subject. On the one hand, DeHirsch and colleagues (1966) found that children's ability to name letters predicts their reading achievement through Grades 1, 2, and into 3. On the other hand, there is no evidence that there is a causal relationship between the two. It may be the case that children who learn letter names at a young age do so because they have an interest in words and this same interest makes them better readers. But if interest is such an important factor, and we saw earlier that both the parents' and the child's interest correlate positively and strongly with later reading ability; thus it would seem that teaching children the names of letters might be beneficial.

Another cognitive correlate of reading ability which preschool children attain is phonemic awareness. However disparate their views of the reading process, most experts agree that *some* degree of sensitivity to the fact that words consist of individual sounds is important to successful reading. Children learning to read English and other alphabetic languages must understand, at the least, that words consist of letters and those letters represent separate sounds that may also exist in other words. Evidence is mounting that the kind of phonemic awareness that is most helpful is that of onsets and rimes (see Chapter 2 and Chapter 10), but there is no compelling evidence that children's understanding of phonemic awareness need be much more sophisticated than this. The reason is that the ability to divide a word into its component sounds is the converse ability to the one required in reading, which is to blend the sounds together to form a sequence of sounds that is sufficiently familiar to permit word recognition. It *is* clear, though, that word recognition is essential to the task of learning to read.

What strategies do preschool children develop that enable them to identify words? Word recognition is a necessary prerequisite to reading, and it is a complicated process to describe. To simplify the procedure greatly, children must examine the printed words and then locate the corresponding entry from long-term memory. Whether they use a phonologically based method or a visually based method of retrieval, this aspect of the task is the same. Using a phonologically based method, they will first recode the printed word into a sequence of sounds and search for a corresponding sound sequence. Using visually based retrieval, they will search for a visual match, skipping the sounding out stage. Children who are especially adept at phonological retrieval will not need to recode the entire word, and even children who normally adopt a visual procedure may occasionally recode the first letter or two of a word.

Although these two methods of retrieval correspond to two approaches to reading instruction, the phonics-based and the whole-word, there is evidence that without instruction children genuinely differ in the strategy they prefer. The traditionally held belief that children begin by sounding out words and then graduate to visual recognition is simply not true for all children. Obviously, many children need to begin with phonological recoding; others recognize the word on the basis of its visual configuration and the context. On confronting the word *stop*, for example, one child may assign a hissing noise to the first letter, a voiceless alveolar stop to the second and so on until a pronunciation is reached which corresponds with one already in memory. Another child may learn the word *stop* by making the association with the red hexagonal sign on which it usually appears. In order to become efficient and fluent readers, all children must eventually abandon phonological recoding as a general strategy although it may be reactivated as a backup strategy when others fail. To illustrate that even proficient readers use a phonological attack strategy when confronted with unfamiliar words, we have only to consider our own behavior with unfamiliar words. If we encounter the pseudoword *grane*, for example, and search our memory on the basis of the visual information alone, we will fail. What we do instead is to assign it a pronunciation on the basis of our knowledge of sound-symbol correspondence, and then search for a match. We then conclude that it is a misspelling of *grain*, a mistyped version of *crane*, or simply a nonsense form, depending on the context. A phonological strategy is available in problem situations such as this, but it is too inefficient as a general strategy, and children who rely on it exclusively will never become proficient readers.

In order to become proficient readers, it is necessary that children acquire more than letter perception skills, phonemic awareness and word identification strategies. In order to become true readers, they must be able to recreate meaning from printed text. Although we use the word *comprehension* to refer to this ability, it is not meant to convey a passive process. On the contrary, reading comprehension is likely one of the most cognitively active and complex activities in which we engage. It is also one of the most important in the lives of young children. To a very large degree, success in reading comprehension will predict children's success in school, but just as important, it will give them the means for developing and pursuing new interests for the rest of their lives, to escape boredom and to acquire a vast amount of information about the world around them and about worlds they may never experience directly. What occurs during the preschool years that serves to shape children's facility to comprehend text?

To answer that question fully is beyond the scope of this book, but it is possible to describe the basic processes involved in comprehension. Notice that in the last sentence, I wrote *comprehension* and not *reading comprehension*. That is because reading comprehension is not an isolated cognitive phenomenon. It involves many of the same processes as listening comprehension. Both listening and reading require us to form and integrate propositions and to draw inferences about what is read or heard and to relate it to what is already known. The fundamental difference between listening and reading comprehension lies in an additional step in reading; the reader must be able to identify individual words, which makes possible the identification of propositions. Perfetti (1984) has postulated two broad components of text comprehension. Local processing refers to "those processes that construct elementary meaning units from text over a relatively brief period" (p. 33). He includes as local processes the identification of words (lexical access) and the building of propositions (proposition assembly). Text modeling

> refers to the processes the reader uses to combine local processes with knowledge about concepts, knowledge about inferences (inference rules), knowledge about the forms of texts, and general knowledge about the everyday world . . . to form a representation of the text meaning. It is this representation that the reader consults at some later time to recall or to answer questions about what has been read. (p. 40)

As an example, let us consider how a proficient reader might come to understand the following sentences.

1. Joe and Jen went to a used car lot.

2. They waited for a salesman to appear.

3. After awhile, they began to look around for themselves.

4. They spotted a blue truck sitting in the shadows.

5. Just as they approached the truck, a smiling man appeared.

Using local processes the reader would construct a rudimentary level of meaning. To begin with, the reader would have to have some kind of recognition and retrieval system to match the words on the printed page with the words stored in memory. Also, the reader would have to select the contextually appropriate meaning for words with more than one meaning. *Lot* in the first sentence is a good example. Its position in the sentence as well as the meanings of the words around it will lead the reader to discount the "large number" lot in favor of the "plot of land" lot. Locating, or encoding, the individual words permits the reader to encode the elementary units of text propositions. The first sentence in the example has eight.

1. Joe exists.
2. Jen exists.
3. The lot exists.
4. Cars exist.
5. They go to the lot.
6. They go at some time in the past.
7. Cars are located at the lot.
8. The cars are used.

Ignoring the fact that the eighth proposition probably contains at least one other proposition, these are the basic meaning elements that the reader has to encode. Each sentence consists of a number of such propositions and so a text can be said to comprise a set of propositions embedded in a set of sentences. The next step in the local processing of these sentences is to assemble and integrate the propositions for longer term memory. By *integrate* is meant the combining of "successively occurring propositions with each other" (Perfetti, 1984, p. 38). The eight propositions of the first sentence must be integrated with each other and then with propositions in successive sentences. There are a number of conventions of writing which facilitate the reader's doing this. One is the use of pronouns. Notice how *they* in sentences two through five serves to link these sentences to each other and to the first sentence which carries the referent, Joe and Jen. Another is the use of the definite article. When the truck is first introduced into the text in the fourth sentence, the indefinite *a* is used. When it appears again in the fifth sentence, the use of *the* reminds the reader that he already knows about the existence of this truck. The definite article is used in a different way in the fourth sentence where we find the truck sitting "in the shadows" even though there has been no previous mention of shadows. In this case, the definite article serves as a signal to the reader's inferencing mechanism. If the reader knows that lots *can* have shadowy places, then the proposition is integrated easily with the others. As Perfetti (1984) puts it, " . . . integrative processes depend on linguistic triggers and the accessibility of linking propositions in memory" (p. 40). In very young children, these triggers and links are largely based in their experience of oral language.

We have not yet achieved comprehension of our short text, though. A useful way of demonstrating the non-local or long-term comprehension process is to reconsider the five sentences we saw earlier. As I write this paragraph, those sentences no longer appear on my computer monitor—I have typed three or four screens beyond them. I shall now reconstruct them from memory and see what variations occur.

1. Joe and Jen went to a used car lot.
2. They were looking around.
3. They didn't see a salesman present.
4. They saw a blue truck sitting in the shadows.
5. As they approached the truck, a smiling salesman appeared.

In my recall of the passage, I correctly reproduced only the first sentence. But I did reconstruct the propositions in the other sentences more or less correctly. Notice that I included a proposition not included in the original, namely that the man who appeared was a salesman. This is an inference that was made possible by my knowledge of the world of car lots. My comprehension of the passage, then, resulted from the three local processes combined with my general knowledge about the everyday world.

It does not sound like a very complicated process, but in fact it is. What has to develop in the young child to make reading comprehension possible? Siegler has suggested that it is a product of five different processes. First, children need to be able to recognize and identify words quickly, with minimal attention to the task, and while simultaneously attending to higher-level tasks. This is called *automatization of lexical access* and means simply that the child must be able to recognize words without conscious effort. Second, children's short-term memories need to expand so that they can remember longer and longer pieces of text. The ability to remember what they have just read is important because it makes it possible for them to integrate previous propositions and to draw inferences among them.

The third dimension of development which children must undergo in order to become proficient readers has to do with background knowledge. Specifically, as children learn more about the worlds in which they live and learn to structure that knowledge in some coherent way, they stand a chance of becoming better readers. As an example, children who are familiar with the standard organization of fairy tales can recall new fairy tales more easily than children who have never heard fairy tales. When it comes to reading an unfamiliar fairy tale, the child who knows how they are structured has a head start on comprehension over the child who does not know. This is true of other types of reading as well. The child with experience of how knowledge is organized for the particular reading task will fare better than the one without.

A fourth area in which children must develop if they are to become successful readers is in monitoring their comprehension. Researchers have demonstrated that better readers within all age groups are the ones who monitor their understanding of the text they are reading and adopt strategies for dealing with any problems they have. These strategies include returning to the source of the problem, correcting words they have identified incorrectly, slowing down, and creating concrete examples for abstract characterizations (Forrest & Walker, 1979; Clay, 1973; Baker & Brown, 1984).

The fifth facet of development which drives reading comprehension is children's increasing ability to adapt their reading strategies to the demands of the particular task. Different types of reading require different reading strategies. As adults, most of us can read a novel in a busy airport or even in front of the television set. Most of us probably could not read a chapter from a university-level physics text in the same setting. Moreover, if we *tried* to read the physics text in the same way as the novel, we would likely not understand or remember very much of what we read. This is because our strategies for comprehending different kinds of text depend on our purpose and on the way the material is structured and presented. Different material makes different demands on us as readers. The ability to adjust our reading behavior to those demands is a significant part of our development as readers.

Very similar cognitive processes operate as we listen to oral language and similar kinds of cognitive development must occur to make us proficient listeners. The fact that listening and reading comprehension have so much in common has led parents and educators to raise the obvious question of why so many children fail to become proficient readers. In their quest for an answer, it has also led many of them to concentrate their attention on that aspect of reading comprehension which most notably differs from listening comprehension, namely lexical access or word identification. Following such reasoning, a reading teacher's thrust would be word-attack skills—if the children can identify the words, they can create the meaning. And for some children this *seems* to be the case. Unfortunately, such reasoning ignores a number of other differences between listening and reading. Children, from birth, have been exposed to oral language being used for communicative purposes. No attempt was made to teach them to listen and the internal knowledge structures (the general knowledge about the everyday world necessary to comprehension of oral or written text) were built at the same time as the language was being created. From birth, they have known the structure of talk and the purpose of talk and no one ever expected them to participate without knowing those things. For some children, there is a genuine difference with reading. If they have not had direct experience with reading, they may not know about the forms of text or about the world of text, or the kinds of things that are written about. They have general knowledge about the everyday world, but this may not be enough to see them through the reading comprehension process if they are lacking in the other kinds of information needed to construct a "text model." If we think of words as blocks and the task of reading as building a castle from blocks, then the problem is easy to see. Having the blocks is essential, but unless you know what a castle looks like, there is little hope of succeeding in getting it built. No amount of block identification activity would help but some pictures of castles or some kind of building plan for a castle would help a great deal.

Most children *do* become proficient readers, eventually, and the foundation for their success is laid in early childhood. It is a simple fact of human nature that most people like to do those things which they are good at doing. Children who have learned to love stories from infancy and who have thus developed an avid interest in print will succeed as readers *unless* the educational system somehow manages to negate all the positive influences of those early years. We will see in a later chapter that this is entirely (and unfortunately) possible. For now, we shall turn our attention to the other side of the reading coin, writing.

Early Learning Associated with Writing

On a number of occasions, Donald Graves has remarked that learning to write should be as easy as learning to read. When we think about their obvious relationship to one another, reading and writing would seem to be essentially mirror images of each other. And perhaps they are. We simply do not know as much about how children learn to write as we do about how they learn to read, although fortunately, researchers are beginning to study young children's writing. They are beginning to find that it makes many of the same demands as speaking, but it is in some ways more demanding.

The business of committing to paper a first draft, whether it be a story told by a 6-year-old or a term paper written by a university student, requires a complex network of interactive processes. In both cases, the writer faces the demands imposed by unfamiliar topics and by multiple goals as well as the mechanical chore of getting thoughts recorded whether to paper or computer memory. Both the child drafting the story and the university student drafting the term paper must begin by retrieving information stored in long-term memory, information relevant to the topic at hand. If the idea for the story (or the term paper) is the writer's own, he has a slight advantage over the writer who is assigned his story or term-paper topic and may have little relevant material stored in long-term memory on which to call. Even when there is information stored, the writer may not have it conveniently organized, and may have to pull it from diverse regions of memory. A paragraph from a first-year university examination paper and a story written by a child in Grade 3 illustrate:

> Linguistics is the study of language. It is a popular course at many universities and is useful for people studying to be teachers, daycare workers, social workers, doctors, lawyers and dentists. One branch of linguistics which is widely studied is psycholinguistics. This is quite unlike historical linguistics which almost nobody studies anymore and would not be useful to daycare workers, social workers, doctors or dentists but might come handy for very old teachers and lawyers. And historians, of course. People who study linguistics are called linguists. They know a lot about languages but do not know how to speak them.

This student was obviously unprepared for the topic demands of this exam and was forced to pull from his long-term memory every bit of information he could about linguistics. The child who wrote the next passage solved a similar problem in much the same way:

> About Deserts
>
> Deserts are hot places wear the wind blose. Not very many peple liv on deserts. Kaktus and tubble weeds grow and maybe some animals but I don't no wich ones. There is a big desert somewear in California and another one in Sehaira, but none in Nova Scotia. The End.

A second demand made on the writer is to formulate goals, or plans, and to keep them in mind long enough to complete the draft. We can see the difficulty with planning in the child's piece on deserts. It is organized in the sense that all the sentences relate to the title, "About Deserts." There is little connection between any of the sentences except that they relate to the title. Unfortunately, this is true of the university student's paragraph as well. Apparently, this kind of organization is typical of children in Grades 2 through 4 (McCutchen & Perfetti, 1982) and demonstrates their difficulty with keeping track of both the point of the topic sentence and the details of other sentences. The result is that their writing sounds more like a list than exposition, narrative, or description.

Finally, the process of drafting makes complex mechanical demands on children. The job of coordinating small fingers to form letters and getting them ordered into words demands so much attention that children may lose track of what they want to say. Research has shown that when children are permitted to dictate their stories rather than write them, they write better quality stories (Bereiter & Scardamalia, 1982). In brief, children's writing ability, where ability consists of being able to tell a story or form a coherent description, is underestimated if we consider only the words they write down. Their sense of story, developed in early childhood, will carry them a long way if they are freed, in at least some writing tasks, from the mechanical demands of writing.

Language and Academic Skills from the Child's Perspective: Six Characteristics of Children's Preschool Learning

It is adults, not children, who categorize some learning as academic and other learning as not. For children, it is all part and parcel of the same thing and it is driven by their natural curiosity in the context of real problems. Margaret Voss relates a story of her son's early learning about reading which makes this point clearly.

> One summer afternoon just a month before his third birthday, Nathaniel sat at the picnic table in our backyard. He had just enjoyed a treat, a jar of apple blueberry baby food. As I turned the jar to examine the label, wondering if I'd just given my son some added sugar, Nathaniel suddenly proclaimed, "Make way for applesauce." Amused and confused, I asked, "What?" "Make way for applesauce," he repeated, pointing to the label. Then he reached out and ran his fingers underneath some words, just as I sometimes do as I read book titles to him. He continued, pointing to and "reading" one word at a time: "it say, 'Make . . . way . . . for . . . applesauce.'" (Voss, 1988, p. 272)

Nathaniel had obviously worked out from his previous experience that print says something—Voss reports that she had been reading his current favorite, *Make Way for Ducklings*, over and over. But he also knew that the print on the label likely related to the contents of the jar, which he also knew. He extrapolated from his prior experience in trying to make sense of a new one. Nathaniel had begun to teach himself to read more than 2 years before the schools would get their chance.

It is parents and educators, not children, who insist on dividing and packaging learning. But before they get to school, children have learned a great deal in general, and they have learned a great deal about learning. Several centuries of research has provided no small amount of insight into the nature of children's early learning, but we hardly need to review it all to make some common-sense observations about what goes on in children's worlds as they build their worldviews, which to adults is the basis for their academic learning.

There are six characteristics of children's preschool learning that are of particular importance to teachers of children.

1. *Children's learning progresses according to their degree of readiness.*   The degree of physical, cognitive, emotional, and social maturity they have attained governs what they learn and when. The most obvious example is language itself. It does no good for a mother to coax and coach her month-old son to say Mama or Dada. The child has not yet achieved sufficient motor control over his articulators to produce the sound reliably. He has not the memory capacity to make the correct associations or to re-produce the correct sequence of sounds reliably. Neither will he be able 6 months later to produce three- or four-word sentences, no matter how much teaching occurs, which brings us to another characteristic of early learning.

2. *Young children are, for the most part, in charge of their own learning.*   This is not to say that they know they are in charge, but simply that they determine what and when they will learn. These decisions are governed, in part, by maturity but also by their natural and robust curiosity about the world around them. My older son, Kerry, could put together wooden jigsaw puzzles with several pieces well before his second birthday. Initially, he was driven to try to put the puzzles together by his desire to see the picture as a whole and, I suspect, by an equally compelling desire to find out if he could do the task. By the time he was 3, he had taught himself to read, by watching *Sesame Street* and by repeatedly asking me to identify words in his books, on signs, everywhere he saw them. Figuring out the relationship between the sounds of words and their written form was very likely another kind of puzzle that he needed to solve.

My other son, Christopher, had no interest in the puzzles at all, possibly be-cause he had seen his brother playing with them so often and knew too well what they were supposed to look like. But long before his second birthday, he wanted to learn to count. He insisted that I count his fingers, my fingers, his toes, books on his shelf, plates at the table, all sorts of things, over and over. He would repeat after me, one-two-three at first and gradually into the 10s, 20s and 30s. This child, incidentally, went on to achieve a near-perfect score on the math SAT some 15 years later. Chris decided not only what he was going to learn but how he was going to learn it. In this he was not unusual. Children are born with curiosity and the drive to satisfy it is the essence of learning.

3. *Play plays an important role in children's learning.*   A great variety of learning oc-curs as they are playing. Playing on swings, monkey-bars, on tricycles, wagons, and even on stairs helps them to acquire gross motor skills and bodily coordination. Playing with smaller objects such as the puzzles Kerry loved or pencils, crayons, or small blocks, helps them develop fine-motor skills as well as eye-hand coordination. But play is also significant to academic learning. Parents who play games with children to keep them from getting bored are providing more opportunities for learning than they re-alize. When they play rhyming games, I Spy, read road signs and license plate num-bers, or count red cars and white cars, they are providing occasions for children to sharpen their recognition and discrimination powers and providing experiences im-portant to literacy. All children play pretend games and benefit from them in at least two ways. First, they are wonderful for the imagination, giving children opportunities to think about the past and to integrate it with the future. Second, fantasy games provide important opportunities for children to use language that is not bounded by the present. They begin, in short, the process of decontextualizing language, of using language that does not refer to real objects in present time.

4. *The role of parents in early learning is facilitator, not instructor.*   As much as I might be tempted to do so, I cannot take credit for my older son's ability to put together puzzles or the fact that he was a very early reader nor for my younger son's learning to count. I helped, of course, but with both children, my job was to sense their readiness (though they made it fairly obvious), provide the help they requested and a number of different materials which would help them to extend their understandings—different kinds and progressively more difficult puzzles for Kerry and an abundance of things to count for Chris.

Perhaps the most important contribution parents make to children's early learning is as partners in daily interaction. Whether the activity be routine, such as washing hands and putting on pajamas, or special, such as decorating a birthday cake or trimming the Christmas tree, the dialogues which occur between parents and children are the means by which children learn. The very first thing they learn, as John Holt (1989) points out, is that speech has purpose:

> Children get ready to speak by hearing speech all around them. The important thing about that speech is that the adults, for the most part, are not talking in order to give children a model. They are talking to each other because they have things to say. So the first thing the baby intuits, figures out, about the speech of adults, is that it is serious. (p. 10)

Once children have learned that the talk around them is purposeful, parents begin to play another role in their dialogues with their children. That role is not as teacher so much as it is facilitator. Gordon Wells (1986) explains:

> Meaning making in conversation should be a collaborative activity. But where there is a considerable disparity between the participants in their mental models and their linguistic resources, the more mature participants must make adjustments in order to make collaboration possible. (p. 89)

Parents, as the more mature participants, make those adjustments which make meaningful dialogue possible. If they are wise they do so not by appropriating the child's conversation as their own, or by interfering with the child's attempts to make meaning, but by holding the conversational doors open in an effort to understand the child's intended meaning. Parents who understand that their own perspective, their own knowledge, cannot be transmitted directly also understand that their role is to gently guide their children as they rebuild the world for themselves.

5. *Interaction is essential to children's early learning.*   This was the principal theme of Chapter 8. We return to it here. Children are not passive participants in the business of learning, vessels awaiting someone to pour in knowledge. Possessed of a boundless curiosity, they eagerly seek answers, test hypotheses and reconfirm those hypotheses as they essentially reconstruct the world through their own experiences.

In the simple act of questioning, children find out what they need to know, extend their knowledge, and open themselves to new ideas on which to build. Consider the following exchange between Matthew, age 3, and his father.

Matthew: What that?
Daddy: Screwdriver. It's called a screwdriver.
M: What do?
D: Well, I'm using it now to put this thing—see it, it's called a screw—into the wood here so horsie's head won't fall off.
M: Horsie head. What that? (Again asking about the screwdriver.)
D: Screwdriver.
M: 'tew . . . (he falters)
D: Screwdriver.
M: Tew diver.
D: Good.
M: Tew diver. Tew diver. Here? (He points to a screw holding on one of the wooden horse's legs.)
D: Yes. That's a screw. I can use the screwdriver to take the screw out. (He begins to remove the screw.)
M: Tew diver. Out.
D: Right. It takes the screw out, too.
M: (Watches his father loosen the screw.) No!
D: Don't worry. We'll put it back again. (Begins reversing the screw.)
M: Tew diver. In.

It is doubtful that Matthew fully understood his father's explanation, but in this situation, he discovered a new label for something in his environment. He doesn't have to wait until he has perfect understanding (or pronunciation) of the word to use it. As he uses it in a variety of contexts, its use will be refined. That refinement will come in dialogues similar to this one, in collaboration with adults. But, of course, in this and other such dialogues, Matthew has learned far more than single words. John Holt (1983) points out that word learning may come nearer the end of children's language learning than the beginning. Before they learn words, children learn

> . . . the large idea of communication by speech, that all those noises that come out of people's mouths mean something and can make things happen. Then, from the tones of people's voices and the contexts in which they speak . . . a very general idea of what they are saying . . . Then they begin to intuit a rough outline of the grammar—i.e., the structure—of the language. Finally, they begin to learn words, and to put those words into their proper slots in the very rough models of grammar which they have invented. (p. 93)

There is an important distinction to be marked here concerning what children learn in dialogue with adults. It is not possible for an adult to pass along a whole, perfectly formed word meaning or concept to a child. What is passed on is the infrastructure which, in continuous interaction with adults and other children, children will build upon. Sometimes, children show a great deal of creativity in the language constructions they build, creating forms or categories which bear little resemblance to those accepted by the adult community. John Holt (1983) relates another story of a child named Jackie, a 2-year-old, who had created in his mind a class of objects that we would call "dry, crumbly things to eat—cookies, crackers, dry toast—to which he had given the name 'Zee.' Neither his father nor his mother knew how he had come to pick that word . . . . Clearly the baby had decided for himself that it was a good name for this class of things" (p. 91). This child had created a category that does not exist in his native language and a word to label it. Such behavior should suggest to us that the role adults play in children's language is not and should not be to teach language. In the dialogue between Matthew and his father, we see an honest, companionable exchange with little if any covert teaching going on. Let's compare it with a dialogue between Barbie, age 2;10, and her mother:

Mother: Do you want peanut butter or cheese today?
Barbie: Peanut butter.
M: And jelly or—
B: No jelly.
M: You don't want jelly. What do you want?
B: Fuff.
M: Marshmallow fluff?
B: Yep. Fuff.
M: Can you say "marshmallow"?
B: No.
M: Sure you can. Try. Marsh-mal-low.
B: Mawo.
M: Good. Marsh-mal-low.
B: Fuff.

This dialogue differs from the one between Matthew and his father in one important way: Barbie's mother takes advantage of the opportunity to do a little language teaching. In this instance, she isn't very successful, but we have to wonder whether such thinly disguised attempts to teach language to young children are good, bad, or unnecessary. Barbie herself shows that they do little good, and John Holt (1983) points out that "billions of children learn to speak who have never been spoken to in this way" (p. 96). And so, we have to consider the strong possibility that surreptitious teaching is a waste of everyone's time. If children do not benefit from it, then we must next decide whether it may do harm. Probably not, but there is at least a slight possibility it does for the simple reason that if children find talk useless or uninteresting, they might not bother with it, and that could be detrimental to their learning it.

What, then, is the role of dialogue with adults in children's language and learning? To answer this, we need to look at the adult's role not as *talker* but as listener. Parents who work hard at understanding what young children say to them contribute significantly to their children's learning. Children catch on quickly when people aren't really paying attention, and if they too frequently have the experience of not being able to make themselves understood or to get a response to their overtures, they may conclude that there is no point in even trying to make themselves understood. Parents who persist in trying to understand children's attempts to communicate and make sense of the world will foster in their children a positive attitude toward language and learning. Finally, Holt captures the essence of the role of the adult when he says that if children find talk to be honest, companionable, and fun, then they will want to do it and will learn to do it. Talk related to activity, talk about things of significance to children, talk introduced by children—all kinds of *real* talk—inspire children to figure out how to do it.

6. *Learning is embedded in the process of socialization.*   Children's lives are not like school curricula. They are not divided up into components and assigned different periods of time—an hour to work on motor development, half an hour for memory development, 20 minutes for hygiene, and an hour and a half for socialization into the family and community. Their learning occurs in an unfragmented whole as part of the process of acquiring full membership in the local society of the family and community. Humans are social animals; they live in groups, and children's early learning is directed toward achieving group membership. They don't learn to say words because it is biologically time to do so or even because language is part of their internal curriculum. They learn language because that is the means through which people connect with one another. From the perspective of children, their preschool years are spent not in learning words, improving their memory, learning concepts, or acquiring the bases for academic learning, but in learning to become like the people around them.

CONCLUSION

This chapter has been about the duality between children's language and learning in the preschool years. In the first section, we examined the intertwining of language and learning by viewing learning through the lens of language. In particular, we saw that parents and teachers can gain valuable insights into children's learning by examining the functions to which children put language in their lives. We identified and traced the development of five functions of these language functions.

In the second section, the duality was examined from the perspective of cognitive growth. In particular, we looked at the development of memory, conceptualization, and academic thinking and the role language plays in each. Throughout, an attempt was made to understand the relationship between language and learning from the child's point of view. Out of all these discussions came six characteristics of children's preschool learning.

If they are to understand what happens in school and, in particular, why some children experience difficulty in school, parents and teachers should understand how children learn before they get to school. They then have the basis for understanding why the environment of the classroom is so alien to some children. In Chapter 10, we continue to explore the dual relationship between language and learning, taking our investigation into the school years and the environment of the classroom.

EXERCISES AND QUESTIONS FOR DISCUSSION

1. Read the following list of words twice and then close the book and attempt to repeat them. Which words did you not recall? What strategies did you adopt to remember the words?

Cook	Joyful
Data	Acne
Boy	Tonic
Book	Gymnasium
Matches	Caldron
Sugar	Rabbit

   See how many of the words you can remember one day later.

2. Repeat the same exercise with the following list, only this time write down the words first and then try to recall them without looking. Were you more successful than in the previous exercise? Why?

Misery	Cup
Cape	Romania
Tuna	Juice
Picture	Market
Secretary	Anger
Dust	Convention

3. What is the role of motivation in learning to read?

4. Sir Edmund Huey once observed that "an understanding of all that is involved in the reading system would be 'the acme of a psychologist's achievement'"(Dickinson et al., 1993, p. 377). Explain what you think he meant by this statement and why he believed it was true.

5. To what degree can reading be thought of as socially interactive?

6. How do you think the process of learning to read differs in a child who has a significant hearing impairment?

CHAPTER TEN

Schooling and Language Growth

Researchers who study language acquisition tend to concentrate on infants and young children. The unofficial canon is that by the time they reach school age, most of children's language learning is complete. They have mastered the major feats of phonology, morphology, and syntax and have a large vocabulary. This is certainly an impressive accomplishment, but the task has not ended. Teachers know that children have a great deal more language to learn, both oral and written. When they come to school, children begin to build upon their experience as language learners, but that experience will only carry them so far because, as we have seen, there are fundamental differences between the language of the home and the language of the school. The former is, for the most part, grounded in tangible reality while the latter tends to be more closely linked to the abstract world of concepts and ideas.

At the end of the last chapter were outlined six characteristics of early learning outside school. If we were to condense those characteristics into a single observation, we could do no better than to borrow from Gordon Wells' (1986) fine book *The Meaning Makers*:

> In the preschool years . . . talking and learning go hand in hand. Children talk about the things that interest them and try to increase their understanding; and, for much of the time, their adult conversational partners sustain and support their efforts, seeking, where appropriate, 'to add a pebble to the pile.' What is characteristic of such learning is that it is spontaneous and unplanned and, because it arises out of activities in which one or both of the participants are engaged, it is focused and given meaning by the context in which it occurs. (p. 67)

In his book, Wells makes direct and systematic comparisons between children's language and learning in the home and in the school, his principal argument being that the mismatch between the two goes a long way toward accounting for the lack of success that some children experience. This chapter makes similar comparisons, extending them to certain minority groups, and reiterates the argument not to change the child but to change the attitude of mainstream education.

THE ATTITUDES OF SOME EDUCATORS

The business of teaching and of planning educational curricula should be governed by two fundamental questions: What is the nature of human learning? and What is the best way of teaching to facilitate that learning? It is probably important to ask a third question as well: What is to be learned? Certainly, in teacher education programs, various forms of those three questions form the basis of the curriculum, although the degree to which they are answered is arguable. In the next chapter, I will argue that the question of what is to be learned is historically and societally constrained, and, thus, largely outside the control of individual teachers. Here, then, I will concentrate on the first two questions. Refining the questions slightly, educators should be asking what *experience* of learning children bring when they begin school and how educators can build upon that experience in preparing for the next stage of children's education. In other words, it would make sense if we thought of schooling not as the beginning of education but as the next stage in a process that began 5 or 6 years earlier. With regard to language learning, and literacy in particular, we would think of the school years as providing new opportunities for children to acquire more language and more uses for their language, to grow in and with their language.

Some educators might view education exactly in that way, but they are likely in the minority. That, at least, is the view of leading educators such as Gordon Wells, John Holt, Judy Lindfors and a number of other researchers and writers in the last two decades. Indeed, I would claim that it is not the way most teachers of elementary school children think about their jobs. Rather, they assume the canonical view that equates education with schooling.

> When children arrive at school, things begin to change. Now a child is one among many, known by teachers in ways less intimate. A child is no longer known in her entirety; it is as if her life history begins again when she walks through the classroom door. (Kuschner, 1989, p. 45)

The first day of school has always been a momentous occasion, one which most of us remember even after the passing of several decades. In the past and for some children, the significance of the occasion may have resided in the fact that school marked the beginning of separation from home and parents. But it remains a noteworthy event for children today, many of whom have already spent a number of years in day care or nursery school. As David Kuschner says of his daughter, Emily:

> Somehow my daughter knew that there was something special about going to kindergarten, that there was something special about starting school. Even though she had attended a day care center for two years, knew what it was like to move through activity times and learning centers, knew what it was like to have 'school friends' as something different from neighborhood friends, and knew what it was like to have teachers, she had it in her mind that kindergarten would be different.
> . . . I don't know when or how she had learned about school, but somehow she knew it would be different. And she was right. (Kuschner, 1989, p. 44)

Schools take responsibility and credit for all manner of "new" learning, chief among which is literacy, even though many children know a great deal about reading and writing when they arrive at school. All in all, we carry on as though learning is what begins when the child first puts a tentative foot inside the classroom door, as though children's minds are blank slates to be written upon or soft clay to be molded. But despite the fact that there may be much writing and molding yet to be done, children arrive at school neither blank nor unformed.

Change the Child

It is just common sense to assume that children who are comfortable in the school setting, who do not find their daily activities to be much different from those they have engaged in at home, will adapt to school more easily and be more successful. This is an assumption shared by schools and parents and borne out by research. Both Heath and Wells show rather conclusively that schools are essentially middle class institutions, and the children who best succeed there are those from middle class homes with middle class values. Educators have known this for a very long time, and although they are to be commended for their efforts in creating equal educational opportunities, the response has been dubious. Most educators are likely unaware that their response is not to change the school in any fundamental way, but to change the child. Rather than to make the school environment (over which they have nearly complete control) more welcoming, educators choose to try to change the child. The evidence abounds. Programs such as Head Start have traditionally concentrated on compensating for or overcoming sociological disadvantage (read "Change the child") rather than on changing the school.

This is a totally unreasonable attitude for a number of reasons. In the first place, such solutions view the child as having a deficit. I find this to be arrogantly objectionable in itself, but even if it were true, from a practical perspective, we probably cannot "undo" the home experience of the child, even if such action were necessary or defensible. In the second place, it ignores what we have discovered in the past decade about sociocultural bias. As David Dillon (1989) writes in an editorial for an issue of *Language Arts* dedicated to home-school relationships,

> . . . there are different kinds of literacies characteristic of different cultural, religious, and especially socioeconomic groups. Being literate according to the norms of one social group does not mean being literate within another social group. (p. 7)

He also points out that research hasn't even begun to address the effect this kind of thinking has on non-mainstream children. We only have to look at the disproportionally high referral rates of Native American (First Nations) children to special education classes or the high incidence of misdiagnosis of learning disabilities (Bailey, 1994) to realize that our first response is almost always to fix the child. It is telling that researchers have to point out that a change in attitude and expectation among all parties to the educational enterprise—parents, community, and educators—is required if Native American children are to have anything approaching equal educational opportunity (Bailey, 1994). Experienced and sensitive teachers have always known this, however. They could tell us that thinking about education in such a narrow way means that we fail to take advantage of the assets, the experience children already have of the world and of learning, and makes the job of teaching harder rather than easier. In short, the direction of educational thinking has traditionally been on preparing children for school rather than on preparing schools for children, and it has resulted in failure for too many children.

Change the Language

When educators set about to change children, one of the first things they identify as needing change is their language. Sometimes, misinterpretation or misapplication of sociolinguistic theory is to blame. In the 1970s, a British sociolinguist named Basil Bernstein hypothesized the existence of two kinds of oral language. The first, called the elaborated code, was the language used in formal situations (such as school) and was characterized by complex syntactic and stylistic conventions. It was considered to be the language for representing abstract thought, its meaning created by linguistic means alone. The other, called the restricted code, was used in informal situations and was characterized by a simpler stylistic and syntactic range and a restricted vocabulary. It was also thought to rely more heavily on accompanying context (situation and gestures, for example) to make its meaning clear and to be incapable of expressing abstractions. Bernstein's observation that middle class children have access to both codes and that some lower class children may have access only to the restricted code led many educators to take the view that children from lower socioeconomic classes have a language deficit that must be overcome if they are to succeed in school.

The hypothesis has largely been discredited now, due in part to the work of Labov (1982) and Wells (1986). Labov demonstrated that the so-called restricted code is perfectly adequate for expressing abstract concepts. More recently, researchers have shown concrete differences between the discourse style of non-mainstream children and that of teachers and middle class white children. A number of studies (Wells, 1986; Heath, 1983; Lindsay, 1992; Michaels & Cazden, 1986) have all examined one aspect or another of the relationship between children's sociolinguistic background and the language of the school. Attempting to discover precisely what it is about the language of the school that makes it relatively "unlearnable" for non-mainstream children, researchers have found that one of the chief differences lies in narrative style. Black children and Native American children (*first nations* children in Canada) tend to use a style of narrative discourse termed *topic associating* as opposed to the *topic centered* style favored by white teachers and middle class white children. There are, in fact, many different styles within the broad category of topic associating, and it would be a mistake to assume that all native children or all minority children acquire the same discourse style. The point is that it is different from the topic centered discourse style of middle class white children. This style typically features tightly organized plot structure—a beginning, middle, and end—with lexical devices (*and then, because, and so . . .*) providing cohesion to the narrative. A topic associating discourse style is marked by "frequent shifts without explicity lexical markers" and cohesion provided chiefly through intonation (Lindsay, 1992, p. 205).

Since most published stories for children are topic centered, it is easy to understand why Gordon Wells' study, and many others, have shown that children who have engaged in the school-like activities of reading and storytelling, and whose narrative styles thus more closely match the teacher's, are most successful in school. This research points educators in the right direction, but it is a direction that is usually ignored. Rather, the research is used as a justification for the less than stellar achievement levels of non-mainstream children and also for the practice of trying to change the child's language to make it fit the mainstream. It is easy to evade responsibility for high rates of illiteracy, for example, if we can blame the children for bringing to school the wrong kind of language.

Based on his monumental and impressive longitudinal study of children acquiring language in Bristol, Gordon Wells reached what he considered to be his most important finding: ". . . up to the age of 5, there were no clear differences between the middle- and lower-class groups of children in their rate of development, in the range of meanings expressed, or in the range of functions for which language was used" (Wells, 1986, p. 142). In describing his findings, Wells disclosed one fact that helps to account for the tenacity of the belief that lower class children come from linguistically deficient homes. He noted that the "half dozen or so most advanced children . . . did tend to come from the better-educated, professional homes" and that "the half dozen or so least advanced children came from homes where the parents were minimally educated and worked, or had worked, in unskilled or semiskilled occupations." But he was quick to point out that for 90% of the 128 children he studied, "there was no clear relationship between family background and level of language development attained" (Wells, 1986, p. 134).

The myth should be put finally and forever to rest. We can proceed in confidence that the language of the children we meet in school has served well the demands placed upon it, and there is no evidence that children from one socioeconomic class makes more demands on it than children from another. The problem is that the language of the child may differ from the language of the school, and it is the school that refuses to change. I have collected a number of accounts over the years that taken together constitute evidence that when it comes to children's language, some classrooms are far from being user-friendly. Incredibly, some take what seems to be an openly hostile attitude to children's talk. Even mainstream children whose own language more closely matches the school norm find much of what happens in classrooms to be strange if not inane. They are simply better at making the necessary linguistic adaptations—they learn to play along. But not all are successful, and in this chapter, we will learn some of the reasons why.

We will look at the language of schools and in schools. Ideally, anyone interested in finding out about the language experience of children in schools will spend time in schools watching and listening. But this is not possible for everyone, and, even when it is, some preparation is necessary to make the observations worthwhile experiences. This kind of background is provided, in part, by the observations of others. Some are anecdotal: the stories told by teachers and children and others who have had experience in classrooms. Others are more formal: reports of studies conducted by researchers interested in children's language growth through the school years.

WHAT'S WRONG WITH LANGUAGE IN SCHOOL

I must begin this section with a cautionary note. Finding fault is easy, but that is not my purpose. I realize that I run two tangible risks here. The first is that by selecting anecdotes to make my points about the disparity between natural language and school language, I present only the negative when in fact I have never visited a classroom where nothing good occurred. The second is that I present a view that seems to undermine my own belief in teachers and in education. Both are dangerous, so let me attempt to control the damage before it is done.

First, even in a poor educational setting, there is likely a great deal of learning, and that may not be apparent in the anecdotes related here. Second, *all* teachers work under conditions that are less than ideal. In recent years, salaries and benefits have improved in some states and provinces, but rarely have they kept up with relative gains in the economy. Teachers have been beleaguered by attacks on their professionalism and made the scapegoats of a political bureaucracy keen to make change (and political impact). Most importantly, classroom conditions have worsened. The demands on teachers have increased dramatically in the latter half of the 20th century. As the structure of the family has become more fragile, teachers have had to assume roles and responsibilities that once belonged exclusively to families. The need to educate children to the dangers of drugs, protect them from abuse, act as advocates, and generally prepare them for a life that is harder and less friendly than it was a half century ago, has left teachers with less time to devote to what were once major goals of schools. Because teachers work under such hardship, we must be *very* careful not to sit in judgment of them, particularly when it is as uninformed as ours is on such scant evidence. That is not my intent, and I hope that I need not reiterate my support for and belief in the teachers who take on the responsibility for education but receive so little of the credit for what goes right.

Later in this chapter, we will meet two teachers who provide good, healthy experiences; the anecdotes that follow here are offered as extreme examples of how children should *not* experience language in a classroom.

"No Talking" and Other Unfriendly Signs

In 1983, John Holt wrote, ". . . in almost all schools, hardly anything is done to help children become fluent, precise, and skilful in speech" (p. 123). This allegation, and it is a serious one, was made toward the end of a chapter about how children learn to talk. His point was *not* to cast aspersions on schools, though he would hardly cast them bouquets either, but to identify the fundamental disparity between children's language and learning when they are left to their own devices and what they experience in schools.

A few years ago, a research assistant was observing a kindergarten class in which she recorded the following dialogue, which has been edited only slightly:

Teacher: (Pointing to a dog in a picture in a picture book.) Molly, do you know what this is?
Molly: Yes.

T: What is it?
M: A dog.
T: Very good. And what's he playing with?
M: A ball.
T: And what color is the ball?
M: Red.
T: Right. (Pointing to a girl in the picture) What is she wearing?
M: A skirt and blouse.
T: What else?
M: Shoes and socks.
T: That's good Molly. What do you think about this picture?
M: It's nice.

At the time the recording was made, Molly was 5;6. She is of normal academic ability and her first language is English. The teacher was not teaching Molly new English vocabulary or structures. Nor was she reading a story. It is not immediately clear, in fact, just what the teacher was doing. This is, I freely admit, a radical example of bad classroom talk. Yet, for many teachers, this dialogue will be at least vaguely familiar, if not in substance then in character. The really scary thing about this dialogue is that it has not been very many years since we would have identified this as an example of a good classroom exchange and held it up as an example of how to interact with young children.

To illustrate how purposeless this talk is, suppose Molly had responded to the teacher as an adult might have if asked the same questions. The following might have transpired:

Teacher: Molly, do you know what this is?
Molly: Of course I do, don't you?
T: What is it?
M: A dog. Geez! Any 3-year-old knows that.
T: Very good. And what's he playing with?
M: Looks like a dump truck to me. Only kidding. That's a ball.
T: And what color is the ball?
M: Color blind, too? Fuschia with a hint of sienna.
T: Right. (Pointing to a girl in the picture) What is she wearing?
M: How much longer are we going to keep this up? Whadaya think she's wearing, a
   barrel? She's wearing clothes. Okay, I'll play along. A skirt and a blouse.
T: What else?
M: Shoes and socks.
T: That's good. What do you think about this picture?
M: I think that girl's mother must be crazy to let her go out to play with the dog in
   her good clothes. No kid I know wears a skirt to school much less to play in. Come
   to think of it, I don't think I know anyone who owns a skirt.

But this dialogue is fictitious. Molly did not respond in this way because she is a child; in the course of a few months in school, being subjected to talk little more purposeful than that in the first dialogue, Molly had internalized many of the characteristics of school talk. She had learned that in school, language is unreal. People, especially teachers, talk about things that no one cares much about. She had learned that school language is decontextualized. Not only do teachers habitually talk about things that aren't there, they seem to avoid opportunities for talking about real things. In the first dialogue, the teacher didn't relate the picture to a story she was reading or make up a story about the picture or provide any real-world context at all for the child. Nor did she encourage Molly to relate the picture to her own life through talk.

Molly had also learned that people, teachers anyway, ask silly questions. Sometimes, they ask questions for which they have already determined the correct answers. Sometimes, they even ask questions that *everybody* knows the answers to and then praise the answers. *How many fingers am I holding up? Three? Very good!* She had learned that much school talk, devoid as it is of purpose and meaning, is easy. Once she figured out just what game the teacher was playing, it was not difficult to play along.

It is also telling to examine the dialogue from a functional perspective. It doesn't take long. Although superficially, the teacher's questions seem to request information, in fact they do not. She already knows the answers and her questions serve only to instruct—to draw Molly's attention to a picture she probably would not be otherwise interested in. The true function of her language seems to be to control Molly's behavior, to direct it toward the teacher's unclear but likely pedagogical purpose. Beyond this, it is hard to find any other function. She is even less successful in providing opportunities for Molly to use language in different ways. Molly only responds to the questions she is asked, mechanically giving the expected responses. We cannot even claim that she is using language to inform, because both she and the teacher know that they both already know the answers. The teacher is steering Molly through a match game, checking to see if the child's answers are identical to the expected ones.

It is ironic that when children get into minor trouble at school, that trouble is so often "talking." Children learn very soon that although schools purport to value language, they don't much value *talk*, not children's talk anyway. The truth of this observation was driven home to me during a visit to a southern California school a few years ago.

A Canadian teacher, a former student of mine, had been hired to teach ESL in a junior high school, considered by the local Board of Education to be one of the best in the area, a model school in many regards. While I was there, the young teacher took me to visit a number of classrooms, but one stands out in my memory. The room was filled with bright, colorful travel posters of exotic places. A VCR and monitor stood in a prominent place in the front of the room and every piece of furniture, every object in the room was labeled with its name in clear black letters on a white card. What I remember best, though, was the largest sign in the room, placed above the blackboard in letters about 9 inches high. In this ESL classroom where the purpose was to foster children's language learning, the sign said "NO TALKING."

We shouldn't assume that there was no talking in that classroom for most assuredly there was. But this brings us to another problem with classroom talk, and a very serious one: The people who would most benefit from honest, purposeful talk are the ones who get the least opportunity to do it. Teachers don't need the practice; children do. But they get little of it in the worst situations and not nearly enough in the best. We don't need research studies or even samples of classroom talk to tell us that this is true. We only have to consider the normal protocol of the classroom. For the most part, it states that children talk only to the teacher and only when requested to do so.

Teachers Value Talk

The message on a "No Talking" sign is unambiguous, but sometimes school messages are less clear. Every time a teacher asks a question to which there is only a single correct answer that she will accept, she is sending the message that a child's talk is important only if it fits her expectations. It is in this sense, then, that teachers value talk; they *evaluate* it. When he makes a value judgment about a child's language, as he does when he tries to correct it or change it, a teacher is telling the child that her talk does not count. The message is sent in myriad ways. The following dialogue that a student teacher recorded tells a wonderfully revealing story about children with dialect differences that underscores my point:

> A teacher in a Western Canadian school had a number of minority children in her Grade 1 class. Among these children were represented three different aboriginal languages. One of the children, Bob, was a native speaker of English, but it was a non-standard dialect since he had learned it on the Reserve from his parents and their generation who were not native speakers of English. The teacher was of the misguided opinion that these children needed ESL and thus, her lessons sometimes had that flavor. One morning a few days after the beginning of school in September, the teacher was teaching the names of items of clothing, and the following occurred:

> **Teacher:** (Pointing to her shoes.) What are these called?
> **Child 1:** Shoes.
> **T:** Right. And what do you wear with shoes?
> **Bob:** Socks (pronounced *shocks*). I gots green ones.
> **T:** Those are "socks" Bobby. Can you say "socks"?
> **B:** Yeah. Shocks. I got shum blue ones too.
> **T:** Some blue what?
> **B:** Shocks.
> **T:** No, say "socks." Those are "socks" not *shocks*.
> **B:** Das what I say. Shocks.

By this time Bob, and probably the other children as well, wondered why they were dwelling on such an inane topic. Surely there was no one left in the class who didn't know what socks were. This teacher made several mistakes but chief among them were the assumption that talk in the classroom would serve *her purposes* and that *she alone* was the arbiter of correct pronunciation. This teacher should have counted herself very fortunate if Bob ever ventured to speak again. Why would he? This anecdote, like the earlier ones, is extreme in illustrating its point. But there are thousands of dialogues each day between teachers and students, and many of these are characterized by dishonesty and manipulation.

Dishonest and Manipulative Talk

By dishonesty, I do not mean that teachers tell children lies and by manipulation I do not mean to suggest that teachers consciously manipulate children's behavior to selfish ends. Rather, I mean any kind of unnatural classroom talk that is directed toward pedagogical ends and not toward communication with children. Some see this kind of talk as endemic in classrooms. As John Holt writes,

> . . . if we think that every time we talk to a child we must teach her something, our talk may become calculated and fake, and may lead the child to think, like so many of today's young people, that all talk is a lie and a cheat. (Holt, 1983, p. 107)

We saw this kind of dishonesty in the dialogue—it could hardly be called conversation—between Molly and her teacher. It isn't necessary to call upon such extreme examples, however, to make the point. We have only to consider the false tones that primary teachers sometimes adopt when talking to children or the fact that we plan so much of our talk to lead us down some pedagogical path.

A number of researchers have described this "pedagogical register" or "teacher-talk register." Heath has observed that it uses higher pitch than other speech registers, and has exaggerated enunciation and intonation patterns (Heath, 1978, cited in Roller, 1989). Cazden (1987) has mentioned "the myriad expressions of control; the prevalence of 'testing' questions; the use of boundary markers such as *now, well,* and *okay*" (p. 31). We have all heard this kind of teacher talk, and if we recognize it, we can be certain that children recognize it as well. They may not make quite the same judgments about it, but with enough exposure, they must surely come to understand that it is different from the registers used when two people are engaged in an honest conversational exchange. The pedagogical "register proclaims not that 'we are talking together,' but that 'I am teaching you' " (Roller, 1989, p. 497).

Teacher talk also reveals itself as dishonest when it is directed toward a pedagogical point and entirely controlled by the teacher. Cathy Roller (1989) provides a good example of this kind of talk and of the pedagogical register in use in the following example:

Teacher: The first question I'd like to ask you about today is whether or not you've participated in a science fair or some kind of contest where you had to make something. Think for a minute. How did you feel when you were entering this contest? Give me a low signal when you're ready to tell about your past experience. OK, C1.

Child 1: When I was in Cub Scouts we had to make a robot out of boards, bottle caps, and (*unintelligible*). At first I thought I was going to win, but when I got to the judging I saw other things that were a lot better than mine.

T: While you were constructing your robot you thought you probably would win. Were you nervous?

C1: No.

T: Not too nervous. Who else has been in a contest like that?

Child 2: I was in the same thing. I wasn't, I got it done. I knew I wouldn't win anything.

T: Uh, huh.

C2: Turned out I was sick that night so I never got to take it in.

T: You never got to take it in. Child 3, have you ever entered a contest or something like that? Some other kind of competition maybe, where you're up against other people and they're doing the same kind of thing you're doing? Child 4?

Child 4: In fourth grade where we had a Valentine party. We had to make these boxes. When I first made it, I didn't think I was going to win at all because I just got some old things and put it together so.

T: What kind of box was it?

C4: Just a Valentine's box in fourth grade where we used to put our envelopes into.

T: Uh, huh. I can remember doing that in school too. Child 5? Have you ever entered a competition?

Child 5: There was a Halloween where you had to color a picture in or draw it. I entered it but I didn't win anything.

T: How did you feel?

C5: I didn't really care.

T: You didn't care whether you won or not. Well, in the story today is a girl named Maria, and she's entering a science fair, so she has to have a pretty elaborate project. How do you think she feels? Just think about it a minute. The importance of the project. C3?

Child 3: I think she feels really nervous.

T: Nervous. C4, how about you?

C4: She's anxious.

T: OK. Let me get some of these words down. I like these words. Nervous, anxious (*writing on board*). Anybody else? C1.

C1: Scared.

T: Scared. C5, do you agree with those?

C5: Uh, huh.

T: Is that what you think she probably will be feeling? OK. (pp. 495–496)

This is an excellent example of talk that scores of teacher educators in the past touted as good teacher talk, as good preparation for the basal story to follow. After all, as Roller (1989) pointed out, the "teacher initiated the discussion, directed the turns, and, after each child's response, commented" in relentless pursuit of her teaching point which was, we can assume, to relate the children's prior knowledge to the reading they were about to do (p. 496). There was a time when some teachers believed this was as it should be. But is it? Admittedly, it is not as bad as the talk that occurred between Molly and her teacher, but we have only to look more closely at the interchange to see that it is highly controlled and manipulative in a number of ways.

First, it was carried out according to the teacher's agenda. She had a purpose and she manipulated the children's talk to that purpose. She initiated the turns, decided when they were completed and controlled what would be talked about. She conveniently ignored the fact that some of the children's honest responses did *not* lead them in the direction she wanted them led (most of them reported feeling no nervousness or anxiety) for it did not matter. She soon wrested control of the talk back and called on another child who might give a better response.

Second, it was conversationally dishonest. No adult would stay around very long to talk to someone whose only contribution to the conversation was to repeat what was last said and then turn to someone else. The repetitions of the children's responses served no purpose whatever. Had they elaborated or expanded the children's language (and this is likely what the teacher *believed* they did), they would have served some purpose. But they did not. Third, the exchange was dishonest in the sense that although it pretended to draw out children's experiences, it did not do so in any meaningful way. As Roller observed, even though the teacher directed many questions at the children's experience, she also controlled the bounds of the communication. She determined what was appropriate for discussion and made it clear that what was appropriate was what she wanted to hear (p. 497).

This excerpt demonstrates another difficulty with classroom talk. Even if honesty, directness, and high interest for the children had characterized the talk, it did not provide much opportunity for each child to talk. Instead, the children formed a captive audience, witnesses to the teacher's controlling language. She used language to accomplish her own agenda, ostensibly providing opportunities for children to engage in meaningful talk but in fact setting severe limits on the language they used.

Teacher Talk Is Teacher Talking

At home, most children have ample opportunity to talk even if they have to share the time with a number of siblings or members of an extended family. But that changes when they get to school. As Cazden (1987) notes, "In the classroom, the group is larger than even the largest families gathered at meals, and so getting a turn to talk is much harder. . . ." (p. 31). Children need to talk, and for the most part teachers do not, yet we can see that teachers do most of the talking. In the excerpt above, we saw a teacher dominating the proceedings, but a closer examination gives us some idea about the impact of that domination on the air time accorded individual children. We don't need a sophisticated analysis; we can get a rough indication by comparing the number of words uttered by each speaker. Table 10.1 shows the proportion of talk attributable to the teacher and each child measured in words.

Table 10.1 Proportion of Teacher Talk

Participant	Total Words	% of Total
Teacher	288	62.3
C1	48	10.4
C2	33	7.1
C3	6	1.3
C4	59	12.8
C5	28	6.1
Total	462	100

We see that even in comparison to the total amount of talk allowed the children, the teacher gets the lion's share with more than 62%. When we consider what this means to each child, the picture grows even darker. At best, C4 generated a total of 59 words for just under 13% of the total talk.

When he directly compared language of the school with language of the home, Gordon Wells found that the number of child utterances directed to an adult was nearly three times greater at home than at school and that children initiated conversation nearly three times more often at home than at school. The number of child speaking terms per conversation was greater at home, by a ratio nearly two to one, but the most telling of the results were these:

a. The proportion of display questions directed by an adult to a child was seven times greater at school than at home. (These are questions which do not request information but provide an opportunity to display knowledge, such as *What color is the ball?* asked Molly by her teacher.),

b. Adults used language to extend children's meaning twice as often at home as at school, and similarly,

c. By a proportion of two to one, teachers develop their *own* meanings more than parents do when talking to children. (Wells, 1986, pp. 67–94)

Teachers' domination of classroom talk costs dearly. As Wells (1986) points out, "conversation is a reciprocal activity: the more one participant dominates, the more the opportunities for the other participant to make his or her own personal contribution are reduced and constrained" (p. 87). It would seem that classrooms are poor places for developing conversational skills. Not only do teachers control the amount of time children spend in talk, they also control the purposes to which it is directed. The child Molly learned very young that when school talk has purpose, it is usually the *teacher's* purpose. She had recognized the kind of talk John Holt (1983) reviled when he wrote:

> . . . The teacher does most of the talking, and now and then asks the children questions, to make sure they have been paying attention and understand. Now and then a bold teacher will start what they call a 'discussion.' What happens then is usually . . . 'answer pulling.'

The teacher asks a series of pointed questions, aimed at getting students to give an answer that he has decided beforehand is right. Teachers' manuals are full of this technique— 'Have a discussion, in which you draw out the following points. . . .' This kind of fake, directed conversation is worse than none at all. Small wonder that children soon get bored and disgusted with it. (p. 123)

And if they are bored, how can they be expected to learn? Much of the time, they don't. Jon McGill (1988), writing of talk in his history classroom, tells of his efforts to bring his information-dispensing talk to life:

A recent lesson to fourth year CSE [Certificate in Secondary Education] pupils involved lengthy outlines of the origins of trade unions. Though I specifically wanted an information giving lesson I also wanted to entertain. Though I conveyed the information using dramatic language, role play and gesture, I was nonetheless left feeling that, in summarizing the lesson, students would see it simply as the teacher having talked—and remain unimpressed by the pyrotechnics which tried to disguise the fact. The next lesson with these pupils demonstrated that they retained little except the drama and the display. What I said was of little impact and during my 'exemplary' lesson, they had said little. (pp. 78–79)

Claire Staab (1991) reported results of a study which showed that in the Grade 3 and Grade 6 classrooms she studied, 78% of class time was devoted either to the teacher talking or to quiet time. This research showed that although 98.5% of the participating teachers professed to believe that "oral language should be a way to learn all content areas," in practice the oral language tended to be their own (Staab, 1991, p. 44). Staab also found that her results were essentially the same as those reported 20 years ago, suggesting that all the research and writing about the importance of talk in classrooms has had little effect.

Teachers talk, and sometimes children listen. Even less often, it seems, they learn. The same tale is told in thousands of households each day as children return home from school to be asked the time-honored question, What did you do in school today?

Parent: What did you do in school today?
Child: Nothing.
P: Surely, something happened.
C: (Thinking about it for a moment.) Nope.
P: Nothing at all?
C: No. The teacher talked a lot. And Mary Beth got in trouble.
P: What did the teacher talk about?
C: I dunno. Stuff.
P: What did Mary Beth get into trouble for?
C: Talking to Peter and me. She was telling us about how her brother broke his foot. You know James? Well he went skiing for the first time ever and . . .

Teachers will have to learn to value children's talk, genuinely, before they will be able to break out of the mold of talking too much and with too little meaning.

School Talk Is Homogeneous

Talk at home is unstructured and relatively free. Parents do not schedule time for conversation, although they may schedule time for a bedtime story. Conversation happens as the people in the household go about their daily activities. Similarly, most children are exposed to a wide variety of talk—numerous dialects and numerous purposes. Dillon (1980) describes the kinds of language a child encounters in the simple act of getting ready for school in the morning:

> Susan's grandmother, who lives with them, tells Susan that her lunch is in the ice box. Susan is in a hurry as she gets it, and her mother calls after her, "Susan, close the refrigerator door." As she stops to do this, Susan hears the morning weather report. It's an interview of a New England resident and sounds something like "The stawm dumped a lawt of snow heah," and she wishes her own Midwestern town would get some snow soon. She meets her friends on the way to school and greets them one by one. "Hey, what's up?" "Boy, sure is cold!" "Think it'll snow?" As they approach the school, the children meet the principal. "Good morning, Mr. Lawrence," Susan says. "How are you today?" He responds and heads for his office as Susan and her friends hurry to class. (pp. 29–30)

In the course of a few minutes, Susan has been exposed to variations caused by language change over time—her grandmother uses *icebox* and her mother *refrigerator*. She hears and has no difficulty understanding the regional dialect on the broadcast news. She switches easily to the subject and vernacular of her peer group and, when she gets to school, to the more formal requirement of greeting the principal. She hurries to class where she will find *some* variation among her classmates, but chances are that the language she encounters there will be somewhat more homogenized than the language of the home, not only because the teacher does most of the talking but because schools sustain their own brand of language.

Most schools perpetuate a variety of English they call the standard dialect. Even in schools that have dropped the notion of a standard, preferred, or educated dialect, there is still a high degree of conformity. This is true in part because they mostly hear teachers whose speech has likely been sanitized as they acquired the education needed to become teachers. I live in a part of Canada where the residents have a readily distinguishable dialect. Yet a few years ago when a colleague I had known for many years revealed that she was a native of this province, I expressed surprise. She did not sound like a Newfoundlander. "No," she replied. "My mother was an English teacher and she made sure that I grew up speaking properly." I have heard similar stories and recall my own attempt to standardize my Ozark dialect to the norm of the New England university that I attended as an undergraduate. The pressures of the educational system are toward linguistic standardization of a type that *may* lead to greater understanding but also leads to feelings of inferiority and exclusion by those who do not happen to conform.

In the second place, there is a sameness to the kinds of things talked about in classrooms. Routines and rules by which classes are conducted and which teachers talk about are essentially the same throughout English-speaking North America. Many language programs are organized to correspond with the scope and sequence charts detailed in the teachers' manuals accompanying basal readers, yielding even more conformity of language and limiting what is talked about.

Third, as we have seen in a number of different examples, school talk seems to be restricted to a very few functions. Staab's (1991) study, while not directly addressing language function, in identifying the fact that teachers did most of the talking provided strong clues about the nature of the talk. Indeed, teachers spent 49% of the total class activity time talking, mostly lecturing, or instructing, and so we can presume that the most commonly used function was the informing function. They spent an additional 29% of the total time in "asking students to work quietly and independently" thus giving a good indication of the other kind of language which dominates classrooms: the language of getting things done, that is, controlling language, or to use Halliday's term, instrumental language. Of the 22% of time left for students to talk, 15% was described as "informal talk" leaving 7% for all the other kinds of talk which children might engage in.

Fourth, and this is perhaps the most frightening and depressing aspect of homogeneity, schools often assume through the language of teachers and the teaching materials they choose that all children have the same background, interests, and experience of language. The individual child, the private person known wholly to her parents becomes the recipient of a preplanned and largely prepackaged school curriculum. Even if they pay lip service to the facts of individual variation among children, schools are only rarely able to respond in ways appropriate for all children. It is a very strong claim, but one which is supported if not directly then at least obliquely by the research evidence, that one of the chief reasons for children failing in school is the fact that schools make this erroneous assumption. In fact, recent research suggests that the language of instruction and the types of materials that might be appropriate is largely dependent on the needs of individual children, particularly when they are outside the mainstream culture. Homogeneity of classroom talk is, thus, not only unnatural, it is particularly detrimental to non-mainstream children.

School Talk Intimidates

Perhaps one of the reasons that the first day of school is such a momentous occasion is that the oral culture of childhood has spread the word that school is a pretty frightening place to be. We may wonder from our adult perspective how this can be so given all the efforts we make to create comfortable, safe, learning environments. But from the child's perspective, the temporary feeling of safety may be lost when we challenge his ownership of knowing.

> Although it has been 20 years since the incident occurred, I remember clearly the day my older son came home from Grade 1 in tears, a grimy worksheet crunched in his fist. When I asked him to show it to me, the cause of his distress poured out. "I got minus," he sobbed, pointing to the mark at the top of the page. (The teacher used a plus, minus, check system to indicate that the work was excellent, deficient, or satisfactory, respectively). "And I did it right!" he sobbed.
>
> I looked at the worksheet. There was a capital letter *D* at the top and the directions to circle all the items pictured which began with the letter *d*. Kerry had dutifully circled the first two, a dog and a door, but had stopped at that point.

"I think your teacher expected you to circle *all* the things which start with the *d* sound. Why did you stop there?" "Because I knew how to do that."

At age 6, Kerry had assumed that school was for learning to do things he didn't already know how to do. Once he had worked out what he was supposed to do with the worksheet and that he knew how to do it correctly, he abandoned the project and turned his attention to something he didn't know. He may have turned to a science fiction book borrowed from the school library or one that he had borrowed from his father's book shelf. He had failed in school because he chose to read instead of circling *ducks*. His learning at school had come into conflict with his previous experience of learning at home.

> Parents tend to respond to the child's meaning and rejoice in each indication of progress. The role of the teacher is generally different: There is a strong demand for correctness, and teachers tend to view errors as failures rather than partial successes. The responsibility for effective communication and for progress falls upon children. Those who do not succeed may be labeled as being lazy, slow, or even disabled. . . ." (Zutell, 1980, p. 19)

Kerry was in almost continual trouble at school that year—for talking, for not finishing his worksheets, and for not participating in his reading group. When I went to school to discuss "his" problems with his teacher, she opened our conference by saying, "I'm very worried about Kerry. He's a bright little boy, but he's having such trouble in reading." I smiled. Had she told me he was having trouble in music or art, I would have assumed that he had inherited my ear and his father's eye. But this is a child who had taught himself to read before he was 3 years old. At home, he was reading stories from the newspaper and Grades 5 and 6 level science fiction, but at school he couldn't read. What his teacher was really saying, of course, was that he wasn't doing the activities deemed appropriate during the time allotted to reading. Chances are these had little to do with real reading, for Smith (1975) was likely right in his estimate that in every hour assigned to reading instruction in the elementary classroom, children only spend about 4 minutes actually reading (cited in Zutell, 1980, p. 19). He didn't mention circling *ducks*, but my student teachers tell me that children still spend a significant amount of time in worksheet activity during the time officially designated for reading. Staab's (1991) study, though not directed precisely to this question, showed that children in Grade 3 and Grade 6 spent about 15% of their time in activities designated as reading. But more than 40% of this time was taken up by the teacher talking. Children spent 47% of this time in "quiet classroom" activities that surely included reading (although the researcher does not indicate how much of this time was spent actually reading). Estimating generously that 90% of the quiet time was spent in reading, the figures would translate into very few minutes per day.

It would seem that Kerry was one of many children Jerome Bruner was talking about when he said that "much of what we do and say in school only makes children feel that they do not know things that, in fact, they knew perfectly well before we began to talk about them" (Holt, 1983, p. 95). When we lead children to mistrust their own knowledge, then we are using language to intimidate. When we demand that they circle *ducks* to prove they know certain sound-symbol correspondences, we show that we have lost touch with the real business of education.

School Language Is Disembodied

At home, children's language is grounded in the reality of family life. They have parents and sometimes siblings who support in myriad ways their attempts at communication and thus their learning of language. Learning in the home is characterized by demonstration and performance. Children watch their fathers bake cookies or fix tires and ask questions, as we have seen in earlier chapters. In watching and assisting, they learn various kinds of skills and the language associated with them. When they get to school, however, children are instructed in how to do things and then get to practice doing them.

That instruction and practice differ from demonstration and performance is easy to establish. Take reading for example. We found out earlier that children who learn to read at home learn by demonstration—they see parents and older siblings getting meaning from print—and by performance—remember "make way for applesauce." At school, rarely do they witness the teacher reading for her own purposes. When they do witness the teacher reading, no one seriously believes that it is part of the reading lesson. No, teachers tell students what to do in order to be able to read and then children do their reading, except that doing reading is seldom reading. Word-attack skills, spelling lessons, handwriting practice, and a myriad of other language activities come between the child and the reading. Language is no longer the medium; it has become the instructional message. That we routinely disembody language is implied in John Holt's lesson on the teaching of reading:

> What we must do in helping anyone learn to read is to make very clear that writing is an extension of speech, that beyond every written word there is a human voice speaking, and that reading is the way to hear what those voices are saying. (Holt, 1989, p. 31)

What Holt suggests is, essentially, that we embody the language of print. We would do well to consider that advice in all our teaching for it is not only in the teaching of reading that we separate language from reality. Too often, for example, we talk about numbers and their properties rather than demonstrating them with real countable objects and allowing children to do their own manipulations with them.

We can learn a valuable lesson from second language immersion classes in this regard. When children do not understand the language of instruction and when the teacher is responsible for teaching not only the content but the language as well, she cannot talk about numbers in the abstract. She cannot say, "If I have two oranges and give Peter one . . ." and expect the children to understand what she is saying. And if they do not understand what she is saying, they will not understand the subtraction problem she is presenting. Rather, she must use visuals—she must demonstrate the concept with real oranges and real people in real time. Immersion teachers routinely rely on concrete objects and on demonstration to make themselves understood. In the process, the children learn not only the content but the language simultaneously because the language of numeracy is embodied in the concepts of numeracy.

LANGUAGE IN SCHOOL: THE POSITIVE SIDE

Earlier in this chapter, I painted a rather bleak picture of language learning in schools. If I were to end the chapter here, I would leave readers with the impression that schools are language deserts where the only children who flourish are those who are nurtured outside in the oasis of the home. That would be patently unfair. There are fine schools in North America populated with children who are thriving in an environment rich in language and language learning opportunity. Many of these schools have embodied in their curriculum and teaching methods the principles of whole language. In such schools, teachers have taken a critical look at their practice, found it wanting, and in response have embraced a new ideology and its corresponding teaching practices. They have accepted and acted upon the truths about language learning that we have learned already—that children learn language best when it is used for real purposes and when teachers refrain from fragmenting it into meaningless pieces or isolated skills.

Whole language has, in fact, become the dominant educational trend of the past decade. When the tenets of whole language are implemented in a sensible manner, it has been a successful approach. Unfortunately, there has also been some educational malpractice perpetrated in the name of whole language. Teachers or educational administrators who have not fully understood the concepts supporting whole language practice have sometimes used it as an excuse for a type of pedagogical *laissez-faire* that has not had the desired effect on children. But where whole language practice has been consonant with its definitions and principles, the result has been beneficial to children's language development in school.

Whole Language Defined

What, then, is whole language? Undoubtedly, there are nearly as many definitions as there are practitioners, but most definitions will encompass certain common beliefs. The definition provided by Froese in his introduction to the text he edited entitled *Whole-Language, Practice and Theory* (1990), is a representative one: ". . . we define whole-language as a child-centred, literature-based approach to language teaching that immerses students in real communication situations whenever possible" (p. 2). Even in such a short definition can be found the potential for profound change. The approach is *child-centred;* so is the language situation in which most children have been successful language learners. The approach is *literature-based;* children who learn to read are those who are read to, and the stories and books which they hear are chosen for their interest and appeal, and not for the sequence and scope of vocabulary or language structures. The approach immerses children in *real communication situations;* before school, children learn language by talking to people about real events and objects in familiar environments.

Whole Language in Practice

Definitions are useful as broad indicators of an approach to language teaching and learning, but they provide few insights into what actually happens in practice. How do the lofty goals implicit in the definition get realized in classrooms full of children? To

answer the question, we will visit the classrooms of two teachers who claim to be practitioners of whole language and find out how they translate a set of principles into
classroom life. We can't stay long in either class, but even a little time will give us some
insights into whole language in practice.

Teacher #1, Mary Kennedy, Calgary, Alberta. Mary Kennedy teaches Grade 2 in
an urban school in Calgary, Alberta, a city of approximately 750,000 located in the
foothills of the Canadian Rocky Mountains. There are 24 children in the class, and
only eight are native speakers of English. Of the remaining 16, eight are beginners and
the other eight are at various levels of proficiency ranging from low intermediate to
advanced. These children come from a variety of linguistic and ethnic backgrounds—
Sarcee, Chinese, Vietnamese, Korean, Polish, Spanish, and Thai.

The classroom is a warm and inviting place to spend the day. Colorful labels are
stuck almost everywhere, a particular help to the non-native speakers just beginning
to learn spoken and written English. There are bright displays of the children's artwork, a listening center with dozens of audiotapes and corresponding books. In one
large corner of the room is the library where dozens of children's books are arranged
for easy access and chairs and large floor cushions invite children to linger and read.
In a prominent position in the reading area is an oak chair similar to the one which sits
behind the teacher's desk (where I've never seen Ms. Kennedy sit). This oak chair has
stretched across its back a blue banner with gold letters identifying it as the "Author's
Chair." From this chair, children read their finished work to others in the class. For
sharing earlier drafts, they work in other parts of the classroom, usually the tables
where they write, but for the premiere of the published work, the authors come
proudly to the author's chair.

Every morning begins in exactly the same way. For the first 15 minutes or so, Mary
reads to the children. She reads a book from the classroom library, one from the school
library, or one which she or one of the children has brought from home. The book may
be a Big Book, a brightly illustrated book, or even one with few pictures or illustrations. Her main criterion for selection is the children's interest, and so she quite naturally lets them choose the books at least part of the time. Whenever she reads to the
class, Mary turns on the tape recorder. She does this so that at a later time, children
may listen to the story again. All the children enjoy listening to the story at the listening center, but perhaps the most noteworthy benefit is to the non-native speakers,
many of whom cannot yet read in English. These children are often found at the listening center listening to the tape as they follow along in the book, thus closely repli-
cating the experience of being read to by an adult.

After Mary finishes reading the book, the children talk to her about the story. She
actively seeks their reactions, and usually refrains from judging their input. The following dialogue is typical:

Mary Kennedy: Michael, I noticed that you were laughing a lot during the story. What
did you find funny?
Michael: The way they all got stuffed into the mitten! My mitten is too little!

Laura: One time my kitty tried to get in my mitten and she got her head stuck. It was funny the way she tried to get out but couldn't.

M. K.: It would be funny, wouldn't it, to see lots of little animals trying to get into one little mitten?

Yan Hua: (Holding up a child's glove) This?

M. K.: That's very like a mitten, YanHua. It's called a "glove." (She turns and writes the word on the paper chart beside her.) Glove. Can you say that?

M: I've got mittens. I'll show you! (He leaves the group to go to the coat room.)

M. K.: Michael's going to get his mitten to show you, YanHua. While we're waiting, I was wondering if someone else wanted to share how you felt about the story?

Gi Ping: Me! I like 'quirrel!

M. K.: What did you like about the squirrel?

G: Look funny. Not like real 'quirrel.

M. K.: No, you're right. He doesn't look much like a real one, does he? Oh, here's Michael with his mitten. That's a bright color, isn't it?

M: My grandma made it for me! See?

The talk here is genuine; it has not been contrived by the teacher to make *her* point, and it is of interest to all those who take part. It is also allowed to range, as natural conversation frequently does, from topic to topic as attention shifts focus. Notice that it is functionally rich talk. In contrast with some of the examples earlier, we find here informing talk used genuinely—when Mary asks Michael what he finds funny, for instance, she doesn't already know the answer—as well as talk which helps to foster language for meeting social needs. In this discussion with the children, she is also providing them with opportunities for projecting into the experiences of the animals stuffing themselves into the mitten.

Ms. Kennedy organizes her teaching around themes, and she integrates the entire curriculum into those themes. Science, arithmetic, language arts, social studies, art, and music are all focused on a single theme, be it dinosaurs, rivers, Christmas, winter, or outer space. The children never seem to get bored with this approach. On the contrary, they seem to enjoy the opportunity to concentrate on a particular subject and not to have to experience the frustration of becoming deeply involved with a subject only to have the teacher suddenly pry them away because it's time to do something entirely different. One of the reasons for their high interest level is that they are consulted on the choice of themes. Sometimes Ms. Kennedy offers them a choice from several and at other times the children offer their own suggestions. One year when the children wanted to include "transformers" as one of their themes, the teacher-pupil roles were reversed for a time as the children supplied much of the information and ideas for activities needed to develop the theme fully.

Writing has a central place in the classroom lives of these Grade 2 children. They have each written something about each theme. Some themes, such as Christmas, generate books which may be short novels, or collections of stories, poems and drawings. Others generate shorter pieces—whimsical couplets, limericks or even riddles. The choice of form is left up to the children, but they write every day, sometimes for an hour or more. A good illustration of the sophistication of the written language which the children in this class produced after only a few months is the book written by a Vietnamese girl named Doan (pronounced to rhyme with *Joanne*). Doan had been in Canada for only 18 months when she wrote the three-chapter story reproduced below.

The Little Rabbit Princess Named Lindary

Chapter One

Once in a dark, dark forest there lived a young Princess Rabbit. She was only two months old when her grandpa and grandma died. Her mother, the Queen had eighteen kindly witches and two wicked witches. One day it was Princess Rabbit's birthday. Her friends, Tung the bobcat, Tyson the tiger, Thuy the owl, Que the cat, Quy the dog and Tammy the pig, all went to Lindary's hole house. They played hide and seek, tag and frozen tag. They ate ice cream, carrots, potatoes, tomatoes, bugs and they drank orange juice and also they drank apple juice. They were very polite at the party.

"These friends are very kindly and wild animals," said Lindary's dad the king. Soon her birthday was over. Her friends went home.

Chapter Two

It was 19 years later and her mother the queen and her dad the king died at last. Her mother and father died because they were too old. She lived alone in the hole.

It was Christmas. One frozen winter day she went up the hole to get a small pine tree to fill in the hole house. But she couldn't carry the tree because it was too heavy for her.

So she called to some of her friends Tung bobcat, Tyson the tiger, Thuy the owl, Que the cat, Quy the dog and Tammy the pig. They tried to carry it. At last they got it in the hole. They celebrated Christmas the other day.

Chapter Three

Soon Lindary was 20 years old. Just then she met a Prince rabbit and Lindary talked to the prince but while she was talking to the prince, the prince replied, "I want to marry you." "So do I" answered the rabbit princess. The next day they got married and they lived happily every after.

The End

Teacher #2, Colleen Maguire, Halifax, Nova Scotia. Ms. Maguire (a pseudonym) teaches Grades 3 and 4 in a neighborhood elementary school located within view and easy walking distance of the Bedford Basin. Split grades are not common in this district any longer, but a few remain and Ms. Maguire says that she enjoys teaching the 3/4 split. She teaches all subjects in the curriculum although an art teacher comes once each week to supplement the activities planned by Ms. Maguire. She does music herself because music is important in her life. She has made it an important part of the children's daily lives as well.

Each morning after the children arrive and put away their coats, mittens, and boots, they gather around a low table in the back of the room where Ms. Maguire has put cartons of apple juice, orange juice, and milk as well as miniature whole grain muffins that a local baker makes each day for the school. Most of the children will have had breakfast at home, but for those who haven't, the nutritious food is welcome. For all, it is an opportunity to begin the morning in a friendly and relaxed way. After 15 minutes, the two children who have been designated as helpers for the week put the milk and juice in the refrigerator, put the remaining muffins away to be eaten later, and the other children select their instruments for the morning rhythm band concert.

Ms. Maguire goes to the piano to begin what has quickly become a ritual for the children. The words and music for the day's song are displayed on an overhead projector and, if the song is new to them, the children listen while Ms. Maguire plays and sings the song once, their fingers or feet tapping along with the rhythm of the piano. She then plays through the song again, explaining as she goes what each instrument is supposed to do. She is not highly directive in her explanation and often invites the children to participate when and how they see fit. Some children prefer singing to instrumentation and sing along with her.

Ms. Maguire does not introduce a new song every day; sometimes the class will work on one song for a week or more, rehearsing it, changing it, enjoying it until it is ready for performance or until they are ready to move on to another song. Performance may be for other classes in the school, for the principal or visitors, or a recording to take home for their families to hear. Though the day begins musically, it is not spent entirely in song. After the children have put away their instruments, they go to look in their mailboxes and spend the next 20 minutes or so in dealing with the morning mail. The mail is the medium through which Ms. Maguire responds to the children's writing. The writing may be in the dialogue journals the children keep with her or pieces at various stages of development which they wish to share with her. Sometimes they simply write her or each other letters. One morning, a third-grade girl named Beth was responding to a letter from a fourth-grade boy named Lyle. The letters are reproduced, with the permission of Beth, Jody, and Lyle, in Figure 10.1.

Once they have attended to the morning mail, the children gather around Ms. Maguire to plan the rest of the day's work. They each make a list of things they want to accomplish. Ms. Maguire joins in this activity, and everyone understands they do not have to complete every task on the list. Everyone tries, however, and most do succeed in finishing the work they've established for themselves. Beth made the list in Figure 10.2 for November 21, 1990.

There are other, more structured, activities in the children's day. On this day, for example, the children were working on problems related to the distances between the earth and the planet which the UFO in a story they had read had come from. Ms. Maguire worked through one problem with the class and then they referred back to their math logs for assistance in completing the rest. For most children, the math log was a reflective account of the process of mathematics as they experienced it in the classroom. It was a combination of notes about how to reach solutions and editorial comment about the difficulty or the mental processes they used to find them.

Figure 10.1

November 21, 1990

Dear Beth,
　　　　I want to tell you a secret but Jody told me not too. Will you promise not to tell if I tell you?

　　　　Your Friend,
　　　　　　Lyle

P.S. It is about Jody.

Thursday, Nov. 22, 1990
Dear Lyle,
I don't want to know any secret about Jody because I think you probly made it all up. Jody is my friend and she tells me all her secrets so you don't know anything that I don't know anyways. Did you know we got a new puppy?
Yours truly,
Elizabeth A. Barnes

Figure 10.2   A third-grader's
agenda

> **Beth's Things "TO DO"**
> 1. Finish picture of UFO
> 2. Write poem to go with picture.
> 3. Listen to story about space monsters [Ms. Mcguire tape records the stories she reads to the children so that they may listen to them later.]
> 4. Recess!
> 5. Work on math log.

Ms. Maguire's class might not seem like a typical whole language class, whatever that might be. Descriptions of whole language classrooms rarely include lengthy accounts of music activities. But Ms. Maguire's class is a whole language classroom in an important sense: her concern is with the *use* of language and not with the *practice* of language. In songs and in the talk that goes on about songs and performance, children are not just rehearsing for communication; they are communicating. In making their "To Do" lists they are not only using language for a real purpose, but even more importantly, they are taking charge of their own learning. In keeping their math logs, they are using language for learning, for monitoring their own experience, and for recalling past solutions to problems.

The Debate: Whole Language or Phonics?

An issue that was once of concern only to elementary school teachers and a few academics is now being hotly debated in the public press. Proponents of phonics methods point to test scores and to research studies showing that children who are taught specifically about the alphabetic code are better at decoding than children who are not. They point to research showing that fluent readers with good comprehension skills are almost always good decoders. In the public debate, this is a compelling argument. Good readers can decode; hence we should teach children to decode. The fallacy of this argument is easy to uncover. No model of the fluent reader is particularly useful as a description of how she got to be a fluent reader. A thorough catalogue of a competent reader's skills does not map the path between illiteracy and literacy. A good reader, for example, is good at prediction—the next word, the next sentence, the rest of the story. And yet, no one would seriously suggest that prediction be taught as an initial strategy for beginning readers—certainly not the *only* strategy. Even proponents of phonics-based instruction concede this point. Answering their critics' observation that children learn print relationships by reading real, continuous text, Foorman and her colleagues concur, observing that "there is a period during beginning reading instruction when all children benefit from practicing letter-sound connections in decodable text" (*Globe and Mail*, March 18, 1997). This brings us to the second problem with the argument, that of exclusivity.

There is a tendency, both in the scholarly literature and particularly in the popular media, to polarize the issue: phonics *or* whole language. In fact, responsible educators will admit that neither approach is right for every child in every situation if it is the only one used. Inherent in the definition of whole language, in fact, is the recognition that individual children differ in ability, interest, and learning style. Teaching sound-symbol correspondence is entirely compatible with whole language so long as it is balanced by other more natural language activities. Barbara Foorman and her colleagues at the Universiy of Houston provide very strong evidence that children who receive "direct instruction in the alphabetic code" are significantly better at reading comprehension than are children who are taught using a mainly literature-based approach (*Globe and Mail*, March 18, 1997). Moreover, whole language advocates can take considerable comfort in the knowledge that the artificial segmentation tasks that characterized the teaching of phonics 30 years ago have largely been replaced by a more sensible and more natural approach. Onset rime phonology, as described in Chapter 2, has begun to revolutionize teaching materials and practice. By focusing on units that are larger than individual phonemes and that are easier for children to identify, teachers can hope to build upon children's natural abilities, or when they are lacking, help them to develop those phonological abilities that will help them to learn to read. The research evidence is mounting that these abilities include the detection of onsets and rimes. Wimmer et al. (1994) demonstrated, for example, that while rhyme awareness before reading instruction has no predictable impact on reading and spelling at the end of Grade 1, by the end of Grade 3, there is a substantial relationship. Awareness of onsets had less predictive impact, and only on Grade 1 reading.

Although common sense would suggest that there is little to be gained by polarizing the argument between whole language and phonics, for it neither resolves the debate nor provides any useful direction for teachers of young children, the debate rages on. It is almost endemic to the business of education that such polarities exist. For whatever reason, educators tend to be extremists. Walter MacGinitie (1991) points out that instead of revising or improving educational practice, educators are forever "revolutionizing" it. He makes the point that by focusing on what is new rather than on improving what works, educators run the risk of throwing away established procedures that work simply because they may be superficially at odds with the new doctrine. This happens when new methods or approaches are carried to extremes.

> A recent and familiar example of the extremes to which most educational fads are carried can be seen in the way we broke down reading into innumerable skills. We all know of classrooms where most of the children are quite capable of doing independent reading but where there is little time for it. The children are fully occupied, instead, with a mandatory and seemingly interminable series of exercises and skills tests. (p. 56)

Whole language, MacGinitie (1991) argues, is susceptible to the same extremism and thus carries a similar educational risk. He writes of the danger: "because whole language is entering the scene in the guise of a replacement, many will interpret whole language as a total rejection of phonics, and the progression of fads will continue" (p. 58). In other words, the total rejection of phonics will eventually cause a reaction that will lead educators again to overemphasize skills instruction. His prediction has, as we well know, come true in a great many places.

What MacGinitie is advocating is essentially principled eclecticism, or using what works even if it happens to seem to be incompatible with a currently accepted approach. As reasonable as this may sound, not all educators agree. Kenneth Goodman, in a panel discussion on literacy sponsored by the International Reading Association, warned against eclecticism:

> I want to say a few bad words about eclecticism, because it's comfortable to say teachers should listen to everything and then pick and choose. It's comfortable to say that if there appear to be polar positions, then the truth must lie some place safely in the middle. The middle of the road is a very thin, white line, and it's a dangerous place to try to stand. (Aaron et al., 1990a, p. 310)

That may be, but extremism is equally dangerous. Whole language may be lost as an important pedagogical approach if educators insist on taking Goodman's view. There is another danger, of course, and this is in the practice that sometimes results from the misinterpretation of whole language tenets.

Whole Language in (Mis)practice

The debate among language teachers is not only about whether or not to adopt whole language. Among those who profess to believe in whole language, there is a great deal of variability in what they believe, in how they actually teach, and in the class activities in which their pupils engage.

In her forward to *Portraits of Whole Language Classrooms* (Mills & Clyde, 1990), Virginia Woodward acknowledges the misconceptions surrounding whole language pedagogy. She quotes the observations of a number of educators to illustrate that the approach is widely interpreted. Four of the remarks made by different educators reveal the spectrum of conceptions about whole language and suggest, as well, the breadth of practice they mandate.

1. I do whole language; I use Big Books.
2. It seems like whole language is just glorified language experience.
3. We do whole language activities on Fridays.
4. Whole language is what good teachers do naturally. (from Mills & Clyde, 1990, p. ix)

Closer examination of these observations, selected but not unrepresentative of those held by a great many educators, say much about the assortment of practices that take place in the name of whole language.

1. *I do whole language; I use Big Books.* Using big books is certainly consistent with whole language. They allow what Judith Newman (1985b) refers to as "shared reading . . . an important component of a whole language curriculum." She continues:

> The enlarged books allow the teacher to create an intimate atmosphere with a number of children at once. The large book sets a stage for involvement with both the story and the print since the children are all able to see what's on the page as they listen to and watch

the teacher read along. It is through such shared reading that children begin to understand how print and meaning are related. (pp. 62–63)

But does using big books mean that a teacher is using a whole language curriculum? Or, is it necessary to use big books in a whole language curriculum? The answer to both is no. It would be entirely possible to use big books within a skills-based curriculum that fragmented language into modes (listening, speaking, reading, and writing) and modes into discrete skill areas (writing into printing, handwriting, spelling, sentence construction, paragraph construction, etc.). On the other hand, it is quite possible to take a whole language approach even with young pupils and *not* use big books. Teachers without the budgets to buy a great many big books have managed very well using a number of alternatives. Moreover, whole language is implemented in the higher elementary grades where big books would not be appropriate. The important thing is the shared experience of reading, which can be accomplished in a number of ways.

2. *It seems like whole language is just glorified language experience.* Again we have a practice that is consonant with a whole language curriculum but does not define it. Language experience may be incorporated into a whole language curriculum because

> Language, whether oral or written, is learned through active "play" with language, through experimenting with different ways to express ideas, and exploring relationships between the children's language and their knowledge. Language experience stories evolve from the children's interests and activities. . . . Language experience stories are an excellent tool for helping children make sense of written language because they emphasize the importance of the connection between a reader's experiences and written language. (Newman, 1985b, p. 62)

Although it might be argued that language experience is one of the cornerstones of whole language, there is a great deal more to it than language experience. Moreover, it is possible to use language experience activities in ways that are fundamentally incompatible with whole language. For example, I once visited a classroom in which the teacher used language experience, in her words, "to teach reading," and allotted it a set period of time. But once reading instruction time was over, the children turned to their "language" activities, an unrelated lesson on antonyms. Nor did this teacher use big books, sustained silent reading, or any of the other practices commonly associated with a whole language curriculum.

3. *We do whole language activities on Fridays.* We can only wonder what happens the rest of the week. Clearly, this teacher has no understanding of what whole language is and why it works. Perhaps it is better for a teacher to practice whole language one day a week than not at all, but it is a little like following a 1000 calorie diet on Monday and eating indiscriminately the rest of the week. Children may enjoy the Friday activities more, and they probably won't do any harm. Neither will they contribute much to their language learning.

4. *Whole language is what good teachers do naturally.* This is my favorite, partly because I wish it were true. What I wish were true, however, is not quite what the educator who made this comment meant. What I wish were true is that all teachers, having given a great deal of time to reading and thinking about language acquisition, would come to realize that language teaching and language learning could and should have much in common, and that they would plan their curricula accordingly. What the person who made the comment implied was that whole language is just common sense, that whatever an effective teacher does is by definition whole language. It would be impossible to identify all the traits that make some people good teachers, but even if we could, we could not make the claim that whatever they did constituted whole language. Doubtless, there are effective teachers who use other methods and these other methods work because the teachers are so committed and dedicated to the method and to the children they teach. It is also the case that what many teachers do naturally has more to do with the way they were taught than what they truly believe about children's language learning.

These four observations have served to crystallize the divergence there is in how educators think about whole language. Collectively, the four remarks indicate misunderstanding about what whole language is. Even among teachers who *do* understand it, however, there are vast differences in the classrooms they inhabit. The description of the diversity is beyond the scope of this book, although we saw in the last chapter brief sketches of whole language in practice and will get glimpses into the approach again in Chapter 11.

Whole language is not the only teaching practice on which educators fail to reach agreement; it is simply the current one and the one which has received the greatest amount of attention in recent years. It is discussed here because it is also the approach to language teaching that is most consistent with our best understanding of how language acquisition occurs. Since a teaching approach should be informed by both a theory of language and a theory of language learning (Richards & Rodgers, 1986), then whole language merits special consideration in any book on language acquisition that encompasses the school years.

Public Perceptions and Whole Language

In recent years, whole language has been the subject of a great deal of public debate. Partly as a result of a general movement toward accountability of the public schools to the society that supports them and partly as a result of a broad societal concern with literacy, whole language has come under attack as an educationally soft approach to teaching. Among the more vociferous critics are some parents and business leaders who argue that the schools are not doing an adequate job in what *should be* their fundamental task, the teaching of reading and writing. They blame whole language, and argue for, indeed *demand*, a return to phonics.

Those who carry the standards banner highest, who proclaim accountability loudest, tend to blame whole language and other child-centered approaches for what they consider to be a crisis in education. They equate standards with basics and basics with reading, writing, and arithmetic taught by traditional methods such as phonics. What many fail to realize, and this is a point to which I return in Chapter 11, is that there is a tendency among would-be reformers to recall a standard of achievement from the past that, in fact, never existed. In other words, close analysis of the test scores reveals that as school retention rates improve, children who once would have dropped out before taking the tests are now taking the tests. They bring down the overall average, that's true, but they are accomplishing far more than their counterparts several decades ago. Let's take an actual example. A school district in Newfoundland has typically had some of the lowest reading scores in Canada as measured by the Canadian Test of Basic Skills. During the last 20 years, the scores have shown only a modest improvement. And yet, during the same period, the school district's retention rate has improved dramatically. Where the dropout rate was once 85% (before Grade 12), it is now only 15%. More children are learning more, but the gross measure of the Basic Skills test does not show the gains. We must also remember that the demands placed on literacy are greater than ever before while the time to teach reading and writing has shrunk. As the demand for "relevant" subjects has increased and as teachers' time has been increasingly devoted to roles once held by parents, social workers, and others in the child's community, they have had less time to spend in teaching basic literacy. Furthermore, the society has changed in ways that impact fundamentally on schooling. Children spend more time watching television than they did in the past, for example, as well as playing computer games. This is not to blame the child, but only to say that gross measures do not give a very clear indication of the true state of literacy or the best method of achieving it. Nevertheless, there is a substantive debate going on over whole language, and it is not likely to be resolved in the foreseeable future.

SIX CHARACTERISTICS OF LEARNING: A COMPARISON

This chapter began with a statement from Gordon Wells which served to crystallize the six characteristics of children's preschool learning from Chapter 8. In the following pages, we saw that there are still many schools which are a long way from reproducing these characteristics. Let us now return individually to those six characteristics to see how each fares under the harsh scrutiny of the classroom lights.

1. *Children's learning progresses according to their degree of readiness.* I am certain that there are schools that can make this claim, but I am equally certain that many more cannot. Some engage in educational practices that purport to recognize and provide for individual children's needs. But even some of these are bastardized. A good example is the notion of reading readiness. This term *should* imply that children learn to read when they are ready to learn. But in practice, it has come to mean that the school has to *do* something to children to get them ready. As John Holt pointed out in *Learning All the Time*, one of the more foolish notions advocated by educators was "that the way to get children 'ready to read' is to show them a lot of books full of nothing but pictures and ask them a lot of silly questions about them. . . . What children need to get ready for reading is exposure to a lot of print. Not pictures, but print." (p. 10)

The simple fact of the matter is that well-intentioned educators find it difficult if not impossible to tailor educational practices in accordance with individual children's readiness to learn. One of the reasons for this difficulty is that most schools are still organized around a common curriculum for each grade, a narrow range of instructional modes, and a limited variety of materials. It is not difficult to understand why schools organize themselves in this way; they are institutions charged with the responsibility of educating large numbers of children within a finite time and budget. That they would attempt to regularize the task in some way is understandable. But the regularization of schools means necessarily that learning cannot proceed according to the child's degree of readiness but must proceed according to some predetermined syllabus.

This is not the case in whole language classrooms. The goals of whole language are entirely consistent with the fact that children proceed according to their degree of readiness. Whole language is, after all, child-centered, and it would be impossible to have a child-centered curriculum which set rigid goals and dictated means for achieving them. The goals of whole language tend instead to be more flexible—to help each child continue to grow in language in the way and the time which best suits him or her. Whole language practitioners recognize that there are many ways for children to achieve those goals and that they will do so according to their own developmental schedule. Comparing whole language practice with this particular characteristic of children's learning results in a close fit, one that can be seen even on a daily basis. For example, it was Beth's decision to put "write a poem" on her "To Do" list, and because it was her idea and she was ready to carry it out, the experience was likely more satisfying for her than it would have been had the assignment been handed down by her teacher.

2. *Young children are, for the most part, in charge of their own learning.* If schools are unable to respond to children according to their individual level of readiness to learn, it is to be expected that they will be unable to provide environments which permit children to take charge of their own learning. Allowing children to decide what they want to learn and how they want to learn it requires a great deal of faith in children's desire to know and it requires the relinquishing of control, or as John Holt would have said, relinquishing the *illusion* of control.

First, it is easy to understand why educators would doubt children's ability to take charge of their own learning. Schools take away children's independence as learners and then complain about the results. Holt recognized this phenomenon in a number of his writings. Describing a child's learning when left to his own devices, he wrote of a boy learning to write who was not content to repeat his successes but kept moving on to harder tasks, setting himself increasingly difficult tasks. Generalizing to other children, Holt (1989) wrote:

> This is what all children do as they grow up—until they get to school. What all too often happens there is that children, seeing school challenges as threats, which they often are—if you fail to accomplish them, you stand a good risk of being shamed . . .—fall more and more *out* of the habit of challenging themselves, even outside of school. (p. 17)

Second, to permit children to set, meet and evaluate their own challenges, schools— and teachers in particular—must be willing to relinquish absolute control of learning. It is an illusion anyway since it is quite impossible to determine what another human being will or will not learn. We *do* have control of curricula, materials, and the mode of teaching, but we are deluding ourselves very seriously to believe that we can truly control what children learn. So why not give up the illusion and begin to let children, who are not inexperienced at the business of learning and who are the true experts on how they themselves learn, guide their own learning?

This is, of course, exactly what whole-language classrooms have done. We saw even in the snapshots of Ms. Kennedy's and Ms. Maguire's classes children taking charge of their own learning—writing their "To Do" lists, reading and writing letters from their mail boxes, keeping in their math logs whatever they thought would help them to remember, deciding what kind of response they want to make to a story they have heard in class, or helping to choose the theme they will study next. An incident which I observed in Ms. Kennedy's class one day illustrates that even practices which might not ordinarily be thought of as consistent with whole language principles may, in fact, in the environment of whole language reveal children to be in charge of their own learning.

One little girl named Jill was highly resistant to invented spelling. She had observed the consistency of the spelling in books and, quite of her own accord, wanted her writing to be "right." Frustrated with her attempts to spell *through*—she had tried *thru*, *thoug*, *tough*, and *thrugh*—she finally asked Ms. Kennedy: "Wouldn't it be easier if you just *taught* me how to spell?"

Jill's point is a good one. There is a danger in our zeal to adopt whole language that we overlook the need of some children to be taught in more traditional ways. That is a danger inherent in any new educational practice—that established methods will be abandoned in favor of newer ones even though, for some children at least, there may be merit in the older methods.

3. *Play plays an important role in children's learning.* Part of the hidden culture of schooling is the idea that school is serious business. Children such as Emily (p. 234) know this to be the case before they get to school. It is one of the things that makes school different from kindergarten. They learn when they get there that recess is not just an opportunity to get a breath of fresh air; it is *the* time for play and represents a distinct break from the hard business of schoolwork. That learning and play might happily coexist is an alien notion to many educators, particularly those who put up "No Talking" signs.

It is hard to imagine how classrooms in which "No Talking" was an important rule of behavior could possibly value play as a medium for learning. How can children play without talking? It is equally hard to imagine how teachers who need to control and manipulate talk to their own purposes could place any educational value on the talk which children use for *their* purposes. In contrast, the tenet of whole language which emphasizes immersing children in real communication situations is entirely consistent with this characteristic of children's learning. What could be more natural to a child than play?

4. *The role of parents in early learning is facilitator, not instructor.* When we transport this characteristic from the home into the school situation, the obvious parallel is for the teacher to act as facilitator rather than director of learning. Yet in example after example earlier in this chapter, we saw that this was not the case. Many teachers attempt to control learning from the curriculum planning stage right through to manipulating children's talk to push them toward a particular teaching objective. We saw the teacher-as-director in Molly's dialogue with her teacher and we saw it again in Jon McGill's history account of the information-dispensing talk in his history class.

The model of teacher as instructor is deeply ingrained in our culture. Our entire pedagogical history is of the teacher as the giver of information, the holder and grantor of wisdom. To abandon this view of the teacher's role means bucking 2,000 years of tradition. Even teachers who want to change may find it very hard to give up the notion of teaching as the dispensing of information. After all, they went to university for 4, 5, or 6 years to learn all that information; surely it's their duty to teach it to someone else. It takes a great act of faith, or as Ms. Kennedy put it "many years of experience. I don't know why it took me so long to give up the old ways since my better judgment told me years ago that they weren't working anyway." Mary's conversion began before the label "whole language teacher" existed and was completed when she went back to university for graduate study and learned that her instincts were consonant with a change that was taking place in language education.

Relinquishing control of and thus some of the responsibility for learning to the child is at the heart of whole-language thinking. Teachers who create the kinds of environments conducive to learning and to wanting to learn are playing a role that is every bit as important and a great deal more effective than teacher-as-instructional-director.

5. *Interaction is essential to children's early learning.* Before they come to school, children learn their language and most other things they know through their interactions with people and the environment. In school, they continue to learn through interactions but the quality of those interactions may not be comparable to those of the home. We saw in many of the earlier anecdotes in this chapter that children's interactions with teachers are often contrived by teachers toward a particular goal established by teachers. The fact that some teachers believe that all their talk must be directed toward a pedagogical end is evidence that their interaction is suspect. We heard in the register adopted by some teachers and in the asking of questions which both teacher and child know not to be real questions a falseness that disclosed the truth of their intent. We heard teachers trying to teach language. These behaviors do not constitute true interaction.

In contrast, we saw in the two whole language classrooms a quality of interaction that was similar to that which occurs in children's homes. We saw and heard teachers not attempting to teach language but talking with children honestly, in real voices, and toward purposes that had legitimacy for both teachers and children. When Ms. Maguire wrote letters to the children in her classes and responded to their letters to her, when the children in Ms. Kennedy's class told her what they liked and didn't like about the stories they heard and when Ms. Kennedy declined to pass judgment on those opinions, we were witness to productive interaction. Because it is partly defined by its emphasis on real communication for real purposes, the whole language approach should always result in quality interaction between teachers and children. And where there is quality interaction, there is more likely to be learning.

6. *Learning is embedded in the process of socialization.* There are doubtless many reasons and many conditions under which humans learn. During our earliest years and, if we are fortunate, throughout our lifetimes, we learn for the sheer pleasure of it, for the delight in knowing something previously unknown. But our learning is also driven by more pragmatic drives—the *need* to have information, knowledge, or skills for a particular purpose. It is also motivated by less obvious drives—to achieve group membership, for example. As we saw in Chapter 8, as children learn language in the home, they are being initiated into the rituals and expectations of family membership. As they venture forth into the world, they become members not only of the family but of the larger community, and a significant part of that community is the school. It is through schooling, in fact, that children in western society learn much of what they need to know to become lifelong participants in society.

It would be expected that language learning, and indeed all learning, during the school years would provide the means for socializing children to the role of community member, of citizen. To some degree, it does. The knowledge they acquire in schools takes many forms. Part of it is factual—the history of the nation in which they live, its system of government, its laws. These facts provide the basis for citizenship just as the facts of mathematics provide the basis for their coping with the worlds of finance and science. What they acquire in school also includes linguistic knowledge which cannot be quantified as a list of facts. I have already suggested earlier in this chapter that the lessons they learn about language may not be the ones we want them to learn. When their talk is not valued, children may well internalize a rule to the effect that some people's talk, namely those in positions of authority, is more important than other people's talk, namely those not in power. When they witness the use of language to manipulate their own behavior, they learn the power of language to corrupt. When they experience the homogenized talk of the school, children may fail to develop appreciation of the linguistic diversity which does not divide us but which helps to identify us as individuals and as distinct groups within the larger English-speaking society. When their talk is channeled and controlled as it so frequently is in school, they risk losing the spontaneity and whimsy that is the stuff of verbal creativity. These are the lessons taught, perhaps unwittingly, but too often and by still too many schools.

But not by all. In some schools, as we saw earlier, language is not scheduled into the school day as a subject to be dissected, analyzed, or memorized. Rather, it is part of the process of children's learning and part of the process of their joining the community of educated people. These rather lofty-sounding goals can be accomplished. To do so requires teachers and children who communicate with one another and share responsibility for growth in language and in learning.

QUESTIONS FOR DISCUSSION

1. Claire Staab also found that women teachers provided "significantly more opportunities for students to speak formally than did male teachers." Speculate on the effect this fact likely has on both male and female children.

2. Gordon Wells and Shirley Brice Heath have demonstrated that the progress of non-mainstream children may be hampered "by the difference in the ways in which language is used and questions are posed in homes and schools" (Commins, 1989, p. 29). What can the primary school teacher do to ensure success of children from these homes?

3. When whole language is the subject of public debate, critics frequently attack invented spelling in particular. Why do you think this is true? What defense can you mount for invented spelling?

4. Find a recently published critique of or attack on whole language and write a rebuttal.

5. Find a recently published critique of or attack on phonics instruction and write a rebuttal.

CHAPTER ELEVEN

Language, Technology, and Schooling in the 21st Century

If I had written this chapter 5 years ago, it would have been very different. The danger even as I write it today is that by the time I finish writing it, it will be out of date. Such is the speed at which the world of technology is changing. Or to put it another way, such is the speed that the world is changing because of technology. Five years ago, in a chapter on technology and education, I would have talked about computers, of course, and possibly about television. I'd have talked about the educational benefits and risks of having computers in the classroom. I would have mused about how the process of writing has changed and will continue to change since the word processor has made editing and revision so much easier and publication so much faster. I probably would have borrowed from a 1989 article by Daniel Lake that described children's classroom work as augmented by computers, an article that extolled the virtues of networked computers in the classroom. I'd have wondered aloud whether we are really being better served by what often amounts to electronic workbooks. I hope I would have questioned the wisdom of putting young children, many of whom already spend 4 or more hours a day in front of a television set, in front of a computer monitor for any appreciable length of time. All valid points, then. But technology has changed so much in the last 5 years that these matters are now of little consequence. It is almost trite to observe that it will continue to change, but I mention it because I am fully aware that by the time you read these words, some of the technologies I write about will be dated. The issues surrounding technology, however, will likely remain.

Nevertheless, there are important issues surrounding emerging technologies and the classroom, and I want to discuss four of them below. The four topics are intricately interrelated, and so the discussions will spill into each other somewhat. I have, nonetheless, divided the discussion to clarify the focus of each of the four issues. I will begin by discussing the impact of emerging technologies on the quality of human interaction in the classroom and, to a lesser degree, in the home. The second issue I will take up is the changing nature of literacy followed by some observations on the role of the teacher. I will conclude this chapter by identifying some of the larger issues of education and schooling that arise out of the technological revolution. But first, a sketch of the present and a glimpse of the future.

THE FUTURE *IS* NOW: SCENES FROM THE PRESENT

The sun has barely risen when Mary Macklin pulls into the school parking lot. Through the glass front doors she can see the lights of the main hall although the classrooms are still dark. She has arrived early in order to get a head start on the day. She is a substitute teacher, taking over from the regular fourth-grade teacher, Helen Kelly, who broke her leg in a fall on the ice while skating with the children the previous day. She'll be back after the weekend, but today and tomorrow, Mary is on her own.

In the classroom now, she glances at the scrap of paper on which she has written Helen's password, moves the mouse and clicks open the daily schedule. Mary is relieved to find that Helen has left plans with substantial detail. Mary has been told that Helen integrates most of the subjects in the curriculum, and so she double clicks to see the long-term plan. She sees that the current topic around which most of the content areas are structured is whales. For the most part, Helen's intent is discernible, and mostly, Mary thinks she can follow it. But there is one problem. The CD-ROM containing some of the most important material is nowhere to be found. Many of the days activities are organized around the material on that compact disk. Mary glances at the clock. The children will arrive in less than an hour. Should she call Helen? She is likely still at the hospital where she spent the night, and even if she had the disk with her, the hospital is a good 20-minute drive from the school, longer during rush hour. Trying to locate the disk is out of the question. Besides, she is a substitute teacher, used to improvising. She has no doubt that she can cope. But Mary has more help than she has in some of the other schools in which she teaches. She has more help than she had in this school 2 years earlier.

Mary studies the plan, makes a few notes and picks up the phone on her desk. She dials an 800 number, puts the phone on speaker and while she waits for an answer, moves to the television set to check the channel. "Good morning, this is Julie. What can I do for you this morning?" Mary turns back toward the phone and explains her problem. "I'm sure we can help," Julie assures her. "Will you hold while I pull up a few things for you?" While she waits, Mary goes around the room checking to see that the six workstations used by the children are all turned on. Julie's voice comes back on the speakerphone. "Mary, we've got some great footage of whales shot at Marine Land last summer. That runs about 10 minutes. We've also got an interview with Dr. _____ from Woods Hole and a film essay shot off New England. We've got some good supplemental print material with the interview. I can also show you some related web sites."

"Could I have a look at the film essay?"

"Sure can. I'm going to send on Channel 78. Stand by."

Before a minute has passed, the monitor blinks to life and the narrator begins. After a few minutes, Mary speaks again to the speaker phone. "That's a little advanced, I think. Could I see the Marine Land footage?"

"No problem. Please hold." A few seconds later, the screen blinks to life again. Mary watches, nodding with approval. "That will do nicely, Julie."

"Right. We'll send that to you right away." The video will be sent in compressed form, decompressed and recorded on the VCR in the classroom before the children arrive for the day. "Is there anything else you need this morning?" Julie asks.

"I could use some help with the math class this afternoon. That's not my strongest subject." They talk for a few minutes about the objectives for the lesson, what the children have had in the previous lesson, and what Helen Kelly's long-term goals are. Together they conclude that another teacher will teach a portion of the lesson, a teacher whom the children will see and hear on the television monitor and who will be able to interact with them, asking and answering questions just as if she were present in the classroom. Mary hangs up the phone and uses the remaining minutes before the children arrive to finish the day's planning.

A thousand miles and a time zone away, Carolyn Boyd sits alone in her classroom planning a unit based on her first graders' enthusiasm for a popular animated film. She picks up her telephone and dials the same 800 number that Mary Macklin just dialed. She explains the unit she is planning and makes a few routine requests that are duly scheduled. Then she asks for something special. "Would it be possible for the children to meet one of the animators?" she asks. She believes that it is important to keep the fantasy grounded in reality, especially educational reality.

Three weeks later, 20 excited children sit on the floor with large name tags pinned to their clothes. The screen flickers to life and a familiar cartoon character dances lightly across gossamer clouds and seemingly stares into the room. "Good morning boys and girls," she says. "Why Corey, that's a pretty blue sweatshirt you're wearing. What does it say—I can't quite see."

Corey is delighted but shy about answering. One of his classmates, Starla, answers for him. "It's a dolphin."

"Ooh," says the animated star, clapping her hands. "I love dolphins. Do you remember seeing me ride a dolphin in the movie?"

"Yes," the children chant in unison.

"He was a very special dolphin. Do you remember why?" She continues to talk about the movie with the children for a few minutes more and then smoothly segues into the main part of the program when the children get to meet the animator who gives them a brief demonstration of how animated films are made. They watch intently, ask questions and delight in the changes he makes to the characters at their suggestion, but like most children their age, really prefer the familiar appearance of the character.

While the children in Mrs. Boyd's class interact with the animator, children in Bob Bertram's Grade 1 class in Burbank, and in Marge Smith's class in Scottsdale are watching along with the first graders in Cindy Sharpe's class in Newport,

Massachusetts where the school day is almost over. These children are not interacting with the animator, but they are able to hear the children in the other class. Later, one of the girls in Bob's class will be in email correspondence with a girl in Carolyn's class. Both use invented spelling and their messages are short, but they will be engaged in real and meaningful correspondence about a topic that is currently important to both of them.

Down the hall in the same school, however, a group of seventh graders is also watching. The material might seem a bit juvenile for them, but these students are working on computer animation, and have other questions. When the animator finishes with the first graders, he goes on live with the seventh grade class to work with them on the particulars of animation. They are joined by another class in Texas. The two classes spend about 15 minutes with him, live via satellite, but they will continue to draw upon his expertise over the next weeks by email that they access from any of the 15 computers in the classroom.

A teacher in Texas needs Spanish language Christmas stories for her kindergarten class; a teacher in North Dakota needs examples of a familiar Christmas carol sung in Danish and Norwegian; and in Newfoundland, a teacher needs some very specific information on global warming. All these teachers will have their needs met by an educational resource company that not only has a massive resource base but which creates material to the precise specifications of teachers, sends it to them by satellite and then makes it available to other teachers around the world. Digital technology has revolutionized education, but unlike some revolutions, it is one that is welcomed by teachers who see not only the benefits to the children but a welcome change in their own roles.

A day in the future? No, Mary Macklin's day was a real one and what was described in the other examples is possible now. Mary Macklin was drawing from a massive resource base, delivered by satellite into her school every day at her request or at the request of any teacher in the school. The teachers in the school have access to an amazing array of resources including computer software, interactive video, compressed video, the Internet, and traditional print materials delivered to the classroom by fax or downloaded to the teacher's computer and printed. What is perhaps more impressive is that the school in which Mary was substitute teaching is one of the poorest in the state. Its *per capita* spending on education is, in fact, one of the lowest in the country, and yet school officials have managed this technology-based transformation within their regular budgets. One of the sources for revenue makes Mary's life a little harder, and that is the reduced number of substitute teaching days required. According to the principal of the school, Connie Seifert, both student and teacher absenteeism has decreased dramatically since the introduction of the service described above. She attributes improved attendance rates to greater interest on the part of the students and less stress on the part of the teachers.

These examples are of schools that use technology almost to its fullest capacity, or at least some teachers use it that way. Some teachers use it in rather more limited ways, and there is no pressure on them to adopt any technology with which they are uncomfortable. Ms. Seifert reports, however, that all teachers do use it. They do so, she thinks, because it is easy to use and does not require that they go to night school to learn to use it. "They very quickly learned its value as a tool," she explains, "and that they had control of when and how to use the tool. It's been a liberating experience for them."

For anyone who hasn't seen this kind of technology in use, a number of things about the descriptions might cause some worry. It isn't too hard to imagine, for example, children sitting in front of computers, clicking and typing and not talking to anyone throughout the school day, communicating with their teacher and with each other via email and visiting each other in virtual chat rooms organized according to subject or topics of interest. What will happen to classroom talk? We have too recently learned that talk is a "tool of thought as well as of communication" that it "forms part of the very texture of learning to understand the world" (Barnes, 1995, p. 2), that it allows us to relive events to interpret and thus bring meaning to them. Can we really consider any teaching tool, no matter how seductive, that endangers that nurturing talk that goes on in classrooms?

HOW DOES TECHNOLOGY AFFECT CLASSROOM INTERACTION?

The introduction of computers into schools, classrooms, and homes was a mixed blessing. While they undoubtedly simplified the more routine aspects of teaching, they brought with them a variety of new and potential problems. Central among these was the fear, expressed by many teachers, that the quality of classroom interaction would suffer as children spent more time with machines. Certainly, there are good reasons to be concerned about children who already watch television for four or more hours a day spending any appreciable amount of additional time before a computer monitor. We know the value of talk among children. We also know intuitively that Internet chat rooms and electronic mail cannot substitute for real, live talk among children and between teachers and children in classrooms. So our fears are justified, right? Not necessarily. There is little hard research to answer the question, but anecdotal evidence suggests that computers in classrooms may not impede classroom talk.

Recently, I was working with Roy Cole, principal of Clarenville High School in Clarenville, Newfoundland, on plans for a new mathematics lab for his high school. Based on the knowledge that the size of a mathematics class ranged from 15 to 32, I assumed that he would want 32 computers for the lab. No, he informed me, his teachers were enthusiastic about the use of computers, especially for mathematics classes. They were equally adamant, however, that there be no more than one computer for every two students. Some argued that a one in three ratio was preferable. They had observed that when students worked together at the computer, not only was there more and better interaction among them, there were also better learning outcomes. In the end, we decided on 15 computers, but Mr. Cole warned me that half of them would likely be turned off during smaller classes.

Teachers throughout Canada and the United States report that children engaged in computer-based activities engage in a great deal of meaningful talk with other classmates.

According to Gerry Smith, principal of River Oaks school in Oakville, Ontario, children become engrossed in educational projects that demand collaboration. Visitors to the school find children working together on problems and projects around computers in ways that demonstrate computers are very effective tools which need not diminish quality talk and might actually enhance it.

Effective tools—that is the key concept. As with any educational tool, whether computer, television, videotape, or worksheet, there is the possibility for misuse. Certainly, if a teacher were to use the computer as a classroom "babysitter" or as a sophisticated electronic workbook, he or she would be abusing the tool to the detriment of the children in the class. This is not to say that a teacher would deliberately misuse this tool, but the potential for inadvertent misuse is there if teachers do not know how to use it effectively. That was true of every innovation that came before the computer, even books. The potential for misuse is always there. With computers, though, it seems easier. Thus, it is especially important that teachers be comfortable with and know how to use computer software appropriately. Because technological change happens so rapidly, it is unrealistic to expect teachers to keep up with the best, most effective and efficient uses of computer software. This is a subject I will return to below.

As with all tools, the computer must be put toward solid educational practice. But unlike others, the computer has a seemingly limitless potential for providing information, interaction with other people all over the planet, for improving the teaching of writing and for freeing teachers and students alike from routine classroom chores that sap valuable teaching time. Computers also underscore the need for a very high degree of basic literacy while simultaneously providing new ways of providing it.

What Is the Impact of Technology on Literacy?

This morning when I sat down at my desk to write, I jiggled the mouse for the computer that is always left on. A little five note song played to announce that I had new mail. I had, in fact, 14 new messages. Sometimes, especially if I have been AWK (Away from Keyboard) for 2 or 3 days, the number will be as high as 60 or more. I scan the list and choose the ones, either by writer or topic, that are most urgent or most interesting to deal with first, but before the day is over, every one will be dealt with along with those that arrive during the course of the day. Anyone who has dealt with volumes of email knows as I do the importance of skimming and scanning skills as well as the significance of context, or, more frequently, the absence of concrete context that can lead to ambiguity and confusion. If anything, we have to be better readers now than ever before in order not to be enslaved by the electronic post office. By better, I do not mean only faster, although speed helps. By better, I mean dealing with unfamiliar or missing context, dealing with unedited text at times, and dealing in general with the business of constructing meaning from a text written under a variety of very different circumstances—different from one another and different from most of the circumstances in which traditional print text is produced.

With the Internet, the possibility of being instantly and widely published, whether on a home page or by a distributed text, exists as it never has before. Our writing is very much on view by the world. With this possibility comes the responsibility for producing clear, coherent, and, we would hope, relevant writing. There is little doubt that effective use of computers requires a high degree of literacy. What is of greater interest to teachers is the potential of the computer to assist in the teaching of reading. To begin to understand this potential, we will take a closer look at one model of reading and its compatibility with computerized instruction.

The model we will assume is an interactive one for there is general agreement among educators "that reading is an interactive process in which readers call upon both visual and non-visual sources of information to make sense of the text" (Zakaluk & Sealey, 1988, p. 93). The interactivity in this definition refers to the fact that "highly skilled readers take advantage of not only lower level sensory information as represented by the letters and their sounds, but also higher level information inherent in the meaning of the text" (Zakaluk & Sealey, 1988, p. 93). The implication for reading instruction is that approaches should be holistic, that is, constructed to encourage children to make use of the four knowledge sources that they draw upon to construct meaning from text. These four sources include:

1. *The reader's orthographic knowledge or the sense of how sounds and letters are related and how they behave in text.* This kind of knowledge would tell the reader, for instance, that the printed letter *a* has a great many possible sounds, none of which is /b/ or /o/. It would also suggest to the reader that the *g* in *gospel* is probably pronounced even though the *g* in *gnome* is not and tell him that *snbkklic* is not a possible English word.

2. *The reader's knowledge of words and morphemes.* This kind of knowledge would help the reader to identify prefixes and suffixes and thus recognize plurals, past tenses, and other regular word formation processes. Faced with an unfamiliar text, the reader could rely on this knowledge to tell certain important things about *Der muggsy wibbles critched smibbely ip der spelen glabul.* He or she would know that there are likely two nouns in the sentence, *wibbles*, probably plural, and *glabul*, probably singular, that the verb is *critched* and that it is in the past tense. It would also be a reasonable guess that *muggsy* somehow describes *wibbles*, that *spelen* tells us something about *glabul*, and that *der* is an article of some kind.

3. *The reader's knowledge of how sentences are formed.* Syntactic knowledge would tell the reader, for instance, that in the sentence above, the subject is *der muggsy wibble*, that it did something (*critched*) in some relation to *der spelen glabul*. These three kinds of knowledge about language give the reader a head start on the task of determining meaning. Without the fourth kind of knowledge, however, the reader would be left guessing about what a *wibble* is, whether all *wibbles* are *muggsy*, what the particular *wibble* did to warrant attention by the writer, and how the *spelen glabul* figures in the action.

4. *The reader's knowledge of the world as related to the topic at hand.* Every reader brings to every reading task a particular experience of the world, some of which may be related to the topic of the text. In the example above, of course, the reader is unlikely to have any previous experience with *critching muggsy wibbles*, but in any normal reading task in a language known to the reader, he or she will have some amount of relevant experience to contribute.

To see how these levels of knowledge interact, let's consider an English sentence *Catherine's solo on the tickle this morning* which I read on a video news service provided by the local cable television company. I recognize all of the words and know how to pronounce them. I also know the meanings of the individual words and the fact that *Catherine's* is an abbreviated form of *Catherine is*. My syntactic knowledge tells me that whoever Catherine is, she (presumably a female if my lexical knowledge that it is a female name is accurate) is doing something alone and probably I am being told where she is doing it. That is as far as I could have gone with interpreting the meaning of the sentence had I just arrived in Newfoundland. As it happens, however, I had been in the province long enough to know that *Catherine* is the name of one of the two ferries that transport commuters between Bell Island and St. John's on the main island. This one item from my fourth or semantic knowledge store allowed me to hazard a guess that a *tickle* is a body of water, since that's where ferries do their work, and I could then decode the sentence: The only ferry running between Bell Island and St. John's on this particular day was the *Catherine*. Reaching farther into my fourth-level store of knowledge, I could hazard a guess at the relevant meaning for commuters: there would be delays getting to work.

The question before us now is how computers can help children to acquire or improve all four levels of knowledge and enhance their ability to integrate them and thus become effective readers. Let us first assume a non-reader. Can a computer contribute to the first level of knowledge, knowledge about the sound system and orthographic correspondence? Research using computer software to assist in reading remediation suggests that possibly it can.

The Computer as a Tool in Remediation

The Colorado remediation project (DeFries et al., 1991; Olson & Wise, 1992) used a computer program to assist in the remediation of children's deficits in word recognition and phonological decoding. On the whole, the results were impressive, showing that children working with a specifically designed computer program made almost twice the gains as children working with traditional remediation techniques. Moreover, children with the most severe problems at the beginning of the study made the greatest gains in both word recognition and phonological decoding. This study does not speak to higher level comprehension processes, but as Olson and Wise (1992) sensibly point out, programs for developing these higher-level processes "will have limited success when basic word-recognition processes are deficient" (p. 109).

The details of the program are unimportant for our purpose here except to say that the researchers used synthetic-speech feedback. It might even be argued that this rather low level skill is best taught by a machine, that is, a talking computer, thus leaving the teacher free to deal with higher level skills. At the time the research project was conducted, synthesized speech was easier and cheaper to produce than digitized human speech. In the past few years, however, the cost of digitizing human speech has greatly decreased due to the decreasing costs of magnetic and CD-ROM memory. Using digitized human speech would make the sound, if not the task itself, a little more natural.

Emphasis is on the computer as a *tool*. Pointing out that many reading-disabled children might well progress using more traditional methods such as reading interesting stories with a teacher to provide individual feedback for word-decoding problems, the researchers express a regretable reality. "Unfortunately, limited resources in the schools and parents' time and/or parents' limited reading skills often constrain the availability of effective tutoring for the additional needs of disabled readers" (p. 110). This is a hard fact of life in schools at the end of the 20th and beginning of the 21st century. We face more educational and social problems than ever before in our history, but we have fewer financial resources with which to cope. We will simply have to learn to conduct the business of education differently. Smarter. More efficiently. More effectively.

As we have seen, the computer has an important role to play in remediation on this level, but does this mean that it should be used instead of more natural methods? Certainly, the capacity is there to teach sound symbol correspondence and word identification to novice readers. Without going into detail about specific programs (likely out of date before this chapter is published), it is sufficient to imagine what a program would have to accomplish. It is easy to imagine the graphics and the game-like activities that could teach the alphabet, sound-symbol correspondence and basic phonic relationships in English. It might even be argued that having a machine to handle such routine tasks would free the teacher to deal with the more advanced aspects reading instruction. Certainly, the bright color and fast-moving images appeal to most children, but the danger is that the medium will overshadow its purpose. There is the possibility that children will be seduced by the medium to the detriment of the message. It is easy to imagine how children might pay a great deal of attention to the game but not make the connection with real reading behavior. This is a danger that exists at other levels of reading instruction (and for other educational uses of computers) and to which I will return below. But is the danger any greater or any different than it was with *Sesame Street?* I think they are similar. My children, like millions of others in North America grew up with Big Bird, Ernie, and Bert and all the *Sesame Street* family. They learned basic sound symbol correspondences there as well as a few words of another language—Spanish when we lived in the United States and French when we lived in Canada. But can *Sesame Street* be credited for the fact that my younger son, now a graduate student in biochemistry, spends his free time reading Shakespeare, Vonnegut, Eddings, and Margaret Laurence? We cannot say with any certainty that *Sesame Street* inspires a life-long love affair with reading; it is the medium that attracts children and through which they learn limited lower-level reading skills. Without strong support from home and school, these children will simply continue the habit of the medium—television watching. And so it will be with computers and the teaching of lower level skills. Unless the computer can facilitate three higher levels of knowledge and the interactions among them, then we should consider other less expensive alternatives.

What, then, of the other three knowledge levels? I contend that readers' knowledge of words and morphemes comes largely from their knowledge of the oral language and that this cannot and should not be taught by computer. What can be taught using the computer is the intersection of this knowledge with the first level. In other words, computer software has excellent potential for teaching not the regular processes of word formation (for children learn these at a very young age) but how these are realized in English orthography, that is, how to recognize them in print. Computer software also has the potential for vocabulary building. It is extremely important, however, that the teacher recognize that computer programs have the same inherent dangers of workbooks, that is, monotonous, non-contextualized segmentation of language into meaningless parts. Teachers, too, must guard against seduction by the medium.

I would apply the same arguments to the third level of knowledge, readers' knowledge of sentence structure, but I would make one additional observation. While it is certainly true that children need little help in learning to construct sentences in their native language, it is also true that written sentences have different characteristics than spoken ones. Writing is not just speech written down. If it were, everyone who could speak could write, and we all know that this is not the case. Written sentences are governed by more stringent rules, some of which are anything but easy to articulate. I have seen some excellent software in development that demonstrates rather effectively the construction of complex sentences as well as the rules about subject and verb agreement. Much of this has more potential as a tool for the teaching of writing than for reading, something which I think is generally true of computer software.

The real potential of computers, I think, comes with the fourth level of knowledge but not in the way that most people would predict. The fourth level is readers' knowledge of the world as it applies to what they are reading about. The potential for increasing world knowledge is starting to seem limitless. Last night I was working at home on a cookbook I am writing with a friend. Although I have a collection of cookbooks and magazines, none of them had the nutritional breakdown of squid. Since I am providing a full nutritional analysis with each recipe, I needed to know the calories per ounce, grams of fat, calcium content, etc. None of my print resources could give me the information I needed. I had just about resigned myself to a trip to the University library when it occurred to me that the same laptop computer I was using to produce the book might also help me to find the information. I plugged in the phone line, clicked the icon to connect me with the University computer and within a minute was into the Internet. Using a popular search engine, I typed in *squid* and within another minute had over 4,000 sources. Typing in *nutritional analysis* I narrowed the search to a few hundred, and in a few more minutes had the information I needed. I often spend time browsing the Net and always find something new to read and inform. It is much like browsing through magazines and books, but it is faster and cheaper. That is the strength of the medium, I believe—the capacity to provide virtually unlimited information very rapidly and thus expand children's world knowledge. The strength also lies in the motivation. I would not have been able to retrieve and use the information about squid had I not been able to read. The Internet provides a powerful stimulus to children to read in order to find out what they really want to know. It probably won't be squid, but whatever it is, it will be there for the asking and the reading. That brings us, of course, to the interaction of the four knowledge levels and the crux of my argument. It is simply this: While the computer has the potential for teaching the lower level skills, its greatest potential lies in the ability to make available to all children the best libraries and the best minds in the world. But a word of warning. My search for information yielded over 4,000 sources; other searches have yielded as many as 15,000. As of this writing, the information is unfiltered and overwhelming in its quantity. For many users it would be, for this very reason, unuseable. **It is the role of the teacher to make it useable.** That is a subject to which I will return below.

Before I leave this topic, however, I would like to reiterate a concern about computers in education. The medium itself is so seductive that it risks overshadowing the message. As an analogy, television has not lost its capacity to educate, but the attractiveness of the medium has seduced most of the population into thinking of it as an entertainment device. The same danger exists for computers. Most educators agree that television has been detrimental to reading. The more time children spend watching television, the less time they spend reading. If we add the time spent in front of a computer monitor playing glitzy, sophisticated games, for example, we can see that the time spent *not* reading is increasing. Anything beyond basic literacy is, thus, threatened.

Will books become obsolete? I'd like to say no unequivocally, but I can't. The best I can say is, not for the generation reading this text. Probably not for the next one, either, but with every decade that passes, we get closer to that day. There are simply too many presses—satellite television computers, environmental concerns over the production and use of paper, etc. Television hasn't made books obsolete but it has affected the time spent reading and is in danger of making literacy obsolete, at least literacy as we traditionalists know it. This is dangerous but points a clear direction for the teacher's role in the computer age.

How Is the Teacher's Role Changing?

This is a question that has been asked many times in the last half of the 20th century. The question has been prompted by changes in our societies other than technological ones. As the social fabric has changed—some would say deteriorated—the teacher and the school have had to assume roles other than those that are, strictly speaking, educational. Schools have become social agencies and teachers have become foster parents as well as counselors and social workers. Most teachers would consider these changes to be daunting enough without adding those being wrought by the computer revolution. I would like to suggest, however, that while there is little doubt that the teachers roles will change, it may well be the case that the changes will be welcome ones that actually give teachers the opportunity to do what they do best. Teach.

We saw in the anecdotes at the beginning of this chapter descriptions of teachers' activities quite unlike anything we could have imagined a quarter century ago. But what *did* we see, exactly? Was it really so different from what we normally find teachers doing? What we saw was a teacher integrating the subjects in the curriculum. What we saw was a substitute teacher coping with missing materials. We saw a teacher doing advance planning for her classes. We saw a teacher seeking the best resources available to meet the learning objectives that she set. True, those resources were purchased from a commercial provider, but then so are textbooks. What we did not see was a teacher using a canned curriculum or trying to force someone else's lesson to fit her own objecives. We did not see teachers delegating their responsibility to teach to the computer. No, what we saw was teachers using different tools. These particular tools were faster, more convenient, and tailor-made. The teachers' role as described were as facilitators. In the computer age, the teacher's role is to set direction, pose questions, respond and evaluate. It is, in short, as we have always wanted it to be. It's simply that now the tools exist for making it possible.

What Does the Future of Education Look Like?

The world has been reduced to numbers. Two numbers, to be exact. Zeroes and ones. The ability to reduce information—print, visual, sound—to zeroes and ones has permitted it to be transmitted rapidly and accurately, providing a degree of communication and information transfer that we hardly fathomed 10 short years ago. We are only beginning to realize the educational capacities of these existing and emerging technologies.

All schools will benefit from new technologies, but for small schools, the advent of satellite and computer technologies may mean the difference between extinction and survival. In much of North America, and especially in Canada, there are a great many small schools. Some of these are community schools in urban centers, but most are in rural communities, especially in Canada where the small population is dispersed over a massive geographical area. The relatively high per-pupil cost of running small schools means that the full range of courses and programs available in larger schools is not feasible. If the school is very small, the threat of closure always exists. In remote areas, however, the closure of a school means either long and sometimes hazardous busing of children over long distances or the death of a community. It is, thus, extremely important that educators find ways of keeping small schools open and offering high quality programs.

Technology offers hope to these schools. While the teacher cannot and should not be replaced, satellite delivery systems make it possible to offer certain courses that the school might not otherwise be able to deliver. In Newfoundland, for example, where a large proportion of the schools are designated as small schools and many of these in very remote areas, certain high school courses such as advanced mathematics, physics, and French have been delivered from the capitol city by distance methods for nearly two decades. The advent of digital and satellite technologies only serves to improve the quality of these courses.

Teachers in small rural schools have fewer resources available to them than their peers in urban centers. This need not be the case, however, since the classrooms augmented by satellite technology that we saw earlier in this chapter could easily have been in small schools. What is available for the urban teacher is becoming available for every teacher.

Perhaps the most exciting possibilities offered by technology are for integrating special needs students.

> The personal computer, when modified with special hardware and software, has opened up exciting and empowering new worlds of education and employment for persons with varying disabilities. Speech synthesis provides spoken output for users who are blind. Screen-enlarging software enables persons with limited vision to read a computer monitor.

> People with varying motor disabilities can use alternate input systems to enable their using computers. (Coombs, 1995, pp. 28–29)

It's about independence and productivity. The author of the quote above is a blind history professor. He notes further:

> . . . while I functioned professionally for years without a computer, the use of an adapted computer has dramatically increased my independence and my professional output. Students submit their work to me in e-mail, which my computer and synthesizer read to me, freeing me from dependence on a human reader. (p. 28)

Although teachers of young children might have some justifiable reservations about freeing children from human contact, the point about independence cannot be ignored for children whether they have disabilities or not. There is also some very promising software being developed for assisting people with hearing impairments and motor impairments.

Independence is one advantage conferred by the computer. Independence is a kind of opportunity; there are others. The great libraries of the world are having their materials digitized. In this format, any work, whether print, audio, or video, can be transmitted accurately and quickly to anyone who requests and has the equipment to receive it. In theory, a child in Plum Point, Newfoundland, or one in Browning, Montana, will soon be able to browse the collections of Harvard or Oxford libraries, or for that matter the resource room of any school in the world. Universities already are linked in this way, either through the Internet or intranets, demonstrating the benefits of such technology.

Of course, the same system that transmits information can be used to transmit communication between people. This communication might be in the form of electronic mail or it might be in the form of video and audio clips. Even as I write this, all the teachers in the province of Newfoundland are connected to one another and to the Internet through the provincial network, STEMnet. This permits a great deal of sharing of ideas and resources. By the time this chapter is in print, children will have equal access and the network will include all the schools in Canada and, through the Internet, all those on-line in the world. The pen pal of an earlier time is now a visitor to a chat room or to a web site or an email correspondent. This communicative potential is a mixed blessing. Those of us who use electronic mail for conducting routine business have learned that the instantaneous nature of electronically transmitted messages has forced changes in the way we work. There is an intrusiveness to electronic communication that some people find troubling, and there are those who are troubled by the fact that the medium is impersonal. It is easy enough to tell people to turn the machine off, and teachers will have to be particularly vigilant about doing so when the medium threatens to overwhelm the message, but we all know that it isn't that easy. Just as parents have a very hard time convincing children that it is in their best interest to turn the television set off from time to time, both teachers and parents will have a hard sell to convince children to go outside and look at the real world, instead of the virtual world, or to read a book. Television took us one giant step away from reality. The computer age threatens to take us galloping even farther away.

Like any tool, the computer has the potential for misuse. It may be obvious, too, that the larger the potential for use, the larger the potential for misuse. Certainly, we cannot be complacent about the danger inherent in the marriage of commercial interests and technology. In the anecdotes at the beginning of the chapter we can see one kind of danger. In this one, a great deal of responsibility for creating content is placed in the hands of a company whose *raison d'etre* is profit. While it may be argued that the company's profit is dependent upon their ability to create and deliver a quality educational product, there is nonetheless reason for concern. This concern could turn into a real worry if teachers were, in effect, to join in the conspiracy by turning over full control of the content in their classes to an educational corporation such as the one described earlier. We can imagine an Orwellian world in which every child in the country is taught exactly the same material by the same teacher who is seen only on a television screen. The classroom teacher thus becomes a media manager or executive producer, choreographing, perhaps, but taking little part in the dance. Imagine, then, what would happen if the educational corporation, after establishing a firm following in the schools, were sold to a special interest group, political or religious, for example. They would have the ability to create and publish only materials consistent with their interests. The potential for education to become the tool of propagandists is thus much larger than it was with textbooks, particularly when teachers and schools had a choice about which textbooks to use. I have, of course, stated an extreme situation, but it is one that we must be mindful of in the years to come.

We ignore to our detriment the possibility for commercial interests to dominate educational ones. Some educators see the marriage of business and education as inevitable. At the same time that educational technologies as well as increased demands on the curriculum are driving up the cost of delivering education, governments are steadily decreasing the amount of money they spend on education. This has forced educational administrators to form partnerships with the business community. A popular soft drink company builds a new recreation facility for a high school. In return, the school gives the company exclusive rights to sell its beverage on school grounds. The only protection that educators have against the domination of commercialism is to become as knowledgeable as possible about technology, to be clear and articulate about their educational goals and the role technology is to play in realizing them, and to clarify their expectations about the part the business community might reasonably play. In other words, technology is an educational reality. It is a very expensive reality, and in order to take full advantage of it, we will have to establish mutually beneficial partnerships with the business community. Otherwise, we will find ourselves and our children working toward goals that are not our own.

QUESTIONS FOR DISCUSSION

1. What are the implications for the teaching of writing in light of the fact that it is now possible to be almost instantly and very widely published?

2. What can a teacher do to protect conversation in a classroom increasingly dominated by machines?

3. Is there any more danger inherent in using "published" courseware through computers or interactive television than in using books?

4. Writing in the *Times of London*, Simon Jenkins observed:

> A house without books is a shelter but not a home. Children who do not read novels may be trained but not educated. Computer literacy is an essential tool for living, like being able to handle money, law and personal relationships. It has nothing to do with literacy.

> Do you think this is an overstatement? What can we do to protect the future of literacy as implied in Jenkins' quote?

Note: Further information about River Oaks Public School can be found on their home page. The URL is http://www.leta.edu.au/smith.htm.

CHAPTER TWELVE

Language and Learning: Reconciling the Home and School Years

In earlier chapters we explored the nature of language acquisition in early childhood and throughout the school years in both monolingual and bilingual children. We looked at children's experience of language learning in the home and in the school, and we explored the differences. The purpose in doing so was not to attack or defend a particular teaching method but to try to gain insights that will help teachers to reach rational and effective decisions about children's language. The task of the teacher is to provide the learning environment in which every child can succeed. It is a formidable task, to say the least, and it would be foolhardy of me to attempt to tell teachers or prospective teachers how it might be accomplished. Nevertheless, I believe that we have learned enough about language acquisition, about children, about schools, and about teaching to reach some conclusions about how to approach the job.

TEN PRINCIPLES FOR RECONCILING DIVERSE VIEWS

At this point, it might seem that the task of the teacher simply cannot be done. There are just too many masters to please—the researchers and theorists who tell us how language is learned (even though they seem rarely to agree among themselves), the parents of the children in school who may have their own ideas about their children's learning, the larger community, which consists of a variety of interest groups, including those of business and industry, and other educators who influence teachers' attitudes about language teaching as well as what goes on in the classroom. Indeed, the

285

job is a monumentally difficult one and one to which few people are well suited. But it can be done. The purpose of this chapter is to extract and synthesize from the previous chapters not a teaching method nor even a formula for finding one, for these are things that all teachers must do for themselves, but a set of principles that are intended to assist teachers in reconciling the disparate views, in pleasing the different masters.

There are 10 of these principles. The first six address the issue of reconciling theory and practice, specifically what we know about language acquisition in the home and school and how that should inform our teaching. The next three are concerned with how to deal with the divergent views of the other communities who are stakeholders in language education policy, and the final one synthesizes the issues and discussion so far into a single maxim: **There are many right ways to teach.**

We saw in Chapter 4 that there are a number of competing theories about how children acquire language, and that there is no one that accounts for all the available data nor answers all the questions that parents, researchers, or teachers might ask. Fortunately, as teachers we do not have to construct a theory of language learning so the fact that these disparate theories cannot be readily coalesced into a single theory of language learning need not concern us greatly. We are more concerned with the facts of language development and how these inform our teaching practice. Since there is no single theory that accounts for all the facts of language *acquisition*, it is not surprising that there is no single theory of language *teaching;* and that there are many ways which work.

Consistent with our best knowledge about language acquisition, there are a number of ways of planning for children's language development in the school years. The facts of language acquisition do not dictate any single method, although they would constitute strong evidence against some, such as the rote learning of vocabulary items out of context. The important thing is to remember to incorporate our best information about language acquisition into all language activities for children. That information includes the five attributes of language set forth in Chapter 1: Language is linked to cognition; language is natural; language is culturally bound; language has structure, and language has many varieties. It also includes the following attributes about language learning which were discussed in later chapters.

Children Learn and Use Language in a Social Setting

Children do not learn to talk in isolation. Social interaction provides the motivation, the opportunity, and the models for language learning. Children are most successful in all aspects of language learning if they are full participants, that is, if parents and teachers talk *with* rather than *to* them and join with them in reading and writing activities. In Janet, Quy, Lucy, Jani, and Michael we saw children learning language in very different circumstances. What was common to all, however, was the fact that they learned language within a setting of real use and with the encouragement of parents and teachers.

Children Need to Be Taught Very Little about Language

None of the children we met was taught English, yet all learned it. In the environment of their homes and communities, they had all they needed to learn language. This is not to say that the teacher does not play an important role in the language learning of school-aged children, but only that the role may be more usefully "seen as 'leading from behind' by supporting the language learning capabilities of students indirectly through the activities we offer them" (Newman, 1985a, p. 5). This may be a difficult part for some teachers to play, accustomed as they are to dispensing information to children. Certainly it is a very demanding role, but the demands are offstage, so to speak, as when the teacher takes the time to get to know as much as she can about all the children in her class by observing them carefully and by meeting with or writing to parents, or when she sits down at the end of the day to make her journal entries, recording the insights she or the children may have had into the learning process or notes about one child's progress and another's frustrations. In short, when she takes the time to consider the needs and to plan for each individual child, she is teaching in a way that may not be readily apparent to a casual visitor to her classroom but which is extremely important to her pupils' success.

Principle #1: Second Language Acquisition in Children Bears a Strong Resemblance to First Language Acquisition

A corollary to this principle is, the younger the child, the stronger the resemblance. The story of Lucy's language learning provides authoritative testimony to the truth of this claim. Her acquisition was native-like in nearly every way, in part because of her early exposure to English. The implication for teachers is that with some adaptation of materials and plans and with some extra time given, teachers can use many of the same methods for teaching ESL learners as native English speakers. This is not to say that the ESL learner should be ignored but only that teachers who base their teaching on children's language needs and on good information about first and second language acquisition will usually be effective. While it is always important to consider the needs of individual children, it is not necessary to start from scratch with ESL learners. There are a great many techniques and activities which work well for both native and non-native speakers. This is especially true of the primary grades (K–3).

In planning for the ESL children in their classes, teachers should remember that these children bring an abundance of cultural and linguistic experiences to the task of language learning. They also bring curiosity and the need to learn English they can use immediately. It is necessary but not sufficient to surround ESL children with all kinds of oral and printed language; that language has to be comprehensible. Teachers who remember to use all the resources at their command to get meaning across—other children, pictures, photographs, pantomime, whatever it takes—will give ESL children the kind of input they need to begin to make sense of the new language.

It is especially important to involve ESL learners as early as possible in the same activities being done by the other children in the class. For example, when the others are writing in journals, ESL children can dictate their journal entries using whatever

English they have or using the opportunity to learn new words from the teacher to express their meanings, or by drawing or even writing in their native language (a parent or older child can usually help you to translate). Whatever the language activity the class is engaged in, it is usually possible to adapt that activity so that ESL children can take part as well.

Less Rehearsal, More Production

We should remember that in acquiring their first language, children do not need an extended rehearsal period before they are permitted to speak in public. Rather, they get on with the business of communicating from the very beginning. It is the desire to communicate and to participate in the immediate society that motivates them to learn language. This single fact should remind us of a great many things we should *not* do in school while simultaneously reminding us of a great many worthwhile activities— reading quality books and engaging in real discussion about them, and writing for a real audience, for example.

Even ESL learners need to communicate in their new language from the very beginning. Our task of teachers is not to oversee or direct their practice until they are ready to use the language but to find ways in which they *can* communicate successfully from the first day they arrive in class. In order for them to do so, they must understand that their language need not be perfect, which means that teachers should keep in mind two corollaries to this axiom.

First, teachers should be more concerned with fluency than with accuracy. In other words, they should expose second language learners to and encourage them to use as much language as possible with little regard for correctness. Children will work out the rules in their own way in their own time, asking for help or otherwise indicating that they are ready to be taught the standard forms. Early or overemphasis on form will send the message to children that how they say something is more important than what they say, and this is not a message which is consonant with an environment which is conducive to language learning.

Second, language learning, indeed all learning, involves risk. In language learning, writing provides a good example. Even proficient writers cannot grow in their craft if they stay within comfortable modes. Journalists need to try short stories, novels, and poems in order to expand their skills and their understanding of their art. Short story writers need to experiment with drama, poetry, and magazine articles. I remember an incident which occurred when I was a student of Donald Murray's at the University of New Hampshire. For several weeks, I had been writing competent expository pieces on a variety of safe topics. Even though he had repeatedly encouraged me to try something a little different, I stayed with a formula I knew to be successful because it had worked with countless English teachers before. Finally, in one of our weekly conferences, he wadded up my most recent effort and threw it at me. "You've demonstrated that you can write competent prose. But you're never going to get any better unless you take some risks. I don't like to tell anyone what to write about, but if you can't write something a little riskier next week, don't bother writing anything at all." I took his advice and it was from that point on that I truly began to learn about writing.

It is neither necessary nor desirable to create a risk-free environment. What is important is to permit learners to take chances in order to optimize their learning. It is essential to create conditions which say to children that it is all right to take chances and to make mistakes, that it is more important for everyone, including the teacher, to try than to be correct.

Principle #2: Know Why You Do What You Do

One of the major purposes of this book has been to provide teachers a basis on which to make informed decisions about their language teaching practice. We examined in earlier chapters a number of competing theories of language acquisition and concluded that each one has its strengths. Clearly there is something that educators can learn from each one. If we learn nothing else from behaviorism, for example, we learn that children cannot learn language without being exposed to it. From the nativists, we learn that there is something unique about language learning, that it enjoys special status in human learning. From the cognitivists, we can take the highly significant notion that language learning involves children's active participation. It does not just seep into their heads; children do not learn by watching or listening; they have to *do* language. From the social interactionists, we draw the conclusion that language acquisition is influenced by a number of factors, physical, linguistic, and socioenvironmental. We may also conclude that because these factors differ among children, the interaction among them may produce different effects in different children. In other words, there will be certain differences among children in how they acquire language, in what they acquire and when. These insights from theory provide some help, but applying the principle articulated here means finding a specific answer each time we ask ourselves why we make a particular curricular decision or choose a language activity.

Admittedly, there may be instances when "because it works" is an acceptable answer to the question of why a teacher does a particular activity. But this answer should only be given after careful reflection about whether the method or activity really works and why. In her introduction to her fine book on whole language, Judith Newman (1985a) asserts that ". . . the clearer we are concerning our beliefs about language and learning, the sharper our focus on what is happening in front of our eyes." She goes on to articulate the questions that she and the other researchers continually asked themselves as they prepared the book:

- What do I believe about language and language learning?
- What do I want this activity to demonstrate about reading, writing, and learning?
- Why is this a useful activity for some particular student or group of students? (p. 5)

These are questions that teachers should regularly ask themselves as they plan for the children in their classes and as they assess themselves at the end of a day or a week. It is especially important for teachers to have a clear understanding about language acquisition against which to measure their practice. They must also have well-defined ideas about language learning because otherwise it is impossible to evaluate their effectiveness as teachers. As Meredith Hutchings (1986) observed about writing in her classroom, "Only after I have identified my own beliefs about the writing process can I begin to answer the questions: What am I actually demonstrating about the writing process to my learners?" (p. 43).

Having examined and specified their beliefs, if teachers then find that they are habitually planning activities that are incompatible with their beliefs about language and language learning, then they should seriously reconsider their entire approach to teaching. If they cannot state their expectations or objectives or if these are frequently inconsistent with their beliefs about language learning, then they probably should abandon the activity. And surely it goes without saying that if they find that they cannot specify how an activity benefits at least some if not all the children who participate in it, then they should replace that activity with one with clearer relevance.

What this principle advocates is practice informed by research and theory. Those whose teaching is guided by a solid grounding in language acquisition and who regularly ask themselves the three evaluative questions above may make mistakes, for who indeed does not, but they will make fewer. They will also be better able to correct the mistakes they do make, to learn from them and to avoid them as they proceed along the course of learning with the children in their classes.

Principle #3: Remember That Language Learning Is a Whole-to-Part Enterprise

This principle might have been included within the discussion of the first principle above. But since it is rather more specific and is such a vitally important one, I gave it separate treatment here. It is crucial because its violation in the past has led to some of our worst failures in language education. It would be tempting to blame the linguists for these communal errors in judgment. After all, as we saw in Chapter 2, their analysis of breaking down language into its component parts has been crucial to our understanding language's complex structure. But they did not dictate practice. It was educators who misapplied linguists' methods and their findings to language teaching. By breaking language down into its component parts and thereby rendering it meaningless, generations of teachers greatly complicated the business of language learning, particularly reading and writing, for countless children. By treating language as something separate from the child which could be done in assigned periods of time, the same teachers robbed it of its inherent appeal. By thinking about language analytically rather than synthetically or functionally, they reduced it to a series of exercises in manipulation, memorization, or worse, and many thousands of school children developed reading problems or failed to learn to write clearly. Their problems with literacy eventually resulted in the reactionary movement which has come to be known as the accountability or back-to-basics movement.

Real language is whole and should stay that way. That does not mean that teachers should never talk about parts of language, how to spell or how to pronounce a particular word, for example. It only means that these activities should take place within a larger language context. A simple example will clarify the distinction. Teacher X spends one half hour in round-robin reading of a story in a basal reader. She follows that up with a writing exercise in which the children complete worksheets based on the reading. The worksheet has four columns headed by four words from the story. The children's task is to circle all the words in the column that begin with the same letter (or that rhyme with, or which have the same vowel sound as) the word at the top. Because the words at the top also appeared in the story the children read, it might appear that the worksheet phonics activity is contextualized within the larger activity of reading the story. But this is nominal context at best and the activity is artificial; the words were isolated from the story and studied for some reason other than the meaning they contribute or the effect they have or the children's reaction to them. In fact, it is hardly relevant at all that they came from the story. The four words do not provide a strong enough connection between the two activities to relate them. The two activities do not support each other in any way.

Teacher Y, on the other hand, takes the same amount of class time in a different way. She begins by initiating a discussion about a field trip she and the children have taken to a chicken hatchery. As they talk, she makes notes on a large flip chart, writing down some of their observations, words that aptly describe something about the trip, or their reactions to what they have seen. Together teacher and students decide that they want to write about the trip and they go off to their writing places to do so. Some children sit at their desks. Some stay near the flip chart in the carpeted reading area. Others prefer the long table at the back of the room. One boy is writing a lengthy entry in his journal. A girl is looking up information about the length of time it takes to hatch an egg in response to a question raised during the discussion. Another girl works on a story about the only red chick hatched in a nest of six, all the rest fuzzy yellow chicks. After she has been working for about 26 minutes, she tells her teacher she would like to read the story aloud. She begins, "Their was a mother chicken named Sandra who layd six big white eggs." Then she interrupts herself. "I know I spelled some words wrong, but I'll fix them later." And later she does. She asks her teacher: "Is that the right 'there'?" "Why do you ask?" responds Teacher Y. "Because I know there's another one like in 'They lost their mittens.' But I can't remember which." Teacher Y then spends a few minutes on *their, there,* and *they're,* offering one or two suggestions for keeping them straight. Before she finishes, three other children are standing nearby listening. One goes away and silently makes a correction; another beams in pride that he has it right in his story.

In the second teacher's class, oral language, reading, and writing all support one another and are not fragmented in any way. The children read what they and others have written, and that writing is based on their earlier talk which was based, in turn, on their mutual experience of visiting the chicken hatchery. All the morning's activities involve the authentic use of language and are related directly and naturally to the children's own experience, in this instance a field trip. There is even a time for the teaching of spelling, but notice that it originates in a question asked by one of the children, a genuine question and not a demonstration question. The teacher has merely taken advantage of a teachable moment, but in doing so she has demonstrated the importance of the next principle.

Principle #4: But Don't Forget the Parts

Attention to the wholeness of language and learning need not and should not mean that the parts are lost. In other words, it is important that children learn the conventions of the language, and doing so may entail for some of them paying attention to discrete segments of the language. Spelling is one example; punctuation, mechanics, and certain aspects of grammar are others. By the time children reach the upper elementary grades, they should have mastery of these conventional aspects of language use. There is evidence that they achieve this mastery in stages. Gunderson (1990) has pointed out, for example, that children go through stages of writing development which take them from the "pre-phonetic" through the "conventional or mature." Chow's (1986) study of children in whole language classes where children were encouraged to write daily in log books but were not instructed in the conventions of writing revealed five stages of development. In the first, the pre-phonetic stage, the children produced letters, numbers and shapes resembling letters, apparently without understanding that there is a correspondence between the symbols and sounds or words. Next, in the semi-phonetic stage, they began to use letters symbolically, to stand for words or parts of words. Writers at the third stage of development, the phonetic stage, demonstrated their awareness that letters stand for sounds and that they know which letters stand for which sounds. Invented spellings were very common at this stage, but for the most part they are rule-governed inventions. That is, children used their knowledge of the relationship between letter and sound to create their own spellings. Many times, of course, these spellings would be the same as conventional spellings.

At the transitional stage, children began "to process words as visual units" (Gunderson, 1990, p. 129). Children at this stage typically continue to use invented spelling, but their writing will also contain conventional patterns as well as patterns which appear irregular. They might spell *through* "though," for instance, not because they do not hear the *r* sound or know how to write it but because they are now working from a visual memory of the word and that memory is sometimes faulty. The final stage of development identified by Chow found mature or conventional writers mostly in command of the conventions of writing. The mechanics of writing had become largely automated, leaving these writers free to write longer and more complex pieces.

Many children will proceed through these stages, achieving mastery of the conventions without requiring any overt intervention at all; they will have learned them from their own reading and writing. Others will have asked the kinds of questions asked by the girl in Teacher Y's class and learned in that way. But some children need more help in passing from stage to stage. It may be necessary for teachers to search for or to foster actively those teachable moments during which such learning is possible.

Principle #5: A Second Language Is an Asset Some Children Bring to School

It has been all too common for teachers to think about ESL children as having some kind of deficit or limitation on their ability to learn. Labels such as LEP (limited English proficiency) perpetuate this misconception. ESL children are deficient only if we persist in looking at what they do not have instead of what they do. What they do have is a well-established and fully functional first language on which to build a second language. When we think of children as missing something, our natural tendency is to provide it. In the case of ESL learners, what we want to provide is language. We may well be tempted to tell them about or to *teach* them language, and while this might not always be a bad idea, it can lead to some disastrous practices, especially with young children. But when we refuse to think of children as lacking something and see them instead as having something very special when they come to school, then our response is not to try to correct or fill the deficit but to build on strength. We can do so with confidence. After all, we have seen in earlier chapters that the particular language which the child learns at home is not as important to school success as the experience of having acquired a first language and the existence of literacy-related activities in the home. By seeing ESL children in this more positive light, it is easier to see that the same language-rich, language-integrated environment which helps native speakers to acquire literacy and to further their oral language learning will also help ESL students to add English to their home language.

Principle #6: Make Sure That the Method of Evaluation Corresponds to What Happens in the Classroom

An experience I had several years ago while engaged in a collaborative research project with a Grade 2 teacher in Calgary underscored the importance of this principle. The teacher's class was an ideal learning environment for Grade 2 children. It was a whole language classroom, before the whole language concept had taken hold in Canada. Writing was a central component of her curriculum and there were no basal readers in the room. The children wrote every day and for much longer periods than the experts claimed children of this age were capable of. They liked to write and enjoyed sharing their writing with their teacher, with me on the days I was there, and with all other visitors to their classroom. More than half the children in this class were ESL learners, and most of them beginners or near-beginners. Nevertheless, they participated fully in all the activities of the class because the teacher made the adaptations that made their participation possible. In short, this teacher was doing a commendable job. Just after Christmas, however, she experienced a minor panic attack when she thought about the fact that the children in her class would be taking a provincial examination in language at the end of Grade 3. This test included a traditional spelling test. The teacher began to worry that the children would not be able to pass such a test because she spent almost no time in teaching spelling. When she talked to me about her concern, I pointed out that, in the first place, the pieces her children "published" had generally excellent spelling. Besides, the invented spellings they used showed them to be well aware of sound-symbol correspondence, and, in some cases, to be in that transitional phase when their spelling shows that they are developing some awareness of what the word looks like in print. She wanted to believe I was right. She even knew I was right. Nonetheless, she worried.

Finally, after a few weeks, she decided to put her mind to rest by administering a standard spelling test. She selected the words by asking the Grade 3 teacher about the words that had appeared on the previous year's examination and then deleting those she was sure the children wouldn't know and adding a few that she knew they had encountered. The results did nothing to abate her concern. The children did very poorly on the test, the only test they had written that year. Many of the children expressed surprise at having to do such an activity; several expressed anxiety over the outcome. The teacher talked to me again. "I really wanted them to do well just to prove that my way is as good as the skills method. What's going to happen to them when they have to write the provincial test next year?" I asked her what she was going to do. "I just can't go back to that way. They're doing so well. You've seen their stories and you've seen how eager they are when they come to school every day."

"Yes," I replied. I had listened to them read their wonderful stories. I pulled one I had copied from my desk drawer and read it aloud to her. It was a Vietnamese child's account of her neighborhood and is reproduced in Figure 12.1. "Do you want to give this up to teach spelling?"

"No, of course not, but will they be all right?"

We then talked for a long while about why the children did so poorly on the test and what she wanted to do about it. In this case, as she pointed out, the test was a completely alien experience. Imagine what it must have been like for children accustomed to spending their time writing and revising real stories to be asked to write down decontextualized, unrelated words that the teacher read aloud. These children had never had a spelling test, had, in fact, never had a formal spelling lesson. In giving them the test, she had asked them to do things with language that were unnatural and outside their experience of language inside or outside the classroom. It is small wonder that they did so poorly.

"What do the results mean?" I asked. After thinking for a few seconds, she replied that they only meant that the children were not very good at performing on this particular task. It said nothing about their development as spellers or even about how they would spell those words at this time under normal circumstances. It didn't take this teacher long to conclude that the results of the test were meaningless and should not influence her decision about how to proceed with the children who, by all reasonable standards, were progressing marvelously. She decided that if she had to, she could in a very short time teach them how to take such a test, but that she would neither change her curriculum nor, until that time, subject the children to further tests of this type. She decided to put her trust in her knowledge of language acquisition and in her own experience with the children. She was right, of course, and the next year, after the Grade 3 teacher had taken a little time to teach them how to take the test, the children performed well above the provincial average on all aspects of the language arts test. On the way to learning to write and loving to write, they had learned to spell as well.

The test in this example was a provincially mandated examination of the type that is coming back into vogue in many U.S. states and Canadian provinces. Some of these tests are constructed and scored in such a manner as to permit children to demonstrate their facility with language. Others are not; they consist of a series of unrelated questions requiring children to perform unnatural acts with language. If such tests cannot be avoided, then some time may have to be spent in teaching children how to take the tests. What is more important is that the teacher work to convince the school and the public that results of such tests reveal very little either about what children have learned or how well they have been taught.

I would like to live in a neighborhood that is peaceful in Viet Nam because there are war and some people break their arm's and legs by the soldiers. I would like to live in a neighborhood that is nice and quiet all around the neighborhood. I would like to live in a neighborhood that has alot of my friends. I would like to live in a neighborhood that has a school beside my house. I would like to live in a neighborhood that has alot of birds. I would like to live in a neighborhood that has a place for me to play.

Figure 12.1   Thuy's neighborhood

Unfortunately, teachers may have little control over government-decreed tests. But they do have control over the evaluation which occurs in their own classrooms and here it is especially important that the test match the task. As Serebrin (1985) observes of children's writing:

We must not confuse the products of their efforts with the processes operating within particular contexts. This means that their efforts must not be evaluated by the yardstick of correct form—conventional spelling, punctuation, and sentence structure—but rather in terms of decision-making events within specific contexts. To see only their products would be to miss the significant "language events"—language users bringing all they currently know to bear upon the task with which they are faced. (p. 53)

Evaluation is the part of the job that many teachers like least, yet most realize that it is a necessary part of the teaching and learning process. While a complete discussion of assessment in language education is beyond the scope of this chapter, a few observations must be made not only about what is to be evaluated but by whom. Since language is social in nature, since most meaningful language activities in the classroom involve the learner and at least one other person, and since we have accepted the principle that the test should reflect the task, it is also reasonable to involve the learner and possibly others in the task of evaluation. Children should be involved in making the decisions about how their learning will be evaluated, and it may be that peer evaluation will prove useful as well. Certainly, teachers should make sure that parents understand how their children's learning will be evaluated and why. They might also be invited to participate. But no matter whom the teacher involves in the evaluation process, the paramount principle to remember is the one stated above: Children should not be evaluated in ways that are incompatible with the ways in which they have experienced learning.

These first three principles are intended to guide teachers as they attempt to reconcile the diverse views of theorists, parents, other educators, and the wider community in which they all live. But first a comment about why it is necessary to do so. First, for obvious reasons it is desirable to create as much harmony as possible between children's homes and the school. If there is discord, then children are the ones who suffer. Most teachers realize, too, that their jobs are hard enough without having disgruntled parents to deal with. The second reason is that schools are funded by public money, and it is not in the interest of educators to have a large portion of the public dissatisfied with what they do. This is not to say that teachers should be governed by public opinion, but only that they should take precautions, at the least, not to antagonize the public and, ideally, to involve them actively in education. This is the seventh principle.

Principle #7: Involve Parents and the Community

The participation of parents in education is deemed so important today that Chapter 1 legislation in the United States requires that schools foster parental involvement activities. Involvement, under that legislation, means "helping parents understand the academic growth of their children" as well as getting them to participate in "actual reading and writing activities that support classroom learning" (Smith, 1991, p. 700). In Canada, there is a similar move in several provinces to involve parents in the operation of schools. The School Council project in Newfoundland in which parents are elected to serve on a formal advisory board is a good example of such a program.

Parental participation is now deemed such a vital component of literacy education that the term *family literacy* no longer refers exclusively to the level of reading and writing attained by all family members, but to "families working together to promote mutual learning" (Nickse, 1989, cited in Smith, 1991, p. 700). One researcher, Joan

Oldford-Matchim (1995), at Canada's Memorial University has received national funding to work with schools and families on a read-aloud program to promote intergenerational literacy.

While teachers and principals should encourage parents' active participation in the life of the schools their children attend, it would be a mistake to assume that those parents who do not attend meetings with teachers or PTA meetings or who do not respond to letters sent home are disinterested in their children's welfare. A great many children are being brought up by single parents who must work, sometimes at more than one job, and shoulder the entire responsibility for their children's care. They may simply not have the time that other parents have to share actively in their children's school life. Ideally, all parents would fall into the category Snyder calls "available parents." But since they do not, it is imperative that teachers find ingenious ways of enlisting their support if not their active participation. The benefits accrue to the teacher as well as to the children. Writing of the importance of involving parents in whole language programs, Snyder (1990) says,

> When parents accept a broadened view of literacy learning, they become increasingly involved in the educative process, as models, participants and audience. Their children, as excited and achieving learners, become powerful influences for continued parental support. (p. 221)

Snyder implies that most parents participate without realizing it, when they talk with their children, listen to, and read with them. When teachers make the importance of these simple acts known to them, they can expect that many parents will seek to participate in other ways.

One way of involving parents is to keep them informed not only about their children's progress but about what kinds of activities are being planned for the class. If parents know ahead of time that the class is going to do a particular activity and that activity is one about which they have some specialized knowledge, they may volunteer to assist in some way. It would not be inappropriate for a teacher to send home a book with a child with a note requesting the parent to read it aloud to the child, so long as the teacher knows that the parent is literate. If the parent is not, or if there is some doubt, then it is helpful to send home an audio tape with the book so that parent and child may share the experience of reading. If she knows that the family does not speak English, a teacher might send a child home with a book in his native language with a request that the parent and child read it together. Giving children assignments which require them to interview or talk to their parents about specific topics is also a good way of involving parents in their children's language education.

The computer age also provides opportunities for parents and children to learn together. Some Canadian schools are experimenting with programs in which the children teach their parents the computing skills they have acquired at school. While these kinds of activities have obvious benefits to both parents and children, the actual activity doesn't matter so much as the sharing.

Parents, of course, are part of a larger community, and this community is a major stakeholder in language education. Partnership between the larger community and

1. Invite community members to the school to share their expertise or interest with students.
2. Encourage visitors to read a favorite book or tell a favorite story.
3. Encourage repeat visits from guests the students find especially interesting.
4. Ask community members to correspond with students on areas of mutual interest.
5. Encourage community members to become volunteer tutors in the school. Senior citizens are an especially valuable resource.
6. Invite businesses to "sponsor" a class in the school. Their sponsorship may involve having their employees volunteer in the class, buying books or computer software for the class, or sponsoring or helping organize field trips.
7. Have students interview business and professional people about their reading habits, that is, what they read and why.
8. Have students interview community members for the school or class newspaper.
9. Ask businesses to display children's stories or artwork in their establishments thus providing a real "audience" for the students' work.

Figure 12.2   Nine ways to involve the public in language education

schools is essential because full participation in the community means that one needs to be able to read and to express oneself effectively orally and in writing, and these are prominent functions of schools. It is thus imperative that we extend our thinking beyond parents when we think about community participation in language education. Although it may take some effort on the teacher's behalf to engage the community in the life of the school, it is well worth the effort. There are a number of roles community members might play which directly affect language education. Some of the more commonly used techniques are listed in Figure 12.2.

Principle #8: Don't Be Dogmatic

Teachers are professionals, and as such, we may be tempted to think of ourselves as having the answers or, at least, of knowing better than the lay community how children should be taught. Of course, to some degree, this is true, otherwise all those years of specialized education would not be necessary and we could hire teachers through the local employment agency much as we hire waiters, pizza delivery drivers, and janitors. But even though we do have specialized education and, most of us, fairly strong opinions about education, it would be a mistake to allow ourselves to become inflexible, to insist that our way is the best and only way. For one thing, from a purely practical perspective, to do so would essentially close the door on much of the community participation for which I have been arguing. For another, we would be forgetting the first principle above. A specific example illustrates the danger.

In recent years, there has been a tendency to view whole language as providing the only way to organize the elementary school curriculum. At least, some supporters of the approach hold such a strong view. Although it is easy to understand why they would hold such an opinion, it is also easy to see how such dogmatism can backfire. I was recently conducting a 2-day materials-development workshop for ESL teachers who came together in the University's resource room to write and assemble ESL materials for their classes. In the district in which most of the teachers work, the Board of Education has made a firm and public commitment to whole language. While they have not mandated whole language for ESL classes, most of the teachers teach both ESL and English speaking children and are thus familiar with the tenets of whole language. Familiar! Their devotion to whole language was so extreme that they dismissed from consideration any materials which even smacked of "skills." In doing so, they denied learners the benefit of materials which were comprehensible and meaningful to them and denied themselves some important tools for managing classrooms in which students' English ability is heterogeneous.

By taking such a strong stance, these also called into question the competence of the few ESL teachers who had learned from experience that many learners need explanation and practice with certain grammar points or with spelling or with certain idioms. Finally, they risked offending (and thus losing the cooperation of) the parents of the ESL children in their classes. Many of these families have come from countries with educational systems which differ greatly from those of the United States and Canada and their children have succeeded within those systems. They have developed certain expectations about learning, and while it is not incumbent on schools to live up to all those expectations, it is incumbent upon them to take into account the previous experience the learner has of language and of learning. Being dogmatic jeopardizes professional harmony and community participation in education.

A corollary of this principle is be willing to compromise. It usually is possible to reach compromise on any issue without abandoning those aspects of a belief that one holds dearest. Besides, it is necessary. Most people are wary of large-scale change but will fairly readily accept small-scale change. Thus, if teachers who want to alter radically the approach to language teaching in a school but are meeting with community resistance, they should consider taking small steps. It probably will take no longer to accomplish their goals, since, this way, they are more likely to have the cooperation of parents and the larger community.

Principle #9: Be Professional

Mary Ashworth (1985) pointed out that if teachers want to be taken seriously and to be treated like professionals, then they must act like professionals. With regard to establishing collaborative relationships with the community, however, certain aspects of professionalism are particularly important. One is that we become and stay informed about the community. The school's relationship with the community is a symbiotic one, and we cannot expect the community to be interested in the school if we show no interest in the community. Another aspect of professionalism, which Ashworth (1985) highlights, improves the credibility of both the individual teacher and the profession. That is to engage in classroom research to support your beliefs about instruction (and possibly to modify them) and, if possible, to write articles describing this research (p. 111). Writing these articles for the lay audience and publishing them in the local press will enhance the school's profile and reputation as well as the teacher's.

One teacher I know used to write an open letter to the local newspaper every week or two in which she described her own struggles with evaluation. She openly shared with the public why she felt she needed to alter the way in which children's language development was assessed and her attempts to find solutions. After a few weeks, others in the community started to write to the newspaper to make suggestions or to praise her for the thoughtful way in which she tackled what was for them a critical issue.

Principle #10: Remember That You Are Teaching Children, Not Language

A beginning teacher may feel overwhelmed by the job ahead. Even an experienced teacher, faced with ever-increasing curricular and social demands and trying to keep up with the professional literature, new theories, and new methods, will be inundated by the responsibility to meet the needs of all the children in every class. The theme of diversity has prevailed throughout the previous pages. Cultural, linguistic, and individual differences have all been shown to have an impact on language and learning. This means that children come to school with individual needs that must be respected if they are to succeed. While it is not possible to structure a totally different instructional plan for each child, it is the teacher's responsibility to be attuned to the needs of each child and to attempt to meet them to the best of his ability. The teacher who puts the child's learning at the top of the educational agenda will naturally assume this responsibility.

These principles do not constitute an exhaustive list of dos and don'ts about teaching nor even about how to reconcile the numerous views about language teaching held by individuals and groups who might be termed stakeholders in the educational process. They are instead guidelines, things to remember that might make the task a little easier. Unfortunately, following these principles will not ensure success but will improve the chances. Following them will also allow us to proceed in the knowledge that we are not compromising the interests of the principal shareholders—the children.

CONCLUSION

No more analysis is needed, and the synthesis is largely done, too. So in concluding this book, I will exercise my prerogative as an author to weave the various threads together in a more personal way.

The Glen Duncan School

Nestled among the lush green rolling hills of Prince Edward Island, in the country that was home to Lucy Maud Montgomery's *Anne of Green Gables*, is a neighborhood school that children still walk to each day except in the worst days of winter. It would be presumptuous to claim that it is a model school, for there are many possible models on which to base an ideal school, but in its faculty, curriculum, and practice, it represents much that is ideal. I first learned of the school when I met some of its alumni, young people in their twenties studying to be teachers at Saint Mary's University in Halifax. Some 10 or 15 years after leaving the Glen Duncan Elementary School (which is not its real name) these neophyte teachers recalled it fondly and told stories about their education that made it sound like a truly progressive place.

Several things struck me as noteworthy. First, it was unusual that so many of the students I encountered had attended this school. Saint Mary's admits only 40 students to the Bachelor of Education degree each year, and these are selected from between 600 and 800 applicants from across Canada. For more than one student to have attended the same elementary school is rare; three or four suggests that the university's selection process is somehow biased in their favor. Second, I have found only infrequently that university students recall their primary education at all; usually, they speak of their high school years, evaluating their experiences with what they read and see of education. But the four students I met during my years in Halifax all spoke well of their years at Glen Duncan. The account that follows is based on the memories of the young man who happened into my office on a summer day. Mark, who was a gold medalist in biology at another University before coming to do his teacher education at Saint Mary's, talked to me about his years at Glen Duncan.

Mark: I didn't know until I started my Early School Experience [a period of observation in schools which students complete prior to beginning their student teaching] that there was anything different about Glen Duncan. But after I'd visited a few classes, I remember thinking "Wow. Times sure have changed." But when I got to talking with some of the others [students in the teacher education program] who had gone to other schools, they said that things seemed pretty much the same to them as always.

Terry Piper: So what was different about Glen Duncan?

M: Well, in retrospect, I have to say that most of what I knew before I went to university I learned there.

T: That's a pretty tall claim. You learned nothing in high school?

M: Well, I'm sure I did. But what I mean is that at Glen Duncan I, we all, learned to learn. It's funny. I remember learning but I don't remember being taught much.

T: Can you explain that?

M: I'm not sure I can. The teachers were always there to help and to make suggestions if we needed them, but, except for one, I can't remember them standing up in front of the room talking to us, telling us about things. I remember that we used to read a lot. Most teachers would read to us at some time in the day, even when we got into the upper grades, and we always loved that. And we had silent reading periods as well when we could read anything we wanted. We wrote a lot, too. Stories, plays, newspaper articles, letters. Every day, we had to write but it was not a chore or anything. I really liked to write. When it was my turn to be editor of the class newsletter, I didn't like the job much. I preferred writing stories to deciding what would go into the paper and editing other people's work.

T: You had a newsletter?

M: Yes, every class had one. There were articles about what the class had been doing, what they were planning to do, that kind of thing. I remember writing the obituary for the class gerbil as well as a lot of birth announcements the year we had a rabbit for a science project.

T: What did you do with the newsletter?

M: It went home to our parents, of course, but it also went to local businesses and to the local newspaper.

T: Tell me about some of your other writing.

M: I wrote a Christmas play in Grade 5. A musical, believe it or not.

T: Was it staged?

M: No, not that one. I tried but I couldn't get enough of my classmates interested. One girl got hers produced, though. I think that was in Grade 6. She wrote the play and several of us helped write revisions and worked on the dialogue. I wrote two songs for it.

T: Was it a success?

M: Well, it didn't make it to Broadway, if that's what you're asking. But it enjoyed a three-night run in Charlottetown and was written up in the local paper.

T: Can you tell me anything more specific about your years at Glen Duncan? How about a typical day?

M: I don't think there was any such thing as a typical day. I remember walking to school most days and wondering what we'd be doing that day. I actually looked forward to it.

T: What might you have been doing one day in, say, Grade 3 or 4?

M: Well, after the morning routine—

T: What was the morning routine?

M: We sang "O Canada" and then had the morning news report. We had to predict one item that would be in the newspaper when it arrived later in the day. That meant that we had had to hear or see the news in the morning or talked to someone else about what was going on. We'd dictate the headlines to Mrs. Marchand— she was my Grade 3 teacher—and she'd write them on a flip chart and leave them until later when the newspapers came. We'd get four or five copies in the class and we'd divide them up and comb the paper for stories to go with our headlines.

T: What happened after the morning routine?

M: Well, we'd usually settle down to our writing. We kept these large notebooks, and we could write about anything we chose but there were also certain writing assignments we had to do each week.

T: The teacher gave you topics to write about?

M: No, not exactly. She gave us tasks. One week I might have to write a letter for the class inviting someone famous to visit.

T: Did you send the letter?

M: Oh, yes, definitely. That's one of the things that I remembered when we were talking in the methods class about whole language and authentic language. Even then, most of the writing assignments were real. I already mentioned the school paper, but sometimes she would ask some of us to write a piece for the local newspaper— to collaborate on an article. Sometimes our required writing was related to other things we were studying. I remember one of my assignments was the description of one of my classmate's entries in the Science Fair. That was for the local paper.

T: Why not your own?

M: Because I already knew about my own. I guess she figured that if I wrote about someone else's I'd have to learn about it.

T: What would happen after writing time?

M: That would sometimes go on for the entire morning. Other times, though, we would work on math or science until lunchtime.

T: What do you remember about math and science?

M: That it was fun, then. We used to do a lot of experiments, but before we did them, we had the most interesting discussions. She would encourage us to ask all kinds of questions and then think of all kinds of ways of finding the answers. She'd ask us "What do you think will happen if . . .?" or "What will it mean if . . .?" questions.

T: Such as?

M: Well, when we were on our way to "discovering" Archimedes' Principle—and, you know, we really thought we *had* discovered it?—we had designed an experiment on water displacement using a marble, a baseball, a softball, and a 12 lb. bowling ball. We thought we had it all worked out and then she asked, "What will happen if the bowling ball is the same diameter but weighs only 10 pounds?" The discussion on that was pretty animated but going nowhere until she asked "Suppose the ball is made of Styrofoam?"

T: You have very clear memories about that.

M: Yes, probably because I went on into science and I've even borrowed that technique from her. But I remember the talk about science to be the most interesting thing about it. The same was true about social studies.

T: Oh, right, the newspaper.

M: Yes, the newspaper seemed to be the starting place for all our social studies lessons. The end of the Vietnam War was in the news then and we spent a lot of time trying to understand what had happened and why. We learned about other wars and talked a lot about beliefs and trade and all the reasons that countries get into wars. We learned about negotiation and compromise in our discussions based on those news stories.

T: Were there any children who didn't speak English when you were at Glen Duncan?

M: Yes, but only a few. There was a French-speaking girl who came in Grade 2 and stayed until Grade 4 and a boy who came in Grade 3.

T: What do you remember about them?

M: Well, there were no ESL classes. But there weren't many ESL kids either. I remember that the teacher would assign each new kid a "buddy" every week, and that buddy would help them to understand what was going on in class and on the playground. I don't remember much more except that eventually, they learned English. The girl went on to university, too. She was a biology major, like me.

T: Do you remember learning to read?

M: Not really. I remember that our Grade 1 teacher read to us a lot. Oh yeah, and she'd have us tell her stories, and she'd write them on a big piece of paper and we'd read them out loud.

T: Language experience?

M: Is that what it's called? But if you're asking whether I remember being taught what sound a *b* makes, no, I don't. I guess I must have been, 'cause I learned to read at some point and I always liked it.

T: Were all your classes and teachers like the ones you've described?

M: With one exception, yes. There was a Grade 5 teacher who came to the school the year I was in Grade 6. She was my brother's teacher and she was very rigid compared to the other teachers in the school. She gave a lot of tests and seatwork and I don't think anyone was very happy. She left after only 1 year.

T: In the years since you left Glen Duncan, have you thought about why it was that that one school attracted so many fine teachers?

M: Actually, until I started my teacher education program, I hadn't thought about it at all. I thought all teachers were like the ones at Glen Duncan. But now I realize that they aren't, and thinking about it, I'd have to say that it was the principal who probably made the difference.

T: How so?

M: He was really special. He didn't just stay in his office the way I see some of these guys doing now. He spent a lot of time in the classrooms working with the kids. He knew all the kids in the school and their parents, too. I think the parents all liked him. He was really good at getting them involved in the school.

T: How did he go about that?

M: Well, the school couldn't afford a full time librarian and so he wrote to the parents.

T: Asking for volunteers?

M: Yes. I remember because my mother was thinking about working there. He wrote a long letter explaining why library was so important to the life of the school and why he had had to make the hard decision to eliminate the librarian's position. His idea was to turn the library into a community resource. He got enough volunteers—qualified ones, too—that the library could stay open three nights a week.

T: Was there material in an elementary school library to interest adults?

M: There was when he finished lobbying all the local businesses. He held an annual library fund raising drive and managed to get enough contributions to keep a good collection. Parents and former students also donated a lot of books and magazines. It was an odd assortment, for sure, but it was an interesting place to spend time.

T: It sounds like all of Glen Duncan might fit that description.

M: Yes, it was. I learned to read and to write and to think and to learn there. I'd really like to go back there to teach one day. If they'll have me.

Mark attended the Glen Duncan school from 1972 until 1978. His recollections of his years there raise a number of intriguing questions. The first and most obvious is whether the school was special or was it typical of most others of its time. We can say with a fair degree of certainty that the Glen Duncan School would be considered special today even if measured against the strictest criteria of excellence in language teaching. That it was special nearly 20 years ago cannot be doubted. The second question is Why? To anyone reading the chapters that preceded this one, the answers should be obvious. Nevertheless, it is appropriate as a conclusion to the book to summarize them.

Accounting for Success

Mark's account was by no means exhaustive, but it provided a window not only on the personal experience of one child, but on the curriculum, the teachers and the principal which contributed to the school's effectiveness. While there are doubtless many reasons for its success, five stand out from reading his recollection.

1. Children participated daily in authentic tasks involving authentic language.
2. They used both reading and writing as means of discovery, as a way of learning.
3. Subject areas were integrated so that language played a central role across the curriculum.
4. ESL students were not segregated but participated fully in the life and activities of the class.
5. Education was a joint-venture enterprise whose success depended upon the partnership of teachers, principal, and community.

It seems obvious to me that these are axioms which could guide any elementary school. This is true, I believe, not because they are profound statements of educational philosophy nor even particularly insightful statements about the nature of human learning. They are basically just common sense if we take to heart the truths about children's language and learning that we explored in the previous chapters. Let us consider the five axioms individually.

Children Participated Daily in Authentic Tasks Involving Authentic Language.
This participation began with the morning routine. In asking children to predict the stories and the headlines in the afternoon paper, the teacher was engaging the children in genuine talk in which they used language for a number of functions. The primary function was forecasting and reasoning. Children would speculate about the probability that various events would make the afternoon news, talk about causes and effects and discuss the reasons. This daily routine would also provide opportunities for children to engage in the informing function of language in telling each other about the newscasts they had already heard. In the simple act of constructing headlines for their predicted stories, the children would have learned a great deal about the message-carrying properties of language—that some words carry more meaning than others which can be left out—and about ambiguity that resulted when they left out too much information or the wrong information.

Later in the day, when the newspapers came, the purposeful language continued. Children read the paper, searching for stories to match their predicted headlines and then talked about the stories they read. It is not difficult to imagine the language and the functions involved:

Hey, look at this. Here's the story about the hurricane. (Controlling; informing)

Where do you think they'd put a story about the school play? (Informing using the subfunction of requesting information)

I don't think it's here. That's strange. I guess they thought the story about the whale was more important. (Forecasting and reasoning; projecting)

Look! There's a story about the zoo on page six but I can't find anything about the aquarium. Why do you think that is? (Controlling; informing; reasoning)

As in much classroom talk, there were undoubtedly many opportunities for children to use the social language required for maintaining relationships with teacher and peers. An important point to remember was that the talk which engendered so many functional possibilities was not contrived but purposeful.

The authenticity of language use continued in the routine of morning writing. It is necessary to give children the freedom to write about whatever they want and in whatever form. That is the nature of much true writing, after all. Except for journalists who may be assigned particular stories from time to time, most writers have a great deal of freedom in deciding what and how they will write. Children were thus encouraged to write whatever they wanted, and in doing so they likely employed all five functions of language although it is likely that some were more heavily used than others. The social and projecting functions, for example, would be rather more heavily used in personal letters with the informing, forecasting, and reasoning functions used more in letters attending to classroom business.

It is also necessary to their development as writers that children experience a variety of different writing formats. The teachers at Glen Duncan assigned tasks to provide that variety. Notice, however, that the tasks Mark remembered were legitimate writing tasks of the type that all of us might have to do in real life. They were not just realistic; they were real. This is an important distinction, I believe, because even very young children understand the difference between pretend and real activities. Like adults, they will care more about the letters they write to the President of the United States, the Prime Minister of Canada, or to Santa Claus if they have a reasonable expectation that they will be read. The more they care, the more they will learn. They will ask questions about the form their letters should take, about the way to state a thought more clearly, or the exact word they need to express a particular idea. In asking these questions and getting them answered, they engage in even more purposeful talk.

They Used both Reading and Writing as a Means of Discovery, as a Way of Learning. Reading and writing were not separate, independent subjects in the curriculum of Glen Duncan but formed an integral and essential component of all classroom learning. We saw in the newspaper exercise one example of purposeful reading. Mark's account does not specifically mention others, but it is perhaps interesting that he cannot recall a reading period or "learning to read" as a separate activity. He remembers his Grade 1 teacher's using a language experience technique, apparently with success since he became a successful reader. Later, in his account of the principal's support of the school library, he conveys a school atmosphere in which reading is a vitally important but a natural part of school life.

Mark's recollection of one of his required writing tasks is telling. In being assigned to write an article about a classmate's science project rather than his own, he was forced to learn something that he might not otherwise have learned except superficially. In writing as a journalist about a scientific experiment for an audience who knew nothing of it, Mark had to understand it in far more detail than he might have, had he been interested only in his role as classmate. Notice, too, that the emphasis on reading and writing did not come at the expense of oral language. Mark's account of his day is of one rich in talk. Talk about current events, about war and negotiation and compromise, talk about science, hypothesizing and predicting the results of experiments, talk to get the newsletter produced, to write and stage plays—this was the talk of his school years and always it was connected to reading and writing and to the real world in which he lived. Here are many excellent examples of language and learning authentically supporting one another.

Subject Areas Were Integrated so That Language Played a Central Role Across the Curriculum. Language across the curriculum was a popular educational notion of the late 70s and early 80s, but long before that, there were elementary teachers for whom this was standard practice. Obviously, it was so for the teachers at Glen Duncan. We have already seen how language was linked to social studies. Reading the newspaper was the starting point for lively class discussions about current events and their causes. It is easy to imagine how much more vital these classes must have seemed than the all-too-typical history or social studies class of the "open-your-book-to-page-10" variety. Children in these classes put language to a great many authentic uses and learned about the world around them at the same time. Skeptics about the unifying capacity of language in integrating the subjects of the curriculum might argue that language and social studies are naturally compatible in ways that language and math or science are not. The teachers at Glen Duncan demonstrated the falsity of this argument. Mark's memory of the excitement engendered by his science classes was of the talk that they fostered. It is probably not an exaggeration to say that children learned to reason scientifically through the questions and answers raised in their discussion of scientific experiments. The hypothesizing they did before the experiment provided excellent use, not practice, of forecasting and reasoning language. Without this talk, most of the children would never have achieved the reasoning. As we saw in Chapter 9, children's language and cognitive growth go hand in hand. This is as true of the kind of reasoning required in science as it is of memory or conceptual development, other aspects of cognitive growth.

The generalizations Mark and the others had to reach as a result of their experimentation, as for instance in their discovery of Archimedes' Principle, were examples of informing language. The forecasting and reasoning and the informing functions are fairly typical school functions, that is, purposes to which language is more typically put in schools; but the ways in which these functions were embodied were interesting, authentic, and memorable. It is also reasonable to assume that in the talk that surrounded the experiments the children carried out, as well as in the talk which the teacher engaged them in, there was also much use of the less formal functions of language, the social and the projecting functions. In Mark's case, the interdependence of language and science had a noteworthy result. It was out of the talk in which science was embedded (or perhaps it was the other way around) that grew the love of science that led to his later career choice.

ESL Students Were Not Segregated but Participated Fully in the Life and Activities of the Class. A few years ago, an elementary teacher explained to me that the ESL children in her class were always involved in the activities of the class. When I asked how they were involved, she answered, "Oh, in lots of ways. I read and they listen. And they always sit and listen while other children share the stories they've written." While I had no doubt that the children derived some benefit from such involvement, I could not help but think of the distinction Joan Kirner made between participation and involvement:

> It was Farmer Brown's birthday. The hen and the pig, who loved her dearly, were discussing what to buy for a birthday present.
> They found it a difficult task to think of a present for one whose material needs were few. Suddenly the hen hit on an idea, "I know," she said, "we can take her home-grown, home-made fresh bacon and eggs for breakfast. She'd love that. If we made it ourselves, she'd know we really cared."
> The pig thought about the hen's idea for a minute, then firmly snorted in reply, "No way am I going to give her bacon and eggs for breakfast."
> "Why not?" said the hen, disappointed.
> "Simple," snorted the pig. "You'd be involved but I'd be participating!" (Cited in Potter, 1989, p. 32)

At the Glen Duncan School, the evidence points to the ESL children's participating rather than simply being involved. Although Mark could not speak from their perspective, what he did tell us of the school and of ESL learners in the school suggests that they played active roles. It is difficult to imagine that teachers who were so caring in their fostering and nurturing of language learning in the English-speaking children would forsake all their principles in providing for ESL learners. What Mark's recollection does tell us is encouraging. ESL children were not segregated but stayed in the same classroom as the English speakers. It is hard to imagine that they did not derive considerable benefit from the rich environment which Mark described.

Indeed, teachers who have insisted on their ESL children's remaining in the classroom rather than being segregated have made a number of helpful suggestions for ESL children that would be useful for mainstream students as well. Writing of the Fair Oaks School in Redwood, California, Lois Bridges Bird stresses the importance and the effectiveness of authentic language. The mostly Spanish-speaking children at Fair Oaks write real memos requesting that the furniture be repaired, they write letters in protest of government policies in Central America, and they even broadcast a half-hour radio program to the community every Friday morning. Teachers provide support and guidance but also encourage the importance of self-reflection in the learning process. The freedom, support, and respect that their language program provides gives the students at Fair Oaks a sense of belief "in themselves as capable, creative learners, knowing what they need and how to get it" (Bird, 1991a, p. 92).

Freedom does not mean that the children are not taught. But as one of their teachers, Roberta Lee, points out, they learn by doing. In producing their radio show, they have to write letters of invitation to potential guests (including the Queen of England!) as well as thank you letters to people who appear; they have to write the scripts for the show, and learn to conduct interviews on the show. Obviously, there must be some instruction as to the form these letters, scripts, and interviews should take, but it is directed toward a real purpose that the children understand (Bird, 1991b, p. 93). Precisely because it is an authentic radio show, the language learning that it fosters will be linked to a number of subjects. Social studies is an obvious one but one can also envision a science or environment spot as well as music, drama, and literature. It is an ideal learning situation. Moreover, it is one which is ideal for both first- and second-language learners.

Education Was a Joint-Venture Enterprise Whose Success Depended upon the Partnership of Teachers, Principal, and Community. In order for such a partnership to work, there should be no silent partners, although it is reasonable to assume that one might speak with a louder voice than the other. At Glen Duncan, it appears that the principal was a senior partner. The fact that Mark remembered him well led in part to that conclusion. These days, it is not unusual for elementary children not to know the principal at all or to know her only as a remote figure who does paperwork, meets with parents and perhaps dispenses discipline. For a child to remember a principal as an active member of the school, someone who spent a lot of time in the classroom and devoted his energies to improving the library, speaks well of that principal.

His way of getting parents to solve the library problem was effective because the solution brought benefits not only to the school but to the community as well. There were the indirect benefits of securing and channeling the parents interest in the school, but there were also direct benefits as well. The small community gained a stationary library where previously it had had only the mobile branch from the nearby city. The library and the school became a community center where it was quite natural for parents and others in the community to find out about the life of the school. Of course, I am not suggesting that any of this made up for the loss of the librarian, for the librarian is a central figure in helping to establish a relationship between children and print. But when the principal could not save the librarian's position, he turned a potential disaster into an advantage for the school and for the community. Moreover, the incident demonstrated his understanding that the library's collection of print, visual, and audio materials was crucial to the school's function.

Shortly after my interview with Mark, I telephoned the school to find out whether the principal was still there. It was a long shot that he would be, after nearly 20 years, but he was. So were some of the teachers who had been there when Mark attended. I went to Prince Edward Island to visit the school, and my visit confirmed that the school probably had been as unique 20 years ago as Mark had indicated, since it is still a very special place to be.

Looking Ahead . . .

Writing so near to the end of the millenium, I cannot resist the urge to look forward. The technological revolution is in full swing, and there will be no going back. There is more to know and there are more ways of finding out than ever before, and the amount of information is increasing faster than we can imagine. It is an exciting time to be a teacher, an even more exciting time to be a learner, but it is also rather daunting, especially for the teacher. The generation of teachers who will read this book will complete the job begun at the end of the 20th century of moving education beyond the industrial age. But even in this new age, there are certain truths that will endure. The first is that in the life of the child and in the life of the school, language is special and will remain so. It is the subject children know best when they begin school and it is the one that will largely determine their success in all the other subjects they encounter. It is the medium by which we will always communicate whether by pen, the Internet, or satellite. The second is that language requires little teaching; children will learn it if they are given the opportunity to do so. For second language learners the opportunities may have to be more numerous and more attention may have to be paid to meaning in the language they hear and see, but the process is natural enough if we do not impede it with overemphasis on structure and form. Third, no one cultural group has an exclusive claim on language or any aspect of it. Pronunciation, word choice, grammar, function, and even purpose of literacy have many acceptable variations within and between cultures. Respecting children's language is remembering that the particular variety individual children bring to school is as much a part of their identity as the teacher's language is to her. It's a matter of respecting the children's expectations about language based on their lived experience. If we fail to understand, for example, that Chipewyan parents do not expect their children to talk before they are 5 years old because they believe that it takes a lifetime to learn their language and that effective learning requires long periods of observation, we run the risk of taking the children's silence as evidence of language delay or as a void that must be filled. If we assume that children who come from non-literate homes do not know about stories, we may well get off on the wrong foot for there are homes in North America in which the tradition of the story is strongly maintained through oral retelling. Language, and thus learning and school success for all the children who populate our classrooms, is at risk unless we learn to respect the experiences of children and build upon them.

Bibliography

Aaron, I. E., Chall, J. S., Durkin, D., Goodman, K., & Strickland, D. (1990a, January). The past, present, and future of literacy education: Comments from a panel of distinguished educators, Part I. *The Reading Teacher*, pp. 302–311.

Aaron, I. E., Chall, J. S., Durkin, D., Goodman, K., & Strickland, D. (1990b, February). The past, present, and future of literacy education: Comments from a panel of distinguished educators, Part II. *The Reading Teacher*, pp. 302–311.

Abudarham, S. (1980). The problems of assessing the linguistic potential of children with dual language systems and their implications for the formulation of a differential diagnosis. In F. M. Jones (Ed.), *Language disability in children*. MTP Press Ltd.

Allen, P., Swain, M., & Harley, B. (1988). Analytic and experiential aspects of core French and immersion classrooms. *Bulletin of the Canadian Association of Applied Linguistics, 10*, 59–68.

Andersen, R. W. (1981). *New dimensions in second language acquisition research*. Rowley, MA: Newbury House.

Anderson, A. B., & Stokes, S. J. (1984). Social and institutional influences on the development and practice of literacy. In H. Goelman, A. Oberg, & F. Smith (Eds.), *Awakening to Literacy*. Portsmouth, NH: Heinemann Educational Books. (pp. 24–37).

Applebee, A. N., Langer, J. S., & Mullis, I. V. S. (1987). *Learning to be literate in America*. Princeton, NJ: Educational Testing Service.

Ashworth, M. (1985). *Beyond methodology, second language teaching and the community*. Cambridge: Cambridge University Press.

Ashworth, M. (1988). *Blessed with bilingual brains*. Vancouver, BC: Pacific Educational Press.

Asselin, M., Pelland, N., & Shapiro, J. (1991). *Storyworlds, linking minds and imagination through literature.* Markham, ON: Pippin Publishing.

Atkinson, R. C., & Shiffrin, R. M. (1968). Human memory: A proposed system and its control processes. In K. W. Spence & J. T. Spence (Eds.), *Advances in child development and behavior.* New York: Academic Press.

Atkinson-King, K. (1973). *Children's acquisition of phonological stress contrasts.* (UCLA Working Papers in Phonetics, 25). Los Angeles: University of California at Los Angeles.

Bailey, V. H. (1994). *Identifying cues to cultural filters in symbolic behaviors and pragmatic language of Navajo children.* University of New Mexico: Ph. D. Dissertation.

Baker, L., & Brown, A. L. (1984). Metacognitive skills and reading. In P. D. Pearson (Ed.), *Handbook of reading research, Part 2.* New York: Longman.

Baker, N., & Nelson, K. (1985). Recasting and related conversational techniques for triggering syntactic advances by young children. *First Language, 5,* 3–22.

Barik, H. C., & Swain, M. (1974). English-French bilingual education in the early grades: The Elgin study. *Modern Language Journal, 58,* 392–403.

Barik, H. C., & Swain, M. (1975). Three-year evaluation of a large scale early grade French immersion program: The Ottawa study. *Language Learning, 25,* 1–30.

Barik, H. C., Swain, M., & Guadino, V. (1976). A Canadian experiment in bilingual education in the senior grades: The Peel study through grade two. *International Review of Applied Psychology, 25,* 99–113.

Barke, E. M., & Parry-Williams, D. E. (1938). A further study of the comparative intelligence of children in certain bilingual and monoglot schools in south Wales. *British Journal of Educational Psychology, 8,* 63.

Barnes, D. (1995). Talking and learning in classrooms: An introduction. *Primary Voices, 3*(1), 2–7.

Barnes, S., Gutfreund, M., Satterly, D., & Wells, G. (1983). Characteristics of adult speech which predict children's language development. *Journal of Child Language, 10,* 65–84.

Basser, L. S. (1962). Hemiplegia of early onset and the faculty of speech with special reference to the effects of hemispherectomy. *Brain, 85,* 427–460.

Bates, E. (1976). *Language and context: Studies in the acquisition of pragmatics.* New York: Academic Press.

Bates, E. (1979). *The emergence of symbols: Cognition and communication in infancy.* New York: Academic Press.

Bates, E., Benigni, L., Bretherton, I., Camaioni, L., & Volterra, V. (1979). *The emergence of symbols: Cognition and communication in infancy.* New York: Academic Press.

Bates, E., & MacWhinney, B. (1987). Competition, variation, and language learning. In MacWhinney (Ed.), *Mechanisms of language acquisition.* Hillsdale, NJ: Lawrence Erlbaum.

Bates, E., & Snyder, L. (1985). The cognitive hypothesis in language development. In I. Uzgiris & J. M. Hunt (Eds.), *Research with scales of psychological development in infancy.* Champaign-Urbana, IL: University of Illinois Press.

Bear, D. R., Templeton, S., Invernizzi, M., & Johnston, F. (1996). *Words their way.* Upper Saddle River, NJ: Merrill/Prentice Hall.

Beardsmore, H. B., & Kohls, J. (1988). Immediate pertinence in the acquisition of multilingual proficiency: The European schools. *Canadian Modern Language Review, 44,* 680–701.

Beatty, R. (1983). Windyfoggery and bureaucratese. *International Review of Applied Linguistics, 62.* 53–66.

Benton, R. (1964). *Research into the English language difficulties of Maori school children, 1963–1964.* Wellington, New Zealand: Maori Education Foundation.

Bereiter, C., & Scardamalia, M. (1982). From conversation to composition: The role of instruction in a developmental process. In R. Glaser (Ed.), *Advances in instructional psychology.* Hillsdale, NJ: Lawrence Erlbaum.

Berger, J. (1991, January 5). Fernandez proposes placing warranties on graduates in '92. *The New York Times,* p. A1.

Berko, J. (1958). The child's learning of English morphology. *Word, 14,* 150–177.

Berko, J., & Brown, R. (1960). Psycholinguistic research methods. In Paul H. Mussen (Ed.), *Handbook of research methods in child development.* (pp. 517–557). New York: John Wiley & Sons.

Berko-Gleason, J. (1993) (Ed.). *The development of language,* (3rd ed.). Upper Saddle River, NJ: Merrill/Prentice Hall.

Berko-Gleason, J., & Greif, E. (1983). Men's speech to young children. In B. Thorne, C. Kramerae, & N. Henley (Eds.), *Language, Gender, and Society.* Rowley, MA: Newbury House.

Berman, R. A. (1979). The re-emergence of a bilingual: A case study of a Hebrew-English speaking child. (UCLA Working Papers on Bilingualism, 19). Los Angeles: University of California at Los Angeles.

Berns, M. (1990). Why language teaching needs the sociolinguist. *Canadian Modern Language Review, 46,* 339–353.

Bever, T. G. (1972). Perceptions, thoughts and language. In J. B. Carroll & R. O. Freedle (Eds.), *Language, comprehension and the acquisition of knowledge.* Washington, DC: John Wiley & Sons.

Beveridge, M. (Ed.) (1982). *Children thinking through language.* London: Edward Arnold.

Beveridge, M., & Brierley, C. (1982). Classroom constructs: An interpretive approach to young children's language. In M. Beveridge (Ed.), *Children thinking through language.* London: Edward Arnold.

Bialystok, E. (1987). Words as things: Development of word concept by bilingual children. *Studies in Second Language Acquisition, 9,* 133–140.

Bird, L. (1991a). Joyful literacy at Fair Oaks school. In K. S. Goodman, L. B. Bird, & Y. M. Goodman (Eds.), *The whole language catalog* (pp. 92–93). Santa Rosa, CA: American School Publishers.

Bird, L. (1991b). Classroom demonstrations. In K. S. Goodman, L. B. Bird, & Y. M. Goodman (Eds.), *The whole language catalog* (p. 93). Santa Rosa, CA: American School Publishers.

Bissex, G. L. (1984). The child as teacher. In H. Goelman, A. Oberg, & F. Smith, (Eds.), *Awakening to literacy* (pp. 87–101). Portsmouth, NH: Heinemann Educational Books.

Blakeslee, T. R. (1980). *The right brain.* New York: Berkley.

Block, E. (1986). The comprehension strategies of second language learners. *TESOL Quarterly, 2,* 463–491.

Block, E., & Kessel, F. (1980). Determinants of the acquisition order of grammatical morphemes: A reanalysis and reinterpretation. *Journal of Child Language, 7,* 181–189.

Bloom, L. (1973). *One word at a time: The use of single-word utterances before syntax.* The Hague: Mouton.

Bloom, L., & Lahey, M. (1978). *Language development and language disorders.* New York: John Wiley & Sons.

Bloom, L., Lahey, M., Hood, L., Lifter, K., & Fiess, K. (1980). Complex sentences; acquisition of syntactic connectives and the semantic relations they encode. *Journal of Child Language, 7,* 235–261.

Bloomfield, L. (1933). *Language.* New York: Holt, Rinehart, & Winston.

Bohannon, J. N. III, (1993). Theoretical approaches to language acquisition. In J. Berko-Gleason, *The development of language,* (3rd ed.). Upper Saddle River, NJ: Merrill/Prentice Hall.

Bohannon, J., & Stanowicz, L. (1988). The issue of negative evidence: Adult responses to children's language errors. *Developmental Psychology, 24*(5), 684–689.

Bohannon, J. N., & Warren-Leubecker, A. W. (1989). Theoretical approaches to language acquisition. In J. B. Gleason (Ed.), *The development of language* (2nd ed.). Upper Saddle River, NJ: Merrill/Prentice Hall.

Bolinger, D. (1980). *Language, the loaded weapon: The use and abuse of language today.* London: Longman.

Bond, Z. S., Eddey, J. E., & Bermejo, J. J. (1980). VO"t del Espanol to English: comparison of a language-disordered and normal child. *Journal of Phonetics, 8,* 287–291.

Bowen, J. D., Madsen, H., & Hilferty, A. (1985). *TESOL techniques and procedures.* Rowley, MA: Newbury House.

Bowerman, M. (1981). The child's expression of meaning: Expanding relationships among lexicon, syntax, and morphology. In H. Winitz (Ed.), *Native language and foreign language acquisition.* New York: The New York Academy of Sciences.

Bowey, J. A., & Francis, J. (1991). Phonological analysis as a function of age and exposure to reading instruction. *Applied Psycholinguistics, 12,* 91–121.

Bowey, J. A., & Hansen, J. (1994). The development of orthographic rimes as units of word recognition. *Journal of Experimental Child Psychology, 58,* 465–488.

Bowlby, J. (1960). Grief and mourning in infancy and early childhood. *Psychoanalytic Study of the Child, 15,* 9–52.

Bradley, L., & Bryant. P. E. (1983, February). Categorizing sounds and learning to read—a causal connection. *Nature,* 419–421.

Braine, M. D. S. (1963). The ontogeny of English phrase structures: The first phase. *Language, 39,* 1–13.

Braine, M. D. S. (1971a). On two types of models of internalization of grammars. In D. I. Slobin (Ed.), *The ontogenesis of grammar.* New York: Academic Press.

Braine, M. D. S. (1971b). The acquisition of language in infant and child. In C. E. Reed (Ed.), *The learning of language.* Upper Saddle River, NJ: Merrill/Prentice Hall.

Braine, M. D. S. (1974). On what might constitute a learnable phonology. *Language, 50,* 270–299.

Braine, M. D. S. (1976). Children's first word combinations. *Monographs of the Society for Research in Child Development, 41* (Serial No. 164).

Brannon, J. (1968). Linguistic word classes in the spoken language of normal, hard-of-hearing and deaf children. *Journal of Speech and Hearing Research, 11,* 279–287.

Brent Palmer, C. (1979). A sociolinguistic assessment of the notion 'immigrant semi-lingualism' from a social conflict perspective. *Working Papers on Bilingualism, 17,* 137–180.

Britsch, S. (1989). The contribution of the preschool to a Native American community. *Language Arts, 66*(1), 29–43.

Britton, J. (1967). *Talking and writing.* London: Methuen & Company.

Britton, J. (1970). *Language and learning.* Harmondsworth, UK: Penguin.

Brown, H. D. (1980). *Principles of language learning and teaching.* Upper Saddle River, NJ: Merrill/Prentice Hall.

Brown, R. (1973). *A first language.* Cambridge, MA: Harvard University Press.

Bruck, M., Lambert, W., & Tucker, G. R. (1975). *Assessing functional bilingualism within a bilingual program: The St. Lambert project at grade eight.* Paper presented at TESOL Convention.

Bruner, J. (1973). Organization of early skilled action. *Child Development, 44,* 1–11.

Bruner, J. S. (1983). *Child's talk.* New York: Norton Press.

Bruner, J. S. (1984). Language, mind, and reading. In H. Goelman, A. Oberg, & F. Smith (Eds.), *Awakening to literacy* (pp. 193–200). Portsmouth, NH: Heinemann Educational Books.

Bruner, J. S. (1986). *Actual minds, possible worlds.* Cambridge, MA: Harvard University Press.

Bryant, P., MacLean, M., & Bradley, L. (1990). Rhyme, language, and children's reading. *Applied Psycholinguistics, 11,* 239–252.

Bryant, P., MacLean, M., Bradley, L. L., & Crossland, J. (1990). Rhyme and alliteration, phoneme detection, and learning to read. *Developmental Psychology, 26,* 429–438.

Burns, G. E., & Olson, C. P. (1989). Planning and professionalizing other FSL programs. *Canadian Modern Language Review, 45,* 502–516.

Burt, M. K., Dulay, H. C., & Hernandez-Chavez, E. (1975). *Bilingual syntax measure.* New York: Harcourt Brace Jovanovitch.

Cairns, H. S., & Hsu, J. R. (1978). Who, why, when and how: A developmental study. *Journal of Child Language, 5,* 477–488.

Calkins, L. M. (1983). *Lessons from a child: On the teaching and learning of writing.* Portsmouth, NH: Heinemann Educational Books.

Calkins, L. M. (1985). Learning to think through writing. In A. Jaggar & M. T. Smith-Burke (Eds.), *Observing the language learner.* Champaign-Urbana, IL: NCTE.

Caplan, D. (1987). *Neurolinguistics and linguistic aphasiology*. Cambridge, UK: Cambridge University Press.

Carmichael, L., Hogan, H. P., & Walter, A. A. (1932). An experimental study of the effect of language on visually perceived form. *Journal of Experimental Psychology, 15,* 73–86.

Carrell, P. (1983a). Background knowledge in second language comprehension. *Language, Learning, and Communication, 35,* 183–200.

Carrow, Sister M. A. (1957). Linguistic functioning of bilingual and monolingual children. *Journal of Speech and Hearing Disorders, 22,* 371.

Carter, C. (Ed.). (1982). *Non-native and nonstandard dialect students*. Champaign-Urbana, IL: NCTE.

Case, R. (1980). *Intellectual development in infancy: A neo-Piagetian interpretation*. Paper presented at the International Conference for Infant Studies, New Haven, CT.

Cazden, C. (1968). The acquisition of noun and verb inflections. *Child Development, 39,* 433–448.

Cazden, C. (1987). English for academic purposes: The student-talk register. *English Education, 19*(1), 31–44.

Celis 3d, W. (1990, November 22). Growing number of parents are opting to teach children at home. *The New York Times*, p. A1.

Chafe, W. (1982). Integration and involvement in speaking, writing, and oral literature. In D. Tannen (Ed.), *Spoken and written language*. Norwood, NJ: Ablex.

Chen H.-C., & Leung, Y.-S. (1989). Patterns of lexical processing in a nonnative language. *Journal of Experimental Psychology, Learning, Memory, and Cognition, 15*(2), 316–325.

Cheshire, J. (1982). Dialect features and linguistic conflict in schools. *Educational Review, 34,* 53–67.

Chomsky, N. (1965). *Aspects of the theory of syntax*. Cambridge, MA: MIT Press.

Chomsky, N. (1975). *Reflections on language*. New York: Pantheon.

Chomsky, N. (1980). *Rules and explanations*. New York: Columbia University Press.

Chow, M. (1986). Measuring the growth of writing in the kindergarten and grade one years: How are the ESL children doing? *TESL Canada Journal, 4,* 35–47.

Christian, D. (1996). Two-way immersion education: Students learning through two languages. *The Modern Language Journal, 80*(1), 66–76.

Clark, E. V. (1977). Strategies and the mapping problem in first language acquisition. In J. MacNamara (Ed.), *Language learning and thought*. New York: Academic Press.

Clark, M. M. (1984). Literacy at home and at school: Insights from a study of young fluent readers. In H. Goelman, A. Oberg, & F. Smith (Eds.), *Awakening to literacy*. Portsmouth, NH: Heinemann Educational Books.

Clarke, M. A., & Silberstein, S. (1979). Toward a realization of psycholinguistic principles in the ESL reading class. In R. Mackay, B. Barkman & R. R. Jordan (Eds.), *Reading in a second language: Hypotheses, organization, and practice*. Rowley, MA: Newbury House.

Clay, M. M. (1973). *Reading: The patterning of complex behavior.* Auckland, NZ: Heinemann Educational Books.

Clyde, J. (1990). A natural curriculum. In H. Mills & J. A. Clyde (Eds.), *Portraits of whole language classrooms* (chap. 2). Portsmouth, NH: Heinemann Educational Books.

Clyne, M. (1985). Development of writing skills in young second language learners. *International Review of Applied Linguistics, 67–68,* 9–24.

Coady, J. (1979). A psycholinguistic model of the ESL reader. In R. Mackay, B. Barkman & R. R. Jordan (Eds.), *Reading in a second language: Hypotheses, organization, and practice.* Rowley, MA: Newbury House.

Cole, P. G., & Mengler, E. D. (1994). Phonemic processing of children with language deficits; which tasks best discriminate children with learning disabilities from average readers. *Reading Psychology: An International Quarterly, 15,* 223–243.

Commins, N. L. (1989). Language and affect: Bilingual students at home and at school. *Language Arts, 66*(1), 29–43.

Connors, K., Menard, N., & Singh, R. (1978). Testing linguistic and functional competence in immersion programs. In M. Paradis (Ed.), *Aspects of bilingualism.* Columbia, SC: Hornbeam.

Content, A., Kolinsky, R., Morais, J., & Bertelson, P. (1986). Phonetic segmentation in prereaders: Effect of corrective information. *Journal of Experimental Child Psychology 42,* 49–72.

Cook, V. J. (1985). Universal grammar and second language learning. *Journal of Applied Linguistics, 6,* 2–18.

Coombs, N. (1995 March/April). Closing the windows on opportunity. *Educom Review, 30*(2), pp. 28–29.

Corrigan, R. (1978). Language development as related to stage six object permanence development. *Journal of Child Language, 5,* 173–190.

Cotton, E. G. (1978). Noun-pronoun pleonasms: The role of age and situation. *Journal of Child Language, 5,* 489–499.

Crago, M. B. (1990). Development of communicative competence in Inuit children: Implications for speech-language pathology. *Journal of Childhood Communication Disorders, 13*(1), 73–83.

Crago, M. B. (1992). Communicative interaction and second language acquisition: An Inuit example. *TESOL Quarterly, 26*(3), 487–505.

Crago, M. B., and Allen, S. E. M. (1995). Morphemes gone askew: Linguistic impairment in Inuktitut. *McGill Working Papers in Linguistics, 10,* 206–215.

Crago, M. B., Annahatak, B., & Ningiuruvik, L. (1993). Changing patterns of language socialization in Inuit homes. *Anthropology and Education Quarterly, 24*(3), 205–223.

Crystal, D. (1976). *Child language, learning and linguistics.* London: Edward Arnold.

Crystal, D. (1987). *The Cambridge encyclopedia of language.* Cambridge, UK: Cambridge University Press.

Cummins, J. (1978). Educational implications of mother tongue maintenance in minority language groups. *The Canadian Modern Language Review, 34,* 3.

Cummins, J. (1979a). Linguistic interdependence and the educational development of bilingual children. *Review of Educational Research, 49*, 222–251.

Cummins, J. (1979b). Cognitive academic language proficiency, linguistic interdependence, the optimum age question and some other matters. *Working Papers on Bilingualism, 19*, 197–205.

Cummins, J. (1980). The cross-lingual dimensions of language proficiency: Implications for bilingual education and the optimal age issue. *TESOL Quarterly, 14*, 25–60.

Cummins, J. (1984). Wanted: A theoretical framework for relating language proficiency to academic achievement among bilingual students. In C. Rivera (Ed.), *Language proficiency and academic achievement.* Clevedon, UK: Multilingual Matters.

Cummins, J. (1988). From multicultural to antiracist education: An analysis of programmes and policies in Ontario. In T. Skutnabb-Kangas & J. Cummins (Eds.), *Minority education: From shame to struggle.* Clevedon, UK: Multilingual Matters.

Cunningham, A. E. (1990). Explicit versus implicit instruction in phonemic awareness. *Journal of Experimental Child Psychology, 50*, 429–444.

Cunningham, A. E., & Stanovich, K. E. (1991). Tracking the unique effects of print exposure in children: Associations with vocabulary, general knowledge, and spelling. *Journal of Educational Psychology, 83*(2), 264–274.

Curtiss, S. (1977). *Genie: A psycholinguistic study of a modern-day "wild child."* New York: Academic Press.

Curtiss, S. (1981). Dissociations between language and cognition: Cases and implications. *Journal of Autism and Developmental Disorders, 11*, 15–30.

Curtiss, S., & Yamada, J. (1978). *Language = cognition.* Paper presented at the Third Annual Boston University Conference on Language Development, Boston, MA.

Curtiss, S., Yamada, J., & Fromkin, V. (1979). How independent is language? On the question of formal parallels between action and grammar. *UCLA Working Papers in Cognitive Linguistics, 1*, 131–157.

Cuvo, A. J. (1975). Developmental differences in rehearsal and free recall. *Journal of Experimental Child Psychology, 19*, 65–78.

Dale, P. S. (1976). *Language development: Structure and function* (2nd ed). New York: Holt, Rinehart, & Winston.

Dalrymple, K. S. (1989). 'Well, what about his skills?' Evaluation of whole language in the middle school. In K. S. Goodman, Y. M. Goodman, and W. J. Hood (Eds.), *The whole language evaluation book* (chap. 10). Portsmouth, NH: Heinemann Educational Books.

Danesi, M. (1988a). Neurological bimodality and theories of language teaching. *Studies in Second Language Acquisition, 10*, 13–31.

Danesi, M. (1988b). Neurobiological differentiation of primary and secondary language acquisition. *Studies in Second Language Acquisition, 10*, 303–337.

d'Anglejan, A. (1978). Language learning in and out of classrooms. In J. C. Richards, (Ed.), *Understanding second and foreign language learning.* Rowley, MA: Newbury House.

Das, J. P. (1980). On cognitive competence and incompetence: A cross-cultural perspective. *Mental Retardation, 8*(2), 81–95.

Davies, A. (1977). *Language and learning in early childhood.* London: Heinemann Educational Books.

Davies, A., Criper, C., & Howatt, A. P. R. (Eds.). (1984). *Interlanguage.* Edinburgh: Edinburgh University Press.

Davis, K. (1975). Severe social isolation. In S. Rogers (Ed.), *Children and language.* London: Oxford University Press.

Davis, P. S. (1991, April). Parents writing with students. *English Journal,* 62–64.

DeFries, J. C., Olson, R. K., Pennington, B. F., & Smith, S. D. (1991). Colorado reading project: An update. In D. Duane & D. Gray (Eds.), *The reading brain: The biological basis of dyslexia.* (pp. 58–87) Parkton, MD: York Press.

deHirsch, K., Jansky, J., & Langford, W. (1966). *Predicting reading failure.* New York: Harper & Row.

De Keyser, R. M. (1986). Individual differences in first language acquisition and some educational implications. *International Review of Applied Linguistics, 73,* 1–26.

Demetras, M., Post, K., & Snow, C. (1986). Feedback to first language learners: The role of repetitions and clarification questions. *Journal of Child Language, 13,* 275–292.

Derwing, B. L. (1977). Is the child really a 'little linguist'? In J. Macnamara (Ed.), *Language learning and thought.* New York: Academic Press.

Derwing, B. L., & Baker, W. J. (1977). The psychological basis for morphological rules. In J. MacNamara (Ed.), *Language learning and thought.* New York: Academic Press.

deVilliers, J. G., & deVilliers, P. A. (1973). A cross-sectional study of the acquisition of grammatical morphemes in child speech. *Journal of Psycholinguistic Research, 2,* 267–278.

Dickinson, D., & Snow, C. E. (1987). Interrelationships among prereading and oral language skills in kindergartners from two social classes. *Early Childhood Research Quarterly, 1,* 1–26.

Dickinson, D., Wolf, M., & Stotsky, S. (1989). Words move: The interwoven development of oral and written language. In J. B. Gleason (Ed.), *The development of language* (2nd ed.). Upper Saddle River, NJ: Merrill/Prentice Hall.

Dillon, D. (1980). Teaching about language itself. In G. S. Pinnell (Ed.), *Discovering language with children.* Champaign-Urbana, IL:NCTE.

Dillon, D. (1989). Editorial. *Language Arts, 66*(1), 7–9.

Doebler, L. K., & Mardis, L. J. (1980). Effects of a bilingual education program for Native American children. *NABE Journal, 5*(2), 23–28.

Donaldson, M. (1978). *Children's minds.* Glasgow: Fontana/Collins.

Donaldson, M. (1984). Speech and writing and modes of learning. In H. Goelman, A. Oberg, & F. Smith (Eds.), *Awakening to literacy.* Portsmouth, NH: Heinemann Educational Books.

Dulay, H., & Burt. M. K. (1974). Natural sequences in child second language acquisition. *Language Learning, 24,* 37–53.

Dulay, H., Burt, M. K., & Krashen, S. D. (1982). *Language two.* New York: Oxford University Press.

Dunn, L., & Dunn, L. (1981). *Peabody Picture Vocabulary Test-Revised (PPVT-R).* Circle Pines, MN: American Guidance Service.

Durkin, D. (1966). *Children who read early.* New York: Teachers College Press.

Eagan, R., & Cashion, M. (1988). Second year report of a longitudinal study of spontaneous reading in English by students in early French immersion classes. *Canadian Modern Language Review, 33,* 523–535.

Edelsky, C. (1982). Writing in a bilingual program: The relation of L1 and L2 texts. *TESOL Quarterly, 6,* 211–228.

Edelsky, C. (1986). *Writing in a bilingual program: Habia una vez.* Norwood, NJ: Ablex.

Edelsky, C., Altwerger, B., Barkin, F., Flores, B., Hudelson, S., & Jilbert, K. (1983). Semilingualism and language deficit. *Applied Linguistics* 4(1), 1–22.

Ehri, L. C., & Wilce, L. S. (1987). Does learning to spell help beginners learn to read words? *Reading Research Quarterly, 22*(1), 47–65.

Ehrenreich, B. (1981). The politics of talking in couples. *Ms.,5,* 43–55, 86–89.

Eilers, R. E., Gavin, W. J., & Wilson, W. R. (1979). Linguistic experience and phonemic perception in infancy: A crosslinguistic study. *Child Development, 50,* 14–18.

Eimas, P. D., Siqueland, E. R., Jusczyk, P., & Vigorito, J. (1971). Speech perception in infants. *Science, 171,* 303–306.

Elliot, A. J. (1981). *Child language.* Cambridge, UK: Cambridge University Press.

Ellis, R. (1985). *Understanding second language acquisition.* Oxford: Oxford University Press.

Engel, W. von R. (1965). Del bilinguismo infantile. *Archivio Glottologico Italiano, 50,* 175–180.

Engel, W. von R. (1966). Linguaggio attivo e linguaggio passivo. *Orientamenti Pedagogici, 13,* 893–894.

Erikson, E. H. (1959). Identity and the life cycle: Selected papers. *Psychological Issues, 1,* 1–171.

Ervin-Tripp, S. (1981). Social process in first- and second-language learning. In H. Winitz (Ed.), *Native language and foreign language acquisition.* New York: The New York Academy of Sciences.

Ervin-Tripp, S., & Gordon, D. (1986). The development of requests. In R. Schiefelbusch (Ed.), *Language competence: Assessment and intervention.* San Diego, CA: College-Hill Press.

Fagan, W. T., & Hayden, H. M. (1988). Writing processes in French and English of fifth grade French immersion students. *Canadian Modern Language Review, 44,* 653–668.

Fanselow, J. (1987). *Breaking rules: Generating and exploring alternatives in language teaching.* White Plains, NY: Longman.

Ferguson, C., & Farwell, C. (1975). Words and sounds in early language acquisition: English initial consonants in the first 50 words. *Language, 51,* 431–491.

Ferguson, C., & Garnica, O. (1975). Theories of phonological development. In E. Lenneberg & E. Lenneberg (Eds.), *Foundations of language development.* UNESCO: NY.

Ferguson, C., & Slobin, D. (Eds.). (1973). *Studies of child language development.* New York: Holt, Rinehart, & Winston.

Ferreiro, E. (1984). The underlying logic of literacy development. In H. Goelman, A. Oberg, & F. Smith (Eds.), *Awakening to literacy.* Portsmouth, NH: Heinemann Educational Books.

Ferreiro, E., & Teberosky, A. (Translated by Karen Goodman Castro) (1982). *Literacy before schooling.* Portsmouth, NH: Heinemann Educational Books.

Field, T., Woodson, R., Greenberg, R., & Cohen, D. (1982). Discrimination and imitation of facial expressions by neonates. *Science, 218,* 179–181.

Finn, C. E., Jr. (1991, May 27). Accounting for results. *National Review,* pp. 38–41, 61.

Fisher, C. J., & Terry, C. A. (1990). *Children's language and the language arts.* Boston: Allyn & Bacon.

Fishman, J., Cooper, R. L., & Ma, R. (1975). *Bilingualism in the barrio. Language Science Monographs,* (Vol. 7). Bloomington, IN: Indiana University Press.

Fletcher, P., & Garman, M. (Eds.). (1979). *Language acquisition.* Cambridge, UK: Cambridge University Press.

Flower, L., & Hayes, J. R. (1981). A cognitive process theory of writing. *College Composition and Communication, 32,* 365–387.

Foley, K. S., Harley, B., & d'Anglejan, A. (1988). Research in core French: A bibliographic review. *Canadian Modern Language Review, 44,* 593–618.

Foorman, B., Francis, D., & Fletcher, J. (1997, March 18). Breaking the alphabetic code. *The Globe and Mail,* Toronto, Canada.

Forrest, D. L., & Walker, T. G. (1979, March). Cognitive and metacognitive aspects of reading. Paper presented at the meeting of the Society for Research in Child Development, San Francisco.

Foster, J. C. (1991, February). The role of accountability in Kentucky's education reform act of 1990. *Educational Leadership,* pp. 34–36.

Foster, M. (1982). Indigenous languages: Present and future. *Language and Society, 7,* 7–14. Ottawa, Canada: Commissioner of Official Languages.

Fowlie, Gary. (1996, May 17). Pulling weeds from the kindergarten. *The Globe and Mail,* p. A22.

Franklin, E., & Thompson, J. (1994). Describing students' collected works: Understanding American Indian children. *TESOL Quarterly, 28*(3), 489–506.

Freedman, D. G. (1979, January). Ethnic differences in babies. *Human Nature Magazine,* pp. 36–43.

Froese, V. (Ed.). (1990). *Whole-language practice and theory.* Scarborough, ON: Prentice-Hall Canada, Inc.

Gagne, R. M. (1965). *The conditions of learning.* New York: Holt, Rinehart, & Winston.

Galloway, L. (1981). Bilingualism: Neuropsychological considerations. *Journal of Research and Development in Education, 15,* 12–28.

Gantt-Gentry, C., White, H., & Randolph, M. (1994). Laterality effects in Cherokee and anglo children. *The Journal of Genetic Psychology, 155*(1), 123–124.

Gardner, B. T., & Gardner, R. A. (1975). Evidence for sentence constituents in the early utterances of child and chimpanzee. *Journal of Experimental Psychology, 104,* 244–262.

Garnica, O. K. (1973). The development of phonemic speech perception. In T. E. Moore (Ed.), *Cognitive development and the acquisition of language.* New York: Academic Press.

Garnica, O. K., & Herbert, R. K. (1979). Some phonological errors in second language learning: Interference doesn't tell it all. *International Journal of Psycholinguistics, 6,* 5–19.

Gary, J. O. (1975). Delayed oral practice in initial stages of second language learning. In M. Burt & H. Dulay (Eds.), 1975, *New directions in second language learning, teaching, and bilingual education* (pp. 89–95). Washington, DC: TESOL.

Gass, S. (1984). A review of interlanguage syntax: Language transfer and language universals. *Language Learning, 34,* 115–132.

Gathercole, S. E., Willis, C., & Baddeley, A. D. (1991). Differentiating phonological memory and awareness of rhyme: Reading and vocabulary development in children. *British Journal of Psychology, 82,* 387–406.

Genesee, F. (1983). Bilingual education of majority-language children: The immersion experiments in review. *Applied Psycholinguistics, 4,* 1–46.

Genesee, F., & Lambert, W. E. (1983). Trilingual education for majority-language children. *Child Development, 54,* 105–114.

Genesee, F., Tucker, G. R., & Lambert, W. E. (1976). Communication skills of bilingual children. *Child Development, 46,* 1010–1014.

Gibson, E. J., & Levin, H. (1975). *The psychology of reading.* Cambridge, MA: MIT Press.

Giles, H., Bourhis, R., & Taylor, D. (1977). Toward a theory of language in ethnic group relations. In H. Giles (Ed.), *Language ethnicity and intergroup relations.* New York: Academic Press.

Giles, H., & Byrne, J. (1982). An intergroup approach to second language acquisition. *Journal of Multilingual and Multicultural Development, 3,* 17–40.

Gleason, J. B. (Ed.). (1989). *The development of language,* (2nd ed.). Upper Saddle River, NJ, Merrill/Prentice Hall.

Gleitman, L., & Wanner, E. (1982). Language acquisition: The state of the state of the art. In E. Wanner & L. Gleitman (Eds.), *Language acquisition: The state of the art.* Cambridge, UK: Cambridge University Press.

Glucksberg, S., & Danks, J. H. (1975). *Experimental psycholinguistics: An introduction.* New York: John Wiley & Sons.

Godby, C. J., Wallace, R., & Jolley, C. (1982). *Language files: Materials for an introduction to language.* Reynoldsburg, OH: Advocate Publishing Group.

Goelman, H., Oberg, A., & Smith, F. (Eds.). (1984). *Awakening to literacy.* Portsmouth, NH: Heinemann Educational Books.

Goldberg, E., & Costa, L. D. (1981). Hemisphere differences in the acquisition and use of descriptive systems. *Brain and Language, 14,* 144–173.

Golinkoff, R. (1983). The preverbal negotiation of failed messages: Insights into the transition period. In R. Golinkoff (Ed.), *The transition from preverbal to verbal communication*. Hillsdale, NJ: Lawrence Erlbaum.

Goodman, G. (1989). Worlds within worlds: Reflections on an encounter with parents. *Language Arts, 66*(1), 14–20.

Goodman, K. S. (1967). Reading: A psycholinguistic guessing game. *Journal of the Reading Specialist, 32,* 34–41.

Goodman, K. S., Bird, L. B., & Goodman, Y. M. (1991). *The whole language catalog.* Santa Rosa, CA: American School Publishers (Macmillan).

Goodman, K. S., Goodman, Y. M., & Hood, W. J. (Eds.). (1989). *The whole language evaluation book.* Portsmouth, NH: Heinemann Educational Books.

Goodman, Y. (1984). The development of initial literacy. In H. Goelman, A. Oberg, & F. Smith (Eds.), *Awakening to literacy.* Portsmouth, NH: Heinemann Educational Books.

Goodman, Y. M. (1986). Children coming to know literacy. In W. H. Teale & E. Sulzby (Eds.), *Emergent literacy: Writing and reading.* Norwood, NJ: Ablex.

Goswami, U. (1993). Toward an interactive analogy model of reading development: decoding vowel grapheres in beginning reading. *Journal of Experimental Child Psychology, 56,* 443–475.

Goswami, U., & Bryant, P. E. (1990). *Phonological skills and learning to read.* Hillside, NJ: Lawrence Erlbaum.

Grabo, R. P. (1931). *A study of the comparative vocabularies of junior high school pupils from English and Italian speaking homes.* (Bulletin No. 13). Washington, DC: US Office of Education.

Graham, A. (1975). The making of a nonsexist dictionary. In B. Thorne & N. Henley (Eds.), *Language and sex: Difference and dominance.* Rowley, MA: Newbury House.

Graham, L., & House, A. S. (1971). Phonological oppositions in children: A perceptual study. *Journal of the Acoustical Society of America, 49,* 559–569.

Graves, D. (1977). *Balance the basics: Let them write.* New York: The Ford Foundation.

Graves, D. (1983). *Writing teachers and children at work.* Portsmouth, NH: Heinemann Educational Books.

Greenberg, J. H. (1966). *Language universals: With special reference to feature hierarchies.* The Hague: Mouton.

Gregg, K. R. (1984). Krashen's monitor and Occam's razor. *Applied Linguistics, 5,* 79–100.

Grunwell, P. (1982). *Clinical phonology.* London: Croom Helm.

Gunderson, L. (1990). Reading and language development. In V. Froese (Ed.), *Whole-language practice and theory.* Scarborough, ON: Prentice-Hall Canada, Inc.

Gunderson, L. (1991). *ESL literacy instruction, a guidebook to theory and practice.* Upper Saddle River, NJ: Merrill/Prentice Hall.

Halliday, M. A. K. (1975). *Learning how to mean.* London: Edward Arnold.

Halliday, M. A. K. (1976). *System and function in language.* London: Oxford University Press.

Halliday, M. A. K. (1978). *Language as a social semiotic: The social interpretation of language and meaning.* Baltimore, MD: University Park Press.

Halliday, M. A. K. (1985). It's a fixed word order language is English. *International Review of Applied Linguistics, 67–68,* 91–116.

Hammermeister, F. (1972). Reading achievement in deaf adults. *American Annals of the Deaf, 116,* 25–28.

Hansen, Jane. (1983). First grade writers who pursue reading. In P. L. Stock (Ed.), *Forum: Essays on theory and practice in the teaching of writing* (pp. 155–162). Upper Montclair, NJ: Boynton-Cook.

Harding, C. G., & Golinkoff, R. M. (1979). The origins of intentional vocalizations in prelinguistic infants. *Child Development, 50,* 338–340.

Harlin, R., Lipa, S. E., & Lonberger, R. (1991). *The whole language journey.* Markham, ON: Pippin Publishing.

Harris, G. A. (1985, September). Considerations in assessing English language performance of Native American children. *Topics in Language Disorders,* 42–52.

Harste, J. C., Woodward, V. A., Burke, C. (1984). *Language stories and literacy lessons.* Portsmouth, NH: Heinemann Educational Books.

Hatch, E. (1978a). *Second language acquisition.* Rowley, MA: Newbury House.

Hatch, E. (1978b). Acquisition of syntax in a second language. In J. Richards (Ed.), *Understanding second and foreign language learning: Issues and approaches.* Rowley, MA: Newbury House.

Hatch, E. (1978c). Discourse analysis and second language acquisition. In E. Hatch (Ed.), *Second language acquisition research.* New York: Academic Press.

Hatch, E. (1978d). Discourse analysis, speech acts and second language acquisition. In W. Ritchie (Ed.), *Second language acquisition research.* New York: Academic Press.

Hatch, E. M. (1983). *Psycholinguistics.* Rowley, MA: Newbury House.

Haugen, E. (1956). *Bilingualism in the Americas.* Tuscaloosa, AL: University of Alabama Press.

Haussler, M. M., Tompkins, C., & Jeanne, L. M. (1987). Young Hopi writers and readers. *NABE Journal,* 83–93.

Hayes, C. W., Ornstein, J., & Gage, W. W. (1987). *The ABC's of languages and linguistics.* Lincolnwood, IL: The National Textbook Company.

Heath, S. B. (1978). *Teacher talk: Language in the classroom.* Washington, DC: Center for Applied Linguistics.

Heath, S. B. (1983). *Ways with words: Language, life, and work in communities and classrooms.* Cambridge, UK: Cambridge University Press.

Heath, S. B. (1986). Separating 'things of imagination' from life: Learning to read and write. In W. H. Teale & E. Sulzby (Eds.), *Emergent literacy: Writing and reading.* Norwood, NJ: Ablex.

Heath, S. B., & Thomas, C. (1984). The achievement of preschool literacy for mother and child. In H. Goelman, A. Oberg, & F. Smith (Eds.), *Awakening to literacy.* Portsmouth, NH: Heinemann Educational Books.

Heatherington, M. E. (1980). *How language works.* Cambridge, MA: Winthrop.

Hersov, L. A., Berger, M., & Nicol, A. R. (Eds.). (1980). *Language and language disorders in childhood*. Oxford: Pergamon Press.

Hickman, J., & Kimberley, K. (Eds.). (1988). *Teachers, language and learning*. London: Routledge.

Hills, E. C. (1914). The speech of a child two years of age. *Dialect Notes, 4*, 84–100.

Hirsh-Pasek, K., Treiman, R., & Schneiderman, M. (1984). Brown and Hanlon revisited: Mothers' sensitivity to ungrammatical forms. *Journal of Child Language, 11*, 81–88.

Hoff-Ginsberg, E. (1986). Function and structure in maternal speech: Their relation to the child's development of syntax. *Developmental Psychology, 22*, 155–163.

Hofstadter, R. (1963). *Anti-Intellectualism in American life*. New York: Alfred A. Knopf.

Holm, A., & Holm, W. (1990). Rock Point, a Navajo way to go to school: A valediction, *Annals, AAPSS, 508*, 170–184.

Holt, J. (1967). *How children learn*. New York: Merloyd Lawrence (Dell).

Holt, J. (1983). *How children learn* (Rev. ed.). New York: Merloyd Lawrence (Dell).

Holt, J. (1989). *Learning all the time*. Reading, MA: Addison-Wesley.

Horgan, D. (1978). The development of the full passive. *Journal of Child Language, 5*, 65–80.

Huang, H. S., & Hanley, J. R. (1995). Phonological awareness and visual skills in learning to read Chinese and English. *Cognition, 54*, 73–98.

Hulit, L. M., & Howard, M. R. (1986). *Born to talk*. Upper Saddle River, NJ: Merrill/Prentice Hall.

Hurtado, A., & Rodriguez, R. (1989). Language as a social problem: The repression of Spanish in south Texas. *Journal of Multilingual and Multicultural Development, 10*(5), 401–419.

Hutchings, M. (1986). What teachers are demonstrating. In J. Newman (Ed.), *Whole language theory in use*. Portsmouth, NH: Heinemann Educational Books.

Ingram, D. (1974). Phonological rules in young children. *Journal of Child Language, 1*, 49–64.

Ingram, D. (1976). *Phonological disability in children*. New York: Elsevier.

Ingram, D. (1979). Phonological patterns in the speech of young children. In P. Fletcher & M. Garman (Eds.), *Language acquisition*. Cambridge, UK: Cambridge University Press.

Ingram, D. (1989). *First language acquisition, method, description and explanation*. Cambridge, UK: Cambridge University Press.

Itoh, H., & Hatch, E. (1978). Second language acquisition: A case study. In E. Hatch (Ed.), *Second language acquisition*. Rowley, MA: Newbury House.

Jacob, E. (1984). Learning literacy through play: Puerto Rican kindergarten children. In H. Goelman, A. Oberg, & F. Smith (Eds.), *Awakening to literacy*. Portsmouth, NH: Heinemann Educational Books.

Jagger, A. (1980). Allowing for language differences. In G. S. Pinnell (Ed.), *Discovering language with children*. Champaign-Urbana, IL: NCTE.

Jago, C. (1989). Whose book is it anyway? *Language Arts, 66*(1), 29–43.

Jakobsen, R. (1941). *Kindersprache, Aphasie und Allgemeine Lautesetze*. Uppsala: Almquist und Wiksell.

Jakobson, R. (1968). *Child language, aphasia, and phonological universals* (A. Keiler, Trans.). The Hague: Mouton.

Jakobson, R., & Halle, M. (1956). *Fundamentals of language*. The Hague: Mouton.

Johnson, D. (1990, November 4). Indian rootlessness. *The New York Times*, Sec. 4A, p. 27.

Johnston, R. S., & Rugg, M. D. (1989). Rhyme judgment ability in good and poor readers. *Language and Education, 3*(4), 223–232.

Just, M. A., & Carpenter, P. A. (1987). *The psychology of reading and language comprehension*. Newton, MA: Allyn & Bacon.

Kasten, W. C. (1987). Medicine men, Bethlehem, and Pacman: Writing in a cultural content. *Anthropology and Education Quarterly, 18*, 116–125.

Kasten, W. C. (1992). Bridging the horizon: American Indian beliefs and whole language learning. *Anthropology and Education Quarterly, 23*, 108–119.

Kavanagh, J. F., & Mattingly, I. G. (1972). *Language by ear and by eye*. Cambridge, MA: MIT Press.

Kellerman, E. (1979). Transfer and non-transfer: Where we are now? *Studies in Second Language Acquisition, 2*, 37–57.

Kellerman, E. (1984). The empirical evidence for the influence of the L1 interlanguage. In A. Davies, C. Criper, & A. P. R. Howatt (Eds.), *Interlanguage*. Edinburgh: Edinburgh University Press.

Kerr, A. (1984). Language and the education of immigrants' children in Sweden. In C. Kennedy (Ed.), *Language planning and language education*. London: George Allen and Unwin.

Kessler, C. (1971). *The acquisition of syntax in bilingual children*. Washington, DC: Georgetown University Press.

Khubchandani, L. M. (1978). Multilingual education in India. In B. Spolsky & R. L. Cooper (Eds.), *Case studies in bilingual education*. Rowley, MA: Newbury House.

Kinsbourne, M. (1981). Neuropsychological aspects of bilingualism. In H. Winitz (Ed.), *Native language and foreign language acquisition*. New York: The New York Academy of Sciences.

Kiparsky, P., & Menn, L. (1977). On the acquisition of phonology. In J. MacNamara (Ed.), Language learning and thought. New York: Academic Press.

Kirtley, C., Bryant, P., MacLean, M., & Bradley, L. (1989). Rhyme, rime, and the onset of reading. *Journal of Experimental Child Psychology, 48*, 224–245.

Kornfeld, J. (1971). Theoretical issues in child phonology. *PCLS*, Seventh Regional Meeting, 454–468.

Kossan, N. (1981). Developmental differences in concept acquisition strategies. *Child Development, 52*, 290–298.

Krashen, S. D. (1973). Lateralization, language learning, and the critical period: Some new evidence. *Language Learning, 23*, 63–74.

Krashen, S. D. (1977a). The monitor model for second language performance. In M. Burt, H. Dulay, & M. Finocchiaro, (Eds.), *Viewpoints on English as a second language*. New York: Regents.

Krashen, S. D. (1977b). Some issues relating to the monitor model. In H. Brown, C. Yorio, & R. Crymes (Eds.), *On TESOL '77*. Washington, DC: TESOL.

Krashen, S. D. (1978). Individual variation in the use of the monitor. In W. Ritchie (Ed.), *Second language acquisition research*. New York: Academic Press.

Krashen, S. D. (1979). A response to McLaughlin, 'The monitor model: Some methodological considerations.' *Language Learning, 29*, 151–167.

Krashen, S. D. (1981). *Second language acquisition and second language learning*. Oxford: Pergamon Press.

Krashen, S. D. (1982). *Principles and practices of second language acquisition*. Oxford: Pergamon Press.

Krashen, S. D. (1985). *The input hypothesis: Issues and implications*. London: Longman.

Kuschner, D. (1989). From the personal world of childhood to the public world of school. *Language Arts, 66*(1), 44–49.

Labov, W. (1972). *Sociolinguistic patterns*. Philadelphia: University of Pennsylvania Press.

Labov, W. (1982). Objectivity and commitment in linguistic science; The case of the Black English trial in Ann Arbor. *Language in Society, 11*, 165–201.

Lake, D. T. (1989). Computers in the classroom: Teaching writing in the 1990s. *English Journal, 78*(7), 73–74.

Lalonde, R. N., Lee, P. A., & Gardner, R. C. (1987). The common view of the good language learner: An investigation of teachers' beliefs. *Canadian Modern Language Review, 44*, 16–34.

Lamendella, J. (1979). The neurofunctional basis of pattern practice. *TESOL Quarterly, 13*, 5–19.

Lanauze, M., & Snow, C. (1989). The relation between first- and second-language writing skills: Evidence from Puerto Rican elementary school children in bilingual programs. *Linguistics and Education, 1*, 323–339.

Language Files, (4th ed.) (1988). Columbus, OH: The Ohio State University Department of Linguistics.

Laosa, L. M. (1975). Bilingualism in three United States Hispanic Groups: Contextual use of language by children and adults in their families. *Journal of Educational Psychology, 67*(5), 617–627.

Larsen-Freeman, D. (1983). Second language acquisition: Getting the whole picture. In K. M. Bailey, M. H. Long, & S. Peck (Eds.), *Second language acquisition studies*. Rowley, MA: Newbury House.

Larsen-Freeman, D., & Long, M. (1991). *An introduction to second language acquisition research*. New York: Longman.

Lasky, R. E., Syrdal-Lasky, A., & Klein, R. E. (1975). VOT discrimination by four to six and a half month old infants from Spanish environments. *Journal of Experimental Child Psychology 20*, 215–225.

Leichter, H. J. (1984). Families as environments for literacy. In H. Goelman, A. Oberg, & F. Smith (Eds.), *Awakening to literacy*. Portsmouth, NH: Heinemann Educational Books.

Lenneberg, E. (1967). *Biological foundations of language*. New York: John Wiley & Sons.

Leopold, W. F. (1939). *Speech development of a bilingual child: A linguist's record* (Vol. 1). Evanston, IL: Northwestern University Press.

Leopold, W. F. (1947). *Vocabulary growth in the first two years* (Vol. 2). Evanston, IL: Northwestern University Press.

Leopold, W. F. (1948). Semantic learning in infant language. *Word, 4,* 173–180.

Leopold, W. F. (1949a). Sound learning in the first two years. (Vol. 3). Evanston, IL: Northwestern University Press.

Leopold, W. F. (1949b). *Grammar and general problems in the first two years.* (Vol. 4). Evanston, IL: Northwestern University Press.

Letts, C. A. (1991). Early second language acquisition: A comparison of the linguistic output of a pre-school child acquiring English as a second language with that of a monolingual peer. *British Journal of Disorders of Communication, 26,* 219–234.

Leung, C. (1989). The multilingual classroom: The case for minority pupils. *Journal of Multilingual and Multicultural Development, 10,*(6), 461–472.

Levelt, W. J. M. (1978). Skill theory and language teaching. *Studies in second language acquisition, 1,* 53–70.

Lewis, M., & Rosenblum, L. A. (Eds.). (1977). *Interaction, conversation, and the development of language.* New York: John Wiley & Sons.

Liberman, I. Y., Shankweiler, D., Fischer, F. W., & Carter, B. (1974). Explicit syllable and phoneme segmentation in the young child. *Journal of Experimental Child Psychology, 18,* 201–212.

Lieven, E. V. M. (1982). Context, process and progress in young children's speech. In M. Beveridge (Ed.), *Children thinking through language.* London: Edward Arnold.

Limber, J. (1973). The genesis of complex sentences. In T. E. Moore (Ed.), *Cognitive development and the acquisition of language.* New York: Academic Press.

Lindfors, J. W. (1987). *Children's language and learning.* Upper Saddle River, NJ: Merrill/Prentice Hall.

Lindsay, A. (1992). Oral narrative discourse style of first nations children and the language of schooling. *Reflections on Canadian Literacy, 10*(4), 205–209.

Lipka, J., & McCarty, T. L. (1994). Changing the culture of schooling: Navajo and Yup'ik cases. *Anthropology and Education Quarterly, 25*(3), 266–284.

Loban, W. D. (1963). *The language of elementary school children.* Champaign-Urbana, IL: NCTE.

Lorenz, K. (1971). *Studies in animal behavior.* Cambridge, MA: Harvard University Press.

Luria, A. R., & Yudovich, F. I. (1971). *Speech and the development of mental processes in the child.* Middlesex: Penguin Books.

Lynwander, L. (1990, October 7). Pupils get financial incentives. *The New York Times,* Sec. 12, p. 6.

MacGinitie, W. H. (1991, March). Reading instruction: Plus ça change . . . *Educational leadership,* pp. 55–58.

Mackay, R. (1990). Bridging the gap between practice and research: Inuit students and English instruction. *Bulletin of the Canadian Association of Applied Linguistics, 12*(1), 9–21.

Mackay, R., Barkman, B., & Jordan, R. R. (Eds.). (1979). *Reading in a second language: Hypotheses, organization, and practice.* Rowley, MA: Newbury House.

Macken, M. A. (1979). Developmental reorganization of phonology: A hierarchy of basic units of acquisition. *Lingua, 49,* 11–49.

Macken, M. A., & Barton, D. (1980). The acquisition of the voicing contrast in English: A study of voice onset time in word-initial stop consonants. *Journal of Child Language, 7,* 41–75.

MacNamara, J. (1966). *Bilingualism in primary education.* Edinburgh: Edinburgh University Press.

MacNamara, J. (Ed.). (1977). *Language learning and thought.* New York: Academic Press.

MacNamara, J. (1977). On the relation between language learning and thought. In J. MacNamara (Ed.), *Language learning and thought.* New York: Academic Press.

MacWhinney, B. (Ed.). (1987). *Mechanisms of language acquisition.* Hillsdale, NJ: Lawrence Erlbaum.

MacWhinney, B. (1987). The competition model. In B. MacWhinney (Ed.), *Mechanisms of language acquisition.* Hillsdale, NJ: Lawrence Erlbaum.

Madrid, D., & Torres, I. (1986). An experimental approach to language training in second language acquisition: Focus on negation. *Journal of Applied Behavior Analysis, 19,* 203–208.

Maguire, M. H. (1989). Teaching English and French as first languages: Are changes necessary? *Bulletin of the Canadian Association of Applied Linguistics, 11,* 29–50.

Major, D. (1974). *The acquisition of modal auxiliaries in the language of children.* The Hague: Mouton.

Malsheen, B. (1980). Two hypotheses for phonetic clarification in the speech of mothers to children. In G. Yeni-Komshian, J. F. Kavanagh, & C. A. Ferguson (Eds.), *Child phonology, Perception* (Vol. 2) New York: Academic Press.

Maratsos, M., Gudeman, R., Poldi, G., & DeHart, G. (1987). A study in novel word learning: The productivity of the causative. In B. MacWhinney (Ed.), *Mechanisms of language acquisition.* Hillsdale, NJ: Lawrence Erlbaum.

Markman, E. M. (1979). Realizing that you don't understand: Elementary school children's awareness of inconsistencies. *Child Development, 50,* 543–655.

Marler, P. (1970). A comparative approach to vocal learning: Song development in white-crowned sparrows. *Journal of Comparative and Physiological Psychology, 71,* (Pt. 2) 1–25.

Marler, P. (1977). Sensory templates, vocal perception, and development: A comparative view. In M. Lewis & L. A. Rosenblum (Eds.), *Interaction, conversation, and the development of language.* New York: John Wiley & Sons.

Marshall, R., & Tucker, M. (1992). *Thinking for a living.* New York: Basic Books.

Martin-Jones, M. (1986). Review of 'Bilingualism or not: The education of minorities.' *Journal of Multilingual and Multicultural Development, 7*(4), 319–324.

Martin-Jones, M., & Romaine, S. (1986). Semilingualism: A half-baked theory of communicative competence. *Applied Linguistics, 7*(1), 26–38.

Mattes, L. J., & Omark, D. R. (1984). *Speech and language assessment for the bilingual handicapped.* San Diego, CA: College-Hill Press.

Mayfield, M. I. (1985, December). Parents, children and reading: Helping Canadian native Indian parents of preschoolers. *The Reading Teacher.*

Mazurkewich, I., & White, L. (1984). The acquisition of the dative alternation: Unlearning overgeneralizations. *Cognition, 16,* 261–283.

McCarty, T. L., Wallace, S., Lynch, R. H., & Benally, A. (1991). Classroom inquiry and Navajo learning styles: A call for reassessment. *Anthropology and Education Quarterly, 22,* 42–59.

McCutchen, D., & Perfetti, C. A. (1982). Coherence and connectedness in the development of discourse production. *Text, 2,* 113–139.

McEachern, W. R., & Luther, F. (1989). The relationship between culturally relevant materials and listening comprehension of Canadian native children. *Language, Culture, and Curriculum, 2*(1), 55–60.

McGill, J. (1988). In the history classroom. In J. Hickman & K. Kimberley, (Eds.), *Teachers, language and learning.* London: Routledge.

McLaughlin, B. (1978). *Second language acquisition in childhood.* Hillsdale, NJ: Lawrence Erlbaum.

McLaughlin, B. (1981). Differences and similarities between first- and second-language learning. In H. Winitz (Ed.), *Native language and foreign language acquisition.* New York: The New York Academy of Sciences.

McLaughlin, B. (1984). *Second-language acquisition in childhood: Preschool children* (Vol. 1)(2nd ed.). Hillsdale, NJ: Lawrence Erlbaum.

McLaughlin, B. (1985). *Second-language acquisition in childhood: School-age children* (Vol. 2)(2nd ed.). Hillsdale, NJ: Lawrence Erlbaum.

McLaughlin, B. (1987). *Theories of second language acquisition.* London: Edward Arnold.

McLaughlin, B., Rossman, T., & McLeod, B. (1983). Second-language learning: An information-processing perspective. *Language Learning, 33,* 135–158.

McLeod, B., & McLaughlin, B. (1986). Restructuring or automaticity? Reading in a second language. *Language Learning, 36,* 109–123.

McNeill, D. (1966) Developmental psycholinguistics. In F. Smith & G. Miller (Eds.), *The genesis of language: A psycholinguistic approach.* Cambridge, MA: MIT Press.

Menn, L. (1971). Phonotactic rules in beginning speech. *Lingua, 26,* 251–255.

Menn, L. (1976). *Pattern, control, and contrast in beginning speech: A case study in the acquisition of word form and function.* Unpublished doctoral dissertation, University of Illinois.

Menn, L. (1983). Development of articulatory, phonetic, and phonological capabilities. In B. Butterworth (Ed.), *Language production* (Vol. 2). London: Academic Press.

Menn, L. (1989). Phonological development: Learning sounds and sound patterns. In J. B. Gleason (Ed.), *The development of language* (2nd ed.). Upper Saddle River, NJ: Merrill/Prentice Hall.

Menyuk, P. (1969). *Sentences children use.* Cambridge, MA: MIT Press.

Menyuk, P. (1971). *The acquisition and development of language.* Upper Saddle River, NJ: Merrill/Prentice Hall.

Michaels, S., & Cazcen, C. (1987). Teacher/child collaboration as oral preparation for literacy. In B. B. Schieffelin (Ed.), *Acquisition of literacy: Ethnographic perspectives.* Norwood, NJ: Ablex.

Mills, H., & Clyde, J. A. (Eds.). (1990). *Portraits of whole language classrooms.* Portsmouth, NH: Heinemann Educational Books.

Milon, J. P. (1975). Dialect in the TESOL program: If you never knew better. In M. Burt & H. Dulay (Eds.), *New directions in second language learning, teaching, and bilingual education.* Washington, DC: TESOL.

Mitchell, C. A. (1989). Linguistic and cultural aspects of second language acquisition: Investigating literature/literacy as an environmental factor. *Canadian Modern Language Review, 46,* 73–82.

Mollica, A. (1989). The immersion experience. *Canadian Modern Language Review, 45,* 434.

Moore, T. E. (Ed.). (1973). *Cognitive development and the acquisition of language.* New York: Academic Press.

Morrow, L. M. (1989). *Literacy development in the early years: Helping children read and write.* Upper Saddle River, NJ: Merrill/Prentice Hall.

Moskowitz, A. (1973). On the status of vowel shift in English. In T. E. Moore (Ed.), *Cognitive development and the acquisition of language.* New York: Academic Press.

Moskowitz, B. A. (1980). Idioms in phonology acquisition and phonological change. *Journal of Phonetics, 8,* 69–83.

Murrell, M. (1966). Language acquisition in a trilingual environment: Notes from a case study. *Studia Linguistica, 20,* 9–35.

Myers, D. T. (1964). *Understanding language.* Upper Montclair, NJ: Boynton-Cook.

Nakazina, S. A. (1962). A comparative study of the speech developments of Japanese and American English in childhood (1): A comparison of the developments of voices at the prelinguistic period. *Studia Phonologica, 2,* 27–46.

National Commission on Excellence in Education. (1983). *A nation at risk: The imperative for educational reform.* Washington, DC: U.S. Government Printing Office.

Nelson, K. (1973). Structure and strategy in learning to talk. *Monographs of the Society for Child Development, 38,* 149.

Nelson, K. (1977). The conceptual basis for naming. In J. Macnamara (Ed.), *Language learning and thought.* New York: Academic Press.

Netten, J. E., & Spain, W. H. (1989). Student-teacher interaction patterns in the French immersion classroom: Implications for levels of achievement in French language proficiency. *Canadian Modern Language Review, 45*(3), 485–501.

Newman, J. (Ed.). (1985a). *Whole language theory in use.* Portsmouth, NH: Heinemann Educational Books.

Newman, J. (1985b). Using children's books to teach reading. In J. Newman (Ed.), *Whole language theory in use* (chap. 4). Portsmouth, NH: Heinemann Educational Books.

Newman, J. (1985c). What about reading? In J. Newman (Ed.), *Whole language theory in use* (chap. 9). Portsmouth, NH: Heinemann Educational Books.

Newport, E. (1976). Motherese: The speech of mothers to young children. In N. Castellan, D. Pisoni, & G. Potts (Eds.), *Cognitive theory* (Vol. 2)., Hillsdale, NJ: Lawrence Erlbaum.

Nickse, R. S. (1989). *The noises of literacy: An overview of intergenerational and family literacy programs* (ERIC Document Reproduction Service No. ED 308 415). Washington, DC: Office of Educational Research and Improvement.

O'Connor, N. M., & Rotatori, A. F. (1987). Culturally diverse special education students. In A. Rotatori, M. M. Banbury, & R. A. Fox, (Eds.), *Issues in special education*. Mountain View, CA: Mayfield Publishing.

Oksaar, E. (1970). Zum Spracherwerb des Kindes in zweisprachiger Umgebung. *Folia Linguistica, 4*, 330–358.

Oldford-Matchim, J. (1995). *Help your child become a better writer.* Clearwater, FL: Global Publishing.

Olson, D. R. (1977). The contexts of language acquisition. *Language learning and thought.* New York: Academic Press.

Olson, D. R. (1984). "See! Jumping!" Some oral language antecedents of literacy. In H. Goelman, A. Oberg, & F. Smith (Eds.), *Awakening to literacy.* Portsmouth, NH: Heinemann Educational Books.

Olson, R. K., & Wise, B. W. (1992). Reading on the computer with orthographic and speech feedback. *Reading and Writing: An Interdisciplinary Journal, 4*, 107–144.

O'Malley, J. M., Chamot, A. U., & Walker, C. (1987). Some applications of cognitive theory to second language acquisition. *Studies in Second Language Acquisition, 9*, 287–306.

Omark, D. R., & Erickson, J. G. (Eds.). (1983). *The bilingual exceptional child.* San Diego, CA: College-Hill Press.

O'Neill, C. (1989). Dialogue and drama: The transformation of events, ideas, and teachers. *Language Arts, 66*(2), 147–159.

Page, M. M. (1966). We dropped FLES. *Modern Language Journal, 50*, 139–141.

Paradis, M. (Ed.). (1978). *Aspects of bilingualism.* Columbia, SC: Hornbeam.

Parlee, M. (1979). Conversational politics. *Psychology Today, 5*, 48–56.

Peal, E., & Lambert, W. (1962). The relation of bilingualism to intelligence. *Psychological Monographs, LXXVI 27*, 1–23.

Pease, D. M., Gleason, J. B., & Pan, B. A. (1989). Gaining meaning: Semantic development. In J. B. Gleason (Ed.), *The development of language*, (2nd ed.). Upper Saddle River, NJ: Merrill/Prentice Hall.

Penfield, W., & Roberts, L. (1959). *Speech and brain mechanisms.* Princeton, NJ: Princeton University Press.

Penner, P. G., & McConnell, R. E. (1980). *Learning language.* Toronto, ON: Gage Publishing Ltd.

Penner, S. (1987). Parental responses to grammatical and ungrammatical child utterances. *Child Development, 58*, 376–384.

Perera, K. (1984). *Children's writing and reading: Analyzing classroom language.* Oxford: Basil Blackwell.

Perfetti, C. A. (1984). *Reading ability.* New York: Oxford University Press.

Perozzi, Joseph A. (1985). A pilot study of language facilitation for bilingual, language-handicapped children: Theoretical and intervention implications. (1985). *Journal of speech and hearing disorders, 50*, 403–406.

Pflaum, S. W. (1986). *The development of language and literacy in young children.* Upper Saddle River, NJ: Merrill/Prentice Hall.

Phillips, C. J., & Birrell, H. V. (1994). Number learning of Asian pupils in English primary schools. *Educational Research, 36*(1), 51–62.

Phinney, M. (1981). Children's interpretation of negation in complex sentences. In S. L. Tavakolian (Ed.), *Language acquisition and linguistic theory*. Cambridge, MA: MIT Press.

Piaget, J. (1955). *The language and thought of the child*. Cleveland, OH: World Publishing.

Piaget, J. (1962). *Play, dreams and imitation in childhood*. New York: Norton.

Piaget, J., & Inhelder, B. (1969). *The psychology of the child*. New York: Basic Books.

Pinker, S. (1984). *Language, learnability and language development*. Cambridge, MA: Harvard University Press.

Pinnell, G. S. (Ed.). (1980). *Discovering language with children*. Champaign-Urbana, IL: NCTE.

Piper, D. (1992). *Language theories and educational practice*. San Francisco: Mellon Research University Press.

Piper, T. (1983). Phonics for ESL learners. *Reading-Canada-Lecture, 2*, 56–62.

Piper, T. (1984a). Phonological processes in the ESL learner. *TESL Canada Journal, 1*, 71–80.

Piper, T. (1984b). Observations on the second language acquisition of the English sound system. *The Canadian Modern Language Review, 40*, 542–551.

Piper, T. (1984c). Successive approximation in second language acquisition. *Canadian Journal of Linguistics, 29*, 2.

Piper, T. (1986a). A tale of two learners. *Canadian Children, 11*(1), 41–60.

Piper, T. (1986b). The role of prior linguistic experience on second language acquisition. *Reading-Canada-Lecture, 4*, 68–81.

Piper, T. (1986c). Learning about language learning. *Language Arts, 65*, 466–471.

Piper, T. (1987). On the difference between L1 and L2 acquisition of phonology. *Canadian Journal of Linguistics, 32*, 245–259.

Piper, T., & McEachern, W. R. (1988). Content bias in cloze as a general language indicator. *English Quarterly, 1*, 41–48.

Pisoni & G. Potts (Eds.), *Cognitive theory* (Vol. 2). Hillsdale, NJ: Lawrence Erlbaum.

Porter, J. (1977). A cross-sectional study of morpheme acquisition in first language learners. *Language Learning, 27*(1), 47–62.

Potter, G. (1989). Parent participation in language arts programs. *Language Arts, 66*(1), 29–43.

Power, D., & Quigley, S. (1973). Deaf children's acquisition of the passive voice. *Journal of Speech and Hearing Research, 25*(16), 5–11.

Premack, A. J. (1976). *Why chimps can read*. New York: Harper & Row.

Premack, D., & Premack, A. J. (1983). *The mind of an ape*. New York: Norton.

Priest, G. E. (1985). Aboriginal languages in Canada. *Language and Society, 15*, 13–19. Ottawa, ON: Commissioner of Official Languages.

Pyles, T., & Algeo, J. (1970). *English: An introduction to language*. New York: Harcourt, Brace, & World.

Quigley, S., Montanelli, D., & Wilbur, R. B. (1976). Some aspects of the verb system in the language of deaf students. *Journal of Speech and Hearing Research, 19*, 536–550.

Quigley, S., Smith, N., & Wilbur, R. B. (1974). Comprehension of relativized sentences by deaf students. *Journal of Speech and Hearing Research, 17,* 325–341.

Quigley, S., Wilbur, R. B., & Montanelli, D. (1974). Question formation in the language of deaf students. *Journal of Speech and Hearing Research, 17,* 699–713.

Quigley, S., Wilbur, R. B., & Montanelli, D. (1976). Complement structures in the language of deaf students. *Journal of Speech and Hearing Research, 19,* 448–457.

Raffler E. W. von (1973). The development from sound to phoneme in child language. In C. A. Ferguson & D. Slobin (Eds.), *Studies of child language development.* New York: Holt, Rinehart, & Winston.

Rasinski, T. V., & Fredericks, A. D. (1989, December). What do parents think about reading in the schools? *The Reading Teacher,* pp. 262–263.

Ratner, N. B. (1989). Atypical language development. In J. B. Gleason (Ed.), *The development of language,* (2nd ed.). Upper Saddle River, NJ: Merrill/Prentice Hall.

Ratner, N. B. (1993). Atypical language development. In J. Berko-Gleason (Ed.), *The development of language,* (3rd ed.). Upper Saddle River, NJ: Merrill/ Prentice Hall.

Reich, P. A. (1986). *Language development.* Upper Saddle River, NJ: Merrill/Prentice Hall.

Resnick, D. P., & Resnick, L. B. (1985). Standards, curriculum, and performance: A historical and comparative perspective. *Educational Researcher, 14*(4), 5–21.

Richards, J. (Ed.). (1978). *Understanding second and foreign language learning: Issues and approaches.* Rowley, MA: Newbury House.

Richards, J., Platt, J., & Weber, H. (1985). *Longman dictionary of applied linguistics.* London: Longman.

Richards, J. C., & Rodgers, T. S. (1986). *Approaches and methods in language teaching.* Cambridge, UK: Cambridge University Press.

Ridley, L. (1990a, May). Enacting change in elementary school programs: Implementing a whole language perspective. *The Reading Teacher,* pp. 640–646.

Ridley, L. (1990b). Whole language in the ESL classroom. In H. Mills & J. A. Clyde (Eds.). *Portraits of whole language classrooms* (chap. 11). Portsmouth, NH: Heinemann Educational Books.

Rigg, P., & Allen, V. G. (Eds.). (1989). *When they don't all speak English.* Champaign-Urbana, IL: NCTE.

Ritchie, W. (Ed.). (1978). *Second language acquisition research.* New York: Academic Press.

Roeper, T., Lapointe, S., Bing, J., & Tavakolian, S. (1981). A lexical approach to language acquisition. In S. L. Tavakolian (Ed.), *Language acquisition and linguistic theory.* Cambridge, MA: MIT Press.

Rogers, S. (Ed.). (1975). *Children and language.* London: Oxford University Press.

Roller, C. (1989). Classroom interaction patterns: Reflections of a stratified society. *Language Arts, 66*(5), 492–500.

Romney, J. C., Romney, D. M., & Braun, C. (1989). The effects of reading aloud in French to immersion children on second language acquisition. *Canadian Modern Language Review, 45,* 530–538.

Rondal, J. A. (1980). Fathers' and mothers' speech in early language development. *Journal of Child Language, 7*, 353–369.

Ronjat, J. (1913). *Le développement du langage observé chez un enfant bilingue.* Paris: Champion.

Rosch, E., & Mervis, C. B. (1975). Family resemblances: Studies in the internal structure of categories. *Cognitive Psychology, 8*, 382–439.

Rosch, E., Mervis, C. B., Gray, W. D., Johnson, D. M., & Boyes-Braem, P. (1976). Basic objects in natural categories. *Cognitive Psychology, 8*, 382–439.

Rosier, P., & Farella, M. (1976). Bilingual education at Rock Point—some early results. *TESOL Quarterly, 10*(4), 379–388.

Roth, F. P., & Davidge, N. S. (1985). Are early verbal communicative intentions universal? A preliminary investigation. *Journal of psycholinguistic research, 14*(4), 351–363.

Ruke-Dravina, V. (1965). The process of acquisition of apical /r/ and uvular /r/ in the speech of children. *Linguistics, 17*, 56–68.

Ruke-Dravina, V. (1967). *Mehrsprachigkeit im Vorschulalter.* Lund: Gleerup.

Sachs, J. (1989). Communication development in infancy. In J. B. Gleason (Ed.), *The development of language*, (2nd ed.). Upper Saddle River, NJ: Merrill/Prentice Hall.

Saer, D. J. (1922). An enquiry into the effects of bilingualism upon the intelligence of young children. *Journal of Experimental Pedagogy, 6*.

Saville-Troike, M. (1980). Discovering what children know about language. In G. S. Pinnell (Ed.), *Discovering language with children.* Champaign-Urbana, IL: NCTE.

Schacter, F. F., Kirshner, K., Klips, B., Friedrickes, M., & Sanders, K. (1974). Everyday preschool interpersonal speech usage: Methodological development and sociolinguistic studies. In *Monographs of the Society for Research and Child Development.* Chicago: University of Chicago.

Schickedanz, J. D., York, M. E., Stewart, I. S., & White, D. (1990). *Strategies for teaching young children* (3rd ed.). Upper Saddle River, NJ: Merrill/Prentice Hall.

Schieffelin, B. B., & Cochran-Smith, M. (1984). Learning to read culturally: Literacy before schooling. In H. Goelman, A. Oberg, & F. Smith (Eds.), *Awakening to literacy.* Portsmouth, NH: Heinemann Educational Books.

Schieffelin, B. B., & Ochs, E. (1983). A cultural perspective on the transition from prelinguistic to linguistic communication. In R. M. Golinkoff (Ed.), *The transition from preverbal to verbal communication.* Hillsdale, NJ: Lawrence Erlbaum.

Schlesinger, I. M. (1977). The role of cognitive development and linguistic input in language acquisition. *Child Language, 4*, 153–169.

Schumann, J. (1978a). *The pidginization process: A model for second language acquisition.* Rowley, MA: Newbury House.

Schumann, J. (1978b). Social and psychological factors in second language acquisition. In J. Richards (Ed.), *Understanding second and foreign language learning: Issues and approaches.* Rowley, MA: Newbury House.

Schumann, J. (1978c). The acculturation model for second language acquisition. In R. Gingras (Ed.), *Second language acquisition and foreign language teaching.* Arlington, VA: Center for Applied Linguistics.

Schumann, J. (1981a). Discussion of 'Two perspectives on pidginization as second language acquisition.' In R. Anderson (Ed.), *New dimensions in second language acquisition research.* Rowley, MA: Newbury House.

Schumann, J. (1981b). Reaction to Gilbert's discussion of Andersen's paper. In R. Andersen (Ed.), *New dimensions in second language acquisition research.* Rowley, MA: Newbury House.

Schumann, J. (1982). Simplification, transfer and relexification as aspects of pidginization and early second language acquisition. *Language Learning, 32,* 337–366.

Scollon, R., & Scollon, S. (1981t). *Narrative, literacy and face in interethnic communication.* Norwood, NJ: Ablex.

Scovel, T. (1982). Questions concerning the application of neurolinguistic research to second language learning/teaching. *TESOL Quarterly, 16,* 323–331.

Scoville, R. (1983). Development of the intention to communicate: The eye of the beholder. In L. Feagans, C. Garvey, & R. Golinkoff (Eds.), *The origins and growth of communication.* Norwood, NJ: Ablex.

Segalowitz, N. (1986). Skilled reading in the second language. In J. Vaid (Ed.), *Language processing in bilinguals: Psycholinguistic and neuropsychological perspectives.* Hillsdale, NJ: Lawrence Erlbaum.

Selinker, L. (1972). Interlanguage. *International Review of Applied Linguistics X,* 209–230.

Selinker, L., & Lamendella, J. (1976). Two perspectives on fossilization in interlanguage learning. *Interlanguage Studies Bulletin, 3,* 144–191.

Selinker, L., Swain, M., & Dumas, G. (1975). The interlanguage hypothesis extended to children. *Language Learning, 25,* 139–191.

Serebrin, W. (1985). Andrew and Molly, writers and context in concert. In J. Newman (Ed.), *Whole language theory in use.* Portsmouth, NH: Heinemann Educational Books.

Seymour, P. H. K., & Elder, L. (1986). Beginning reading without phonology. *Cognitive Neuropsychology, 3,* 1–36.

Shacter, F. F., Kirshner, K., Klips, B., Friedrickes, M., & Sanders, K. (1974). Everyday preschool interpersonal speech usage: Methodological development and sociolinguistic studies. In *Monographs of the Society for Research and Child Development.* Chicago: University of Chicago Press.

Shafer, R. E., Staab, C., & Smith, K. (1983). *Language functions and school success.* Glenview, IL: Scott, Foresman & Co.

Shapiro, J. (1990). Research perspectives on whole language. In V. Froese (Ed.), *Whole-language practice and theory* (pp. 268–305). Scarborough, ON: Prentice-Hall Canada, Inc.

Shvachkin, N. (1973). The development of phonemic speech perception in early childhood. In C. A. Ferguson & D. I. Slobin (Eds.), *Studies of child language development.* New York: Holt, Rinehart, & Winston.

Siegler, R. S. (1986). *Children's thinking.* (1st ed.). Upper Saddle River, NJ: Merrill/Prentice Hall.

Siegler, R. S. (1991). *Children's thinking* (2nd ed.). Upper Saddle River, NJ: Merrill/Prentice Hall.

Sinclair, H. (1977). The cognitive basis of the comprehension and production of relational terminology. *Journal of Experimental Child Psychology, 24,* 40–52.

Skinner, B. F. (1957). *Verbal behavior.* Upper Saddle River, NJ: Merrill/Prentice Hall.

Skuktnabb-Kangas, T. (1984). *Bilingualism or not: The education of minorities.* Clevedon, UK: Multilingual Matters Ltd.

Slobin, D. (1966). Comments on developmental psycholinguistics. In F. Smith & G. Miller (Eds.), *The genesis of language: A psycholinguistic approach.* Cambridge, MA: MIT Press.

Slobin, D. (1971). *Psycholinguistics.* Glenview, IL: Scott, Foresman & Company.

Slobin, D. (1973). Cognitive prerequisites for the acquisition of grammar. In C. A. Ferguson & D. I. Slobin (Eds.), *Studies of child language development.* New York: Holt, Rinehart, & Winston.

Slobin, D. (1979). *Psycholinguistics* (2nd ed.). Glenview, IL: Scott, Foresman & Company.

Slobin, D. (1982). Universal and particular in the acquisition of language. In E. Wanner & L. Gleitman (Eds.), *Language acquisition: The state of the art.* Cambridge, UK: Cambridge University Press.

Slobin, D. (Ed.). (1985). *The cross-linguistic study of language acquisition: The data.* (Vol. 1). Hillsdale, NJ: Lawrence Erlbaum.

Slobin, D., Dasinger, L., Aylin, K., & Toupin, C. (1993). Native language reacquisition in early childhood. *Proceedings of the twenty-fourth annual child language research forum.* San Francisco: Center for the Study of Language and Information, 179–196.

Smith, C. (1991). Family literacy: The most important literacy. *The Reading Teacher, 44*(9), 700–701.

Smith, E. B., Goodman, K. S., & Meredith, R. (1976). *Language and thinking in school* (2nd ed.). New York: Holt, Rinehart, & Winston.

Smith, F. (1975). *Comprehension and learning: A conceptual framework for teachers.* New York: Holt, Rinehart, & Winston.

Smith, F. (1983). *Essays into literacy.* Portsmouth, NH: Heinemann Educational Books.

Smith, F. (1984). The creative achievement of literacy. In H. Goelman, A. Oberg, & F. Smith (Eds.), *Awakening to literacy.* Portsmouth, NH: Heinemann Educational Books.

Smith, F. (1985). *Reading without nonsense* (2nd ed.). New York: Teachers College Press.

Smith, F. (1988). *Joining the literacy club: Further essays into education.* Portsmouth, NH: Heinemann Educational Books.

Smith, F., & Miller, G. (Eds.). (1966). *The genesis of language: A psycholinguistic approach.* Cambridge, MA: MIT Press.

Smith, M. E. (1933). A study of the speech of bilingual children in Hawaii. *Psychological Bulletin, 30.*

Smith, M. E. (1935). A study of the speech of eight bilingual children of the same family. *Child Development, 6,* 19–25.

Smith, N. V. (1973). *The acquisition of phonology: A case study.* London: Cambridge University Press.

Smolkin, L. B., & Suina, J. H. (1996). Lost in language and language lost: Considering native language in classrooms. *Language Arts, 73,* 166–172.

Snow, C. (1972). Mother's speech to children learning language. *Child Development, 43,* 549–565.

Snow, C. (1979). The role of social interaction in language acquisition. In W. A. Collins (Ed.), *Minnesota symposia on child psychology* (Vol. 12). Hillsdale, NJ: Lawrence Erlbaum.

Snow, C., & Ninio, A. (1986). The contracts of literacy: What children learn from learning to read books. In W. H. Teale & E. Sulzby (Eds.), *Emergent literacy: Writing and reading.* Norwood, NJ: Ablex.

Snowling, M. J., Hulme, C., Smith, A., & Thomas, J. (1994). The effects of phonetic similarity and list length on children's sound categorization performance. *Journal of Experimental Child Psychology, 58,* 160–180.

Snowling, M., Stackhouse, J., & Rack, J. (1986). Phonological dyslexia and dysgraphia—a developmental analysis. *Cognitive Neuropsychology, 3*(3), 309–339.

Snyder, G. (1990). Parents, teachers, children and whole-language. In V. Froese (Ed.). *Whole-language practice and theory.* Scarborough, ON: Prentice-Hall Canada, Inc.

Soldier, L. L. (1985). The whys and wherefores of native American bilingual education. *The Urban Review, 17*(4), 225–232.

Soudek, L. I. (1981). Two languages in one brain: Recent work in neurolinguistics and its implications for second-language learning. *English Language Teaching Journal, 35,* 219–224.

Spolsky, B. (1978). *Educational linguistics.* Rowley, MA: Newbury House.

Spolsky, B. (1985). Formulating a theory of second language learning. *Studies in Second Language Acquisition, 7,* 269–288.

Spolsky, B., & Cooper, R. L. (Eds.). (1978). *Case studies in bilingual education.* Rowley, MA: Newbury House.

Staab, C. (1990). Talk in whole-language classrooms. In V. Froese (Ed.), *Whole-language practice and theory* (chap. 2). Scarborough, ON: Prentice-Hall Canada, Inc.

Staab, C. (1991). Teachers' practices with regard to oral language. *Alberta Journal of Educational Research, 37*(1), 31–48.

Stampe, D. (1979). *A dissertation on natural phonology,* J. E. Hankamer (Ed.). New York: Garland Publishing Company.

Steiner-Khamsi, G. (1990). Community languages and anti-racist education: The open battlefield. *Educational Studies, 16*(1), 33–47.

Stephens, D., Huntsman, R., O'Neill, K., Story, J., Watson, V., & Toomes, J. (1990). We call it good teaching. In H. Mills & J. A. Clyde (Eds.), *Portraits of whole language classrooms* (chap. 15). Portsmouth, NH: Heinemann Educational Books.

Stern, D., Beebe, B., Jaffe, J., & Bennett, S. (1977). The infant's stimulus world during social interaction: A study of caregiver behaviors with particular reference to repetition and timing. In H. Schaffer (Ed.), *Studies in mother-infant interaction.* New York: Academic Press.

Stevick, E. W. (1990). *Humanism in language teaching.* Oxford, UK: Oxford University Press.

Strickland, D. S. (1994). Educating African American learners at risk: Finding a better way. *Language Arts, 71*(5), 328–336.

Strickland, D. S., & Morrow, L. M. (Eds.). (1989). *Emerging literacy: Young children learn to read and write.* Newark, DE: The International Reading Association.

Strickland, R. G. (1962). The language of elementary school children: Its relationship to the language of reading textbooks and the quality of reading of selected children. *Bulletin of the School of Education, 38*(4). Bloomington, IN: University of Indiana.

Stringer, D., Bruce, D., & Oates, J. (1973). *Generative linguistics: An introduction to the work of Noam Chomsky; Language acquisition: Language and cognition.* Milton Keynes, UK: The Open University Press.

Stuart, M., & Coltheart, M. (1988). Does reading develop in a sequence of stages? *Cognition, 30,* 139–181.

Stubbs, M. (1986). *Educational linguistics.* Oxford, UK: Basil Blackwell.

Sullivan, M. W., Rovee-Collier, C. K., & Tynes, D. M. (1979). A conditioning analysis of infant long-term memory. *Child Development, 50,* 152–162.

Swain, M. (1974). French immersion programs across Canada: Research findings. *Canadian Modern Language Review, 31,* 117–129.

Swain, M. (1976). Bibliography: Research on immersion education for the majority child. *Canadian Modern Language Review, 32,* 592–596.

Swain, M. (1978). French immersion: Early, late or partial? *Canadian Modern Language Review, 34,* 557–585.

Swain, M. (1979). Bilingual education: Research and its implications. In C. Yorio, K. Perkins, & J. Schachter (Eds.), *On TESOL 1979: The learner in focus.* Washington, DC: TESOL.

Swain, M., Barik, H., & Nwanunobi, E. (1973). *Bilingual education project: Evaluation of Elgin County Board of Education partial immersion program for grades one, two and three.* Unpublished Paper. Toronto, ON: Ontario Institute for Studies in Education.

Swain, M., & Lapkin, S. (1982). *Evaluating bilingual education: A Canadian case study.* Clevedon, UK: Multilingual Matters.

Swacher, M. (1975). The sex of the speaker as a sociolinguistic variable. In B. Thorne & N. Henley (Eds.), *Language and sex: Difference and dominance.* Rowley, MA: Newbury House.

Tabouret-Keller, A. (1962). L'acquisition du langage parle chez un petit enfant en milieu bilingue. *Problemes de Psycholinguistique, 8,* 205–219.

Tager-Flusberg, H. (1989). Putting words together: Morphology and syntax in the preschool years. In J. B. Gleason (Ed.), *The development of language,* (2nd ed.). Upper Saddle River, NJ: Merrill/Prentice Hall.

Tardif, C., & Weber, S. (1987). French immersion research: A call for new perspectives. *Canadian Modern Language Review, 44,* 67–78.

Tarone, E. (1982). Systematicity and attention in interlanguage. *Language Learning, 30,* 417–431.

Tavakolian, S. L. (Ed.). (1981). *Language acquisition and linguistic theory.* Cambridge, MA: MIT Press.

Taylor, D. M., Wright, S. C., Ruggiero, K. M., & Aitchison, M. C. (1993). Language perceptions among the Inuit of arctic Quebec: The future role of the heritage language. *Journal of Language and Social Psychology, 12*(3), 195–206.

Teale, W. H. (1986). Home background and young children's literacy development. In W. H. Teale & E. Sulzby (Eds.), *Emergent literacy: Writing and reading.* Norwood, NJ: Ablex.

Teale, W. H., & Sulzby, E. (Eds.). (1986). *Emergent literacy: writing and reading.* Norwood, NJ: Ablex Publishing.

Teitelbaum, H., & Hiller, R. J. (1977). The legal perspective. In *Bilingual education: Current perspectives (Law), 3,*(pp. 1–64). Arlington, VA: Center for Applied Linguistics.

Temple, C., & Gillet, J. W. (1989). *Language arts: Learning processes and teaching practices.* Glenview, IL: Scott, Foresman, & Company.

Templin, M. C. (1957). *Certain language skills in children: Their development and interrelationships.* (Institute of Child Welfare Monograph 26). Minneapolis, MN: University of Minnesota Press.

Terrace, H. S. (1980). *Nim: A chimpanzee who learned sign language.* New York: Knopf.

Tierney, R. J. (1983). Writer-reader transactions: Defining the dimensions of negotiation. In P. L. Stock (Ed.), *Forum: Essays on theory and practice in the teaching of writing* (pp. 147–151). Upper Montclair, NJ: Boynton-Cook.

Tierney, R. J., & Pearson, P. D. (1984). Toward a composing model of reading. In J. M. Jensen (Ed.), *Composing and comprehending.* Champaign-Urbana, IL: NCRE/ERIC.

Titone, R., & Danesi, M. (1985). *Applied psycholinguistics: An introduction to the psychology of language learning and teaching.* Toronto, ON: University of Toronto Press.

Tittle, C. E. (1973). Women and educational testing. *Phi Delta Kappan, 55*(2), 118–119.

Torrey, J. W. (1973). Learning to read without a teacher: A case study. In F. Smith (Ed.), *Psycholinguistics and reading.* New York: Holt, Rinehart, & Winston.

Totten, G. O. (1960). Bringing up children bilingually. *American Scandinavian Review, 48,* 42–50.

Tough, J. (1977). *The development of meaning.* London: Allen & Unwin.

Tough, J. (1979). *Talk for teaching and learning.* London: Ward Lock Educational.

Toukomaa, P., & Skutnabb-Kangas, T. (1977). *The intensive teaching of the mother tongue to migrant children of pre-school age and children in the lower level of comprehensive school.* Helsinki: The Finnish National Commission for UNESCO.

Treiman, R. (1985). Onsets and rimes as units of spoken syllables: Evidence from children.

Treiman, R., & Zukowski, A. (1988). Units in reading and spelling. *Journal of Memory and Language, 27,* 466–477.

Trybus, R., & Karchmer, M. (1977). School achievement scores of hearing impaired children: National data on achievement status and growth patterns. *American Annals of the Deaf, 122,* 62–69.

Tucker, G. R., & Gray, T. C. (1980). The pursuit of equal opportunity. *Language and Society, 2*, 5–8.

Tulving, E. (1983). *Elements of episodic memory.* New York: Oxford University Press.

Vaid, J. (Ed.). (1986). *Language processing in bilinguals: Psycholinguistic and neuropsychological perspectives.* Hillsdale, NJ: Lawrence Erlbaum.

Valian, V., Winzemer, J., & Erreich, A. (1981). A 'little linguist' model of syntax learning. In S. L. Tavakolian (Ed.), *Language acquisition and linguistic theory.* Cambridge, MA: MIT Press.

Van Buren, P. (1975). Semantics and language teaching. In J. P. B. Allen & S. P. Corder (Eds.), *The Edinburgh course in applied linguistics: Papers in applied linguistics* (Vol. 2). London: Oxford University Press.

Van Lawick-Goodall, J. (1971). *In the shadow of man.* Boston: Houghton Mifflin.

Velten, H. V. (1943). The growth of phonetic and lexical pattern in infant language. *Language, 19*, 281–292.

Vihman, M. M., & McLaughlin, B. (1982). Bilingualism and second-language acquisition in preschool children. In C. J. Brainerd, & M. Pressley (Eds.), *Progress in cognitive development research: Verbal processes in children.* Berlin: Springer Verlag.

Vocolo, J. M. (1967). The effect of foreign language study in the elementary school upon achievement in the same language in high school. *Modern Language Journal, 51*, 463–469.

Vorih, L., & Rosier, P. (1978). Rock Point community school: An example of a Navajo-English bilingual elementary school program. *TESOL Quarterly , 12*(3), 263–269.

Voss, M. M. (1988). "Make way for applesauce": The literate world of a three year old. *Language Arts, 65*(3), 272–278.

Vygotsky, L. S. (1962). *Thought and language.* Cambridge, MA: MIT Press.

Wagner, R. K., & Torgesen, J. K. (1987). The nature of phonological processing and its causal role in the acquisition of reading skills. *Psychological Bulletin, 101*(2), 192–212.

Walkerdine, V. (1982). From context to text: A psychosomatic approach to abstract thought. In M. Beveridge (Ed.), *Children thinking through language.* London: Edward Arnold.

Ward, A. (1990). Communicative inequality: The participation of native Indian and non-native children in instructional dialogue in a cross-cultural kindergarten class. *Reflections on Canadian Literacy, 8*(1), 22–28.

Warren-Leubecker, A. W., & Bohannon, J. N. (1989). Pragmatics: Language in social contexts. In J. Gleason (Ed.), *The development of language,* (2nd ed.). Upper Saddle River, NJ: Merrill/Prentice Hall.

Waterhouse, L. H. (1986). Problems in facing the nature/nurture question in child language acquisition. *Language Sciences, 8*(2), 153–168.

Wells, A. S. (1991, January 6). In the market for a public school? *The New York Times,* Sec. 4A, p. 6.

Wells, G. (1986). *The meaning makers: Children learning language and using language to learn.* Portsmouth, NH: Heinemann Educational Books.

Westby, C. E., & Roman, R. (1995, August). Finding the balance: Learning to live in two worlds. *Topics in Language Disorders,* 68–88.

Wexler, K. (1982). A principle theory for language acquisition. In E. Wanner & L. Gleitman (Eds.), *Language acquisition: The state of the art*. Cambridge, UK: Cambridge University Press.

Whitaker, H. A., Bub, D., & Leventer, S. (1981). Neurolinguistic aspects of language acquisition and bilingualism. In H. Winitz (Ed.), *Native language and foreign language acquisition*. New York: The New York Academy of Sciences.

White, R. W. (1960). Competence and the psychosexual stages of development. In M. Jones (Ed.), *Nebraska symposium on motivation* (pp. 97–141). Lincoln, NE: University of Nebraska Press.

Whitehurst, G., & Vasta, R. (1975). Is language acquired through imitation? *Journal of Psycholinguistic Research, 4*, 37–59.

Whorf, B. L. (1975). The organization of reality. In Rogers, S. (Ed.), *Children and language*. London: Oxford University Press.

Wieczkiewicz, H. C. (1979, May). A phonic reading program for Navajo students. *Journal of American Indian Education*, 20–27.

Wiggins, G. (1991, February). Standards, not standardization: Evoking quality student work. *Educational Leadership*, pp. 18–25.

Wilbur, R. B., Montanelli, D., & Quigley, S. (1976). Pronominalization in the language of deaf students. *Journal of Speech and Hearing Research, 19*, 120–140.

Wilkerson, I. (1990, November 4). Blacks look to basics. *The New York Times*, Sec. 4A, p. 26.

Willis, F., & Williams, S. (1976). Simultaneous talking in conversation and the sex of speakers. *Perceptual and motor skills, 43*, 1067–1070.

Wimmer, H., Landerl, K., & Schneider, W. (1994). The role of rhyme awareness in learning to read a regular orthography. *British Journal of Developmental Psychology, 12*, 469–484.

Winitz, H. (Ed.). (1981). *Native language and foreign language acquisition*. New York: The New York Academy of Sciences.

Winter, M., & Rouse, J. (1990, February). Fostering intergenerational literacy: The Missouri parents as teachers program. *The Reading Teacher*, pp. 382–386.

Wiss, C. (1989). Early French immersion programs may not be suitable for every child. *Canadian Modern Language Review, 45*, 517–529.

Wode, H. (1980). Operating principles and 'universals' in L1, L2 and FLT. In D. Nehls (Ed.), *Studies in language acquisition*. Heidelberg: Julius Groos.

Wootten, J., Merkin, S., Hood, L., & Bloom, L. (1979, March). *Wh-questions: Linguistic evidence to explain the sequence of acquisition*. Paper presented at the biennial meeting of the Society for Research in Child Development, San Francisco.

Wright, T. (1987). *Roles of teachers and learners*. Oxford: Oxford University Press.

Yamada, J. (1981, August). On the independence of language and cognition: Evidence from a hyperlinguistic retarded adolescent. Paper presented at the International Congress of Child Language, University of British Columbia, Vancouver.

Yardley, A. (1973). *Young children thinking*. London: Evans Brothers.

Yopp, H. K. (1988). The validity and reliability of phonemic awareness tests. *Reading Research Quarterly, 23*, 159–177.

Yule, G. (1985). *The study of language.* Cambridge, UK: Cambridge University Press.

Zakaluk, B. L., & Sealey, D. B. (1988). Teaching reading to Cree-speaking children: Instructional implications from an interactive model of reading. *Reading-Canada-Lecture, 6*(2), 93–99.

Zappert, L. T., & Cruz, B. R. (1977). *Bilingual education: An appraisal of empirical research.* Berkeley, CA: Bay Area Bilingual Education League/Lau Berkeley Unified School District.

Zareba, A. (1953). Jezyk polski w szwecji. *Jezyk Polski, 33,* 29–31, 98–111.

Zutell, J. (1980). Learning language at home and at school. In G. S. Pinnell (Ed.), *Discovering language with children.* Champaign-Urbana, IL: NCTE.

Subject Index

Accommodation, to children by caregivers, 177
Accommodation theory, of second language learning, 105, 116, 225
Acculturation theory, of second language learning, 105, 115, 116
Adverbs, in young children's speech, 84
Alphabetic writing systems, 10
    Reading of, 36
Amnesia, infant, 209–210
Animal communication systems, 3, 147, 149
    Bees (waggle dance), 3, 147, 148
    Chimpanzees, 148
    "Clever Hans," 148
    Jackdaws, 3, 147, 148
    Properties of, 3
Aphasias
    Defined, 173
    Expressive, 173
    Global, 173
    Receptive, 173
Applied linguists, 29–30
    Educational linguist as, 29–30
Aptitude, as a variable in second language learning, 104
Articles, acquisition of in young children, 85–86
Articulation disorders, 171–172
    Lisping, 171
    vs. delay, 171

Assimilation processes in phonology
    Defined, 72
    Examples, 72–73
Attention, 1
Autism, 191

Babbling, 59–61
Basic Interpersonal language skills (BICS), 124, 137, 175–176, 177
Behaviorism, 105, 143–149
    Case against, 145–149
Bilingual programs, 100–103
    Evaluation of, 101
    Maintenance, 100–101
    Transitional, 100–101
Bilingual Syntax Measure (BSM), 124, 129, 130, 181–182, 186
Bilingualism, 10–13, 91–117
    Defined, 92
    Home, 93–96, 124
    Language mixing in, 94–95
    School, 96–103
    Simultaneous or successive, 92–93, 133
        Exemplified, 124–136
    Stages of development in young children, 95

Caretaker speech, 162, 163, 177

Cognition
    And language development, 15–16, 207–231
    And oral language, 3–4, 26
    And written language, 4
Cognitive Academic Language Proficiency (CALP),
        138, 175–176, 177
Cognitive style
    Types of learning, 106
    As a variable in second language learning, 106
    Variation in personal cognitive style, 107
    Variation in strategy, 106
Cognitive theories
    Bruner's, 157
    case against, 158–159
    Luria's, 157
    Piaget's, 155–157
    of second language learning, 113–115, 142,
        155–159
Communication disorders, 167–189
    Assessing bilinguals, 171, 172, 186–189
    In Michael, 179–186
    vs. differences, 168–169
Communicative competence, 184, 185–186
Computer
    Impact on literacy, 274–276
    As tool in remediation, 276–279
Conditioning, in behaviorism
    Classical, 144
    Operant, 144
Conjunction
    Different uses of *and*, 81–82
    As preferred syntactic strategy, 81
    As recursive device, 48
Consonants
    Clusters, 35–36
    Disorders in, 172
    Onsets, 33–34, 35–36, 258
    Production of, 32
Conversation
    Building skills in, 192–195
    Gender-based differences in, 194–95
    Indirect requests in, 194
    Repairs in, 193–194
    Rules of, 83
    And sensitivity to listener's perspective, 192
    And sensitivity to relevance, 193–194
"Conversational bouts," 161
Critical period for language acquisition, 151–153, 154
Culture, language linked to, 6–8

Descriptive/theoretical linguists, 22–23
Developmental forms, 14–16, 130
Developmental processes, in phonology, 71–74
Discourse analysis, 28–29
Discourse studies, 110–111
Discourse theories of second language acquisition, 105

"Elaborated code," 236
Embedded sentences, 48–49
English
    History of, 24–25
    Middle English, 24–25
    In Newfoundland, 9, 10
    Old English, 24
    Spelling, historical basis of, 24–25
    Standard dialect of, 9, 11, 247
    As a world language, 55
English-only legislation, 91
Environment, importance to language learning, 17,
        150–155, 160, 163
Evaluation, methods of, 293–296

Field dependence/independence, 107
FLES (Foreign language teaching in the elementary
        school), 98, 99
Foreigner talk, 109–110
French
    Immersion, 97–98, 175
    Influence on English, 24
    Language use in teaching, 250

Great Vowel Shift, 25

Hearing impairment, 173–174
    And effect on reading ability, 174
Historical linguists, 23–25
Homophony, 64

Idioms, 40
Imitation, behaviorist view of, 144
    Social interactionist view of, 162
Immersion (*see also* French immersion), 97–99
    double, 98
    early, 97–98
    early partial, 98
    language use in teaching, 250
    late, 98
    two-way, 99–100
Information processing, 142, 157–158

Interlanguage hypothesis
    And communication strategies, 111
    And first language transfer, 111
    And learning strategies, 111
    And overgeneralization from the target language, 111
    And second language acquisition, 105, 109, 111, 182
    And transfer of teaching process, 111
Internet, 274–275, 278
Intonation, 31
    Contrastive, 38
    Defined, 37–38
Inuit children
    Communicative behavior of, 177
    Diagnosing communication disorders in, 178
Invented spelling, 292

Janet
    in infancy, 57–61
    introduction to, 56
    from 1;6 to 2;0, 66–68
    from 1;0 to 1;6, 63–66
    the preschool years, 61–82
Japanese kana, 9

Language
    Role of in development of academic skills, 217–231
    In school, 233–266
Language acquisition
    First
        Compared to second, 17, 95
        First words, 61
        Precursors to, 57–61
        Preschool years, 61–82
    Regression in, 145
    Second
        Conditions for success, 136–139
        Stories of, 119–139
        Theoretical issues in, 103–117
        Theories of (*see also* individual theories), 105
    Social aspects of, 192–205
    Theories of, 141–164
    Uniformity of, 147
Language acquisition device (LAD), 149–150, 151
Language awareness, 57, 127–128
Language comprehension, 1, 125
    And Lucy, 16
    And Michael, 181–182

Monitoring of, 223
    As process of language behavior, 26
    In reading, 221–224
Language data
    Longitudinal vs. cross sectional, 142
    For use in theory construction, 141–142
Language disorders, 172–175
Language fluency, 125, 130–131
    Communication disorders involving, 170–171
    Cluttering, 170
    In Michael, 183–184
    Stuttering, 170
    Temporary dysfunction in, 170
Language functions, 196–204
    Analysis, 196–197
    In children's lives, 197–203
    Across cultures, 203
Language mixing in bilinguals, 95, 188
Language perception, 26
Language production, 26
Language register, 14, 93, 128, 132
Language structure, 10–12, 30–53
Language switching in bilinguals, 126, 127
Language varieties, 8–10, 29
Learner variables, in second language acquisition, 104, 105
Learning, characteristics of in preschool children, 226–231
Lexicon, (*see also* vocabulary)
    Acquisition of, 126
Linguistic nativist
    Case against, 153–154
    As theory of language acquisition, 149–155
Linguists
    Applied linguists, 29–30
    Descriptive/theoretical, 22–23
    Educational linguist, 29–30
    Historical, 23–25
    Neurolinguists, 27–28
        And brain research, 28
    Psycholinguists, 25–27
    Sociolinguists, 28–29
Literacy (*see also* reading *and* writing)
    The home as a factor, 88–89
    Importance of social interaction to, 89
    And the sound system, 36
    As subject of study by applied linguists, 29–30
    In young children, 88–89
Lucy, 13–18

Memory, 1
   Basic capacities of, 208–209
   Role of language in, 208–211, 212
   Strategies in, 210–211
Metamemory
   Content knowledge in, 212–213
   Defined, 211
   Monitoring in, 211
   Role of language in, 212
Minimal pairs, 31–32
MLU (mean length of utterance), 62
Mnemonics, as memory strategy, 210
Monitor model, of second language acquisition, 111–113
   And the acquisition-learning hypothesis, 112
   And the affective filter hypothesis, 112, 113
   And comprehensible input, 113
   And the input hypothesis, 112–113
   And the monitor hypothesis, 112
   And the natural order hypothesis, 112
Morpheme Acquisition Order (MAO), 151
Morphemes
   Bound, 39
   Derivational, 39
   Grammatical/inflectional, acquisition of, 39–40,
      70–71, 78–79, 87, 150, 151, 156–157
   Lexical, 39
   And other languages, 49–50
Morphology
   Compounding in, 40
   Defined, 39
   Second language learning of, 130
Morphophonology, 86–87

Naming rituals, in Inuktitut, 135
Narrative
   Components of, 195
   Construction of, 195–196
   Differentiated from conversation, 195
   Style,
      Of minority children, 236
      And school success, 237
Neurofunctional theories of second language
      acquisition, 105, 116
Neurolinguists, 27–28
   And brain research, 28
Noun phrase, development of in young children,
      84–85
Novel forms, production of, 145

Occam's Razor, 153–154
Onsets (see consonants)
Overgeneralization, 80, 150

Parallel distributed processing (PDP), 158
Passive voice
   Acquisition of, 81
   Structure of, 46–47
Peabody Picture Vocabulary Test (PPVT), 128, 129
Phonemes, 31–32
   Defined, 32
Phonics
   Rules, 36
   Sound/symbol correspondence, 22
   And whole language, 258–259
Phonological processes
   Assimilation, 34
   Dissimilation, 35
   Simplification process, 72
   Substitution process, 73–74
   Syllable structure processes, 72
   Vowel alteration, 34
   Vowel reduction, 34
Phonology (see also sound system)
   Acquisition of, 63–65, 68, 71–74, 79–80, 82
   Distinctive vs. non-distinctive differences (see also
      minimal pairs, phonemes), 31
   Regression in, 65
Play, importance to children's learning, 227–228
Poverty of the stimulus argument, 149, 154
Pragmatics, 75, 83–84
   Conventions of, 51–52
   Defined, 51
   Gender and, 52, 194–195
   Narrative construction, 195–196
Preconceptual thought, 62
Precursory language behavior, 57–61
   Distinguished from true language behavior,
      60–61
Prepositions, early acquisition of, 71
Proficiency
   And accommodation theory, 115–116
   And the acculturation model, 115
   And fossilization, 115
Pronouns, acquisition of, 69–70
Psycholinguist
   Teachers as, 25
   Work described, 25–27

Reading
 Of alphabetic languages, 36
 Comprehension, 221
 Phonics method, 230, 258, 259
 And phonological awareness, 36
 Proposition construction in, 222–223
 Readiness, 262–263
 Role of language in learning, 218–224
 Strategies, 224
 Teaching methods compared, 291
 Whole word method, 220
Reduplication, in Janet's phonology, 63
Reinforcement, role of in language learning, 146–147
Relative clause
 Acquisition of, 62, 80–81
 As embedded sentences, 47–48
"Restricted code," 233
Rhyming
 And alliteration, 89
 As historical evidence, 23
 Importance of, 88–89
Rime, 31, 33–34, 258
Rule-governed behavior, 22
 Children's learning of, 150

Semantics
 Children's acquisition of, 214–215
 And syntax, 51, 75–78
 Theoretical perspectives of, 214–216
Semilingualism, 176, 178, 186
Semivowels, 31
 Defined, 32
Sensorimotor period, 62
Sign language, 5
"Silent letter," 36–37
Situational appropriateness, and second language use, 16
Situational variables
 Categories of, 108
 In second language learning, 107
Social interaction, importance to early learning, 228–229
Social interaction theory, 159–163
 Case against, 162–163
 Compared to behaviorism, 159
 Compared to cognitivists, 160
 Compared to nativism, 159
 Defining traits, 159
Socialization and learning, 231

Sociolinguists, 28–29
Sound system
 Avoidance as a strategy in learning, 65
 Children's learning of, 16–17, 63–65, 68
 Simplification of, 72
 Systematicity in, 65
Speech
 As input to language acquisition, 161–162
 Simplified (*See also* caretaker speech and accommodation)
 Synthetic, 276
Stress
 Defined, 37
 Syllabic, 37, 87
Submersion, 101–103
 Compared to immersion, 102–103
Syllabic writing systems, 9
Syntax
 Acquisition of, 67, 68, 75–79, 80–82, 84–86
 Ambiguity and, 43–45
  Defined, 43
  Exemplified, 43
 Clause structure, 84–86
 Constituents, 41–42
 Defined, 40
 Hierarchical structure, 69, 150
 Linear order, 41
 Of negative sentences, 45–46
 Of other languages, 49–50
 Paraphrase in, 44, 45, 83–84
 Of questions, 45–46
 TG grammar as theory of, 46–47
  Phrase-markers, 46
  Recursion in, 48

"Teachable moment," 291
Technology
 Impact on literacy, 274–276
 And small schools, 280
 And special needs children, 280–281
Test of Auditory Comprehension of Language, 187
Threshold hypothesis, 175
Transformational Generative (TG) grammar, 46–47, 154
 Recursion in, 48
  Conjunction as method of, 48
  Embedding as method, 48–49
  Phrase-markers, 46
Translation, by young bilinguals, 127

Uniqueness of human language, 2, 14–16, 18, 147
Universal grammar, as theory of second language
    acquisition, 105

Verb complements, acquisition of, 62
Verb, irregular/strong, 34
Verb phrase
    Development in young children, 85
    As major constituent of sentence, 46, 47
Vocabulary (*see also* lexicon)
    Abstract, 147
    Acquisition of, 63, 79, 82, 83, 87–88, 126, 153
Voice disorders, 169–170
Vowels
    Acquisition of, 65, 71

Alteration, 34
Defined in terms of production, 32
Diphthongs, 33
Lax and tense, 33
Quality, 33
Reduction, 34
In syllables, 65

Whole language
    Defined, 251
    As mispracticed, 259–261
    And phonics, 257–259
    In practice, 251–257
    And public perception, 261–262
Writing, early learning associated with, 225–226

Author Index

Aaron, I. E., 259
Abudarham, S., 175, 176, 187
Altwerger, B., 175, 176
Ashworth, M., 299
Atkinson-King, K., 87
Aylin, K., 117

Bailey, V. H., 235
Baker, L., 223
Barik, H. C., 98
Barke, E. M., 175
Barkin, F., 175, 176
Barnes, D., 1, 273
Barten, D., 74
Basser, L. S., 152
Bates, E., 61, 156, 158
Bear, D. R., 25
Beebe, B., 160
Bennett, S., 160
Benton, R., 109
Bereiter, C., 226
Berko, J., 15, 150
Berko-Gleason, J., 160, 195
Berman, R. A., 117
Bernstein, B., 236
Bird, L., 308, 309

Bissex, G. L., 89
Block, E., 156
Bloom, L., 57, 60, 80, 81, 151
Bloomfield, L., 143
Bohannon, J. N., 154, 155, 156, 159, 162
Bolinger, D., 52, 53
Bourhis, R., 105
Bowey, J. A., 34
Bradley, L., 34, 35, 88
Braine, M. D. S., 69, 146, 150
Brown, A. L., 223
Brown, H. D., 106, 107
Brown, R., 15, 62, 70–71, 146, 147, 151
Bruce, D., 157
Bruck, M., 109
Bruner, J., 61, 155, 157, 198, 249
Bryant, P., 34, 35, 88
Bub, D., 27
Burt, M. K., 107, 108, 112, 113, 124
Byrne, J., 105

Carmichael, L., 208
Carrow, M. A., 175
Caxton, W., 24
Cazden, C., 70, 151, 236, 242, 244
Chall, J. S., 259

Chomsky, N., 22, 46, 105, 149, 154, 156
Chow, M., 292
Christian, D., 100
Clark, E., 214
Clay, M. M., 223
Clyde, J. A., 259
Cochran-Smith, M., 7–8
Cohen, D., 160
Commins, N. L., 267
Connors, K., 98
Coombs, N., 281
Cotton, E. G., 84
Crago, M. B., 135, 177, 178, 186, 189
Cruz, B. R., 101
Crystal, D., 49, 67, 76, 78, 79, 80, 82, 87, 88, 91, 95, 96, 149, 153, 156, 170, 171, 173, 190, 216
Cummins, J., 138, 175, 176
Curtiss, S., 153, 159

Danesi, M., 27, 58
Danks, J. S., 131
Dasinger, L., 117
DeFries, J. C., 276
DeHirsch, K., 219
Demetras, M., 155
deVilliers, J. G., 151
deVilliers, P. A., 151
Dickinson, D., 4, 128, 196, 218, 232
Dillon, D., 235, 247
Doebler, L. K., 100
Donaldson, M., 96–97, 216
Dulay, H., 107, 108, 112, 113, 124
Dunn, L., 126
Durkin, D., 219, 259

Eddings, D., 277
Edelsky, C., 175, 176, 195
Ehrenreich, B., 195
Eilers, R. E., 209
Eimas, P. D., 58
Ellis, R., 105, 111, 113, 115, 116
Engel, W. Von R., 60, 94, 95, 96
Ervin-Tripp, S., 194

Farella, M., 100
Farwell, C., 65
Ferguson, C., 64, 65
Ferreiro, E., 89

Field, T., 160
Fiess, K., 80, 81
Fletcher, J., 257, 258
Flores, B., 175, 176
Foorman, B., 257, 258
Forrest, D. L., 223
Foster, M., 135
Francis, D., 257, 258
Francis, J., 34
Freedman, D. G., 29
Friedrickes, M., 197, 198, 199
Froese, V., 251
Fromkin, V., 159

Gagne, R. M., 106
Gardner, B. T., 148
Gardner, R. A., 148
Garnica, O., 58, 64
Gary, J. O., 108
Gass, S., 105
Gavin, W. J., 209
Genesee, F., 98
Giles, H., 105, 115, 116
Gleason, J. B., 87, 142, 214, 215
Gleitman, L., 158
Glucksberg, S., 131
Golinkoff, R. M., 61, 161
Goodman, K. S., 4, 156, 259
Goodman, Y., 5
Gordon, D., 194
Goswami, U., 34, 35
Grabo, R. P., 175
Graham, A., 52
Graham, L., 58
Grammont, M., 93, 96, 132
Graves, D., 6, 225
Gray, T. C., 101
Greenberg, J. H., 105
Greenberg, R., 160
Gregg, K. R., 105
Greif, E., 195
Grunwell, P., 72, 74, 79
Guadino, V., 98
Gunderson, L., 292

Halliday, M. A. K., 161, 196, 197, 198, 199, 201, 202, 248
Hammermeister, F., 174

Hanley, J. R., 36
Hansen, J., 4
Harding, C. G., 61
Harris, G. A., 29
Hatch, E., 95, 105, 111, 137
Hatch, E. M., 28, 107, 110, 114, 115
Haugen, E., 92
Haussler, M. M., 100, 101
Heath, S. B., 163, 164, 235, 236, 242, 267
Hernandez-Chavez, E., 95, 124
Hirsh-Pashek, K., 155
Hoff-Ginsburg, E., 162
Hogan, H. P., 208
Holt, J., 228, 229, 230, 234, 238, 242, 245–246, 249, 250, 262, 263
Hood, L., 80, 81, 151
Horgan, D., 81
House, A. S., 58
Howard, M. R., 159, 192, 194
Huang, H. S., 36
Hudelson, S., 175, 176
Huey, E., 232
Hulit, L. M., 159, 192, 194
Hulme, C., 35
Hutchings, M., 290

Ingram, D., 59, 62, 64, 65, 71, 73, 82, 87, 144, 171, 198
Invernizzi, M., 25
Itoh, H., 95, 137

Jaffe, J., 160
Jakobson, R., 141
Jansky, J., 219
Jeanne, L. M., 100, 101
Jenkins, S., 283
Jilbert, K., 175, 176
Johnson, S., 25
Johnston, F., 25
Jusczyk, P., 58

Karchmer, M., 174
Kessel, F., 156
Khubchandani, L. M., 101
Kinsbourne, M., 28
Kirshner, K., 197, 198, 199
Kirtley, C., 34
Klein, R. E., 209

Klips, B., 197, 198, 199
Kossan, N., 215
Krashen, S. D., 105, 107, 108, 111, 112, 113, 152
Kuschner, D., 234

Labov, W., 236
Lahey, M., 57, 60, 80, 81
Lambert, W. E., 98, 109, 175
Lamendella, J., 105
Landerl, K., 35, 258
Langford, W., 219
Lapkin, S., 98
Larsen-Freeman, D., 105, 106
Lasky, R. E., 209
Laurence, M., 277
Lenneberg, E., 152
Leopold, W. F., 65, 93, 94, 96, 124, 141
Levelt, W. J. M., 114
Leventer, S., 27
Lifter, K., 80, 81
Limber, J., 80
Lindfors, J. W., 234
Lindsay, A., 236
Loban, W. D., 85
Long, M., 105, 106
Luria, 155, 157, 198

MacGinitie, W. H., 258, 259
Macken, M. A., 74
MacLean, M., 34
MacNamara, J., 175
MacWhinney, B., 158
Major, D., 86
Mardis, L. J., 100
Markman, E. M., 211
Marler, P., 152
Martin-Jones, M., 176
Mattes, L. J., 168, 170, 171, 188
McCutchen, D., 226
McGill, J., 246
McLaughlin, B., 91, 92, 93, 94, 95, 99, 104, 105, 106, 112, 113, 114, 138, 146, 153
McLean, M., 88
McLeod, B., 105
Menard, N., 98
Menn, L., 59, 60, 87, 145
Menyuk, P., 80
Meredith, R., 4, 156

Merkin, S., 151
Mervis, C. B., 215
Michaels, S., 236
Mills, H., 259
Milon, J. P., 109
Moskowitz, A., 87
Murray, D., 216
Murrell, M., 94

Nakazina, S. A., 60
Nelson, K., 146
Newman, J., 259, 260, 287, 289
Newport, E., 162
Nickse, R. S., 296

Oates, J., 157
Ochs, E., 163
Oksaar, E., 95
Oldford-Matchim, J., 297
Olson, R. K., 276
Omark, D. R., 168, 170, 171, 188

Page, M. M., 99
Pan, B. A., 214, 215
Parlee, M., 194
Parry-Williams, D. E., 175
Peal, E., 175
Pearson, P. D., 4
Pease, D. M., 214, 215
Penfield, W., 152
Penner, S., 155
Pennington, B. F., 276
Perera, K., 69, 84, 85, 86
Perfetti, C. A., 221, 222, 226
Pflaum, S. W., 89, 163
Piaget, J., 59, 87, 155, 156, 158, 160
Piper, D., 196
Piper, T., 65
Platt, J., 157, 175–176
Porter, J., 112
Post, K., 155
Potter, G., 308
Premack, A. J., 148
Premack, D., 148
Priest, G. E., 135

Ratner, N. B., 174, 207
Reich, P. A., 15, 98, 101, 102, 146, 152, 154, 209
Richards, J., 157, 175–176

Richards, J. C., 261
Roberts, L., 152
Rodgers, T. S., 261
Roller, C., 242, 243, 244
Romaine, S., 176
Ronjat, J., 93, 94, 96, 124, 141
Rosch, E., 215
Rosier, P., 100
Rovee-Collier, C. K., 209
Ruke-Dravina, V., 94

Sachs, J., 60, 61
Saer, D. J., 175
Sanders, K., 197, 198, 199
Scardamalia, M., 226
Schieffelin, B. B., 7–8, 163
Schneider, W., 35, 258
Schneiderman, M., 155
Schumann, J., 105, 115
Scollon, R., 163
Scollon, S., 163
Scoville, R., 61
Sealey, D. B., 275
Segalowitz, N., 105
Selinker, L., 105, 111
Serebrin, W., 295–296
Seuss, 61, 88
Shacter, F. F., 197, 198, 199
Shafer, R. E., 197, 198, 199, 200, 201, 202
Shakespeare, W., 23, 53, 277
Shepard-Kegl, 5
Shvachkin, N., 58
Siegler, R. S., 208, 209, 211, 214
Singh, R., 98
Siqueland, E. R., 58
Skinner, B. F., 105, 143
Skutnabb-Kangas, T., 175, 176
Slobin, D., 114, 147, 150, 151, 156
Slobin, D. I., 117
Smith, A., 35
Smith, C., 296
Smith, E. B., 4, 156
Smith, F., 5, 7, 74
Smith, K., 197, 198, 199, 200, 201, 202, 249
Smith, M. E., 175
Smith, N. V., 65
Smith, S. D., 276
Snow, C., 155, 196
Snowling, M. J., 35

Snyder, G., 297
Spolsky, B., 103, 104, 105, 112, 113, 115
Staab, C., 197, 198, 199, 200, 201, 202, 246, 248,
    249, 266
Stampe, D., 72
Stanowicz, L., 155
Stern, D., 160
Stotsky, S., 4, 128, 196, 218, 232
Strickland, D. S., 7, 9, 84, 259
Stringer, D., 157
Sullivan, M. W., 209
Swacher, M., 194
Swain, M., 97, 98, 175
Syrdal-Lasky, 209

Tabouret-Keller, A., 94
Tager-Flusberg, H., 81, 82, 151
Taylor, D., 105
Teberosky, A., 89
Templeton, S., 25
Templin, M. C., 71
Terrace, H. S., 148
Thomas, J., 35
Tierney, R. J., 4
Titone, R., 58
Tittle, C. E., 52
Tompkins, C., 100, 101
Torrey, J. W., 89
Totten, G. O., 93, 94
Tough, J., 197, 198, 199
Toukomaa, P., 175, 176
Toupin, C., 117
Treiman, R., 34, 155
Trybus, R., 174
Tucker, G. R., 98, 101, 109
Tynes, D. M., 209

Van Lawick-Goodall, J., 149
Vasta, R., 144

Velten, H. V., 141
Vigorito, J., 58
Vihman, M. M., 92
Vocolo, J. M., 99
Vonnegut, K., 277
Voss, M. M., 226
Vygotsky, L. S., 4, 149, 160, 198

Walker, T. G., 223
Walter, A. A., 208
Wanner, E., 158
Warren-Leubecker, A. W., 154, 155, 156, 159, 162
Weber, H., 157, 175–176
Wells, G., 228, 233, 234, 235, 236, 237, 245, 262,
    267
Whitaker, H. A., 27
Whitehurst, G., 144
Williams, S., 194
Willis, F., 194
Wilson, W. R., 209
Wimmer, H., 35, 258
Wise, B. W., 276
Wiss, C., 98
Wode, H., 105
Wolf, M., 4, 128, 196, 218, 232
Woodson, R., 160
Woodward, V., 259
Wootten, J., 151

Yamada, J., 114, 159
Yardley, A., 207, 217
Yopp, H. K., 35
Yudovich, 157

Zakaluk, B. L., 275
Zappert, L. T., 101
Zareba, A., 94
Zutell, J., 249